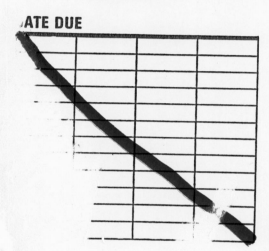

ATE DUE

A Half Century of Municipal Reform

A Half Century of Municipal Reform

The History of the
National Municipal League

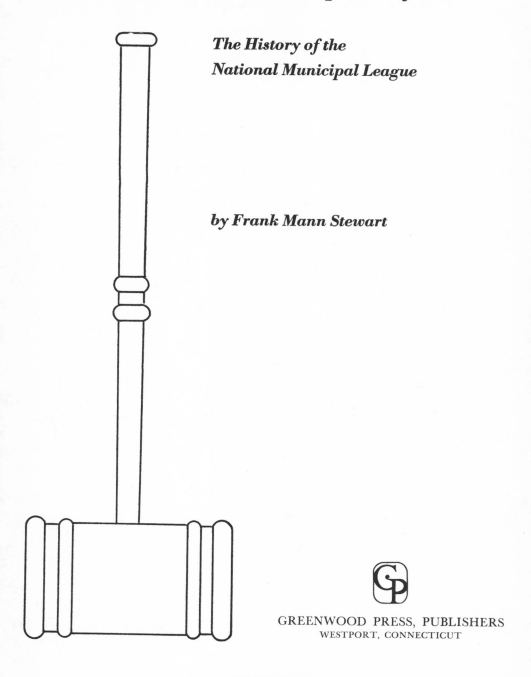

by Frank Mann Stewart

GREENWOOD PRESS, PUBLISHERS
WESTPORT, CONNECTICUT

The Library of Congress has catalogued this publication as follows:

Library of Congress Cataloging in Publication Data

Stewart, Frank Mann.
  A half century of municipal reform.

  Bibliography: p.
  1. National Municipal League. 2. Municipal
government--United States. I. Title.
JS302.N64S8 1972   352.073   74-168967
ISBN 0-8371-6240-8

To the Memory
of
Charles Grove Haines
1879–1948

Preface

THIS STUDY records the history of the National Municipal League, outlines the conditions which brought this citizens' organization for better government into existence, describes its program for the improvement of local government, analyzes its methods, techniques, and problems, and attempts to evaluate the contribution of the League to fifty years of municipal reform, 1894–1944. It does not purport to discuss all phases of the struggle for municipal reform during this period. In a few instances reference is made to events up to the fall of 1948.

The publications and files of the League furnished most of the material for the story of the League's activities. Examination was also made of all the data available in public and university libraries in New York City, Philadelphia, Los Angeles, and Berkeley, California. Many interviews with League officials and friends helped to clarify important points.

To the former Secretaries of the League—Clinton Rogers Woodruff, Harold W. Dodds, Russell Forbes, and Howard P. Jones—I am especially indebted for many valuable suggestions, and for counsel and criticism. Mr. Woodruff permitted me to examine his personal files for the early years of the organization. To Secretary Alfred Willoughby and the League staff, I owe a debt of gratitude for numerous courtesies during the preparation of the study. Mr. Richard S. Childs made available to me his extensive collection on the short ballot.

I wish also to acknowledge the financial assistance furnished by the Bureau of Research in the Social Sciences of the University of Texas.

Before their deaths Provost Clarence A. Dykstra and Professor Charles G. Haines, of the University of California, Los Angeles, read the manuscript and contributed sound advice and encouragement.

Finally, I must express my appreciation to my wife, to Ronald M. Ketcham, and to the members of the staff of the Bureau of Governmental Research of the University of California, Los Angeles, all of whom have been of great assistance in the preparation of the manuscript.

F.M.S.

June, 1950
Los Angeles, California

Contents

I

Municipal Government in the Spoils Era

Significant political and social movements often are quickened by certain notable events. Municipal affairs, for example, were of little prominence before the Civil War. After 1865 cities assumed an increasingly important place in the national economy. Conditions in municipal government during the thirty years following the end of that war constitute a dismal chapter in the evolution of local institutions.

General Conditions of National Life

The Civil War had a profound effect on the American scene. Politically, national issues achieved a new and distinct position in the popular interest. National party politics became the chief concern of the voters. The controversies of the reconstruction era overshadowed local government and municipal affairs. Cities were scarcely regarded as political entities, but served only as another jurisdiction in which the major party machines might operate. The spoils system reached its peak in both federal and local governments.

The postwar years were notable in our economic history. Inventive genius made possible machine production, speeded up transportation and communication, and developed a vast extension of facilities for business and agricultural activity. The great conflict intensified economic activity in an unparalleled way. It lifted industrial development to new peaks. It gave impetus to railway construction and expansion. Particularly in the North, and later in the South, business enterprises grew rapidly to meet new demands. During and after the war, contracts for government supplies, generous distribution of land grants, and financial speculation led to vast increases of capital in the hands of private groups.[1] These were the beginnings of the trend toward what later was to be called "big business." Improvement of agricultural methods helped to promote city growth and made urban development a major influence on farm conditions.

[1] For notes to chap. i, see pp. 209–211.

It was a golden age of expansion and money making in all sections of the country, with the exception of the southern states. The city was the mecca to which thousands of men turned in the hope of participating in the prosperity of the day. The fortunes of the time were acquired easily, but often unscrupulously. A loose ideology fostered a disregard for honest methods in the conventional sense. Most brilliant minds of the day were absorbed in the acquisitive endeavors of a quick-spreading industrial-commercial expansion. Few promising young men of those times were advised to enter politics. Historians have pointed out that this period did not "possess its due proportion of political leaders of the first rank."[2] In critical review of these years, Henry Adams wrote in his celebrated personal history, "No period so thoroughly ordinary had been known in American politics since Christopher Columbus first disturbed the balance of American society."[3]

Factors Affecting Municipal Progress

In addition to the influence of the general political, economic, and moral conditions in the postwar period, it must be recognized that numerous physical, social, and cultural factors also strongly affected the municipal situation.

A sharp increase in city growth was one of the outstanding characteristics of the period. In 1860 there were 141 cities with a population of 8,000 or more; by 1870 there were 226 such cities. Twenty years later the figure was 445. From a total of 5,072,256 in 1860, the number of city dwellers swiftly mounted to 18,244,239 in 1890. During the thirty years from 1860 to 1890, the urban population increased from 16 per cent to 29 per cent of the national total.[4] By 1890 there were four cities with more than 500,000 people, fifteen with more than 200,000, and twenty-eight with over 100,000.

This was a distinct reversal of trend. During the first ninety years of the federal government's existence, cities consistently had received less than one-third of the population increase. Then in the 'eighties the turn came. By the 'nineties cities were growing three times as fast as rural areas. A new movement was under way.[5]

Concurrent with this growth was a steady increase in municipal functions.[6] The rapid concentration of people into small areas presented numerous problems. Where new communities flourished, services had to be hastily organized. Where older communities expanded, existing facilities often proved hopelessly inadequate. Water supply systems, sewers, and facilities for the removal and disposal of garbage and rubbish had to be provided. Property had to be protected against fire and theft. Especially acute was the problem of public health, which required constant attention. The provision of public utilities such as light, gas, and transportation became a necessity as the small city sprang into urban adulthood. The paving, lighting, and cleaning of streets, planning of boulevard systems, and building of bridges became important aspects of city administration. There were school systems and public libraries to be planned and administered; playgrounds, parks, and other educational and recreational facilities to be provided. As urban communities grew, problems multiplied both in number and in variety.

The surge of expansion found cities woefully unprepared so far as services were concerned. Thus the problem usually became one of expediency rather than of efficiency. As a result, there were vastly increased expenditures. Enormous public works programs were undertaken. Valuable public franchises were given away for political reasons. Unprecedented borrowing led to huge public debts. Excessive waste was inevitable for lack of time to plan. In many cases new facilities were only stopgap arrangements. Growth required expansion, however haphazard and poorly administered the expansion might be; yet, despite this, there was a steady advance in the standards of municipal service as compared to those of prewar years and some of the public improvements represented progress of a very definite nature.[7]

Poor planning and administration were not the only weaknesses in urban government. Good government, in large part, depends on the interest of the electorate. One of the most unusual features of the age was the appalling apathy of the self-styled "better class" toward these cancerous municipal conditions. The people who might have provided finances and leadership for local civic betterment were engrossed in other pursuits. Too often their financial and social positions were dependent on the continuance in power of local political machines. Special concessions and privileges were the order of the day; the businessman preferred to pay tribute rather than to insist on integrity of public administration. Some, in fact most, of the fortunes of the period were made through the development and exploitation of major transportation, communication, public utility, and other necessary systems. Many of the lesser fortunes and portions of the larger holdings were gained through the complicity of corrupt municipal politicians.

Any appraisal of the situation would be incomplete without some reference to the literature on local government that was available after the Civil War. As is true today, the daily press theoretically afforded the greatest means of publicity but never featured municipal affairs except when they approached the scandalous.[8] There was no really sustained interest in local politics and administration on the part of newspaper publishers. However, at least one historian of the period believes that sensationalism in the press did assist in promoting civic welfare, even if in a spasmodic way.[9] Certainly the New York *Times* played an important role in exposing the Tweed Ring in New York City.[10]

A number of the general literary journals of the day gave some consideration to municipal problems. Among them were the *Atlantic, Century, Cosmopolitan, Harper's, Nation, North American Review,* and *Scribner's.* Although discussion of public questions occupied about one-third of the space in twelve outstanding periodicals during the 'nineties, fiction still predominated.[11] But from 1886 to 1890 several magazines concerned almost entirely with public matters were established. These included: *Current Literature, Literary Digest, Public Opinion, Review of Reviews, Arena,* and *Forum.*[12] The last two were of the crusading type and led the way to the muckraking years of the twentieth century.[13]

The periodical press, although somewhat more productive than newspapers, accorded slow recognition to local issues. However, a sharp upswing began in the 'eighties. A survey of the only reputable general index of the periodical literature of the nineteenth century shows more articles on conditions in municipal government in the decade 1882–1892 than had been listed in the previous eighty years.[14]

Even more striking is the fact that during the period from 1892 to 1902 nearly twice as many articles were printed as had been published during the ninety years preceding. In 1897 the first magazine entirely on municipal subjects was established; it was a quarterly, *Municipal Affairs*, and continued publication until 1902. However, one critic, in evaluating the current literature on local matters, called it "void of scientific method."[15]

Comprehensive books on municipal government were practically nonexistent.[16] The first adequate commentary on American cities was written in 1888 by the distinguished British observer, James Bryce, and included in *The American Commonwealth*. But during the 'nineties a number of textbooks on municipal problems appeared.[17] Several reports of investigating commissions and memorials of civic organizations revealed the general condition of municipal government.[18]

This dearth of books is not surprising when we realize the nature of higher education in the United States during this time. The historical function of higher education had been to train for the ministry. Before the Civil War most students went to European universities to take advanced study. Their interests lay primarily in philosophy and literature.[19] The study of politics was approached mostly through moral philosophy.

Following the war, university instruction took on a new character. The number of institutions increased from about 350 in 1878 to nearly 500 in 1898.[20] Registration of nonprofessional graduate students rose from slightly more than 400 to nearly 5,000.[21] The scientific study of politics and institutions was greatly expanded.[22] Johns Hopkins University inaugurated the study of "history and politics" in 1876. Columbia University's School of Political Science was founded in 1880.[23] Chicago, Harvard, Pennsylvania, and Wisconsin followed with the establishment of departments in politics, economics, sociology, and history. Andrew D. White, president of Cornell University, John W. Burgess and Frank J. Goodnow at Columbia University, A. Lawrence Lowell at Harvard University, Woodrow Wilson at Princeton University, Theodore D. Woolsey at Yale University, and Edmund J. James at the University of Pennsylvania, were among the leaders in this new field. By 1890 the beginnings of study in public administration were discernible. Even then, it was not until 1894 that the first independent lectureship on municipal government under the direction of Professor Leo S. Rowe was instituted at the University of Pennsylvania.[24]

There were other developments which had some bearing on the situation of which the most significant were the beginnings of several national associations in the social sciences. The American Social Science Association had been established in 1865, but it was the 'eighties that saw the creation of the American Historical Association, the American Economic Association, the American Statistical Association, and the American Academy of Political and Social Science. Just after the turn of the century, in 1903, the American Political Science Association and the American Sociological Society were organized. Each of these groups at some time during its existence has given close attention to municipal problems.[25] The periodical publications of these various learned societies have provided a national vehicle for discussion of the pressing problems of local government.[26]

On the whole, it may be said that before 1890 cities failed to receive recognition proportionate to the importance of the issues involved. The general neglect by the press and by publishers and the slow development of organized instruction in universities was reflected in the deplorable character of city government. There was little exchange of information, and consequently only a very sketchy impression of civic problems and possible solutions was available even to the most interested citizens. As ignorance is prone to do, this circumstance promoted bad government, or at least lent no assistance to efforts to cure, or, better, to prevent the disease.

From this sketch of the general background of municipal government during the spoils era we turn to an analysis of the then current forms of city government, and a discussion of the manifestations of some of the local political machines.

FORMS OF CITY GOVERNMENT

Social change and governmental readjustment are usually complementary processes. Thus, during the nineteenth century the shifting composition of cities and the multiplication of municipal services were accompanied by a constant revision of the structure of local government, frequently too late to provide any real remedy.

The degree and kind of municipal progress varied in different sections of the country. In the East, where cities were older and more or less staid in character, resistance to new forms was the general rule. Change came only out of absolute necessity, and the approach was by means of reallocation of authority rather than by remodeling of structure. In the South the trend toward concentration of authority was much slower than elsewhere, probably because of the modified tempo of urban development in that region. As might be expected because of their newness and absence of traditional ties, cities in the central and western states adjusted and modified their organizations and practices with an uncommon ease and regularity. Nowhere, however, does there seem to have been a consistent, methodical, long-term approach to the problems of the city as a social and political institution.

Perhaps of primary interest is the distinct development of the municipal executive.[27] The office of mayor in colonial times had been a copy of the English type. The early American mayor had little or no special power, but merely presided over the common council of which he was a member. In fact, only four out of the seventeen cities in the Colonies had an elective executive. Early in the nineteenth century the idea of popular election of the mayor gained growing acceptance, but progress of the elective plan was slow until 1834, when New York City adopted it; it was an established feature in the system of municipal administration by the 'fifties.

While the position of the mayor was thus developing more independence, the city council still held the major share of authority in most cities before the Civil War.[28] However, as cities grew and their administrative powers expanded, a distrust of the council gradually arose. To prevent the misuse of their increasing authority, appeals were made to state legislatures for stricter state control over local administration, but instead of stopping at control, legislatures interfered in municipal affairs through special legislation of an obnoxious character and by the setting up of numerous independent boards to administer local functions.[29] Often, to all intents and purposes, state legislatures became the policy-making bodies for cities. Municipal councils, thus shorn of their main legislative functions, were rendered impotent. To make matters worse, the usual form of departmental organization was a board or commission which was elected by the people, appointed by the mayor, or, in some cases, designated by the governor of the state.[30]

All of this led to a disintegration of local authority and responsibility. Legislative interference became so objectionable that many states adopted constitutional provisions forbidding special legislation.[31] Although this did not necessarily eliminate the abuses, since the spirit of such provisions was easily evaded, it revealed a new attitude toward cities. Missouri, as early as 1875, was the first state to grant constitutional home rule to cities; yet only four states had done so by 1900.[32]

As Professor J. A. Fairlie has pointed out, municipal problems were dealt with haphazardly before 1870.[33] During the later decades of the nineteenth century there was a more serious and understanding consideration of the plight of cities. Reorganization of government in many important cities was one of the indications of the new outlook. In 1870 New York City received a new charter which abolished state commissions and gave the city its first general power of taxation.[34] Within the next decade Brooklyn, Richmond, Chicago, and a number of other cities also secured new charters. All this was a forward-looking development. The charters agreed in providing for the appointment of many officials by the mayor, subject to the council's consent. In a number of cities the mayor was given authority to remove appointive officials on definite charges. Most of them permitted the mayor a limited veto power over council action, subject to a two-thirds or three-fourths overriding vote by the council.

From this time on, there was a gradual tendency to concentrate authority and responsibility in the mayor. By 1880 this official was generally empowered to appoint the heads of administrative departments and, through them, the city employees. Although it was not the general practice, the mayor of Brooklyn, in 1882, was given the absolute power of appointing the principal department heads. Two years later, the same power was conferred upon the mayor of New York City. Boston and Buffalo followed within the next ten years. As a rule, however, the mayor's appointments required council confirmation. In only a few instances was his power of removal of appointive officers an established fact.[35] Another of the significant developments of the last half of the century was the extension of the mayor's term.[36] The term was extended from one to two years in most cases and sometimes to a period as long as three or four years. This reduced rapid rotation in office and contributed somewhat to administrative stability.

An important innovation appeared in the New York City charter of 1873, which set up a board of estimate and apportionment. This board had complete power over the budget, expenditures, and financial operation of the city. It constituted the first major check on extravagant spending practices, and was copied by a number of cities both large and small. Nevertheless, such communities as Chicago, Dubuque, Duluth, Minneapolis, and Omaha left budget matters in the hands of a council committee. In smaller cities, on the whole, the council remained the central organ in financial affairs.

The form of the city council varied somewhat. Usually each city had a board of aldermen and a common council, which sat separately to act as a check on each other.[37] Most colonial councils had been unicameral, but when the federal Constitution was adopted, the influence of its form extended even into local government. Baltimore, Boston, New York, Philadelphia, Pittsburgh, and St. Louis adopted bicameral systems during the first half of the nineteenth century.[38] By the close of the Civil War city councils were usually fairly large and divided into two bodies; within the next twenty years the size of these legislative groups was reduced, and a movement was begun to return to a single-chambered council, elected at large rather than on a ward basis.[39]

Because of control of the city by the legislature and because of the absence of facilities for exchanging information and ideas, the forms of administration were almost as numerous as the cities themselves. There was a lamentable absence of coördination and of planning in the organization, procedures, and practices of municipal government.

Particularly in the larger communities, responsibility was so widely diffused as to defy either popular or administrative control of government. Most of the political safeguards and aids to management which we now regard as commonplace did not exist. The more or less complete separation of judicial from administrative and legislative functions in local government is of comparatively recent origin.[40] Reform of election methods did not really become effective until this century. The Australian ballot was first adopted by cities in 1888, and the short ballot idea did not take root until the turn of the century.[41] Suffrage for women was generally denied. Proportional representation, the initiative, referendum, and recall are largely twentieth-century developments.[42] It was only after the middle of the century that municipal services were placed on a paid rather than a voluntary basis. The merit system was not introduced in cities until after the passage of the Pendleton Act by Congress in 1883.[43] Modern budgetary methods and controls were practically unknown until after 1900;[44] only two cities had any form of centralized purchasing before that date.[45] The establishment of efficiency agencies in cities followed the period we are considering.[46] The municipal reference library and the privately supported municipal research bureau trace their origin to 1900 and 1906 respectively.[47] University research in public administration was just beginning in the 'nineties, and the growth of academic bureaus of municipal research came after 1900.[48] Only seven state leagues of municipalities were in existence by 1900, and the League of American Municipalities was not organized until 1897.[49]

URBAN MACHINES AND BOSSES

Contemporary observers agree that the era following the conclusion of the Civil War was the period of most flagrant corruption in the history of American cities. In 1888 James Bryce characterized city government as "the one conspicuous failure of the United States."[50] Two years later Andrew D. White, professor and statesman, corroborated Bryce's criticism. He wrote: "Without the slightest exaggeration we may assert that, with very few exceptions, the city governments of the United States are the worst in Christendom—the most expensive, the most inefficient, and the most corrupt. No one who has any considerable knowledge of our own country and of other countries can deny this."[51]

Urban political machines flourished because of a number of conditions, some of which have been pointed out earlier, namely, the unconcern of the more capable citizens and the lack of leadership offered. However, the era produced several outstanding public officials, such as Seth Low, mayor of Brooklyn and president of Columbia University,[52] and Mayors Pingree of Detroit, Strong of New York, Jones of Toledo, and Quincy of Boston.[53] Theodore Roosevelt was beginning his administrative career as a member of the United States Civil Service Commission and was to serve later as president of the New York City Police Board. Only a few cities were fortunate to have such leadership. Almost everywhere else ordinary men with a flair for political manipulation took control of municipal government. It was convenient for them that the prevailing psychology left them largely to their own devices.

But not all of the conditions are to be traced to human limitations. When any organization is growing rapidly, seeking to assimilate new elements and to become adjusted to new conditions, decisions must be made hurriedly; mistakes are unavoidable. Lack of system and ill-defined responsibility in municipal management was a contributing factor. So also was the rapid broadening of the municipal suffrage. Even before the outbreak of the Civil War, except in five states which had established low tax-paying qualifications, there were no restrictions. This situation might not have been so serious had there not been an accompanying increase in immigration. By the middle 'forties immigrants were entering the United States at the rate of 100,000 annually. After the middle of the century came the great influx of Irish, German, and other national groups. These newcomers lived, for the most part, in the larger cities. Politicians were quick to see that unschooled foreigners might easily become major sources of support for local machines. The slowness with which improvements were made in the nominating machinery, in registration facilities, in the printing of ballots, and in the means for casting them also played into the politician's hands.

A peculiar psychology developed in which loyalty to the party and the keeping of faith with political friends were used as excuses to condone financial malpractices. Professor T. H. Reed has shown in his discussion of this period that the possibility of graft was most attractive.[54] Municipal graft generally thrived on three sources. The police department was nearly always a focal point. For a price the letter of the law might be evaded or its enforcement might be omitted altogether. A second major source of corruption lay in the desire of businessmen to receive privileges from the city government. This took many forms, ranging from the unchecked evasion of petty ordinances to the securing of public utility franchises of great value—for a consideration. Finally, direct raids on the city treasury were a characteristic practice of the vicious political machines of the day.

No city, large or small, lay beyond the pale of these evil influences.[55] New York with its Tweed Ring, and Philadelphia with its Gas Ring, were of course, notorious. Washington, D.C., had its real estate group. Cincinnati struggled under Cox's control; St. Louis suffered because of Butler's selling of franchises and contracts;

the Ames regime held sway in Minneapolis; and San Francisco was under the thumb of "Blind Boss" Buckley.

The Tweed Ring in New York City is cited as the classic example of municipal corruption. It certainly deserves whatever infamy has attached to its record. Its tactics were so fundamental to the success of machines during these years that they deserve some mention here.[56] The most frequent abuses arose through frauds in connection with contracts for the construction of public buildings and other municipal facilities, as well as in the purchase of supplies and materials. It was estimated by the Citizens' Association in 1871 that of the 130,000 voters, Boss Tweed could influence about half through the various agencies at his command. By appointment to public office, by the letting of contracts, by employment on public works, by the issuance of licenses, and by either suspended sentences or nonprosecution of indictments, as well as other nefarious means, the power of the Ring was vigorously extended. When it was at last overthrown in 1873, the era of machine corruption had reached its climax. This does not mean that graft disappeared, but that it never reached quite such astounding proportions again.

Philadelphia's experience paralleled that of New York.[57] The ruling group came to be known as the Gas Ring, because it was through appointment as one of the gas trustees that James McManes managed to bring the whole of the gas department under his domination. Other major city departments fell into the hands of the machine. They handled the giving and taking of hundreds of city jobs and the letting of most of the city contracts. In addition, they purchased a controlling interest in the main horsecar company of the city. It was estimated that at one time the Gas Ring could command the support of at least 20,000 workers, voters in the community. Thus, this body became a major factor not only in local but also in state and federal affairs. Finally, in 1881, the Ring was driven from power by an indignant electorate.

In other cities these standard techniques of graft were employed in varying degrees. Municipal utilities were a particularly fertile field for exploitation in many communities. A combination of several capitalists acquired management of the street railways of New York City, Philadelphia, Pittsburgh, Chicago, and scores of other places in New England, Pennsylvania, Ohio, and Indiana. Among themselves, these same capitalists also operated the gas and electric light systems in more than eighty cities, as far as Philadelphia in the East, Minneapolis in the West, and St. Augustine in the South. A lone group held control of most of the local trolley and lighting companies in New Jersey, and there was a similar management of such facilities in San Francisco and other places on the Pacific Coast.[58]

Coöperation of state and local machines in both major parties was a common practice throughout the country. For instance, the Tweed Ring could not have flourished without the complicity of Republican groups both in the city and in upstate New York. Of course, such considerations always involved a *quid pro quo*, which the dominating faction was willing to concede.

From a purely material and financial standpoint, graft and corruption were detrimental to cities. A general demoralization of municipal administration seemed to develop in direct proportion to the interference of sinister politics. Simultaneously, as politics in the worst sense gathered strength, the cost of services increased proportionately. Padded cost figures were in wide use. Cities everywhere were forced to borrow to satisfy the demands of an expanding community. Between the warranted requirements of growth and the unwarranted plundering by political machines, fiscal affairs of cities generally got out of control. These malodorous conditions existed largely because the logical rulers remained uninterested or inarticulate. Usually the excesses of the politicians had to reach shocking proportions before there was an organized movement for municipal reform.

SUMMARY

The era, 1865 to 1895, was one of tremendous physical growth of cities and expansion of municipal activities. From the standpoint of administration, it was a period of disintegration, waste, and inefficiency. Political machines and bosses plundered many communities. Lax moral standards of the times in business life, the apathy of the public, and general neglect of the whole municipal problem by leading citizens, by the press, and by the universities, all contributed to the low state of city affairs. Lack of a common body of knowledge and of definite standards of municipal government, coupled with legislative interference and local politics, produced a confused situation in local organization and responsibility. Corruption in city government was made possible by the prevailing spoils system, by the activities of national political parties in local elections, and by the absence of adequate instruments of democratic control and of scientific methods of administration. Outstanding public officials and administrators were few; municipal reference and research agencies were nonexistent; and organizations of public officials were in their infancy. The period has been justly described as the "Dark Ages" of American municipal history.

II

The Organization of Municipal Reform

IT IS AXIOMATIC in politics that conditions must sink to a very low level before the forces of reform and reconstruction are set in motion. As Professor T. H. Reed says, "There is, happily, a certain rhythm in human affairs by reason of which, when they have swung as near as may be to the nadir, they swing up again toward the zenith. It is in the times of bleakest despair that the forces gather which lift the race higher."[1]

The period 1865–1895, while it witnessed the triumph of the party machine and bosses in many cities, saw also the genesis of the municipal reform movement. Patriotic and civic-minded men and women of many communities organized local reform associations. In 1894 the first nation-wide meeting of local reformers was held in Philadelphia, and from its deliberations came the impetus for the creation of a permanent national organization for municipal reform.

LOCAL REFORM ASSOCIATIONS

Attempts at municipal reform in the 'seventies were mostly spasmodic and temporary. The Council of Political Reform, organized in New York City in 1871, and the Committee of Seventy, created in the same year to fight the Tweed Ring, were notable examples. A Citizens' Reform Association in Philadelphia, established in 1871, was active for nearly a decade. The oldest organization of the sort is the Citizens' Association of Chicago, with a continuous record since 1874. In 1878 the Society for Prevention of Crime was organized in New York City. Under the leadership of Dr. C. H. Parkhurst, who became its president in 1892, it played a prominent part in the exposure of police corruption in New York City.[2]

Reform organizations of a more permanent nature appeared in the 'eighties. In this decade the following associations came into existence: Citizens' Association of Albany, 1881; National Civil Service Reform League, 1881; Massachusetts Re-

---

[1] For notes to chap. ii, see pp. 211–213.

form Club, 1882; International Law and Order League, 1883; Baltimore Reform League, 1885; American Institute of Civics, 1885; Citizens' Municipal Association of Philadelphia, 1886; Citizens' Association of Boston, 1887; Massachusetts Society for Promoting Good Citizenship, 1887; Citizens' Association of Buffalo, 1888; and Library Hall Association of Cambridge, 1889.

The early 'nineties was the time of the full flowering of municipal reform groups. In 1894 there were more than eighty organizations, of which about sixty had been created since 1890. Only three could boast of an origin before 1880. New York City was the home of more than a dozen reform agencies in 1894, to say nothing of numerous local district organizations. More than thirty groups organized for action in 1894. There were reform associations in some sixteen states, with more than half of them concentrated in New York, Pennsylvania, and Massachusetts. Less than one-tenth of the active agencies were found west of the Mississippi River.[3]

Among fifty-two reform organizations described by Tolman,[4] the names most frequently appearing were: municipal league, reform league, city club, civic federation, good government club, citizens' association, improvement society, and committee of fifty or seventy. Voluntary subscriptions or a nominal membership fee or assessment supported these agencies. Work was done by volunteer officers and committees; only eight had a salaried secretary. Nine reported ward and precinct organizations; eight were incorporated. Women were ineligible for membership in twenty-one groups; two limited membership to 100 and 200 respectively. Annual reports and pamphlets constituted their publications; only two reported a regular organ.

The objectives of these associations were both general and specific. According to its constitution the City Club of New Brunswick, New Jersey, sought to "encourage every wise project for adding to the comfort and convenience of our citizens, and to the prosperity and development of our city."[5] The Civic Federation of Chicago had for one of its purposes the advancement of the "municipal, philanthropic, industrial, and moral interests of Chicago. . . ." In Detroit the Civic Federation proclaimed as its objectives the federation of the moral forces of the city and the promotion of the "welfare, order, and prosperity of Detroit."[6] Specifically, their objectives were certain concrete reforms—honest, efficient, and economical administration; reduction of taxes; simplification of government; suppression of the saloon; home rule; improved legislation and charters; civil service reform; full enforcement of existing laws; punishment of those guilty of election frauds, maladministration, or misappropriation of public funds; separation of municipal politics from state and national politics; nomination and election of municipal officials solely on account of their fitness for office; conduct of local government upon nonpartisan and strictly business principles; promotion of intelligent discussion of municipal affairs and the participation of all good citizens in local government.[7]

How were such objectives to be accomplished? By legal action, by criticism and protest, and by coöperation. But principally by two means, the educational and the political. Under the former were included investigations; publication and agitation through papers, reports, discussions, resolutions, public meetings, the press, committees, and the personal efforts of members; and the exercise of every moral influence in behalf of municipal regeneration. Many organizations limited their activities to investigation, agitation, publication, and the massing of moral forces. Others resorted to political methods to accomplish their ends. These included the study of the records of candidates and distribution of the findings; endorsement of or opposition to candidates; furnishing a corps of watchers at the polls; or the nomination and support of independent candidates.[8]

Outstanding as leaders of the reform movement in their respective cities were the City Club of New York and the Municipal League of Philadelphia. The City Club of New York was incorporated on April 4, 1892. One of the club's primary functions was to assist "in the study of honest, efficient municipal government." It sought also to sever municipal from national politics. Politically, the organization was restricted to nonpartisan action having to do with municipal matters. The securing of sound legislation and the preparing of important constitutional amendments was a phase of the practical work. The club maintained a public bureau and issued literature on municipal government and its reform. With nearly one thousand members in 1894, each paying an annual membership fee of fifty dollars, the organization maintained a splendid club house on Fifth Avenue. It may properly be regarded as one of the major influences in this whole movement. Because of the activity of the club, more than twenty Good Government Clubs, with about 6,000 members, were organized in New York City.[9]

These Good Government Clubs fostered by the parent City Club subscribed to the same general principles. They served as local social-political centers where citizens might meet, either for serious discussion or for the enjoyment of leisure. General awakening of public sentiment and nomination of better men to public office were among the claimed accomplishments of these groups. Corruption at the polls was deterred by the recruitment of a corps of watchers in each club district. A Council of Confederated Good Government Clubs was organized in 1894.

The Municipal League of Philadelphia, which later was to join with the City Club of New York in calling the First National Conference for Good City Government, was created in the latter part of 1891. The League worked for the separation of municipal from national and state politics, the honest and efficient conduct of city government upon business principles, and the extension of civil service reform to all municipal departments. It also undertook an extensive publication and propaganda program. It participated vigorously in campaigns to defeat bad candidates and to elect competent representatives to both the Select and the Common Councils of Philadelphia. The organization was sustained entirely by voluntary contributions, there being no dues. It had committees in more than one-third of the wards of the city and a total membership of not less than thirty-five hundred persons.[10]

In addition to the organizations which gave most of their energy strictly to municipal reform, there were also many agencies which divided their interest, making municipal government merely one sector of their activity. The Union League Club of Chicago, established in 1879, is an example of a social-political group which dealt with the problems of municipal reform from time to time, but not as its sole function. The National Civil Service Reform League played an important role in promoting better personnel standards in cities, and the American Institute of Civics sought to promote good government by elevating the standard of citizenship. There were chambers of commerce and business leagues in Cleveland, Minneapolis, Kansas City, Missouri, and other cities which were interested in municipal reform as a means of making their community more attractive to outside business firms.[11] Some groups combined philanthropic, industrial, moral, and municipal programs.[12] Along the outer fringe of reform development during these years was what might be called the ephemeral organizations which were created for the achievement of a given reform and died with its attainment. Such campaigns usually were directed to the defeating at the polls of a particularly oppressive machine.[13]

The movement did not have the support of the more radical municipal reformers nor of many persons drawn from the working classes. "It has been chiefly a movement of business and professional men, its main endeavors being to organize for the enforcement of such laws as we now have and the simplification and purification of administration."[14] Women had an important part in municipal reform as members of civic groups and through societies composed exclusively of their own sex. Public sentiment in behalf of good city government was aroused in many communities through the efforts of the churches and various young people's religious societies. Law enforcement societies in several states formed in 1883 the National Law and Order League. Around Dr. Parkhurst in New York City there rallied a group of young men and the City Vigilance League was formed in 1892.[15]

Space will not permit a detailed discussion of the results of the "Civic Renaissance."[16] In many a spirited moral campaign, the "rascals" of municipal politics were unseated. But early loss of citizen interest in community regeneration often meant that hard-fought victories by reformers were followed by the renewed triumph of the party machine. This only goes to prove "that the course of evolution is not to be indicated by a smooth ever-rising curve, but by an irregular line in which only the general trend is upward."[17]

The work of the pioneers of municipal reform represents a basic and fundamental achievement upon which later advances were made. During this time the tools of a lasting reform were being shaped. Organized groups in various communities were becoming self-continuing forces in the interests of civic betterment. Where the city hall government often changed hands, these reform elements remained active from one city administration to another. With time came experience and keener political sagacity, as well as a sort of local reform tradition. The reform organizations largely achieved their objectives, says Professor Reed. Furthermore, they made "a great and lasting contribution toward awakened popular interest and informed public opinion. They permanently raised the character level of elective city officers."[18]

Leaders of the movement for better city government soon recognized that unity within the single community was not enough. Experiences must be shared. Fundamental strategies must be exchanged. Above all, virile personalities must have a national forum. With well-nigh prophetic foresight, in 1892, one observer wrote:

An association in each city, with small committees, each investigating some branch of municipal work and studying the subject in the light of information gathered both at home and abroad, would be of great assistance to the city officials; and a league of such associations, holding annual meetings, would increase by cooperation the efficiency of them all.[19]

Two years later local reform associations joined in the formation of the National Municipal League.

FIRST NATIONAL CONFERENCE FOR GOOD CITY GOVERNMENT

Preliminary steps were taken by the Municipal League of Philadelphia in the summer of 1893 to call a national conference for good city government. The idea met with encouragement, particularly from the City Club of New York, and it was decided to proceed. At about the same time municipal reformers in Minneapolis were making preparations to assemble such a group in their city. "Without any previous communication or understanding upon the subject, the necessity for the movement was recognized simultaneoulsy by the West and by the East."[20]

CALL FOR THE CONFERENCE

The formal Call for the Conference was issued by the Municipal League of Philadelphia on December 29, 1893.

The Municipal League of Philadelphia, with the co-operation of the City Club of New York, has decided to issue a call for a National Conference for Good City Government, to be held in Philadelphia on the 25th and 26th days of January 1894.

The Principal objects of the Conference will be to determine, so far as is possible by inquiry and debate, the best means for stimulating and increasing the rapidly growing demand for honest and intelligent government in American cities, and to discuss the best methods for combining and organizing the friends of Reform so that their united strength may be made effective. . . .

You are respectfully invited to be present at the meetings and to take part in the discussions. It is believed that by attending this Conference, those who realize the vast importance of the problems to be discussed will accomplish much in arousing public interest, in raising the popular standards of political morality, and in securing for the advocates of Municipal Reform that feeling of brotherhood and co-operation and that unity of actions and methods, which will multiply their strength and enthusiasm, and inspire the people with the hope and confidence essential to final success.[21]

Officers of local reform associations were urged to secure the appointment of delegates to attend the Conference. The call was signed by the Committee of Arrangements of the Municipal League of Philadelphia, consisting of Charles Richardson, Stuart Wood, George Burnham, Jr., S. D. McConnell, Edmund J. James, William I. Nichols, Joseph G. Rosengarten, Francis B. Reeves, W. M. Salter, Herbert Welsh, Clinton Rogers Woodruff, Thomas Martindale, George Gluyas Mercer, R. Francis Wood, and by Edmond Kelly, John Harsen Rhoades, and R. Fulton Cutting, the latter three constituting the committee of the City Club of New York.[22]

The endorsement of the call for the Conference was signed by James C. Carter, president, and Edmond Kelly, secretary, of the City Club of New York, and by many other prominent leaders in the municipal reform movement in different cities.[23]

Approximately one hundred and fifty delegates and invited guests, representing twenty-nine organizations, were in attendance at the Conference.[24] Twenty-one cities in thirteen states, from New Orleans in the South to Minneapolis in the West, were represented by delegates. University representatives were present from Brown University, Cornell University, and the University of Pennsylvania. Prominent lawyers, journalists, clergymen, businessmen, and government officials were there from Philadelphia, Washington, D. C., Boston, New York, Baltimore, Brooklyn, Chicago, Minneapolis, Milwaukee, Columbus, Kansas City, Missouri, and many other cities. All sessions of the Conference were well attended. Women made up approximately half of the audiences, which ranged from 400 to 1,000.[25]

PROGRAM OF THE CONFERENCE

James C. Carter, president of the City Club of New York, served as chairman, and Clinton Rogers Woodruff, secretary of the Municipal League of Philadelphia, as secretary of the Conference. The program, as outlined in the call for the Conference, included:

> *First.* A brief summary of existing conditions in different cities, and a description of Municipal Government and Municipal Officials as they ought to be.
>
> *Second.* Methods for obtaining better Government without resorting to the nomination or support of independent candidates.
>
> *Third.* Methods that involve the nomination or support of independent candidates.[26]

Throughout the two days the program was carried out practically as it was announced. Veteran political reformers reported on the conditions of government in the principal cities of the East—Boston, Brooklyn, Baltimore, Cambridge, Philadelphia, New York—and in Chicago and Milwaukee. The municipal government of Berlin was described. The relation of civil service reform to municipal reform was discussed. Other topics were: separation of municipal from other elections; influence upon officials in office; methods of arousing public sentiment in favor of good city government; methods of bringing public sentiment to bear upon the choice of good public officials; the churches and municipal reform; and practical methods for securing political reform.[27]

Those present were in general agreement that the government of the larger cities of the East was bad, that it was extravagant, inefficient, and corrupt. The weakest part of municipal government was the city council. Chief evils of local government were: the spoils system, national political partisanship, indifference of good citizens, contract system of performing city work, and the predominance of great corporations in city affairs. Solutions suggested included concentration of executive responsibility, divorcement of state and national politics from municipal elections, eradication of the spoils system, elimination of partisanship from municipal affairs, and management of the city as a business corporation. How were these reforms to be accomplished? The answers were: by education, by the activities of the churches and women's organizations, and by the formation of local reform associations to work for the selection of better public officials.

A few quotations from leading speakers will illustrate the practical nature of the discussion:

Theodore Roosevelt: In the end the work [of reform] has got to be done by actual, hard, stubborn, long-continued service in the field of practical politics itself.

Franklin MacVeagh: Our trouble, sir, is your trouble—the indifference and the neglect of the so-called good citizens. Our lack is the good citizenship of the good citizens.

Carl Schurz: I believe, however, that the widest possible application of civil service reform principles to all the departments of municipal government is not merely a desirable, but an indispensable complement of all the other reforms, for it touches the root of the evil. . . .

Mrs. Mary E. Mumford: Good city government is good housekeeping, and that is the sum of the matter.

Rev. James H. Ecob: The redemption of the city is the goal of our civic life.

James C. Carter: . . . We have a great deal better municipal government than we deserve.

Horace E. Deming: The majority of the people of this country will soon live in our cities; the majority of votes on election day will be cast in the cities; the majority of the country's wealth is already there. Most of the public offices are in the cities. If our cities are left impure, of what avail is a national government? We shall not have one very long. If we make our municipalities pure, the future of our institutions is assured.

Moorfield Storey: Municipal reform is only a question of will.

Charles J. Bonaparte: If you wish to secure for the community a better government, you must make the community deserve a better government, and show that it deserves it by getting it.[28]

Three resolutions were adopted by the Conference. One recorded the opinion of the meeting that the attainment of good municipal government required that national politics should be divorced from city elections and the administration of city affairs. The most important action taken was the adoption of a resolution calling for the appointment by the chairman of the Conference of a Committee of Seven to prepare a plan for the organization of a National Municipal League, to be composed of civic improvement associations in American cities. "Upon the completion of the plan and its approval by such associations, or as many of them as the said committee may deem necessary, the committee shall declare the proposed League to be fully organized and prepared to enter upon its work." Later it was voted that the chairman of the Conference should be a member of the committee and that additional members might be added at the committee's discretion. The Conference, by resolution, requested the committee to consider the advisability of holding another assembly at a time and place to be determined by them.[29]

Observers agreed that the principal significance of the Conference lay in its stimulation of interest in municipal reform. The N. Y. *Nation* stated that

> The conference on municipal government, . . . drew out a remarkable number of well-written papers. It cannot be said to have thrown any very new light on the problem of municipal reform, but it was invaluable as a means of rousing and extending interest on the subject among those who think about municipal reform at all. Ten years ago, nay, five years ago, no such gathering would have been possible. . . . It was noteworthy, too, that in the discussion very little, in fact no attention was bestowed on charters or distribution of powers. Nearly every address was devoted to the best means of bringing influence to bear on the voters in favor of better city government.[30]

Concluding its discussion of the Conference, the *Annals* declared:

> It lay in the nature of the situation that no immediate practical outcome should be the result of this Conference. But every citizen who was privileged to attend this Conference must have rejoiced at the evidence of growing interest in the great field of Municipal government. There were, of course, many different opinions as to the practical methods of securing the end desired, but all agreed as to the necessity of arousing public attention and educating public sentiment, if our city governments are to be improved. No subtle devices or complicated machinery will be of any avail unless the sense of civic duty can be aroused in the average citizen.[31]

The *Outlook* noted one omission in the program. "The soundness of these recommendations and the vigorous municipal spirit manifested made the Conference an event of public importance. The only limitation to its usefulness was its failure to consider the social reform measures in which the working class organizations are concerned."[32]

And the New York *Times* said: "The 'National Conference for Good City Government', . . . was, on the whole, most promising and successful. The papers that were read were clear, intelligent, and full of careful and accurate information. The crank who is liable at any moment to break in upon deliberations on any subject of reform was conspicuous by his absence. The range of the interest in the movement was very great."[33]

The committee in charge of the Conference recorded its opinion of the meeting in the introduction to the volume of proceedings.

> The Conference was successful from every point of view: it awakened renewed interest in the subject and effectively increased the zeal of those already engaged in the work; it aroused from indifference and apathy those who had heretofore considered the municipal problem as one of small importance; it brought the subject of needed reforms forcibly before the minds of those who realize that municipal government is the one conspicuous failure in the political system of the United States; it showed that the subject is actually receiving careful study and earnest attention from our ablest and foremost citizens; it has created that *esprit du* [*sic*] *corps* among the workers that will be a source of inspiration and strength; and it has given a substantial impetus to the cause in Philadelphia, and in every city where the evils of municipal maladministration have arrested the attention of its citizens.[34]

Herbert Welsh, a delegate from the Municipal League of Philadelphia, was impressed with the important part which women would probably take in the municipal reform movement. "In no small degree was the success of the Conference due to the work of intelligent, experienced, and enthusiastic women. Their aid was invoked in order to render the effort successful, and they responded to the appeal in various practical ways."[35]

ORGANIZATION OF THE LEAGUE

The Committee of Seven authorized by the Conference at Philadelphia to prepare a plan for the organization of a National Municipal League was subsequently appointed, with Herbert Welsh of Philadelphia as chairman. Other members were Charles Richardson of Philadelphia; James C. Carter, W. Harris Roome, and James W. Pryor of New York; Moorfield Storey of Boston; Charles J. Bonaparte of Baltimore; and Franklin MacVeagh of Chicago.[36] Work was begun immediately and correspondence with cities in all parts of the country ensued. Mr. Welsh recorded that letters giving information about reform organizations and of a desire to associate with similar organizations were received from Albany, Troy, Buffalo, Providence, Boston, Baltimore, Milwaukee, St. Paul, Minneapolis, Columbus, Denver, Pueblo, San Francisco, Los Angeles, Tacoma, Seattle, Birmingham, Sheboygan, and many other places.[37] Secretary James W. Pryor of the City Club of New York reported to the annual meeting of the club in April that correspondence in his office indicated that organizations eligible to membership in the League might be expected to develop in Brooklyn, Buffalo, Albany, Rochester, Troy, Utica, Schenectady, and Yonkers in New York; New Brunswick, New Jersey; Hartford, Connecticut; and Pittsburgh, Pennsylvania.[38]

In the same report the secretary stated that while the two representatives of the City Club on the organization committee were considering the matter, the committee, growing impatient of delay, had adopted the constitution in a form which might require several amendments. The chairman of the committee had submitted the constitution to a number of organizations expected to take part in the formation of the League and proposed to declare the League organized and to call a meeting of the delegates from those associations which had approved the constitution. Since coöperation of the City Club with the other associations was desirable, the only practical course seemed to be the adoption of the constitution as submitted, with strong recommendations to the Board of Delegates to accept certain amendments at its first meeting. The Council of Good Government Clubs had adopted the constitution as revised by the City Club representatives. New York had been suggested by the chairman of the organization committee as the proper place for the first meeting of delegates.[39]

Subsequent to the annual meeting of the City Club, Secretary Pryor communicated to Chairman Welsh the adoption of the constitution and the cordial invitation of the Club to hold the first meeting of the Board of Delegates at the club house.[40]

President Carter of the City Club called to order the first meeting of the Board of Delegates of the National Municipal League, held at the City Club of New York on May 28–29, 1894. Nineteen affiliated associations had appointed delegates, but representatives from only fifteen were present.[41] Charles Richardson of Philadelphia was chosen as temporary chairman, and James W. Pryor of New York, as temporary secretary.

The report of the organization committee (Committee of Seven) was made by Mr. Welsh. The committee had drafted a constitution for a National Municipal League and had submitted it for approval to the Municipal League of Philadelphia, City Club of New York, Municipal League of Boston, Citizens' Association of Boston, Reform League of Baltimore, Citizens' Reform Movement of Baltimore, Advance Club of Providence, and Board of Trade of Minneapolis. Each body had adopted the constitution and named delegates to the first meeting.[42]

It was voted to approve the constitution as submitted by the organization committee. The committee on by-laws reported that it was inexpedient to recommend to the Board of Delegates the adoption of a preamble to the constitution, which had been suggested by the City Club of New York. This preamble outlined the general principles for the conduct of city government. The committee on by-laws recommended the appointment of another committee to prepare an address to the public stating the objects of the League. This duty was later put in the hands of the Executive Committee. With a few changes the by-laws, as recommended by the committee on by-laws, were adopted.[43]

Officers, as provided in the by-laws, were elected as follows: president, James C. Carter, New York; first vice-president, Charles Richardson, Philadelphia; second vice-president, Samuel B. Capen, Boston; secretary, Clinton Rogers Woodruff, Philadelphia; treasurer, R. Fulton Cutting, New York; members of the executive committee: Herbert Welsh, Philadelphia; Dudley Tibbitts, Troy; Matthew Hale, Albany; Louis D. Brandeis, Boston; William G. Low, Brooklyn; Joseph A. Miller, Providence; and Charles J. Bonaparte, Baltimore.[44]

The question of a publication for the League came before the delegates when George G. Mercer of Philadelphia read a letter containing a proposition from William Draper Lewis of Philadelphia regarding the use of the columns of the *Saturday Review*. After some discussion, the matter was referred to the Executive Committee. Before the Conference in Philadelphia there had been some correspondence between the officers of the Municipal League of Philadelphia and those of the National Civil Service Reform League regarding the use of the columns of *Good Government* by the Municipal League of Philadelphia, the City Club of New York, and other similar organizations.[45] The Board of Delegates adopted a resolution reported by the Executive Committee, that the League would favor the establishment of a paper and directing the Executive Committee to promote such a paper if published under a control and auspices in which the Executive Committee should have confidence.[46]

A resolution was adopted approving the proposition that "the nomination and election of Municipal officers upon municipal issues alone and without regard to the national party organizations, is the best method of securing permanent good government for our cities." It was also voted that the Executive Committee should call a meeting of the Board of Delegates and a convention of the League at some time after the elections in the autumn and before the end of the year.[47]

During the second day of the Conference the Executive Committee held two brief sessions. Charles J. Bonaparte was chosen chairman of the committee and Clinton Rogers Woodruff, secretary. The chairman was instructed to prepare an address to the public and to submit it to each member of the committee for approval. Subcommittees on Grievances and Abuses, Finance, Publications, and Law were authorized. It was voted that associate members should pay an annual fee of five dollars and be entitled to receive the publications of the League. The question of a journal for the League was discussed and a resolution reported to the Board of Delegates. The secretary was authorized to have printed 500 copies of the constitution and by-laws, with the names of the officers of the Executive Committee and a list of affiliated associations, and to prepare a circular inviting individuals to become associate members.[48]

Under the auspices of the League a mass meeting was held on the evening of the second day. At this final gathering the purposes of the League, and the experiences of municipal reformers in several major cities, were presented.[49]

Constitution and By-Laws

As stated in the Constitution, the objects of the National Municipal League were:

First.–To multiply the numbers, harmonize the methods and combine the forces of all who realize that it is only by united action and organization that good citizens can secure the adoption of good laws and the selection of men of trained ability and proved integrity for all municipal positions, or prevent the success of incompetent or corrupt candidates for public office.

Second.–To promote the thorough investigation and discussion of the conditions and details of civic administration, and of the methods for selecting and appointing officials in American cities, and of laws and ordinances relating to such subjects.

Third.–To provide for such meetings and conferences and for the preparation and circulation of such addresses and other literature as may seem likely to advance the cause of Good City Government.

Any association in an American city having as its object the improvement of municipal government was declared eligible to membership. A member association might withdraw at any time. The League should have no connection with state or national parties or issues, and should confine its work strictly to municipal affairs. Management of the League was to be in the hands of a Board of Delegates chosen by the member associations. No limit was put upon the number of delegates each association might appoint. The Board of Delegates might admit additional associations to membership and terminate the membership of an association by a vote representing three-fourths of the associations belonging to the League. At League meetings a vote by associations must be taken when demanded by any delegate, and the vote of each association must be cast according to the preference of the majority of its delegates then present. Power to raise funds for necessary expenses was given to the Board of Delegates, but no dues or assessments could be levied and no association could be held liable for any sums except such as it might, from time to time, voluntarily agree to contribute. Admission of individuals as associate members of the League, without the right to vote or act for the League, was placed in the discretion of the Board of Delegates. Amendment of the constitution might be effected at any time by the votes of delegates representing three-fourths of the associations then belonging to the League.[50]

By-laws of the Board of Delegates adopted at the New York meeting required a stated meeting of the Board to be held in May of each year, the time and place to be selected by the Executive Committee. Special meetings might be called by the president or by the Executive Committee, and had to be called by the secretary on the demand of delegates from any five associations belonging to the League and located in as many different cities. Officers of the League, including a president, a first vice-president, and a second vice-president, were to be elected by ballot of the Board of Delegates at each stated or annual meeting. A secretary, a treasurer, and other officers deemed proper by the board were to be elected by the board or it might alternatively authorize the Executive Committee to appoint them. All officers of the Board of Delegates were to be ex officio members of the Executive Committee. Officers of the League were to be officers of the Board of Delegates. Seven delegates elected by the Board at each stated or annual meeting were to constitute the Executive Committee for the ensuing year. This committee, under the direction of the Board, was to have general charge and management of all the affairs of the League.[51]

Such was the original arrangement for the routine handling of the affairs of the League between conferences. However, in 1911 the Board of Delegates disappeared from the picture, and the then Executive Committee became reconstituted as the Council, while the small business committee which, created in 1904 for the sake of transacting business promptly, had carried on most of the work of the Executive Committee, now took over the name as well. This is of some importance for following the work of the League through the years subsequent to 1911 as transacted by the Council and the Executive Committee. The setup of these two bodies under the newer arrangement will be explained more fully in a later chapter.[52]

THREE YEARS' WORK, 1894–1897

From its organization in May, 1894, until the conclusion of the Louisville conference in May, 1897, the work of the League may be classified as (1) holding of four national conferences for good city government, (2) publication of literature on municipal reform, and (3) serving as the coördinator of the municipal reform movement. A brief discussion of each of these items will indicate the nature of the League's activities.

NATIONAL CONFERENCES FOR GOOD CITY GOVERNMENT

Four such conferences were sponsored by the League in this period, at Minneapolis, December 8–10, 1894; at Cleveland, May 29–31, 1895; at Baltimore, May 6–8, 1896; and at Louisville, May 5–7, 1897. At the Minneapolis conference papers were read dealing with the municipal governments of Minneapolis, St. Paul, Cleveland, and Milwaukee. Three papers were presented by university representatives: "The Elements of a Model Charter for American Cities," by Professor Edmund

J. James of the University of Pennsylvania; "Proportional Representation and Municipal Reform," by Professor Jeremiah W. Jenks of Cornell University; and "Some Essentials of Good City Government in the Way of Granting Franchises," by Professor Edward W. Bemis of the University of Chicago. William G. Low of Brooklyn spoke of the results secured by voluntary and temporary movements, and Herbert Welsh of Philadelphia discussed the subject of municipal leagues and good government clubs. Although at the Philadelphia conference veteran reformers predominated, this conference was characterized by the presence of a considerable number of younger men interested in political reform. In another respect the meeting differed from that at Philadelphia; the tone of the papers and addresses was more optimistic. Professor Jenks commented:

The one thing about this Conference that has impressed me more than any other is the general optimistic tone of all the papers and of all the addresses that have been made. Last year, at Philadelphia, the speakers seemed to vie with one another in telling big stories, I regret to say true stories, of the bold, bad men that were running the city governments of Philadelphia, New York, Boston and other cities. . . . Now, here, today the tone of the addresses has been quite different. We, of course, have heard of some places that are practically perfect now, although it is feared that they will not remain so in the future. Nearly all of the speakers have said something to this effect, that while their governments were not now perfect, and there was much to be desired, nevertheless, they were fairly good, and they were reasonably well satisfied with them.[53]

Professor James insisted that it was unfair to condemn all municipal governments in the United States as bad.

What is the present condition of city government in the United States? We are inclined to think sometimes, and it is fair to infer from the remarks that many people make, that city government is in a bad way in every part of the United States, and that in very much the same degree everywhere. I do not think that that is a fair description of the actual state of affairs. Very many of our American cities, particularly our smaller cities, are, I think, well administered, considering the conditions. Many more, I think, are indifferently administered, and I should say only a very few very badly; but of our large cities we may almost turn the statement about, and in the case of our very largest cities there is certainly much to be ashamed of.[54]

A feature of this conference was the defense by D. F. Simpson, city attorney of Minneapolis, of the strong council system of government in that city. It was a surprise to the visitors from the Atlantic states to learn that the strong council plan was as popular in the West as the strong mayor plan in the East. Godfrey Haas of Galesburg, Illinois, suggested that the secretary, in making arrangements for the next conference, provide for devoting part of the discussion to the smaller cities.[55]

Conformably to this suggestion, the program of the Cleveland conference centered about the problems of the smaller cities and the characteristic feature of the meeting was the large representation from municipalities of this class.[56] With regard to the program of the meeting, the *Outlook* commented:

The theme of the Conference is "Present Municipal Conditions in Cities of the Second Class." . . . This is truly a National exhibit, and, inasmuch as the smaller cities of the country are better governed than the large cities, the first-hand reports of the work that is being done in them cannot fail to be full of suggestion as well as information. The large cities have a way of assuming in reform movements a general leadership that does not belong to them. . . . The great cities have been the last places to be reached.[57]

In accordance with its established policy, the Cleveland conference refused to adopt several resolutions which were presented.[58] At the meeting of the Board of Delegates the League's constitution was amended to increase the number of vice-presidents from two to five, and the membership of the Executive Committee from seven to nine. This was to allow representation to western and southern cities.[59] A suggestion was made by N. F. Hawley of Minneapolis that the League organize a bureau of information and statistics. It was voted to refer the matter to the Executive Committee, which, at a subsequent meeting, promised consideration. Another delegate inquired whether the League could issue a digest of the charters of the different cities of the country.[60] Walker B. Spencer of New Orleans wanted more papers at future conferences dealing with such practical features of municipal government as the payment of salaries to city officials, control of cities by an elective council or by boards appointed by the mayor, and the problem of election of councilmen by a small constituency or by the city at large.[61]

The progress of municipal reform during the past sixteen months was proudly related by Secretary Woodruff. Before 1894, few active and aggressive reform bodies existed in cities. Pointing to the recent marked development, Mr. Woodruff indicated that there were forty-eight associations enrolled as affiliate members of the League, with several others awaiting admission. There were one hundred and eighty-five associate members, and League correspondents were active in every political division of the country, except in the Indian, Oklahoma, and Alaska Territories. When the League was organized there were between forty and fifty municipal reform organizations which were established mostly in the eastern states. By the time of the Cleveland meeting, there were one hundred and eighty, spread throughout thirty-one states. Western cities were as well represented as the East. Accompanying this growth, there had been a constant increase in literature on the subject of municipal reform and growing discussion in all the leading newspapers.[62]

A staff correspondent wrote to the *Outlook*:

The pervading tone of the convention was one of practical hopefulness—a hopefulness amply justified by the results which the National Municipal League has already accomplished. Indeed, one of the most interesting and effective reports of the entire Conference was Secretary Clinton Rogers Woodruff's account of the growth of the National Municipal League during the past year, with the organization of vigorous branches in various parts of the country.[63]

Special attention was given to the government of southern cities at the Baltimore conference in May, 1896. Reports were heard of conditions in Baltimore, Richmond, Atlanta, Nashville, Memphis, and of municipal reform in Georgia. Professor Leo S. Rowe of the University of Pennsylvania commented that the favorable accounts of the administration of several of these southern cities were somewhat of a surprise to the convention, which had been accustomed to hearing pessimistic reports from representatives of northern and western cities. Other papers discussed the conditions in Springfield, Massachusetts, Chicago, Albany, and Pittsburgh. Papers dealing with municipal ownership, control of franchises, organization of the council, and payment of salaries to municipal legislators provoked much discussion.[64]

In his annual report Secretary Woodruff congratulated the League on the fact that the municipal reform movement had continued to grow. "It seems to be definitely settled that the movement for good city government has come to stay. For a time it appeared to many to be of a spasmodic and temporary character." Most of the associations mentioned in the report of the last year were still in more or less active existence, and there had been an increase of 65 per cent, bringing the number of enrolled bodies to two hundred sixty-seven. Interest in reform was growing, and not only among lawyers, but among doctors, clergymen, businessmen, wage earners, and women. The correspondence of the League and the demand for the *Proceedings* of the Minneapolis and Cleveland conferences demonstrated that the interest was "deep, general and constantly growing." Since the Cleveland conference there had been much discussion of the problems of municipal government and the League's relation thereto. There had been some criticism that there was nothing more than discussion, that the delegates did nothing but talk. Suggestions had been made that the League should nominate reform candidates for offices in various cities, and furnish platforms for its affiliated associations. Such was not the true function of the League, he said.[65]

The Louisville conference in May, 1897, marked the end of the preliminary descriptive work of the League. Thereafter, few papers on municipal conditions appeared on the programs of the annual conferences. At this meeting, however, reports were received from Providence, New Haven, Rochester, New York, Philadelphia, Charleston, New Orleans, St. Louis, Kansas City, Missouri, San Francisco, and Ohio cities. The following papers were also read: "The Powers of Municipal Corporations," by Professor Frank J. Goodnow of Columbia University; "American Political Ideas and Institutions in their Relation to the Conditions of City Life," by Professor Leo S. Rowe of the University of Pennsylvania; "The Legislature in City and State, 1797–1897," by Horace E. Deming, New York; and "The Business Man in Municipal Politics," by Franklin MacVeagh, Chicago. George Chance, president of the Legislative Labor League of Pennsylvania, discussed the subject, "The Wage Earner in Politics," this being the first paper presented by a representative of labor.[66] Appointment of a committee to investigate and report on the feasibility of a Municipal Program was the most important action taken by the conference.[67] The work of this committee will be discussed later.[68]

Secretary Woodruff reported that the correspondence of the League indicated a continuance of the deep interest in municipal reform. "From all classes and from all sections; from the student and from the businessman; from the professional man and from the laborer, inquiries are daily received; and the newspapers, weeklies and magazines seem to vie with each other in giving information bearing on the numerous points at issue." The number of affiliated reform organizations had increased to 100, located in all sections of the country. Mr. Woodruff concluded his survey of the year's developments with this optimistic statement.

In every direction the outlook is bright and promising, not, perhaps, of the immediate fulfillment of all the hopes and desires of those who are most deeply interested; but of substantial progress and steady growth. The sentiment for better government is gaining day by day. It is not a movement for a particular form of local government nor of specific panaceas for municipal evils; but rather one to bring the citizens, those who are primarily responsible, to a fuller appreciation and a more general discharge of the duties of citizenship—in short, a movement for citizenship reform.[69]

LITERATURE ON MUNICIPAL REFORM

In addition to publishing the *Proceedings* of the Philadelphia, Minneapolis, Cleveland, Baltimore, and Louisville conferences the League prepared four pamphlets and distributed in the first year 24,000 copies.[70] On several occasions the Executive Committee considered proposals of the publishers of municipal journals that their magazine should be selected as the organ of the League, but each time it was voted that it was not the desire of the League either to establish or to adopt an official publication.[71] The League also served as a bureau of information, answering many questions addressed to it on the subject of muncipal government and its reform.[72]

COÖRDINATION OF MUNICIPAL REFORM EFFORTS

An important phase of the League's work was the bringing together for conference and for exchange of opinion and experience those already engaged in the work of municipal improvement. At the conferences held under the auspices of the League there were assembled not only those interested in the general problem of municipal government, but also many with practical experience in the administration of cities.[73] As Secretary Woodruff said in his report to the Cleveland conference, "The League has done and is doing its utmost to coördinate all the forces making for civic righteousness, and to bring into closer and more harmonious relations all workers in behalf of better municipal government."[74]

SUMMARY

In the generally deplorable condition of municipal life in the post Civil War era the mobilization of agencies of civic reform was inevitable. When municipal mismanagement in a community became intolerable, groups were organized to combat vicious political machines, to elect honest men to public office, and to bring about improvements in governmental practice. Although few in number, limited in funds, and confronted with powerful opposition, these determined pioneers laid the foundation for the "great era of reform" of the 'nineties.[75]

Before the Philadelphia conference there had been no harmony of action among municipal reformers nor any effort to unify their forces. This conference brought together veteran reformers from many cities. The practical consequence of the meeting was the appointment of a committee to draft a constitution for a National Municipal League. Organization of the League was accomplished at a meeting in New York in May, 1894. Within the next three years four conferences on good city government were held in different sections of the country. These meetings of the workers in the field and those actively interested in the problem of good city government furnished opportunity for the exchange of information and experience. Those who participated came to a realization that the reform of municipal government was more than a local issue; it was a national problem of significant consequences to the people of the entire country. There was almost universal agreement that municipal government, generally speaking, was bad. But no unanimity existed as to causes and remedies. One theory was that the problem was largely a moral one; there was something wrong in human nature, and the citizenship should be reformed. Another view was that reform could come only through a change in governmental organization.

As a consequence of such diversity of opinion, no attempt was made for several years to formulate the principles of municipal reform into a definite creed. At the Louisville conference in 1897 a Committee on Municipal Program was authorized, and around its investigations and reports centered the activities of the League for the next several years.

III

A Municipal Program

PROFESSOR Frank J. Goodnow, a distinguished student of municipal government, stated in 1897 that there existed "no generally accepted theory of municipal government." The proof of this was to be found in the proceedings of the Minneapolis and Cleveland conferences of the League, where the discussions of the problems of municipal government by speakers from all parts of the country had revealed "an almost complete lack of agreement upon the part of those present as to the proper system of municipal organization for this country."[1]

FIRST MUNICIPAL PROGRAM

It was a general realization of this situation which prompted the Louisville meeting of the League, in May, 1897, to adopt unanimously the following resolution, proposed by Horace E. Deming of New York:

> *Resolved*, That the Executive Committee appoint a Committee of Ten to report on the feasibility of a municipal program, which shall embody the essential principles that must underlie successful municipal government, and which shall also set forth a working plan or system, consistent with American industrial and political conditions, for putting such principles into practical operation; and said committee, if it find such municipal program to be feasible, is instructed to report the same, with its reasons therefor, to the League for consideration. . . .[2]

In accordance with this resolution the Executive Committee nominated ten persons. The secretary was instructed to communicate with the absent members of the committee to secure their approval not later than May 24. Those selected were: Horace E. Deming, Albert Shaw, New York; Frank J. Goodnow, Columbia University; Alfred T. White, Brooklyn; Nathan Mathews, Jr., Boston; George W. Guthrie, Pittsburgh; Edmund J. James, University of Chicago; Charles Richardson, Clinton Rogers Woodruff, Philadelphia; and Leo S. Rowe, University of Pennsylvania. Alternates were named as follows: Moorfield Storey, Louis D.

---

[1] For notes to chap. iii, see pp. 214–216.

Brandeis, Boston; Albert Bushnell Hart, Harvard University; Jeremiah W. Jenks, Cornell University; and John F. Dillon, New York.[3]

A committee of seven, instead of ten, was the final outcome. Horace E. Deming was chosen chairman. Mr. Deming had been engaged in the practice of law in New York City since 1877. Beginning with the organization in 1880 of the Brooklyn Young Republican Club, he had been a founder and officer and member of active committees, of numerous clubs and civic associations working for ballot, civil service, and charter reform. He was counsel to the committee of the New York State Senate that investigated the administration of the civil service, and drafted the bill which became the basis of the present civil service law. He was a member of a special committee of the New York Bar Association to report on a proposed new charter for Greater New York. Mr. Deming was one of the signers of the endorsement of the call for the first National Conference for Good City Government; he attended the Philadelphia conference and was a delegate, appointed by the City Club of New York, to the first meeting of the League in New York, in May, 1894.[4]

Serving also on the committee were Dr. Frank J. Goodnow, professor of administrative law at Columbia University; Dr. Albert Shaw, New York, editor of the *Review of Reviews;* George W. Guthrie, prominent Democratic attorney of Pittsburgh; Charles Richardson, reformer and retired businessman of Philadelphia; Dr. Leo S. Rowe, assistant professor of political science at the University of Pennsylvania; and Clinton Rogers Woodruff, secretary of the League, who acted as committee secretary. Regarding the members of the committee, Secretary Woodruff said: "Of the seven, five had been trained as lawyers—although only three were practicing attorneys, the other two serving as professors in educational institutions—one was a trained journalist, and the other a retired business man with an experience as a civil service examiner in Philadelphia." All members of the committee, except one, were college trained. Three had studied abroad and had published important treatises on European municipal government. The personnel of the committee represented men of strong personal convictions, "belonging to different parties, looking at the question of municipal government from widely different standpoints, trained in different schools of political thought. . . ." It was a cause for congratulation that such a committee was able to present a unanimous report.[5] The *Outlook* considered the committee "as well informed a body of specialists on municipal matters as could easily be secured."[6] Professor J. A. Fairlie recorded: "All had long been interested in problems of municipal government and had given a great deal of attention to the subject. . . ."[7] Members resided in only two states; three lived in New York City, three in Philadelphia, and one in Pittsburgh.

After eighteen months of hard work the Committee on Municipal Program made its preliminary report to the conference of the League in Indianapolis, November 30 to December 2, 1898. The committee said that it had no apology to offer for presenting this outline sketch of its labors. The task assigned to them had few, if any, precedents. They were asked to crystallize the results of the experience of American and European cities into a program applicable to present conditions.

"Under such circumstances it became necessary to proceed with great caution and conservatism. The committee keenly felt the necessity of bringing any system that they might recommend into organic relation with the traditions and accepted political ideas of the American people."[8]

In addition to the text of the Constitutional Amendments and Muncipal Corporations Act the committee submitted papers by four of its members discussing some of the fundamental principles which furnished the basis of the Municipal Program.[9] Each paper had been approved by the several members of the committee and constituted essential parts of its report. The titles were: "The Municipal Problem in the United States," by Horace E. Deming; "The Place of the Council and of the Mayor in the Organization of Municipal Government—The Necessity of Distinguishing Legislation from Administration," by Frank J. Goodnow; "The City in the United States—The Proper Scope of Its Activities," by Albert Shaw; and "Municipal Franchises," by Charles Richardson. These principal papers were discussed in prepared comments by leading students of the municipal problem.[10] The report of the committee and its discussion, formal and informal, constituted the major part of the proceedings of the Indianapolis conference.

Each speaker was in sympathy with the underlying principles of the report, but there was some criticism of details. C. S. Palmer objected to the provision giving the mayor, instead of the heads of departments, the right to appoint subordinate officers and employees. Professor John R. Commons of Syracuse University said that the committee had imitated English and German cities in giving large general powers to the council, but had not provided adequate central supervisory agencies, such as the English Local Government Board. He also thought that the committee had not carried out the principle of separation of powers to its logical conclusion, which was that the mayor should not have the veto power over the council. N. F. Hawley foresaw serious obstacles in the way of adoption of the program by state legislatures. First, it attempted too many reforms and innovations in one document; second, the constitutional amendments contained too many matters of detail; and third, it did not give cities sufficient choice as to the form of their government. He criticized, too, the provision giving the mayor power to appoint and remove the judges of the municipal courts.[11]

At the conclusion of the conference a resolution was adopted referring the report and all criticisms and suggestions to the committee with instructions to complete its work and report to the next annual meeting of the League.[12]

The final report of the committee was made to the Columbus conference, November 16–18, 1899. First vice-president Charles Richardson, in the chair, stated in his introductory remarks, that nearly all of the work of final revision had fallen on Chairman Deming, capably assisted by Professor Goodnow. Denying that the final report was the work of any one man, Mr. Deming explained the method of revision of the report.

> A special addition [sic] of the draft, as amended, was printed and sent out to thinkers and workers on this subject everywhere in the United States. Criticisms short, criticisms long, criticisms cursory and criticisms elaborate

were received. These were copied and copies put into the hands of every member of your Committee. The suggestions were tabulated and classified and these were put into the hands of every member of your Committee. Your Committee met, discussed these criticisms and these suggestions, and your Committee held not only personal meetings, but numerous meetings by correspondence; and when the final draft was reached, that was printed and was in turn sent around to the members of the Committee, and another, and another, and another—and I don't know how many final drafts, until at last, in the form in which it appears here, it was printed.[13]

In connection with the final report five papers were presented discussing different aspects of the program. Three of these were prepared by members of the committee and had been read and approved by their colleagues. The title of Professor Goodnow's paper was "Political Parties and City Government under the Proposed Municipal Program;" Mr. Deming's, "Public Opinion and City Government under the Proposed Municipal Program;" and Professor Rowe's, "Public Accounting under the Proposed Municipal Program." Two papers were presented by persons not members of the committee. Bird S. Coler, controller of New York City, read a paper, "The Power to Incur Indebtedness under the Proposed Municipal Program," and Dr. Delos F. Wilcox of Elk Rapids, Michigan, contributed a paper entitled, "An Examination of the Proposed Municipal Program."[14] The last two papers were incorporated in the final report of the committee. Other papers discussing the Program had been prepared in advance, at the invitation of the committee.[15] Accompanying the committee's report were the revised drafts of the Constitutional Amendments and the Municipal Corporations Act.[16]

As at the Indianapolis conference, there were some suggestions for change. William Dudley Foulke of Richmond, Indiana, thought that there should be a two-thirds vote to carry bond propositions instead of a majority, and that the method of election of the council took that body too far away from the expression of public opinion. He suggested election of one-third of the membership every year, or election of the entire body every two years. Allen W. Thurman of Columbus argued that the report should go further and recommend a compulsory primary election law and municipal ownership.[17] Mr. Deming believed that some of these suggestions could be put into the text of the final report as alternatives or as footnotes. A motion was unanimously adopted approving the report of the committee and referring it to the Executive Committee with power to act, and the Committee on Municipal Program was then by formal vote of the conference discharged, with the thanks of the League.[18]

The text of the constitutional amendments and of the Municipal Corporations Act,[19] together with the nine papers in explanation of the program presented at the Indianapolis and Columbus conferences, and two additional papers, were published the following year in book form.[20] A brief historical sketch, "Municipal Development in the United States," by Dr. John A. Fairlie of Columbia University; and "A Summary of the Program," by Professor Rowe were the other papers included in the volume.[21]

The Municipal Program consisted of three parts: first, five constitutional amendments; second, a Municipal Corporations Act; and third, the eleven supplementary papers mentioned above. A word of explanation may be needed as to why the program contained both a series of constitutional amendments and a Municipal Corporations Act. The committee was proposing a uniform system of municipal government intended to cover the needs of every state. While many of the features of the program could have been carried out by the legislatures in the different states, constitutional amendment was thought necessary to protect the program from future legislative interference, and thus insure a measure of stability and permanence in local government. It was expected by the committee that the Municipal Corporations Act would be generally adopted before the constitutional amendments, and that the acceptance of the act would facilitate the adoption of the amendments.[22] Because of its importance a rather full digest of the municipal program will now be given.[23]

RELATION OF CITY TO STATE

City government is subject to the limitations contained in the constitution and general laws of the state applicable either to all the inhabitants or to all the cities of the state. Special laws for cities may be enacted in the following manner. A special law affecting a city must receive the affirmative vote of two-thirds of all the members of the legislature, and before going into effect must secure the formal approval of the city council within sixty days after passage by the legislature. Should the city council disapprove, the law, to become effective, must be again passed by the legislature within thirty days after such local veto. Such passage must be by the affirmative vote of two-thirds of all the members of the legislature, which two-thirds must include three-fourths of the legislators from districts outside of the city or cities to be affected. Failure of a city council to act at all, either favorably or unfavorably, is to be deemed a disapproval of the special law. Special laws may be repealed by the procedure provided for the passage of general laws.

Any city with a population of twenty-five thousand or more may adopt its own charter and frame of government. Such charters are subject to the constitution and general laws of the state and to such special laws as may be passed in the manner provided above. Procedure for the adoption and amendment of home rule charters is provided.

It is made the duty of the legislature to pass a general municipal corporations act, which shall apply to all cities in the state adopting it by popular vote. All cities created after the passage of the act shall be organized under its provisions.

Every city incorporated under the act shall be the local agent of the state government for the enforcement of state laws within its corporate limits, except as otherwise provided by general law applicable to all cities. The legislature, by general law, may subject every city incorporated under the act to the supervision and control of such state administrative boards and officers as may be established for the purpose.

A financial report containing a statement of the receipts, expenditures, and debt of the city, must be made, at least once a year, to the state controller or other officer or board exercising supervision over local finances. Such reports shall be certified as to their correctness by the state controller, printed, and submitted by him to the next regular session of the legislature. The controller shall have power to examine into the affairs of the financial department of any city, particularly its financial condition and resources, the method and accuracy of its accounts, and to determine whether requirements of the constitution and laws have been met. For this purpose he shall have the power to administer oaths, and to compel the attendance of witnesses and the production of books and papers. A report of each examination must be made, and shall be kept as a public record in the controller's office.

The state governor may remove any mayor for misconduct, as well as for inability or failure properly to perform his duties. A public opportunity to be heard in his defense must be given to the accused official. Decision of the governor, when filed with the reasons therefor in the office of the secretary of state, is final. Pending investigation, the governor may suspend a mayor from office for thirty days.

POWERS OF CITY

Subject to limitations contained in the state constitution, general laws, and special laws enacted in accordance with the provisions above described, every city is vested with "all powers of government," including the power to acquire, hold, manage, control, and dispose of property within or without the city limits, to license and regulate all trades, occupations, and businesses, and to perform and render all public services. "Within its corporate limits, it shall have the same powers of taxation as are possessed by the State." This includes the authority to make local improvements by special assessment, or by special taxation, or both.

The usual corporate powers—perpetual succession, use of a common seal, right to sue and be sued—are conferred upon a municipality. Each city shall also have power to enact ordinances "necessary to protect health, life, and property, to prevent and summarily abate and remove nuisances, and to preserve and enforce the good government, order, and security of the city and its inhabitants." It may enforce its ordinances by reasonable fines and penalties, and establish minor courts to be vested with the civil and criminal jurisdiction of justices of the peace.

Full power is given to the city to establish and maintain streets, sidewalks, bridges, water works, and sewers; to regulate the height of buildings and method and style of construction; to dispose of sewage, refuse, and garbage; to establish, maintain, and regulate wharves, docks, harbors, ferries, markets, abattoirs, workhouses, houses of correction, reformatory institutions, hospitals, charitable institutions; and to establish and maintain schools, museums, libraries, and other institutions "for the instruction, enlightenment and welfare of its inhabitants. . . ." A city may annex territory contiguous and adjacent to its limits in accordance with conditions prescribed in the act. Powers and requirements specified in the act with reference to street and other franchises, indebtedness, tax rate, and city accounts are described below.[24]

THE COUNCIL

The mayor and council-form of government is prescribed by the act. The council is to be a unicameral body, composed of at least nine and not more than fifty members, the exact size to be determined by local conditions. Members are to be elected on a general ticket from the city at large and are to serve for six years, one-third of the membership being elected every two years. Where local conditions make it impractical to hold two elections at different times in the same year, the term of a member of the council could be fixed at three years, with one-third of the council being elected each year. Retiring members are eligible for reëlection. Councilmen shall serve without remuneration. No qualifications are prescribed, but ineligibility is established by the following provision: "No member of the Council shall hold any other public office or hold any office or employment the compensation for which is paid out of public moneys; or be elected or appointed to any office created or the compensation of which is increased by the Council while he was a member thereof, until one year after the expiration of the term for which he was elected; or be interested directly or indirectly in any contract with the city; or be in the employ of any person having any contract with the city, or of any grantee of a franchise granted by the city." The council is the judge of the qualification and election of its own members, subject to judicial review; may elect its own officers; determine its rules of procedure; compel the attendance of members; and punish and expel its members. Conviction of bribery results in forfeiture of office.

A president of the body shall be elected from its own membership. The time and place of regular meetings may be prescribed by ordinance, but the mayor may at any time call a special meeting. All sessions of the council and of its committees shall be public. Final passage of an ordinance or resolution shall not occur on the day of its introduction, "except in case of public emergency, and then only when requested by the Mayor and approved by the affirmative votes of three-fourths of all the members of the Council."

The council "shall have full power and authority, except as otherwise provided, to exercise all powers conferred upon the city, subject to the veto of the Mayor. . . ." It has the power to regulate the assessment and collection of taxes, and to make regular and special appropriations, except that it may not increase the mayor's budget. Its powers with reference to franchises, debts, direct legislation, minority or proportional representation, will be made a matter of detailed discussion in subsequent pages.[25]

Complete authority to organize the administrative service is given to the council. Only one head of a department is created by the charter—the city controller, who is to be elected by the council and subject to removal by it. All other offices are to be created by the council, which has the power to fix salaries and duties, but appointments to all such positions shall be made by the mayor. There shall be no elective city officials other than the mayor and members of the council. All departments and officers of the city may be investigated by the council or a committee of the council, and full power is given to the investigating agency to enable it to secure the facts.

MAYOR AND ADMINISTRATIVE SERVICE

The mayor, chief executive officer of the city, is elected for a term of two years. His compensation is fixed by the council, but may not be changed after his election. The president of the council shall act as mayor, in case of a vacancy or during the temporary absence or disability of the mayor. Procedure in the removal of the mayor by the governor has already been described.[26]

When requested by the council, it is the duty of the mayor and department heads to attend council meetings and answer questions relative to administrative affairs. The chief executive officer and heads of departments have the right to be present and take part in council proceedings, but not the right to vote. A limited veto of council ordinances and resolutions is given to the mayor, and also the item veto of appropriations. He prepares and submits the annual budget to the council, which may reduce or omit any item, but not increase either any item or the total expenses.

All directors of departments, except the city controller, are appointed by the mayor. Subject to the civil service provisions of the act, the mayor has the power to appoint all officers and employees in the subordinate administrative service and to fill all vacancies. Department heads may appoint and remove laborers. No fixed term of office is provided for officers and employees. Subject to the removal provisions of the act, they hold their offices without definite terms, and at the pleasure of the mayor. Power is given to the mayor to investigate the management of any city department or the conduct of any administrative official.

Eleven pages of the act are given to the detailed civil service provisions. A municipal civil service commission, to be composed of three or more suitable persons appointed by the mayor, is charged with the duty of administering the civil service regulations. Such regulations shall provide for the classification of officers and employments based on duties and functions; for appointments to be made on the basis of open, competitive examinations, where practicable (ordinary laborers excepted) ; for vacancies to be filled by the selection of one of the three highest on the eligible list; for temporary appointments not to exceed thirty days; for a probationary period not over three months; and for promotion based on merit, competition, and seniority. Specific regulations are designed to prevent political assessments, subscriptions, or contributions. Restrictions on the power of removal protect the tenure of employees. Removal, reduction in grade or salary, or transfer of any officer or employee shall not be made on account of religious or political beliefs or opinions. Before any official is removed, reduced, or transferred, he must first be given a written statement of the reasons therefor, and a duplicate copy of this statement must be filed in the office of the civil service commissioners. If demanded by the official, the statement of reasons, with his reply, must be made a matter of public record in the archives of the city.

FISCAL AFFAIRS

A city controller, to be elected and subject to removal by the council, is established by the act. He is to head the department of finance and keep the books of accounts and make the financial reports to the state authorities, as required by the act. A separate record for each grantee of a franchise from the city must be kept in his office. He is to audit all bills, claims, and demands against the treasury, and settle all claims in favor of or against the city. He must, before January 15 of each year, give the council a report of the financial transactions of the municipality during the past calendar year.

The city is given power to borrow on the credit of the corporation, "but the credit of the city shall not in any manner be given or loaned to or in aid of any individual, association, or corporation, except that it may make suitable provision for the aid and support of its poor." Total indebtedness shall not exceed a certain per cent (between five and ten) of the assessed valuation of real estate within the city subject to taxation. Two classes of indebtedness are not included in this limitation: revenue bonds issued in anticipation of the collection of taxes, unless they are not paid within two years from the date of issue, and bonds issued for self-liquidating municipal projects, such as the supply of water or other projects from which the city will derive a revenue. Bonds for this latter purpose must have the approval of two-thirds of the members of the council, the mayor, and a majority of the qualified electors of the city casting their votes at the next ensuing municipal election.

City taxes levied against real and personal property or either of them, "in addition to providing for the principal and interest of the then outstanding bonded indebtedness shall not in the aggregate exceed in any one year . . . per centum of the assessed valuation of the real and personal estate subject to taxation by such city. . . ."

Contracts for services rendered, or for goods or materials furnished, shall not be made for a longer period than five years. Except those for services rendered, all contracts must be made upon specifications, and the manner of letting shall be prescribed by general ordinance. Every contract must be countersigned by the controller. Reference has already been made to the executive budget system established by the act.[27]

FRANCHISES AND PUBLIC UTILITIES

Article II, section 10 of the Municipal Corporations Act, provides:

> The rights of the city in and to its water front, ferries, wharf property, land under water, public landings, wharves, docks, streets, avenues, parks, bridges, and all other public places are hereby declared to be inalienable, except by a four-fifths vote of all the members elected to the Council, approved by the Mayor; and no franchise or lease or right to use the same, either on, through, across, under, or over, and no other franchise granted by the city to any private corporation, association, or individual, shall be granted for a longer period than twenty-one years; and, in addition to any other form of compensation, the grantee shall pay annually a sum of money, based in amount upon its gross receipts, to the city.

In case of purchase of the property by the city, upon the termination of the grant, no payment shall be made for the value of the franchise. Every grantee of a franchise from the city must keep books of accounts and make quarterly financial reports to the city controller, who may inspect the grantee's books of accounts.

Before the final vote, all franchise ordinances must be published, at the applicant's expense, not less than twice in each of two newspapers having a general circulation in the city and to be designated by the mayor.

Complete freedom is given to the city to determine its public ownership policy. It may

> ... acquire or construct, and may also operate on its own account, and may regulate or prohibit the construction or operation of railroads or other means of transit or transportation and methods for the production or transmission of heat, light, electricity, or other power, in any of their forms, by pipes, wires, or other means.

Another article germane to this general topic is that which prohibits the legislature from passing "a private or local bill granting to any private corporation, association, or individual, any exclusive privilege, immunity, or franchise whatever."

ELECTORAL METHODS

Legislation shall be enacted providing for the personal registration of voters and for secrecy in balloting. No election for any city office shall be held on the same date as the election for state and national officials. Nomination of elective officials shall be by petition signed by not more than fifty qualified voters of the city, and filed with the mayor at least thirty days before the date of the election. The form of the ballot is determined by the council, "but the names of all candidates for the same office must be printed upon the ballot in alphabetical order under the title of such office."

Direct legislation, minority or proportional or other method of representation in elections, may be established by direct vote of the people. On petition signed by a certain percentage of those voting at the last election, the council must submit the proposition at the next city election and a majority affirmative vote causes the proposal to go into effect immediately.

GENERAL PROVISIONS

Legal actions by citizens are permitted to restrain the execution of any fraudulent contract by the city, the payment of unauthorized claims, or salaries of persons in the administrative service not appointed in accordance with law and regulations.

Sections of the program dealing with the public schools are brief. The city is given power to establish and maintain schools, and the duty of determining the number and salaries of teachers and employees is left to the officer or board in charge of the educational system of the city.[28]

PRINCIPLES OF THE PROGRAM

With the above summary of the principal provisions of the program in mind, we may now consider other aspects of the report. Part of the program consisted, as has already been noted, of a series of articles by members of the committee and others "setting forth the philosophical, political and psychological relations of the recommendations to existing conditions."[29] These papers constituted a very able explanation and defense of the program. Space will not permit a detailed analysis of the arguments and exposition contained in these addresses. But it is possible to select certain passages which will illustrate the theory and philosophy on which the program was based, and also its fundamental principles and nature.

HOME RULE

Special legislation for cities was not absolutely prohibited, but it was surrounded by certain safeguards designed to protect the city from unwarranted interference with its local affairs. Home rule, the right to adopt and amend charters, was given to cities with a population of 25,000 or more. As Chairman Deming said: "The city's independence is guaranteed. The state legislature can not meddle with purely local affairs."[30] Elsewhere Mr. Deming defined the fundamental principle of the program in these words: ". . . ample power in the city to conduct the local government, without possibility of outside assistance or of outside interference save by such supervision of a central state administrative authority as may be necessary to enforce a state law applicable alike to all the cities or all the inhabitants of the state." All else in the program was detail in the application of this principle.[31] And Professor Rowe declared that the object of the program was to provide such a position in the political system of the state and such a framework of government as would give to the city the widest possible freedom of action in formulating the details of its own organization and in the determination of its local policy.[32]

SUBSTITUTION OF ADMINISTRATIVE FOR LEGISLATIVE CONTROL

Professor Goodnow was the first student of American government to point out the great legislative centralization and administrative decentralization which had existed in our political system. He advocated home rule for cities, subject to a considerable control by state administrative agencies, and fortified his argument by the experience of British, French, and German cities under such a plan. Largely through his influence the program included provisions to establish a limited supervision of municipal activities in the field of finance and other activities of interest to the state as a whole.[33]

Mr. Deming pointed out that it was the intent of the program to leave the legislature no excuse to meddle with local government and to give to cities such a grant of powers as to discourage application to the legislature for additional powers. In developing the argument for the substitution of state administrative supervision for legislative control, he said:

> In so far as the municipal corporation is made the agent of the State to enforce and administer general laws within the corporate limits, it should be under the supervision of and responsible to central State administrative departments and not subject to the sport of special legislation.
>
> A municipality thus constituted is not an *imperium in imperio,* but a free self-governing community, subject to State administrative supervision as to all matters of general State policy to be enforced throughout the State. Legislative interference is eliminated. Home rule is not only possible, but compulsory.[34]

ELIMINATION OF PARTISANSHIP FROM MUNICIPAL AFFAIRS

At the Philadelphia conference and every subsequent meeting of the League discussion of the methods of separating municipal from national and state politics was an important feature of the programs. How did the Municipal Program propose to eliminate partisanship from city government? Professor Goodnow mentioned civil service regulations, indefinite tenure of administrative officers and employees, limitations on removals, a uniform system of municipal accounting under state supervision, limited term for franchise grants, restrictions on special legislation, home rule, a simple municipal organization, state central administrative control, permission to adopt direct legislation and minority or proportional representation, separation of municipal from state and national elections, and provisions for nomination by petition, personal registration, secrecy in voting, and a blanket ballot with candidates alphabetically listed for each office.

In concluding his article, "Political Parties and City Government under the Proposed Municipal Program," Professor Goodnow said:

> It has been felt that city government must, to be efficient, be emancipated from the tyranny of the national and State political parties, and from that of the Legislature—the tool of the party. It must, however, be subject to the proper control of the State government as the representative of the interests of the State. To avoid tyranny and preserve control is not easy. The problem may be solved, however, by diminishing both the temptations and opportunities for tyranny and by throwing limitations about the exercise of the control without destroying it. These temptations and opportunities have, it is hoped, been diminished by making special legislation very difficult, by enlarging the powers of the cities, by making the control of the city government of little value to the parties through reduction of patronage and a publicity of accounts, and finally by making it easy for the city voter to separate city from State and national issues, and to insist that these city issues shall receive attention apart from any consideration of national and State politics. The State control has been preserved, but its exercise has been taken from the legislature and entrusted to administrative officers wherever it has been felt that its preservation is absolutely necessary.[35]

GENERAL GRANT OF POWERS TO MUNICIPALITIES

The rule of narrow construction of municipal powers by the courts has been the prevailing one in the United States. As stated by Judge J. F. Dillon, unless a power was specifically granted or necessarily implied in the express grant, or absolutely essential to the declared objects and purposes for which the municipal corporation was created, the legal presumption was against the existence of such a power.[36] The detailed enumeration of powers in a city charter not only restricted the activities of a city but compelled it to appeal to the state legislature for additional authority to meet new conditions.

A bold departure from the existing system was contained in the committee's recommendation that a city should have "all powers of government," subject only to the limitations found in the constitution, general laws, and special laws enacted in the manner provided in the Program.

The comment of Professor Rowe among others was typical:

> This recommendation is unquestionably a departure from the traditional rules of the law of public corporations. The courts have always required a specific grant from the Legislature to justify an exercise of local authority. In giving to the municipality all powers not inconsistent with the general laws of the State, the endeavor has been made to reverse the policy of the past and to create the presumption in favor of the broadest exercise of municipal powers. The history of municipal government clearly shows that the constant appeals to the State Legislature for additional powers has been one of the most unfortunate influences in our public life. It has created the impression that the real seat of city government is in the State Legislature, rather than in the city authorities, and has developed the unfortunate habit of constant interference by the former body in local affairs.[37]

WIDE SCOPE OF MUNICIPAL ACTIVITIES

Article II of the Municipal Corporations Act was intended "to confer a very broad and general liberty upon the municipal corporation to do things, local and municipal in their nature, which do not interfere with the general work of the State government, nor with the rights and immunities of communities or individuals." Dr. Shaw stated that it was the opinion of the committee that nobody could decide so well as the individual municipality how far it would carry its activities and in what variety of ways it would make itself serviceable to its citizens.[38]

In the field of public utilities the committee was unanimous, according to Mr. Richardson, that the city should have the freedom of choosing its own policy, of leasing its franchises or operating services for its own benefit. This did not mean that the committee endorsed the policy of municipal ownership. As announced by Dr. Shaw: "It is not that the proposed Municipal Program advocates the municipal construction, much less the municipal operation, of a transit line. It does not at this moment devolve upon us either to advocate or to condemn any particular innovation or extension of municipal functions. What we contend for is that in all these matters . . . the municipal corporation ought to be in as good a position under the law as any private corporation to engage directly in the business of supply."

The generous grant of governmental powers, including those over street franchises, and the large borrowing and taxing powers insured to the city ample power to control its local development. And, as Secretary Woodruff pointed out, ". . . the control which the state may exercise over cities through its executive and its administrative officers makes it equally certain that the cities will not be able to make use of their large powers contrary to the best interests of the state as a whole."[39]

SEPARATION OF ADMINISTRATIVE AND LEGISLATIVE FUNCTIONS

A favorite theory of Professor Goodnow's was the distinction between legislation and administration. All functions of government were reducible to two: legislation, or the determination of the public policy; and administration, the execution of the policy after it had been determined. These functions should be assigned to separate agencies of government. To employ the precise language of Professor Goodnow:

> It is a distinction based upon a sound psychology. In the case of a single sentient being the will must be formulated, if not expressed, before its execution is possible. In the case of political bodies, which are more and more coming to be recognized as subject to psychological law, not only must the will or policy be formulated before it can be executed, but also the very complexity of their operations makes it almost impossible to intrust the same authority as well with the execution as with the determination of the public policy. This is so not merely because the function of determining the public policy requires deliberation while the function of its execution requires quickness of action, but also because the burden of government is too great to permit of its being borne by any one authority.[40]

Such a principle could easily be applied to municipal government, since it was largely a matter of administration. In recent years municipal government had been frequently characterized as a matter of business and not of government. "What is meant by this characterization is really not that the criteria of municipal government are the criteria of business, industry, or commerce . . . but that success in city government is to be expected only where the officers of that government . . . are efficient. In other words, what people mean, when they say that municipal government is business, is that municipal government is administration."[41]

The committee accepted this fundamental distinction between legislation and administration and recommended in its Municipal Program a city council with large legislative or policy-determining powers and a mayor, in whom was vested all administrative powers.

REHABILITATION OF THE COUNCIL

Perhaps no feature of the program represented a greater departure from existing conditions or drew more criticism from contemporary reviewers than the proposal to rehabilitate the council and to restore it to a position of power and importance in the city government.

Professor Goodnow defended the form of municipal organization recommended by the committee. He pointed out that decline in the powers of the council had resulted in the transfer from the city to the state legislature of the power of determining local policy. "If, then, municipal home rule is of any importance, i.e., if it is important that the local municipal policy shall be locally determined, a city council, i.e., a local legislature, is an essential part of the municipal organization." Another result of the gradual destruction of the council was the vesting of practically all municipal legislative and administrative powers, locally exercised, in the mayor and other administrative officers, for example, the charters of New York, and Brooklyn before consolidation. "Such a plan . . . has the serious disadvantage of making impossible the distinction between legislation and administration and of almost precluding permanence of tenure for administrative officers." Hence, a second reason for the restoration of the powers of the council was that it made possible the distinction between legislation and administration in municipal government. But such a plan, to be successful, must deny to the council the exercise of administrative powers. "Our government will in none of its forms be satisfactory until the general body of the people grasp the conception that administration, i.e., the execution of policy, is a field of governmental activity in which politics, i.e., the function of determining policy, should not enter."[42]

An important power possessed by the council was the right to appoint and to remove the city controller. In support of this provision, Professor Rowe argued that it would help to strengthen the position of the council, that a long term for the controller was desirable and that such could not be secured by popular election, and that appointment by the mayor would be improper, since the controller had the duty of preventing the misapplication of municipal revenues by the mayor and his appointees. Furthermore, his selection by the council would permit the shortening of the ballot.[43] Mr. Deming contended: "The Controller's is in no sense a partisan political office. His duties are purely administrative and, therefore, he should not be elected by popular vote."[44]

STRONG MAYOR PLAN

The extensive powers over administration given to the mayor were in line with the developments in municipal government during the ten years preceding the formulation of the Program. "The concentration of administrative power in the Mayor," said Professor Rowe, "is now regarded as an essential requisite to efficiency."[45]

It was believed by the committee that adequate checks had been provided to prevent the arbitrary use of the mayor's powers. As stated by Dr. Wilcox: "It is believed that the large powers of the mayor will enable him to give an excellent administration if he is capable and conscientious, while the careful restrictions put upon him by the civil service provisions and the checking powers of the governor, the council, and the controller will prevent him from stopping the machinery of government by his blunders if he is inefficient or from turning over the government to a set of rascals if he is a knave." A term of two years for the mayor and the fact that one-third of the council was elected with him every two years would permit a popular review of administrative and legislative policy.[46]

SHORT BALLOT

The short ballot principle was recognized in the program. Only the mayor and members of the council were elective, and the election must be on a general ticket. "By means of this separation [of municipal from state and national elections] and the reduction in the number of elective officers, it is the thought of the commitee," wrote Secretary Woodruff, "that electors will give more attention to local matters, and exercise more care in the selection of officials."[47]

Although the program did not include sections on direct legislation and minority or proportional representation in local elections, provision was made that each city should be left free to adopt any of these features upon approval of the people.[48]

MERIT SYSTEM

Eleven pages of the Municipal Corporations Act, the most detailed provisions contained in the draft, were devoted to the civil service regulations designed to establish the merit system and to keep politics from being injected into the administrative service of the city. Perhaps the most important feature of these provisions was the principle of indefinite tenure established for all persons in the administrative service of the city.[49] These sections had the endorsement of such veteran civil service reformers as Lucius B. Swift of Indianapolis and George McAneny, secretary of the National Civil Service Reform League.[50]

RESPONSIBLE MUNICIPAL DEMOCRACY

The principles thus far discussed have emphasized two fundamental features of the program—freedom and power, the ability and the means for a city to determine its local organization and policy. A third basic feature was the principle of responsibility. Not only was the city to be endowed with freedom and power, but practically every provision of the program was designed to eliminate checks and balances and establish the control of the people over their own local government. Such features as the short ballot; the strong mayor; unicameral legislature; open sessions of the council; electoral methods; actions by citizens; the merit system; the power of investigation given to the mayor, controller, council, civil service commissioners, and state officials; election on a general ticket; separation of municipal from state and national elections; bonding and taxing powers; and many others, gave to the people the instruments of popular control. In the words of Dr. Wilcox, "The proposed Municipal Program has taken democracy for granted, and has attempted to organize municipal government in relation to this great fact."[51]

The democratic features of the program were discussed on several occasions by Chairman Deming. After giving a brief outline of the history of municipal government in the United States, he continued: "The failure of city government in the United States has not been a failure of democracy." And this because "from the beginning there had not been a single city government based upon fundamental democratic principles and adequately equipped to apply those principles in the practical conduct of its public business."[52]

And elsewhere in discussing the program he concluded with this significant paragraph:

Such in brief outline is the city under the proposed Municipal Program. It is a representative democracy. Unable to resort to outside assistance and secure against outside interference, compelled to work out their own local destiny, clothed with ample powers to manage the city's business, its citizens are guaranteed that the public policy which they favor will be the policy of the city government; the very necessity of the case will develop an enlightened public opinion, which will determine the public policy. In such a government the will of the people when deliberately expressed will control, and the people cannot escape expressing their will. The people are the government.[53]

The resolution adopted at the Louisville conference creating the Committee on Municipal Program directed that committee to crystallize the results of the experience of American and European cities, and to present a program applicable to present conditions. In its preliminary report to the Indianapolis conference the committee stated that it had proceeded with "great caution and conservatism" and "keenly felt the necessity of bringing any system that they might recommend into organic relation with the traditions and accepted political ideas of the American people."[54]

To what extent did the committee succeed in doing this? What features of the program were based on European experience? On American experience? What departures were there from American practice? What provisions represented controversial innovations? Was the program theoretical or practical? Radical or conservative?

The fact that three of its members had studied and written of European municipal conditions insured that the committee would have adequate knowledge of the working principles of English and Continental local governments. Among the features of the program definitely based on European practice the following were typical: the idea of a uniform municipal corporations act; indefinite tenure of department heads; separation of municipal from national and state elections; a six-year term for councilmen with one-third elected biennially; nonpartisan ballot; nomination by petition; a unicameral municipal legislature; wide scope of municipal activities; and the practice of administrative instead of legislative control.[55]

For the most part, the program embodied the results of American experience in local government. After enumerating the leading characteristics of the proposed system of municipal government, Professor Fairlie said, "Except the first, [disappearance of detailed enumerated powers], all of these features are in operation in some parts of the United States, and most of them are approved by all students of municipal government." And in the same article he concluded: "The plan of the Municipal Program . . . follows closely the lessons of experience and the tendencies of American municipal development in the past."[56]

The strong mayor plan, state administrative supervision over local government, and the franchise policy recommended were in line with current trends in municipal government in the United States. A local veto on legislation affecting cities was established in the New York constitution of 1894; audit of fiscal accounts by the state was found in Wyoming; three states—Missouri, California, and Washington—had home rule for cities; and the merit system was in successful operation in the federal government and in several of the larger cities.[57]

Several features, however, represented rather distinct departures from American experience. The most important were: the general grant of powers to cities; restoration of the council to a position of importance and power; election of councilmen on a general ticket and for a six-year term; appointment of the city controller by the council; and the prevention of special legislation by clearly defining it in the constitution.[58]

Answering the criticism that the program was not "a historic growth" and "a product of the soil, gradually evolved," John A. Butler, president of the Municipal League of Milwaukee, explained the nature of the committee's work:

> After years of careful study of the condition of American and European cities, it is the result of a final compromise, not upon a basis of theoretical views, but of actual and successful practice; and the component parts of the Program, are what was left after a careful scrutiny of the crude and original formulations of actual municipal experience and methods. . . . The charter is therefore emphatically not an innovation, but the result of historic growth. . . ."[59]

In a comprehensive review of the program, Professor Robert C. Brooks of Cornell University, after summarizing the principal reforms proposed, continued:

> From the foregoing some conception may be obtained of the thoroughness, one might even add boldness, with which the committee has attacked the problem of municipal government in the United States. Changes of such magnitude are proposed that it will necessarily be years, possibly decades, before the public can be educated to demand them or the legislature to grant them. Yet there are few students of municipal government who would consider the Program utopian or despair of ultimate success along the lines laid down by the committee. Of the various reforms proposed, some have already been adopted with success in a number of American cities, others are strongly supported by European experience. The public has formed pretty definite opinions on certain questions dealt with by the committee, and more or less successful attempts at reform have already been made. Special legislation is a case in point. Here the committee simply seeks to carry out the popular will by thoroughgoing reforms which shall take the place of earlier and more superficial legislation. Part of the Program may then be expected to meet with little opposition except that arising from inertia. But on the other hand, the committee found itself obliged to take a decided stand on several controversial questions, and to make more than one distinct break with existing conditions and traditions of municipal government in the United States. Here strenuous opposition must be anticipated. It can hardly be maintained, however, that the Municipal Program violates at any point a definitely established American political principle as did the report of the Tilden Commission, not to mention numerous other drastic municipal reform measures that have been proposed at various times in the United States.[60]

APPRAISAL OF THE PROGRAM

Let us now turn from the discussion of the principles and nature of the program, to see how it was received by professors of municipal government, text writers, and journalists.[61] What criticism and what praise did they have for the report?

Part of the opinion of Professor Brooks has been given above. Several features of the program drew the criticism of this reviewer. "Perhaps no innovation contained in the program will meet with so much opposition as the attempt to rehabilitate the council. Strongly as the members of the committee have put their case, much experience of a sad sort points in the opposite direction." The experience of European cities was quoted too sweepingly in favor of the unicameral municipal legislature. It was questionable whether the provision permitting the setting aside of the debt limit in the case of self-liquidating municipal projects would accomplish all that was anticipated. Limitation of the term of the mayor to two years was contrary to the strong tendency to lengthen it, and retention of the veto power in the mayor violated the strict separation of legislative and administrative functions. Political organizations would have just reason to complain regarding the provision that "the names of all candidates for the same city office must be printed upon the ballot in alphabetical order under the title of the office."

These were criticisms of details. Professor Brooks concluded his review with this favorable comment:

> To attempt to go into details regarding the Program within the narrow limits of a review article is manifestly impossible. So wide a field has been covered by the committee and so thoroughly has it performed its work that we can at best but indicate its scope and commend it heartily to students of municipal government everywhere. In it legislative committees and reform bodies especially will find a mine of well digested information and argument suited to their needs. The articles in support of the Program are generally admirable and serve well the purpose of elucidating the dry text of the Charter and constitutional amendments. No more suitable introduction to the whole work could hardly have been provided than Mr. Fairlie's sketch of municipal development in the United States from colonial times to the present day.[62]

Professor E. Dana Durand of Stanford University prepared the review of the program for the *Political Science Quarterly*. While differing with the committee on certain proposals, he characterized the report as "the most clear and authoritative presentation yet made of the general character and working of American municipal organization and methods and of the changes that are desirable in them." He continued, "No one can doubt that, if enacted, it would prove vastly superior to any municipal system now existing in the United States." He doubted whether the limitation of franchises to a period of twenty-one years would attract private corporations, and also that the limitations on municipal debts and tax rate would produce true economy. He thought the committee might have recommended new forms of municipal taxation rather than the continuance of the almost exclusive use of the general property tax.

About one-half of Professor Durand's review was a discussion of the relations between the mayor and the council. He questioned the possibility of drawing a sharp distinction between administration and legislation in city affairs. More effective supervision over the administration might be secured by making administrative officers continuously responsible to the council, within certain limits, rather than by putting such control in the hands of a mayor elected for a two-year term. "Would it not perhaps be feasible, at least by gradual evolution, to establish in city government something akin to the cabinet system, in which close harmony, rather than separation, of executive and legislature should be sought?"[63]

Whereas Professor Durand was contending for a strong council, Henry de Forest Baldwin of New York City believed that city councils should be abolished and argued that problems of local policy should be determined by administrative officials organized in a manner similar to the New York City Board of Estimate and Apportionment. He criticized the election of the controller by the council instead of by the people and disapproved the proposal for the appointment of all subordinate officers by the mayor. State administrative supervision was not carried far enough, particularly in the field of civil service, he thought.[64]

The views of Dr. Wilcox on the program have already been noted.[65] Later he wrote that the most serious omission in the general plan of municipal organization recommended by the committee was the failure to provide for a cabinet or consulting group of department heads.[66]

It was the opinion of Professor Fairlie that the general ticket method of electing councilmen went too far in ignoring the idea of local representation. "It may be admitted that the present ward system is usually unsatisfactory; but are there not in every city sectional divisions with tolerably distinct municipal interests and some elements of common social life? Such divisions ought to be recognized and emphasized in the political system." Their boundaries should be fairly permanent, and in addition to being used as a district for council elections, might also be employed for the election of members of the state legislature, as well as for such municipal purposes as schools, police, and fire. With such a district system there should be combined also the plan of electing at large a small number of members of the council.[67]

He also recorded his dissent from the idea of excluding the city council from all powers of administration. "It is not entirely clear that all municipal councils should be restrained from exercising any administrative functions. In small cities, where the amount of municipal work is limited, there is no absolute necessity for separating legislative and administrative functions, and council committees may well discharge the latter duties and save the expense of additional officials. In large cities the distinction is much more important. . . ."[68]

A large part of the Municipal Corporations Act was reprinted in a digest of city charters prepared for the use of the Chicago Charter Commission of 1906–1907. In a preface to the volume, Professor A. R. Hatton of the University of Chicago said: "The act is not a slavish adoption of the forms and methods of other countries, but, without neglecting the lessons of foreign experience, it aims to take account of American conditions and American political ideas. It has been pretty generally accepted by leading authorities on municipal government as the best plan yet formulated for the government of cities in the United States."[69]

M. N. Baker, associate editor of *Engineering News*, in reviewing the Municipal Program in the issue of December 1, 1898, while admitting that it would probably never come into universal use in the different states, continued:

> The greatest value of any such program must lie in its exposition of the principles involved. . . . We think, however, that no higher praise could be given the committee than the statement that it has come marvellously near presenting an outline of government capable of universal adoption. The reason for this is that it has confined itself to an outline, instead of falling into the common error of going largely into details.[70]

A year later, in the same journal, he praised the program as "one of the best pieces of constructive work ever done by an organization devoted to the improvement of municipal government," and declared that the Model Charter was "a better and more complete framework for a municipal government than any existing city charter which we now recall."[71]

INFLUENCE OF THE PROGRAM

We should now attempt to estimate the influence of the Municipal Program on American thought regarding municipal government and on the progress of charter reform in cities. The first evaluation is difficult, and we are compelled to call upon the assistance of contemporary students of municipal government. As already noted, Professor Hatton stated that the program had been "pretty generally accepted by leading authorities on municipal government as the best plan yet formulated for the government of cities in the United States." And Dr. Wilcox said:

> This program has attracted wide attention, and has already had a marked influence on new legislation in some states and cities. The program undoubtedly has helped to clear the air and crystallize into practical form the best judgment of students of our municipal problems as to the legislative reforms needed.[72]

Many other quotations could be given to illustrate the influence of the program.[73] But what of the use of the program by charter revision commissions and constitutional conventions? Four years after the promulgation of the program, Dr. Wilcox summed up its use as follows:

> It has nowhere been enacted into law as a whole, but its influence has been felt practically everywhere that charters have been framed, constitutions revised or municipal reform agitated "under the flag." It was published in full in Honolulu for the benefit of the Hawaiian legislature. It was used by the Havana Charter Commission and, I believe, by the Porto Rican and Philippine Commissions. It has left marked traces in the new constitutions of Virginia and Alabama, and has formed the basis for a sweeping amendment to the Colorado constitution. The Charter Commission of Portland, Ore. used it. The Charter Revision Commission of New York City adopted some of its provisions. The Duluth and St. Paul charters are in line with it in important respects. It has formed the basis of agitation for charter reform in Wisconsin, Michigan, Delaware, and doubtless many other States. Its experience in Ohio, however, has been unfortunate. The Municipal Code Commission in that State was at work at the time of the Columbus Conference for Good City Government, at which the Program was adopted. Perhaps on account of their proximity, the commissioners absorbed so many reform ideas that their code was rejected by the Ohio politicians.[74]

Concluding a paper, "Charter Tendencies in Recent Years," at the meeting of the League in 1908, Professor Fairlie remarked:

> In the main, then, the principles of the Municipal Program have been steadily gaining ground. Its influence can be seen in the work of state constitutional conventions, in state laws and in charters for particular cities. In

no one place, however, has it been adopted as a whole; and even where some of its principles have been accepted the details have often been modified. Indeed, in several instances, a distinct improvement has been made over the detailed provisions framed ten years ago. If one general criticism may be made of that Program, it is that the proposed constitutional provisions are much too long, and specify detailed provisions which should rather be left to regulation by statute or local action. But the fundamental principles of the Program still hold good; and should and will continue to be extended even more in the future than in the recent past.[75]

Dr. W. F. Willoughby, assistant director of the Bureau of the Census, wrote in 1910 that the publication of the program marked "an epoch in the history of municipal reform in the United States and . . . exerted a profound influence in bringing about improved conditions."[76]

To Professor Rowe likewise the formulation of the program recorded a turning point in the progress of reform. A serious charge against reform movements had been that they were engaged in destructive criticism and incapable of furnishing a positive basis for improvement. "Anyone who has carefully observed the movement of popular opinion during recent years can not fail to have been impressed with the danger involved in this growing distrust of the ability of reform movements to meet the practical problems of American political life."[77]

In conclusion it may be said that the unity of thought among reformers, and the furnishing of a positive program for municipal action with its consequent influence upon public opinion, constitute the chief significance of the Municipal Program.

IV

A New Municipal Program

THE FIFTEEN YEARS following the publication of the Municipal Program were significant ones in the development of municipal government. New forms of government, the commission and the city manager plans, were in operation in hundreds of cities. The establishment of the first Bureau of Municipal Research in New York in 1906 introduced the scientific research method into municipal affairs. Improved systems of taxation and of accounting and budgeting had been installed in many cities. There was rapid expansion in many municipal functions, such as public utilities, city planning, libraries, courts, and supervision of health. Popular support of the merit system had increased and the need for experts in administration was beginning to be realized. Definite progress had been made in the acceptance of the short ballot principle, home rule, preferential voting, proportional representation, and of the initiative, referendum, and recall. The movement for direct primaries and for nonpartisanship had gained much ground. Cruder forms of municipal corruption had diminished.[1]

As a leader in municipal reform the League had a prominent part in most of these developments. During this period no single League committee, like the Committee on Municipal Program, was set up to study and report on these movements. Rather a dozen or more committees were active. It was the work of these committees, to be described later, which furnished the groundwork for many important features of the New Municipal Program.[2]

SECOND MUNICIPAL PROGRAM

Realization that there had been important progress in municipal government and charter making since the issuance of the Municipal Program led the League to appoint a new committee to study the old document and to report what changes were made necessary by developments since 1900. On November 26, 1912, the Executive Committee authorized the appointment of such a committee to consist of five members of the first Committee on Municipal Program and an equal num-

[1] For notes to chap. iv, see pp. 216–219.

ber of new members, with the president of the League serving as chairman ex officio.[3] This plan did not prove feasible as to personnel, owing to the fact that most of the members of the former committee found themselves unable to serve on it again.

As reconstituted at the Toronto meeting of the Council,[5] the Committee on Municipal Program consisted of William Dudley Foulke, Richmond, Indiana, president of the League, chairman, and eleven other members.[6] Secretary Clinton Rogers Woodruff was the only member who had served on the original committee. The new committee was divided into six subcommittees, namely, home rule and public utilities, mayor and council, taxation and finance, electoral features, administrative features, and franchises. Its first meeting was held in New York on September 11–12, 1914, when reports of subcommittees were discussed. A preliminary report dealing with the sections of the new Model City Charter on the council, city manager, civil service and efficiency board, and a partial draft of a municipal home rule constitutional amendment were submitted to the annual meeting of the League held at Baltimore, November 18–20, 1914. Suggestions developed in the discussion were referred to the committee for consideration.[7] The tentative drafts submitted at the Baltimore meeting were printed in pamphlet form for the use of members of the League.[8]

These sections were revised at a two-day meeting of the committee in New York on April 8–9, 1915, and sections dealing with the initiative, referendum, and recall, and other electoral provisions were approved and added to the Model City Charter. The draft of the home rule constitutional amendment was completed, and this, together with the tentative drafts of sections, was printed and presented to the League members for study and criticism.[9] A meeting of the committee in New York, September 14, 1915, made further changes in the Model City Charter, approved the financial provisions, and added two appendices dealing with proportional representation and franchises.[10]

The annual meeting of the League at Dayton, November 19, 1915, approved certain sections and referred the document back to the committee for further amendments.[11] A final meeting of the committee in Philadelphia, December 27–28, 1915, completed the work and a fourth edition of its conclusions was printed and distributed.[12]

During the formulation of the program helpful suggestions were received from a number of students of municipal government, including Charles Richardson of Philadelphia, member of the first Committee on Municipal Program; Lieutenant C. P. Shaw of Norfolk, Virginia, member of the Advisory Committee of the League; H. S. Gilbertson, executive secretary of the National Short Ballot Organization; C. F. Taylor, editor of *Equity;* and C. G. Hoag, general secretary-treasurer of the American Proportional Representation League. The civil service provisions were submitted for comment to Elliott H. Goodwin, former secretary of the National Civil Service Reform League; the proportional representation provisions to Professor John R. Commons of the University of Wisconsin; and the city planning section to Dr. John Nolen, Cambridge, Massachusetts; Frederick Law Olmsted, Brookline, Massachusetts; and Robert H. Whitten, New York City.[13]

At the annual meeting in Dayton, the committee was authorized, when it had completed the draft, to have it printed and a copy sent to each member of the League for approval. Authority was also given to the committee to fix a final date for the receipt of communications from members.[14]

Chairman Foulke reported to the Council in April, 1916, that the Model City Charter was complete to the extent of the plan contemplated when the committee was appointed. However, certain phases of city government, such as taxation, public libraries, and social centers remained for consideration as subjects of additional legislation. The program had been submitted to the League members by mail with the request that all suggestions for amendments be sent to the secretary by May 1, 1916. He asked that the committee be continued until the criticisms and proposed amendments of members had been received and considered.

The Council voted to continue the committee with authority to consider proposals from individuals and committees of the League, particularly the Committee on Municipal Budgets and Accounting. It was given power to adopt changes involving only details and to report to a later meeting of the Council upon those dealing with matters of substance. The subjects of assessment of property for taxation, the creation of zones and districts, and special assessments were referred to the committee. After discussion of the necessity for model library provisions in the Charter, the president was authorized to appoint a committee of five to draft and to report to the Council a model city library act.[15]

The final draft of the program was sent to members early in April, 1916.[16] A paragraph of the accompanying circular letter read:

> The Committee desires to call attention to the fact that the subjects of taxation, libraries, education, special assessments and public improvements are to be considered subsequently by special committees which are now at work on the subjects. The Committee felt that as these were separate and separable subjects, the publication of the model charter need not be further delayed until reports on them were received, considered and approved.[17]

No votes were cast against the adoption of the program before or after the date fixed by the committee. However, a number of requests for changes were made by Richard Henry Dana, president of the National Civil Service Reform League; by the League's Committee on Municipal Budgets and Accounting; by Lieutenant C. P. Shaw of Norfolk, Virginia; by Samuel H. Ranck, librarian, Grand Rapids Public Library; by C. M. Fassett, Department of Public Utilities, Spokane, Washington; and by D. B. Harvey, of Hackettstown, New Jersey; Charles Mulford Robinson of Rochester, New York; Edward K. Putnam of Davenport, Iowa; and James H. Wolfe of Salt Lake City.[18] These suggestions were concerned with details of procedure rather than of principle, except for that presented by Lieutenant Shaw, which was attached in a note to the chapter on civil service.[19]

Having completed its work, the committee was formally discharged at the Council meeting in November, 1916. Progress was reported on the publication of a volume embodying the arguments for the provisions in the Model City Charter.[20]

At the Detroit meeting of the Council in November, 1917, it was voted to revive the Committee on Municipal Program with substantially the same personnel for the purpose of considering suggested changes in the proportional representation sections, the inclusion of a model library section, and other proposals for altering or adding to the Model City Charter.[21]

The secretary reported to a meeting of the Executive Committee in December, 1917, that the members of the former committee had been invited to serve on a new committee and nearly all had accepted. Recommendations as to the form of the Model City Charter were referred to it for consideration and action.[22]

A report regarding the work of the committee[23] was made by the secretary to the Council meeting in June, 1918. He reported also on the volume, *A New Municipal Program*, and it was the sense of the Council that publication should not be delayed.[24] Edited by Secretary Woodruff, and published in 1919, this book contained the report of the Committee on Municipal Program and its proposals for constitutional municipal home rule and for a Model City Charter. Also included were chapters by members of the committee which were designed to furnish the "philosophical and the practical arguments for the Committee's conclusions."[25]

OUTLINE OF PROVISIONS

Like the first program, the New Municipal Program presented its recommendations in two parts: provisions regarding municipal home rule to be adopted and incorporated in the state constitution, and a Model City Charter.[26]

CONSTITUTIONAL MUNICIPAL HOME RULE

The legislature is given power by general law to provide for the incorporation of cities and villages, and for the organization and government of cities and villages which do not adopt laws or charters in accordance with subsequent provisions of the constitutional amendment. Cities and villages may adopt by popular vote a form of government prescribed by general law.

A city may frame, adopt, and amend a charter for its own government in accordance with the procedure outlined in the amendment. It is required, however, that all "elections and submissions of questions provided for in this article or in any charter or law adopted in accordance herewith shall be conducted by the election authorities provided by general law."

State supervision is provided in the following section: "General laws may be passed requiring reports from cities as to their transactions and financial condition, and providing for the examination by state officials of the vouchers, books and accounts of all municipal authorities, or of public undertakings conducted by such authorities."

Cities are granted "all powers relating to municipal affairs," and as a further protection it is provided that "no enumeration of powers in this constitution or any law shall be deemed to limit or restrict the general grant of authority hereby conferred. . . ." To insure the supremacy of the state legislature and "in order to make it clear to the courts that a distinction between local and general matters is intended," it is provided "that this grant of authority shall not be deemed to limit or restrict the power of the legislature, in matters relating to state affairs, to enact general laws applicable alike to all cities of the state."

Certain powers are enumerated as belonging to cities. These powers refer to taxation and special assessments, local public services, local public improvements, bonds and franchises, public schools and libraries, and local police and sanitary regulations.

Power is given to any city of 100,000 population or more, by popular vote, to organize as a distinct county and to provide in its charter for the consolidation into one municipal government of county, city, and all other local authorities.

ELECTORAL METHODS

Twenty-five pages of the Model City Charter concern the provisions relating to nominations, elections, recall, and direct legislation. Municipal elections are to be held every two years, when there are no state or national elections. If held in even years, they are to be separated from state or national elections by at least thirty and preferably sixty days. Candidates for the council are nominated by petition. Election by the Hare method of proportional representation is preferred by "a substantial majority of the members of the committee" and is included in the text of the Charter. An alternative method, the preferential ballot, is given in the appendix. The party primary and the party form of ballot are thus outlawed by the Model City Charter.

To the council is given power to make rules, not inconsistent with the Charter or general law, for the conduct of elections, the prevention of election frauds, and for recount of the ballots under certain conditions.

The sections on the initiative, the referendum, and the recall have the endorsement of a majority of the committee. Members of the council, the only elective officers provided in the Charter, may be removed from office by the recall. The initiative power applies to ordinances, "including ordinances granting franchises or privileges, and other measures." Power of the people "to approve or reject at the polls any measure passed by the council or submitted by the council to a vote of the electors" is defined as the referendum.

These provisions regarding forms of nomination papers, filing of nomination papers, ballots and voting, rules for counting the ballots, filling of vacancies, and for the exercise of the initiative, referendum, and recall constitute the longest and most detailed sections of the Charter.

THE COUNCIL

Members of the council are elected on a general ticket from the city at large by proportional representation and serve for a term of four years, subject to recall. No salary is fixed in the Charter and a footnote says: "In determining whether a salary shall be paid, and if so how much, it must be borne in mind that the duties of the council are supervisory; and that it is the object of this charter to place the administrative affairs of the city in the hands of the city manager."

The size of the council is left flexible, the number of members and their method of election, at large or from districts, being determined by the size of the city, it is explained in a footnote. A minimum number of five is suggested, and not more than fifty for the largest cities. "Great cities may with advantage be divided into large districts, each to elect five or more members of the council. . . . If proportional representation is not used and the number of councilmen to be elected at large, or from a single district, is more than five, provision should be made for their election—after the first time in groups."

Organization and procedure of the council are outlined and it is given the usual powers to provide for its own rules of procedure, punishment of members, and compulsory attendance of members. All sessions of the council and of its committees must be public.

To this body is given "full power and authority, except as herein otherwise provided, to exercise all the powers conferred upon the city." It is the policy-determining organ of the municipal government, with power to enact ordinances, levy taxes, approve the budget, exercise the city's borrowing power, provide the public services, and authorize the local improvements.

The power to administer does not belong to the council but control over administration is its function. It selects a chairman from its own membership, who bears the title of mayor. The council also elects a clerk, a civil service commission, and a city manager. A councilman may not be chosen as city manager or as a member of the civil service commission.

Definite prohibitions are placed upon the council to prevent improper interference with the city manager in the conduct of public affairs. Conviction renders a member liable to a fine or imprisonment, or both, and to removal from office in the discretion of the courts.

The mayor acts as presiding officer of the council and "shall be recognized as the official head of the city for all ceremonial purposes, by the courts for the purpose of serving civil processes, and by the governor for military purposes." With consent of the council he may, in times of public danger or emergency, assume control of the police, maintain order, and enforce the laws.

CITY MANAGER

At the head of administration there is a city manager, chosen by the council for an indefinite term. The only limitation on the discretion of the council is that the choice of the manager must be made "solely on the basis of his executive and administrative qualifications." Residence in the city or state is not required. His salary, fixed by the council, varies according to the size of the city and the responsibilities of the office. The council may remove the manager at any time. If removal proceedings are started after six months of service, the manager has the right to demand written charges and a public hearing by the council before final removal is made effective. Meantime the council may suspend the manager.

The Charter designates the manager as "the chief executive officer of the city," and he is responsible to the council "for the proper administration of all affairs of the city." He is given the power to make all appointments, except as otherwise provided in the Charter. He prepares and submits to the council the annual budget based on departmental estimates. The Charter gives him the right to be present at all meetings of the council and of its committees and to take part in the discussion. The sole exception arises when the council is considering his removal.

Certain limitations on the powers of the manager are found in the Charter. He does not appoint the civil service board and the personnel regulations constitute important limitations upon the power of appointment. There is also the provision for an annual audit of the accounts of all city officers.

A footnote contains this statement of caution:

> While the manager plan herein proposed is probably the most advanced and scientific form of municipal organization yet suggested, it is of the highest importance that any city adopting the plan should not omit any of the other principal features accompanying it in this draft. Without these provisions, the manager plan, owing to its concentration of executive and administrative authority in the manager, might prove to be susceptible to perversion in the interest of a boss in cities with an undeveloped and inactive public opinion, because the members of the council might then be elected upon a slate pledged beforehand to the selection of some particular candidate as manager.

> It is also true that no form of government can in and of itself produce good results. The most that any plan can do is to provide an organization which lends itself to efficient action and which at the same time places in the hands of the electorate simple and effective means for controlling their government in their own interests.

ADMINISTRATIVE DEPARTMENTS

Six departments are established by the Charter: law, health, works and utilities, safety and welfare, education, and finance. A note indicates that the department of education should be omitted in places where an independent school system is working well. A smaller or a larger number of departments may be established to fit the population or other local needs of the city. New departments may be created, existing departments combined or abolished, or temporary departments for special work established by a three-fourths vote of the entire membership of the council. Functions of all departments are to be determined by the council, unless otherwise provided in the Charter. "The principle underlying the formation of departments and bureaus should be twofold: (1) functional grouping and (2) tasks which demand the time and capacity of the highest grade of administrative heads—i.e., one first-class full-time man to head each department."

Each director of a department is appointed by the manager "on the basis of his general executive and administrative experience and ability and of his education, training, and experience in the class of work which he is to administer." In every case, the person chosen must have served actively in the same service in this or some other city. The manager may remove a director at any time but only after written charges and a public hearing, if the director demands.

It is the duty of directors to administer their departments under the immediate supervision of the manager, who may require their advice in writing on all matters affecting their office.

The power to investigate city affairs is given to the council, the city manager, and any agency authorized by them, or by either of them.

CIVIL SERVICE

Administration of the merit system is vested in a civil service board of three members, appointed by the council for six years, one member being appointed every two years. Members are removable from office for neglect, incapacity, or malfeasance by a four-fifths vote of the council, following written charges and a public hearing. The board is given power, after public notice and hearing, to promulgate rules for the civil service. The competitive service does not include elective officers, city manager, and judges. It "may or may not include the directors of executive departments, or the superintendents, principals, and teachers of the public schools, as may be directed by the council."

Rules of the board are to provide (1) for the standardization and classification of all positions and employments, the classification to be based upon duties and responsibilities, and salaries to be uniform for like services in each grade; (2) for open competitive tests for all positions, including mechanics and laborers, skilled and unskilled, with the proviso that by unanimous vote of the board noncompetitive tests may be given for any position "requiring peculiar and exceptional qualifications of a scientific, managerial, professional, or educational character;" (3) for appointments to be made from the three highest on the eligible lists, which shall be open to public inspection; (4) for the limitation of temporary appointments to sixty days; (5) for a probationary period not exceeding six months; and (6) for promotion "based upon competitive records of efficiency and seniority to be furnished by the departments in which the person is employed and kept by said civil service board, or upon competitive promotion tests, or both." Competitive examinations for higher positions may, with the approval of the board and the city manager, be opened to persons not in the city service.

The board is required to keep a public record of its proceedings, to maintain a complete roster of all employees, to certify payrolls, and to "fix standards of efficiency and recommend measures for coördinating the operation of the various departments and for increasing individual, group, and departmental efficiency." It may conduct investigations regarding the administration of the civil service rules and the general condition of the civil service of the city.

Cause for the removal, suspension, lay off, or reduction in grade of employees, and the procedure to be followed is stated in the Charter. Provisions against fraudulent practices and the prohibition of political activity are very similar to those of the first Municipal Program.

FRANCHISES AND PUBLIC UTILITIES

The Model City Charter does not attempt to set forth "the details of a comprehensive constructive public utility policy applicable to all utilities alike and to all cities alike," yet it does contain, in the form of a note, a declaration of certain general principles for the formulation of a franchise and public utility policy for a city.

The fundamental objectives of a sound public utility program are to secure (1) the best practicable public utility service, (2) fullest control of the streets to the city, (3) removal of obstacles to municipal ownership and operation of public utilities, and (4) public utility rates fixed as low as possible. It is not an objective of such program "to secure compensation for franchises or special revenues for general city purposes by an indirect tax upon the consumers of public utility services."

To carry out the above objectives, every city should conform, as nearly as feasible, to the following principles:

(1) Each utility serving an urban community should be treated as far as practicable as a monopoly with the obligations of a monopoly; and its operation within the city should be based as far as practicable upon a single comprehensive ordinance or franchise grant uniform in its application to all parts of the city and to all extensions of plant and service.

(2) Every franchise should be revocable by the city upon just compensation being paid to its owners, when the city is prepared to undertake public ownership.

(3) The control of the location and character of public utility fixtures, the character and amount of service rendered, and the rates charged therefor should be reserved to the city, subject to reasonable review by the courts or a state utilities commission where one exists.

(4) The granting and enforcement of franchises and the regulation of utilities operating thereunder should be subject to adequate public scrutiny and discussion and should receive full consideration by an expert bureau of the city government established and maintained for that purpose, or, in case the maintenance of such bureau is impracticable, by an officer or committee designated for the purpose.

(5) Private investments in public utilities should be treated as investments in aid of public credit and subject to the public control and should be safeguarded in every possible way, and the rate of return allowed thereon should be reduced to the minimum return necessary in the case of safe investments with a fixed and substantially assured fair earning power.

The specific provisions of the Model City Charter are drafted in accordance with the above policy and principles.

FINANCIAL SECTIONS

A director, appointed by the manager, heads the department of finance with supervision over the fiscal affairs of the city. This department is to keep accounts showing the financial transactions for all departments of the city and is to make reports, quarterly and annually, and for such other periods as may be required by the manager or the council.

A budget for the following twelve months must be submitted by the manager to the council not later than one month before the end of the fiscal year. The annual appropriation ordinance, based on the budget, must be passed by the council not later than one month after the beginning of the fiscal year. Total appropriations for the fiscal year are not to be permitted to exceed the revenues as estimated for the same period.

The tax levy ordinance to raise funds to meet the appropriations and the debt requirements is enacted by the council before a specified date each year. Ad valorem taxes are levied on property at its fair market value.

Special assessments for payment of the cost of a public improvement, including a public utility, may be levied by ordinance of the council upon abutting, adjacent and contiguous, or other property specially benefited. Payments may be spread over a period of not more than ten years. An assessment against property cannot exceed in amount the benefits accruing to the property from the improvement and its operation. Details of assessment procedure are to be provided by ordinance.

Borrowing, through the issue and sale of bonds, is permitted for the purchase of land, construction and equipment of buildings and other permanent public improvements, and for the payment or refunding of previous bond issues. The bond ordinance cannot be passed without public notice at least two weeks before final action by the council. Passage of the ordinance requires approval of two-thirds of all the members of the council, or submission at a regular or special election and approval of a majority of those voting thereon. A percentage limitation of the assessed valuation of property subject to direct taxation is to be fixed by each city with reference to its total indebtedness. The term of issue of bonds cannot exceed the estimated period of utility of the improvement for which issued and in no case more than thirty years. Serial bonds only are to be issued. The ordinance must provide for an annual tax levy to pay principal and interest.

Temporary loans in anticipation of tax receipts may be made, but in the aggregate such loans cannot exceed a fixed per cent of the tax receipts of the preceding fiscal year. All such loans must be paid from taxes collected for the fiscal year in which they are issued. Public notice at least two weeks before final vote and approval of two-thirds of all the members of the council is required for the authorization of temporary loans.

All moneys accruing from taxes, special assessments, and other sources are collected by the department of finance and paid into the city treasury. Such funds are deposited with responsible banking institutions furnishing adequate security and the highest rate of interest. All interest accrues to the benefit of the city.

Except for public utility franchises, no continuing contract can be made for a period of more than ten years. Such contracts require for their validity at least two weeks' notice before final action of the council, approval of two-thirds of all members of the council, or submission at a regular or special election and approval of a majority of those voting thereon.

The director of finance makes an audit and investigation of the accounts of any officer of the city upon his death, resignation, removal, or the expiration of his term. An annual audit of the accounts of all officers, and an audit of the department of finance upon the death, resignation, removal, or expiration of the term of the director of finance is made in accordance with any law for state inspection and audit of municipal accounts. In the absence of such a state law, the council may have the audit made by qualified and disinterested public accountants. An audit of the accounts of any officer or department may be ordered by the council at any time.

CITY PLANNING

A city planning board of three members is created to be composed of the director of public works and utilities and two citizen members chosen because of their knowledge of city planning. The board is to appoint "a person of skill and experience in city planning" as secretary. Authority is given to employ consultatively city planning experts. The city engineer is the chief engineer of the board.

After enumerating the duties of the board, the Charter continues:

> All acts of the council or of any other branch of the city government affecting the city plan shall be submitted to the board for report and recommendations. The council may at any time call upon the board to report with recommendations and the board of its own volition may also report to the council with recommendations on any matter which, in the opinion of either body, affects the plan of the city.... No action by the council involving any points hereinbefore set forth shall be legal or binding until it has been referred to the board and until the recommendations of the board thereon have been accepted or rejected by the council.

In addition to other information, the annual report of the board to the council "shall also contain a program for improvements to the city plan year by year during the three years next ensuing, with estimates of the cost thereof and recommendations as to how the cost shall be met."

PRINCIPLES OF THE NEW PROGRAM

The above analysis of the constitutional provisions and the Model City Charter reveals that the New Municipal Program was based on certain fundamental principles, many of which were found in the first program. A brief discussion of these principles will reveal the progressive nature of the document.

HOME RULE

In the light of the experience with constitutional municipal home rule since 1900 the League reexamined the provisions of its first program and submitted a draft which Professor A. R. Hatton believed "superior in form and principle to the provisions for constitutional municipal home rule now found in any state constitution."[27]

NONPARTISANSHIP IN MUNICIPAL AFFAIRS

As Mayo Fesler said: "The League has consistently stood for nonpartisanship in city elections."[28] To secure this, the Model City Charter provided for the separation of municipal from state and national elections, nomination by petition, and election by proportional representation on a nonpartisan ballot.

RULE OF THE PEOPLE

To the above electoral features should be added the provisions for the short ballot and the initiative, referendum, and recall. This electoral system made possible the control by the voters of their local affairs. "The model charter seeks to simplify the election process, assure the elector that his vote will be given its full weight, and leave to him the responsibility for his own government." Under the electoral conditions provided in the Charter "an alert, intelligent, and active electorate can make its will easily effective." Richard S. Childs commented: "Our goal is democracy."[29]

SEPARATION OF LEGISLATION AND ADMINISTRATION

Abandoning the federal plan of municipal organization, the new Model City Charter adopted the city manager plan, which involved the placing of legislative and administrative powers in separate agencies. Professor W. B. Munro described the relationship of legislation and administration under the proposed system in the following terms:

> The Model City Charter accordingly provides for a council . . . to be the pivot of the municipal system. It is to be the final source of local authority, not sharing its powers with some other body or official but delegating some of them. That is to say, to a city manager chosen by the council and holding office during the council's pleasure, it assigns the entire charge of administrative affairs. The two great functions of municipal government are thus placed in separate but not in independent hands. Legislation is entrusted to a body which is large enough to be adequately representative; on the other hand, the concentration of administrative functions is made complete. The councilors are laymen, without expert knowledge or special interests. The city manager is a professional administrator. There can be no confusion in this arrangement, no deadlocks or lost motion.[30]

EXPERT ADMINISTRATION

One of the most significant discussions of the Model City Charter was the chapter contributed by Dr. A. L. Lowell on experts in municipal government. Defining an expert as "one who has learned his business by long experience, who makes it his work in life, the profession to which he devotes his chief thought and labor until he obtains a command of its problems that other men do not possess,"[31] Dr. Lowell believed that the Model City Charter would facilitate the employment of such experts for municipal work.

> The model charter does all that can be done by providing an organization in which the use of trained men will be as natural as possible, and which will tend to educate the public in their employment. If the city manager is himself a true professional administrator, and remains in office long enough to acquire a powerful influence, it is certain that he will draw to his aid, and maintain, a corps of expert subordinates with the same professional spirit that he has himself. And even if he is not at first a trained expert, yet if the regulations governing the directors of the departments are not grossly violated, these men will have an expert knowledge and a professional attitude that will in time almost inevitably extend itself to the post of city manager.[32]

The comprehensive civil service sections were designed to eliminate the evils of the patronage system and to insure a competent municipal personnel.

INTEGRATED ADMINISTRATIVE ORGANIZATION

Professor H. G. James characterized the administrative organization established in the Charter as one framed in recognition of the principle of "administrative centralization." He continued:

> Every employee in the city is subordinate and responsible to some official, every subordinate official is in the same relation to some superior, every department is under the charge of a director and every director is in every way subordinate and responsible to the city manager. . . . Lest there be the slightest suspicion of our having erected a bureaucracy in creating the administrative hierarchy, the apex of the pyramid, the city manager, is made absolutely and completely subordinate to the city council, the elective body representing the people of the city.[33]

MUNICIPAL OWNERSHIP

In explanation of the franchise policy of the program, Dr. D. F. Wilcox said:

> The National Municipal League is not yet committed to the policy of municipal ownership and operation of all public utilities, and is not prepared to substitute for the idea of municipal home rule in public utility matters a comprehensive and exact public utility policy to be recommended to all cities alike. Nevertheless, the League recognizes that the mere untying of the hands of a municipality so as to give it discretion to solve its utility problems in its own way, does not meet the complete requirements of a national municipal program. While many important franchise and utility questions are still mooted, even among those who look at these problems solely from the public point of view, the time is now ripe for a general declaration of principles, in accordance with which local utility policies should be worked out.[34]

IMPROVED FINANCIAL METHODS

Since the publication of the first program, League committees and other organizations, both official and unofficial, had investigated problems of municipal finance and great progress had been made in the theory and practice of financial administration. In comparing the financial sections of the program of 1900 with that of 1916, Professor J. A. Fairlie pointed out that the new program included many provisions not found in the first document. "For the most part, these represent a logical development from the principles of the previous program; but in some respects there is a distinct departure from the earlier views."[35]

CITY PLANNING

The brief section on city planning represented an addition to the original program. In his chapter on this subject, M. N. Baker thus began the discussion: "When the Municipal Program of the National Municipal League was adopted in 1900 the term city planning was almost unknown in this country. The art itself was even more rare. Rarer still were legally constituted bodies with adequate control of even the street layout, much less of the city plan as a whole."[36]

APPRAISAL OF THE NEW PROGRAM

The articles contributed by the members of the Committee on Municipal Program constitute the best discussion of its features and principles. But the opinions of others—editors, professors, and practical municipal administrators—are also valuable. What did they think of the New Municipal Program?

The *Survey*, commenting on the first program and the progress of municipal reform since 1900, said:

> The skeptics who still see only the failures of American municipal government, as if there had been no progress since the dark ages of two decades ago when graft and corruption and inefficiency were most prevalent, will find food for thought in the fact that the "model city charter" then suggested has so far been paralleled by real charters in actual use that a new model has become necessary. . . .
>
> This model charter demonstrates how modern municipal government has caught up with the reformers. At least a dozen cities with the commission manager form have charters that differ from the model only in minor details. . . .
>
> The old model charter was a lonesome pioneer. The new model charter merely falls in line abreast of Dayton, Springfield, Niagara Falls, Cadillac and Ashtabula. It marks the close of a period in municipal reform—a period of forging good tools for democracy to work with.[37]

Professor Charles A. Beard of Columbia University wrote, "This document . . . represents the mature judgment of that Association which has done such notable service in promoting thinking about city government in the United States." He concluded:

> Adequate evaluation of the document before us would call for a treatise on municipal government and administration. . . . There is nothing esoteric about the program. The proposals are for the most part clearly put and the language employed is far more precise and definite than one usually finds in city charters. The document is stripped of verbiage and compact in form. Some of the sections, such as those on the initiative and referendum might have been reduced, and more faith put in ordinances, but the good and wise will differ on this point. As a whole, the League's program will undoubtedly prove to be a new milestone in the history of American city government, recording many genuine achievements and telling of better things to come.[38]

Text writers on municipal government have praised the League's work in charter making. Professor William Anderson concluded his text with a chapter entitled, "The Programme of Municipal Reform." He placed the League first among municipal reform organizations and continued: "It is, in fact, the reform programme of this league, first adopted in 1900 and then revised and reaffirmed in 1916, which furnishes most of the material for this chapter. This programme covers most of the important phases of the municipal problem in America today."[39] Elsewhere Professor Anderson commented on the striking similarity between the views of John Stuart Mill and the principles found in the Model City Charter.[40]

Charles M. Fassett took the Model City Charter as the basis for his chapter on municipal charters. "It was formulated by a committee of twelve of the most eminent students of municipal affairs in this country, men of close contact with their subject and without any selfish purpose. It has formed the pattern for several charters now in operation and is based upon principles and practices of city government which have been thoroughly demonstrated." The Charter did not cover such subjects as schools, parks, libraries, and harbors, but in most states these functions were carried on under general state laws.[41]

Professor W. B. Munro gave a paragraph in one of his texts to model city charters. Several such charters had been prepared and the League's Model City Charter was considered "the best among these compilations." After outlining the practical difficulties of articulating such documents with the general laws of the state in which the city is located, he concluded: "Nevertheless these model charters have proved useful in that they afford examples of orderly arrangement, clearness of expression, and reasonable conciseness."[42]

One review pointed out that the program did not include discussion of housing, recreation, education, and other aspects of a complete municipal program. Complimenting the editor upon his success in integrating the many papers incorporated into the volume, it concluded: "The result is a book of reference valuable alike to the student and to the charter draftsman. Avowedly propaganda for the program of the National Municipal League, the book seems well calculated to fulfil its function."[43]

The unity of the presentation also received the favorable comment of Professor Howard L. McBain of Columbia University. "For a volume written by a dozen authors *A New Municipal Program* exhibits an unusual degree of unity of purpose and of consistency. . . . Most of the papers are good; some of them are excellent; inevitably, however, where there are so many contributors, there is considerable variation in the matter of interest and of value." As for the influence of the program, he found it difficult to measure the influence exerted by the program of 1900. "Since that time, there has been in the United States a prodigious growth of interest in, knowledge about, and comment upon, municipal affairs. In view of this fact, it will be even more difficult to estimate the results that flow from this later program. Certainly, however, it will be of no small service to those who seek its aid."

Professor McBain thought, however, that too much attention was given to the legal aspects of the municipal problem, city-state relations, the grant of municipal powers, and the structure of the city government. "What we really need is not so much a new program as a new attitude of mind and a better understanding of the nature of the forces that must operate our legal programs. With this other and more serious aspect of our city problem this book does not purport to deal, although special mention should doubtless be made of President Lowell's eminently commonsense chapter on experts in municipal government."[44]

There were two ways of organizing reform movements, said Dr. C. C. Williamson of the New York Municipal Reference Library. One was for a dominant individual to gather under his leadership a group of like-minded enthusiasts and to advance the reform idea by propaganda and skillful publicity. "Another . . . is to bring together intelligent citizens, holding varied and independent views, and construct a reform program from the common ground of principles and methods which all can accept." The latter method was the one adopted by the League in preparing its Municipal Program. For all engaged in drafting constitutional provisions relating to cities or in framing charters the program would be the most indispensable general guide to intelligent discussion. Its influence in shaping legislation and directing the evolution of municipal government in the coming decades was certain to be very marked.[45]

MODEL CITY CHARTER, REVISED EDITION, 1927

In the fall of 1924, Secretary Harold W. Dodds wrote to members of the Committee on Municipal Program stating that during the past two or three years a number of suggestions had been received that the Model City Charter should be revised in important sections or entirely rewritten. He enclosed a copy of the charter and requested an opinion whether revision should be undertaken, and if so, what its scope should be. A similar letter was addressed to a half dozen persons who were not members of the committee.

At a meeting of the Council on November 11, 1924, a motion was adopted that the president appoint a committee to consider the revision of the Model City Charter and to report the redraft to the Council.[46] Because of the inability of some of the members of the 1913 committee to serve again and of the desire to add new talent, the committee was reorganized. Eight former members consented to act and five new names were added.[47]

Meetings of the Committee on New Municipal Program were held in New York on March 20–21, 1925, and on May 17–18, 1926.[48] The revision of the Model City Charter was published in 1927. A foreword to the document stated that the charter had undergone a "thorough revision and rewriting." Special acknowledgment and thanks were extended to Professor Hatton, who acted as draftsman. Frank B. Williams of New York also assisted in the preparation of the city planning and zoning sections.

The committee found the 1916 charter to be still generally satisfactory and hence made no considerable change of principle. The major modifications in substance were summarized as follows:

(1) New rules for counting the ballots prepared by the Proportional Representation League on the basis of the experience of Cleveland, Cincinnati, Boulder and Ashtabula.

(2) More detailed financial provisions, particularly relating to budget and appropriation procedure.

(3) A more carefully designed procedure for the administration of special assessments and the appropriation of property for public improvements.

(4) A civil service department constituted along new lines; more specifically, a director of civil service charged with administering the employment service together with a board consisting of the director and two other members, the board to have a final veto over rules to be promulgated.

(5) New sections on city planning and zoning.[49]

Approximately 10,000 copies of the 1916 draft of the Model City Charter had been distributed. No other single document had rendered such influential service to charter commissions and those promoting the manager plan, said the committee.[50]

MODEL CITY CHARTER, REVISED EDITION, 1933

At a meeting of the Executive Committee in the spring of 1930, Secretary Russell Forbes reported that a number of suggestions had been received during the past year that the Model City Charter should be revised, particularly the sections on personnel administration. The committee voted to instruct the secretary to revive the Committee on New Municipal Program and to confer with the president regarding the appointment of a special committee to prepare revised sections on civil service for the charter.[51] To this special committee President Richard S. Childs appointed: Lent D. Upson, Detroit, chairman; Fred Telford, Chicago, secretary; William C. Beyer, Philadelphia; Robert M. Goodrich, Duluth; H. Eliot Kaplan, New York; and Clarence E. Ridley, Chicago.[52]

During the spring of 1930, Emmett L. Bennett, director of the Municipal Reference Bureau of the University of Cincinnati, at the request of the League, made a meticulous examination of the Charter and submitted detailed suggestions for changing the phraseology and content of the 1927 edition.[53]

Serving on the Committee on New Municipal Program were twenty-three members, twelve of whom had been on previous charter committees.[54] Five experienced city managers were added to the committee and their assistance "materially improved the administrative practicality of the document."[55]

Mr. Childs acted as chairman, and Dr. Dodds as secretary of the committee. Professor George A. Graham of Princeton University materially assisted the committee by preparing a comprehensive digest and comparison of the differences between the present draft and the proposed revision of the Model City Charter. He also wrote a ten-page introduction to the final edition of the Model City Charter, explaining and interpreting its basic features. J. M. Leonard of the Detroit Bureau of Governmental Research, under the direction of Lent D. Upson, prepared the draft of the sections dealing with the appropriation of property and special assessments.

Early in its deliberations, the committee assigned sections of the charter to different members for revision and much of the work was done by correspondence. Four meetings of the committee were held: Cleveland, November 9, 1930; Buffalo, November 8, 1931; Princeton, New Jersey, January 15, 16, 17, 1932; and Washington, D.C., September 19, 1932. Completion of its assignment in March, 1933, was followed by the publication of the fourth edition of the Model City Charter.

In the foreword to the document, the committee stated that this was the third edition in the city manager form. Its work represented "no radical break with the past." The text had been clarified and improved in many places, where experience had shown that improvement could be made. Sections on the department of finance and on city planning and zoning were thoroughly revised; new rules for counting the ballots in proportional representation elections were adopted; sections on slums and blighted areas were added; and important changes were made in the personnel department. "The department of civil service has been changed to a department of personnel. Administrative responsibility has been centered in the director of personnel, and the quasi-legislative and quasi-judicial functions of the personnel board have been clearly limited and defined."[56]

Two new features characterized this edition. One was the introduction prepared by Professor Graham commenting upon the basic provisions of the charter.[57] The other, printed as an appendix, was the report of a committee of the International City Managers' Association entitled "Objectionable Charter Provisions." Eleven specific suggestions were made with respect to provisions to be avoided in charter drafting. This committee was composed of City Managers O. E. Carr, Oakland, California; John N. Edy, Dallas, Texas; R. W. Rigsby, Asheville, North Carolina; Clarence E. Ridley, secretary of the Association; Professors Leonard D. White, University of Chicago; A. R. Hatton, Northwestern University; and Thomas H. Reed, University of Michigan.[58]

The committee reported that more than 3,000 copies of the 1927 revision of the Model City Charter had been distributed.[59]

MODEL CITY CHARTER, FIFTH EDITION, 1941

In May, 1937, President H. W. Dodds took steps to form a committee to revise the Model City Charter so that it would meet the present-day requirements of local government. Of the 1933 edition, 2,000 copies had been sold and it had been necessary to order 500 additional copies.

Twenty-nine persons, fourteen of whom were veterans of former charter groups, accepted appointment on the Committee on Revision of the Model City Charter.[60] Richard S. Childs, chairman of the Council of the League, was chairman, and Professor Edwin A. Cottrell of Stanford University was vice-chairman of the committee. First meeting of the committee was held in Chicago, June 4–6, 1937, in conference with the executive directors of the various public officials' groups established there. Subcommittees were appointed to consider: (1) finance; (2) personnel; (3) special assessments and condemnation; (4) planning, zoning, and housing; (5) public utilities; (6) contractual relations with private agencies. Reports of subcommittees were discussed by the committee at the annual conference at Rochester, New York, in November, 1937. Other sessions of the committee were held in Chicago, in February, 1938, and in July, 1939. All of the meetings in Chicago were financed by the Public Administration Clearing House, of which Louis Brownlow was director.

The articles on finance were greatly benefited by the advice of the League's Committee on a Model Fiscal Program, a group of approximately seventy specialists on different aspects of municipal finance. Coördination of the large amount of material and the drafting of the final document was the responsibility of the committee on style and draft under the chairmanship of Arnold Frye.[61]

Published in November, 1941, the fifth edition of the Model City Charter represents the most comprehensive revision since the 1916 edition. Provisions of the charter were completely rewritten to incorporate new developments in municipal organization and administration. Following the introduction by Arnold Frye, chairman of the committee on style and draft, there is an outline of the charter with comments on its principal features. Next are the constitutional provisions on municipal home rule to be incorporated in the state constitution. Then follows the Model City Charter with twelve articles. Five appendices conclude the document. Pertinent comments by the committee, in the form of numerous footnotes, are scattered throughout the charter.

The form of government provided in the charter is the council-manager plan, a feature of all editions since the original Municipal Program of 1900. A small council is elected from the city at large by proportional representation. If proportional representation is not feasible in a particular city the nonpartisan election-at-large system is recommended. The council enacts local legislation, adopts the budget, determines policies, appoints and removes the city manager, and provides for an annual independent audit of municipal accounts. From its membership the council elects a mayor who presides at council meetings, is head of the city government for ceremonial purposes and for purposes of military law. No regular administrative duties are assigned to the mayor.

Selection of the city manager by the council is to be made solely on the basis of his executive and administrative qualifications and experience. Local residence at the time of appointment is not required. Councilmen are not eligible for the appointment during the term for which they were elected and for one year after the expiration of term. As chief executive officer and administrative head of the city government, the city manager is responsible to the council for the management of municipal affairs. He appoints and removes officers and employees, submits to the council the annual budget and report on finances and administrative activities, and advises the council on finances and other municipal problems.

In recognition of the fact that some cities may prefer not to adopt the city-manager plan, the framers of the Model City Charter recommend as an alternative the strong-mayor plan, with an elective mayor as chief administrator to have all of the administrative powers and control given to the manager in the charter. In Appendix V are included provisions for a method of election of the mayor. The veto power could be given to the mayor if deemed desirable. Discussions in the introduction and outline of the charter suggest that changes in the charter could also be made to provide under the assistant-mayor plan for the appointment of a professional administrative assistant to an elective mayor.

Departmental organization is kept to a minimum in the charter, which creates only departments of finance, personnel, and a city planning commission with a director of planning. Other departments, adjusted to the population and other local needs of the city, may be organized under ordinance upon recommendation of the manager. Details of departmental and divisional organization, with operating rules and regulations, may be included in an administrative code, enacted by the council upon recommendation of the manager. Appendix IV contains provisions regarding a department of law, as an illustration of how such articles should be drafted. It is suggested that in very large cities the council, upon recommendation of the manager, should establish administrative areas or districts, each to be in charge of an administrative assistant appointed by the manager. A variety of services to citizens, often performed by councilmen, could be rendered by the manager's representative in the district. Management of the public library in accordance with the general laws of the state relating to libraries is recommended.

Indicative of the committee's interest in sound and workable principles of finance is the placing of the articles on finance immediately following the articles on the council and city manager. These provisions are longer than in previous editions of the charter and reflect the experience of the depression years and technical improvements in the field. They reflect also the views of the League's Committee on a model fiscal program and follow the model laws prepared by that group. Articles on special assessments and condemnation and on tax administration are included as appendices. The former is based on provisions of the Model State Constitution and the latter conforms in principle to the League's Model Real Property Tax Collection Law.

The director of finance, appointed by the city manager, is head of the department of finance. In small cities the manager may assume control of this department. Principal duties of the director of finance are: compilation of the current expense estimates and capital estimates for the budget; fiscal and accounting control for all offices, departments, and agencies; assessment of property, special assessments, collection of taxes and other revenues, and custody of all public funds; preparation of monthly and annual financial reports to the council and city manager. A division of purchases, under the city purchasing agent, is a part of the department. In large cities a separate purchasing department under the manager would seem preferable, but in a small city purchasing could be the responsibility of either the city manager or director of finance. Expenditure control provisions of the charter are strict but permit sufficient flexibility to meet emergencies.

Provisions on the budget are designed to insure careful financial planning of both current and capital expenditures. Based on departmental estimates procured by the director of finance, the budget is submitted to the council by the city manager at least thirty-five days before the beginning of the fiscal year. Council may insert new items or increase or decrease items, except certain fixed charges. Adoption of the budget must be not later than the twenty-seventh day of the last month of the fiscal year. In the event of the council's failure to act on the budget within the time specified, the budget as submitted goes into effect.

The manager's budget must include a statement of pending capital projects and proposed new capital projects, with a statement of the amounts proposed to be raised out of current income and the amounts proposed to be raised from borrowing during the fiscal year. "The city manager shall also include in the message, or attach thereto, a capital program of proposed capital projects for the five fiscal years next succeeding the budget year, prepared by the planning commission, together with his comments thereon and any estimates of costs prepared by the department of public works or other office, department, or agency." Copies of departmental capital estimates furnished the city manager must also be filed with the planning commission for its use in preparing the capital program. An appropriation of at least five per cent, a "down payment," for each capital project which is to be financed by bonds during the fiscal year must be included in the budget.

Article V, on the subject of borrowing for capital improvements, follows the provisions of the Model Bond Law prepared by the Committee on a Model Fiscal Program. Its debt provisions include such subjects as: definition of a "capital project"; power to borrow by issuing bonds and notes in anticipation of bonds; form, content, and procedure for passage of bond ordinance; referendum on bond ordinance; appropriation for down payment; special debt statement; instalments of bonds; period of usefulness; public sale; and short period of limitations. The article omits such matters as debt limits, detailed provisions as to periods of probable usefulness and procedure about sales of bonds except the general provision requiring public sale of all authorized issues of more than $10,000. Charter draftsmen are advised that the extent of the acceptance of these provisions in a city charter will depend upon the adequacy of the constitution and general laws of the state on the subject of the incurring and payment of debt.

The merit system for city employment is provided in Article VII of the charter. "Appointments and promotions in the administrative service of the city shall be made according to merit and fitness to be ascertained, so far as practicable, by competitive examination." There is established a department of personnel under a personnel director appointed by the city manager. A personnel board of three members, appointed by the council for terms of six years, has advisory, investigatory, and quasi-judicial functions. Rules for the administration of the merit system are prepared by the personnel director and submitted to the personnel board, which has the power to approve, reject, or modify them. When approved by the council rules become effective. A classification plan and a standard schedule of pay for each position in the classified service are prepared for the city manager by the director of personnel. Such plans are then submitted by the manager to the council, with his recommendations, and become effective when adopted by the council. A pension and retirement system for officers and employees, on a jointly contributory basis, may be established by the council. Cost of the system must be determined on an actuarial basis. Provisions are included to prohibit political activity of members of the personnel board and of the classified service of the city.

The organization established by the charter for planning, zoning, housing, slum clearance and blighted areas, consists of a planning commission, a director of planning, and a zoning board of appeals. A city planning commission of five members is appointed by the council, with the mayor and city manager serving as ex officio members. The director of planning, appointed by the city manager with the approval of the commission, is the technical adviser of the commission, and may be designated as its executive secretary. Three members appointed by the council constitute the zoning board of appeals. The planning commission is required to make and adopt the master plan for the physical development of the city and controls the platting or subdivision of land within the city. Plans for slum clearance, rehabilitation of blighted areas, housing, neighborhood replanning and redevelopment, and disaster replanning, prepared by the planning commission, are adopted by the council by ordinance. Power to establish and modify the official map of the city is given to the city council, and also the power to enact zoning ordinances. Special exceptions and variances from the zoning regulations may be made by the zoning board of appeals. A separate housing authority may be created by the council if necessary to take advantage of state subsidies under general law.

Other subjects covered by articles in the charter are the initiative and referendum, general provisions, and succession in government.

In drafting the charter the committee attempted to present a document covering all of the essential matters to be included in a charter for any city regardless of size. It recognized, however, that omissions or additions, might be necessary to adapt the charter to local conditions and the provisions of state constitutions and laws. This factor is emphasized in discussion in the introduction, outline of the charter, and in footnotes throughout the various articles. Furthermore, in five appendices are included articles for the consideration of charter draftsmen, which the committee thought it unnecessary to incorporate in the Charter. These articles deal with the subjects of public utilities, special assessments and condemnation, tax administration, and department of law. Rules for the election of the mayor, under a strong-mayor form of government, are provided in appendix V, and may be substituted for the provisions for a city manager. Another example of alternative provisions is found in Article IX, where a footnote provides rules for the choice of councilmen by the nonpartisan election-at-large system, if proportional representation is not desired.

Discussing the League's model laws and their influence on governmental improvement, President Harold W. Dodds of Princeton University, former secretary and president of the League, made this comment regarding the Municipal Program and the Model City Charter: "A *Municipal Program* was the precursor of the *Model City Charter* which is widely credited with having had more influence than any other single document on the improvement of local government. This model has been revised four times. . . . Basically, however, the *Model City Charter* today is the 1899 *Municipal Program* as modified and extended in 1916. . . . To set patterns clearly and specifically, delineating the best practice and the best thought on a problem, to correct existing defects, to set high standards which would provide something to fight *for* instead of *against*," has been the purpose of all the League's model laws. Of greatest importance, the model laws have brought "stability, dignity, and scientific fact to 'reform.' "[62]

In the introduction to the fifth edition of the Model City Charter it is pointed out that the city manager form of government, which it prescribes, had been adopted by more than five hundred cities. Indicative of the sustained interest in a technical legal document is the widespread distribution of the charter—more than 15,000 copies during the period of its publication, 3,500 of them within the last few years. "Since the *Charter* made its first appearance in 1900," wrote Secretary Howard P. Jones, "it has increasingly become the working tool of legislative draftsmen and a textbook on municipal administration for students of the subject within and without our schools and universities."[63]

To assist local charter commissions in the difficult and technical work of constructing a sound document, the League in 1944 appointed a Committee on a Guide for Charter Commissions to prepare a simple, practical manual of procedure for charter drafting.[64] Financed partly by a grant from the Columbia Foundation of

San Francisco, the committee met in New York in March, 1946, and discussed a preliminary draft. Executive Secretary Alfred Willoughby reported in 1946 that two subsequent drafts had been prepared, final revision was proceeding, and publication was scheduled for early in 1947.[65]

SUMMARY

Since the publication of the Municipal Program in 1900, four revisions of the Model City Charter have been issued. In these successive editions of the celebrated document are recorded the evolution of the best thought regarding municipal government and administration. Drafted by committees composed of lay citizens, professors, governmental researchers, and practical administrators, they have incorporated the latest technical improvements and ideas regarding home rule, corporate powers, municipal organization and management, electoral methods, civil service, finance, planning and zoning, slum clearance, and public utilities. Inevitably they represent some compromises as to details, but unity was achieved on the broad principles involved.

From the time of its issuance as a manager plan charter in 1916, the Model City Charter has served as a guide for practically every city which has considered the council-manager form of government.

The most important report issued by the League during its first quarter century, the charter now has as companions several other model laws and systems prepared by League committees within the past twenty-five years.[66] In many instances these model documents have supplemented and expounded principles originally incorporated in the various drafts of the Model City Charter, as we shall see in the next three chapters dealing with the League's efforts to secure improved governmental organization, responsible, democratic, local government, and higher administrative standards.

V

Improving the Forms of Government

PROGRESS in municipal government since 1888 has been outlined under five heads: (1) increased public interest; (2) development of home rule; (3) changes in municipal organization; (4) new instruments for popular control; and (5) the perfection of administrative techniques in various fields.[1] By combining certain of these categories it is possible to reduce the program of reform to three principal phases: first, the designing of improved forms of government; second, the establishment of effective democratic control of governmental processes; and third, the development of higher administrative standards.

In this and the two succeeding chapters the work of the League in the fields of organization, politics, and administration will be outlined. The program of the League, how it is formulated, and its influence upon government and administration will be discussed. Methods employed by the League to promote its principles will be separately treated in a subsequent chapter.[2]

THE MUNICIPAL EXECUTIVE

The mayor-council form of organization was incorporated in the first Municipal Program. In line with the trends in municipal government at that time the strong-mayor type of executive was provided in the Model City Charter.[3]

COMMISSION GOVERNMENT

A few years after the publication of the Municipal Program the attention of students of municipal affairs was centered on Galveston's experiment with the commission form of government. From 1904 on, discussion of the commission plan—its operation, adoptions, merits, and demerits—found a place on the agenda of the annual meetings of the League.[4]

---

[1] For notes on chap. v, see pp. 219–224.

Many of the papers presented to these meetings were brought together in a book edited by Secretary Clinton Rogers Woodruff, and issued in 1911 as the first volume of a newly established "National Municipal League Series."[5] The preface contained the following statement regarding the attitude of the League toward the new plan of government:

> So far the National Municipal League has not indorsed the commission form of government in its entirety. In fact, there has as yet been no agreement among publicists as to what is the irreducible minimum which can be called commission government. . . . To the extent that the commission government provides a short ballot, a concentration of authority in the hands of responsible officials, the elimination of ward lines and partisan designations in the selection of elective officials, adequate publicity in the conduct of public affairs, the merit system, and a city administration and a city administrator responsive to the deliberately formed and authoritatively expressed local public opinion of the city, it embodies principles for which the League stands. There are many other features upon which it has expressed no opinion.[6]

Before the Richmond meeting in November, 1911, a special Committee on the Operation of Commission Government was appointed to prepare an analysis of the plan. The committee members were: Richard S. Childs, New York, chairman; Charles A. Beard, Columbia University; William B. Munro, Harvard University; Ernest S. Bradford, Washington, D.C.; and Secretary Woodruff. In its report to the Richmond meeting the committee substantially agreed that the relative success of commission government was due primarily to its democratic features, essentials of which were unification of powers and the short ballot. The conclusion of the committee was: "Commission government is in general to be recommended for cities of 100,000 population and under, and possibly also for cities of much larger size in preference to any other plan now in operation in any American city." The trend of the discussion which followed the presentation of the report "was to the effect that the commission was by no means the ultimate form of American municipal government, but a transitional form which was destined to lead on to the wholesale cleaning up of myriad ancient abuses."[7]

Two years later at Toronto, the committee made its second report entitled, "The Coming of the City Manager Plan." The history of the manager plan, the Lockport draft of a city manager charter, and the rapid spread of the plan were noted. Four members of the committee agreed in a majority report that the city manager feature should be recommended to charter makers for inclusion in new commission government charters as a "valuable addition to the commission plan." Twelve advantages of the new plan were listed and discussed. Mr. Bradford presented a minority report in which he contended that the city manager plan differed so widely from the commission form that it should not be classed as a variation of commission government but rather as a new plan. He also urged that the city manager plan should be tested by experience and that its superiority over the commission form should be clearly demonstrated before receiving the endorsement of the League.[8]

COUNCIL-MANAGER PLAN

Mr. Childs is the inventor of the city manager plan in its present form, and to him goes the credit for the early interest of the League in the new plan of government.[9] He once described himself as "the minister who performed the marriage ceremony between the city manager plan as first thought of in Staunton, and the Commission plan in Des Moines."[10]

Discussions of the theory and practice of the new plan, with notes on charter developments, were featured in the early volumes of the *Review*.[11] The Committee on Municipal Program accepted the manager plan and it was incorporated in the 1916 edition, as well as in later editions of the Model City Charter.[12] In 1915 a book on the new city manager profession was published in the League series.[13] A Committee on City Manager as a Profession was appointed in 1916. President A. L. Lowell of Harvard University was the first chairman and his colleagues were: Henry M. Waite, Dayton; R. S. Childs, New York; Charles A. Beard, Columbia University; Ossian E. Carr, Niagara Falls; and Gaylord C. Cummins, Grand Rapids. This committee recommended that the League should maintain a list of city managers and of men eligible for the position. The decision of the Council and Executive Committee was that the names of men who had expressed their willingness to be considered as possibilities for city managerships might be sent in response to inquiries, but no definite recommendation of men to positions should be made.[14]

The Story of the City-Manager Plan, a pocket-size pamphlet published in February, 1921, has had several editions and has proved to be one of the most popular and effective pieces of League literature for the promotion of the idea. In 1923 the League published a *Loose-Leaf Digest of City Manager Charters,* prepared by Professor R. T. Crane of the University of Michigan, and designed for use by charter commissions, charter draftsmen, and civic organizations studying the manager plan.

During the early years of city management the work of promoting the adoption of the plan by new cities was shared by the League with the International City Managers' Association, established in 1914. In 1929 the City Managers' Association discontinued such efforts and the League carried on promotion.[15]

Since that time the League has been the leading national citizen organization engaged in educational work on behalf of the manager plan. Its service to local communities or organizations interested in the adoption of the plan has included the furnishing of League charters and other literature,[16] addresses by members of the staff and others secured through the League office, advice in conducting campaigns, assistance in drafting charters and enabling legislation, and aid in campaigns for the defense of the plan when attacked. Through the *Review* and other publicity media, consistent effort is devoted to the popularization of the features of the plan and its success in operation. Within the past decade this phase of the League's work has been expanded.[17]

As mentioned above, the League and the City Managers' Association shared the work of promotion until 1929. In many other ways the two organizations have co-operated. The League was represented at the organization meeting of the Managers' Association in 1914 and five times (1915, 1916, 1917, 1921, 1923) joint annual meetings of the two groups have been held. City manager notes were published in the *Review* in 1922 and 1923. Representatives of the two associations have worked together on several joint committees. City managers have served on important League committees, including the Committee on New Municipal Program. Two former city managers have been president of the League, Henry M. Waite, 1921–1923, and Clarence A. Dykstra, 1937–1940.

Many members of the League have made significant contributions to the city manager movement, but two deserve special mention, Mr. Childs and Dr. A. R. Hatton of Northwestern University, for years field representative and charter consultant of the League. Professor Leonard D. White said of their work:

> Mr. Childs took a lively interest in the manager movement in the earliest days and contributed powerfully to its establishment. He has often addressed the managers and has always sought to stimulate their imagination and sense of wide responsibility. Dr. Hatton has been actively identified with charter drafting for years, is a close student of the manager plan, has taken an active role in advocating it in all parts of the country, and has been a friendly critic of the managers for a decade. Both have had a leading influence on the manager movement.[18]

METROPOLITAN INTEGRATION

In December, 1914, the Executive Committee created a Committee on City and County Consolidation, consisting of H. S. Gilbertson, East Orange, New Jersey, chairman; Richard H. Dana, Cambridge; Clyde L. King, University of Pennsylvania; Winston Paul, New York; and Mark L. Requa, Oakland, California. A Council meeting in April, 1916, approved the recommendation of the committee that an active effort should be made by the League to eliminate county government where city and county limits coincide, and to confer upon the appropriate city officials and departments any necessary powers, duties, and responsibilities of county government that are not duplications of already existent city functions. The committee was discontinued in 1917.[19]

No reference to the problem of city and county relations was made in the first Municipal Program. Section 8 of the constitutional provisions on municipal home rule which accompanied the 1916 Model City Charter dealt with consolidation of city and county. By vote of the electors any city of 100,000 population or more could be organized as a distinct county, and such city and county might provide in its municipal charter for the consolidation of the county, city, and all other local authorities in one system of municipal government.[20] This provision was omitted from later editions of the Model City Charter "as being no longer of universal application." No general solution of the problem of the government of metropolitan areas had been reached, a footnote to the Charter stated.

Section 88 of the first edition of the Model State Constitution provided that

> Any county with a population of over ——— may be authorized by law to provide in its charter for a consolidated system of municipal government,

providing for the powers and duties of county, city and other municipal authorities within the county and abolishing all officers whose powers and duties are otherwise provided for.

The same provisions were incorporated in the revised edition of 1928.[21]

In 1922 the League published a study, "The Political Integration of Metropolitan Communities," by Professor Chester C. Maxey of Western Reserve University.[22] He described the accomplishments of the integration movement in Baltimore, Philadelphia, San Francisco, St. Louis, New York, Denver, Pittsburgh, Wheeling, and Washington, D.C., and outlined the efforts for unification in Boston; Chicago; Cleveland; Alameda County, California; Portland, Oregon; Los Angeles; Essex County, New Jersey; and other communities. His general conclusion was, ". . . political integration is indispensable to every metropolitan community that aspires to attain its maximum development as a center of industrial, commercial and social activity."

Problems of metropolitan areas were discussed at the annual meetings of the League in 1917, 1920, 1921, and 1923. At Boston in November, 1924, the question was discussed at length and a resolution was adopted requesting the League to appoint a committee to study the government of metropolitan areas.[23] Favorable action on this resolution was taken by the Council a few months later and a Committee on Metropolitan Government was constituted.[24] Dean Frank H. Sommer of New York University Law School was chairman, and Paul Studenski, New York University, secretary. Chairman Sommer, Professor T. H. Reed, and H. W. Dodds acted as an editorial subcommittee.[25]

Application was made to the Russell Sage Foundation for a grant to cover the salary of a secretary and expenses of investigation. In December, 1925, a gift of $10,000 was made by the Foundation for the project, the sum to be expended under the direction of the chairman of the committee and the secretary of the League.[26] Extensive field studies in the United States and Canada were made by Dr. Studenski, who prepared a preliminary draft for criticism by the other members of the committee. The report of the committee, the first comprehensive study of its kind, was published in book form in 1930.[27]

There were presented factual data and experience regarding seven types of organization to solve regional governmental problems: intermunicipal coöperation and exchange of services, consolidation and annexation under a unitary form of government, city-county consolidation and separation, expansion of county government, special metropolitan authorities, the New York Borough plan, and the federated region or city. The conclusions of the committee were summarized in a two-page chapter. The committee could find no panacea or formula applicable to all regions. "There can be no single answer to the problem of metropolitan organization, applicable to all conditions and times." Separate study must be made for each region and a plan devised for its particular needs. Furthermore, "The different types of organization or readjustment so far proposed are not always mutually exclusive. They supplement each other to a large degree." Finally, much more information and experience was needed before dogmatic conclusions could be reached. A great amount of local research into the details of regional relationships was a necessity. "Here is a rich field of investigation which should be cultivated intensively by political scientists."[28]

Professor Charles E. Merriam of the University of Chicago praised the report as "one of the most important contributions to municipal government in recent years," and continued: "No study in recent years, indeed, has presented so rich a store of hitherto inaccessible material regarding a vital phase of the urban process." But he considered the findings, on the whole, "a little inconclusive."[29] Almost the same comment regarding the conclusions was made by Professor Austin F. Macdonald of the University of California, who remarked that ". . . the seven conclusions which it contains are so general in their scope that it is virtually impossible to disagree with them—a sure sign that they have little value." The report was almost solely descriptive and made little effort to solve the problem of regional government. But, wrote Professor Macdonald: "This volume is by far the most important contribution to the field since Dr. Maxey's study of nearly a decade ago. It is well written, comprehensive, and accurate."[30] Declaring it "a pioneer effort," Professor Joseph McGoldrick of Columbia University said: "The chief value of the volume lies in the picture that it presents of the variety now existing in approaching the problem."[31] *Engineering News-Record* welcomed the book as a contribution on a subject that was growing rapidly in importance and that had never before been treated comprehensively.[32] The *American Economic Review* thought that students of economic problems would be interested in the discussion of taxation, public utilities, transportation, and the grouping of population, and that they would find the document "thoroughly annotated."[33]

Texts on municipal government now give more attention to the metropolitan problem and the League's study is constantly cited.[34] Professor Charles M. Kneier expressed the common view of political scientists when he wrote: "This is the most valuable study available on the subject of the government of metropolitan areas."[35]

The Model State Constitution, as revised in 1933, provides that, under regulations made by general law, any powers of cities, villages, and other local units of government may be transferred to the county, with the latter's consent. The rights of initiative and referendum are guaranteed to the people of local units regarding every transfer of power or revocation of transfer, and to the people of the county with regard to every proposal giving or withdrawing such consent.[36]

Power is given to any county to frame and adopt a charter. Further provisions for the assumption of municipal functions by counties are as follows:

> Such charter may provide for the concurrent or exclusive exercise by the county, in all or in part of its area, of all or of any designated powers vested by the constitution or laws of this state in municipalities and other local units of government; it may provide for the succession by the county to the rights, properties, and obligations of municipalities and other local governments therein incident to the powers so vested in the county, and for the division of the county into districts for purposes of administration or of taxation or of both. No charter or amendment vesting in the county any powers of a municipality or other local unit of government shall become effective unless it

shall have been approved by a majority of those voting thereon (1) in the county, (2) in any municipality containing more than 25 per cent of the total population of the county, and (3) in the county outside of such municipality.[37]

Similar provisions are contained in the fourth edition of the Model State Constitution, as revised in 1941 and 1946.[38] The legislature is given power to facilitate agreements between local units for a coöperative or joint administration of any function, and also power to encourage the consolidation of civil divisions or the establishment of coöperative enterprises between them.[39]

In his annual report for 1942 Secretary Howard P. Jones called attention to the serious problems which metropolitan areas would face at the end of the war. Many persons had urged the League to conduct a study of this problem on a national basis. The League sponsored the meeting of a small group in Chicago in July, at which the nucleus of a Committee on Postwar Problems of Urban Peoples was organized. Foundation support to finance the study over a period of five years was being sought.[40]

STATE GOVERNMENT

At the Springfield meeting in November, 1916, Vice-President Childs boldly proposed that the scope of the League's work be expanded to include county, state, and national activities so far as they apply to the structure of government. An interesting discussion ensued, resulting in a reference of the whole matter to the Executive Committee.[41] Subsequent to the annual meeting, Secretary Woodruff sought the views of a considerable number of active members and found the consensus of opinion friendly to the suggestion. The Executive Committee accordingly adopted a resolution in December stating that municipal progress was being increasingly embarrassed by the relative backwardness of state and county government and that the League should thereafter give part of its attention to the problems of county and state government. When this action was reported to the League membership by letter the response was favorable.[42]

A Committee on the Form of State Government was created with Professor A. R. Hatton as chairman. It was agreed to hold a joint meeting of the League and the American Political Science Association and the suggested topic for the conference was "A Model Structure for a State Government."[43]

MODEL STATE CONSTITUTION

The feature of the twenty-fifth annual meeting of the League held at Cleveland, December 29–31, 1919, in conjunction with the American Political Science Association, the Governmental Research Conference, and the National Association of Civic Secretaries, was a Moot State Constitutional Convention to secure the consensus of opinion among civic leaders and political scientists on the problems involved in the revision of a state constitution.

Preparation of proposals for submission to the Moot Convention was divided among seventeen organizations and individuals.[44] Tentative drafts of the provisions concerning the governor and legislature, proportional representation, legislative procedure, the budget, judiciary, initiative and referendum, and state, county, and municipal indebtedness were published in advance of the meeting.[45]

A distinct departure from the traditional forms of state government was the proposal for a state manager submitted by a committee of the National Short Ballot Organization. A single-chambered legislature would select from its own members a legislative council of nine members. The chairman of the council would have the title of governor but with no veto or appointive power. An administrative manager would be appointed by the legislative council to hold office at the pleasure of the council. Powers of the manager would include appointment and removal of heads of departments, execution of the laws, custody of state property, and maintenance of public order. The committee said that its proposal was "to extend logically to state government the principles of unification of powers and complete control by the representative body embodied in its model charter for municipalities—the city-manager plan." According to the committee, "The governor . . . becomes the legislative leader in a position comparable to that of the Prime Minister in the various parliaments of the British Empire. He is the majority floor-leader, . . . the key man whose position and utterances on political questions of the day are momentous and often decisive." A more conservative plan, however, was finally agreed upon, the manager proposal being defeated by a substantial majority.[46]

Votes of the membership on the proposed drafts were in the nature of an advisory opinion to the Committee on State Government, which had referred to it the proceedings of the Moot Convention with instructions to draft a model state constitution for presentation to the next annual meeting of the League. Debate and advisory voting on the progress report of the Committee on State Government on the Model State Constitution was the outstanding constructive feature of the Indianapolis meeting of the League in November, 1920. There was general acceptance of the committee's report with some amendments.[47] A complete constitution was submitted to the Chicago meeting in November, 1921, and was adopted except for the sections relating to public welfare.[48] In 1924 there was published in pamphlet form the final text of *A Model State Constitution*, with explanatory articles: "The Legislature," by H. W. Dodds; "The Executive," by John A. Fairlie; "The Budget," by A. E. Buck; "The Judiciary," by W. F. Dodd; and "Counties," by Richard S. Childs.[49]

Continued demand for copies of the Model State Constitution led to the issuance of a second edition in 1928, incorporating various textual improvements. Dr. Hatton, draftsman of the original document, assumed the principal work of revision.[50] Criticisms and suggestions for amendment were received from various sources outside of the committee: Professor Howard White of Miami University; Charles S. Ascher, assistant director of the Public Administration Clearing House; and the League's Committee on County Government. These resulted in the submission of the document to the Committee on State Government for approval of suggested changes. A third edition, including several textual alterations, not representing changes in fundamental principle, was issued in March, 1933. Acceptance of the recommendations of the Committee on County Government caused the most extensive revisions.[51]

A review of the principal features of the Model State Constitution will indicate to what extent its framers proposed radical innovations or followed the trend of constitutional development in state government. The traditional bicameral legislature is abandoned in favor of a single chamber elected for a term of two years by proportional representation. This body chooses from its own membership a legislative council of seven members, with the governor also a member. Duties of the council are to gather material, prepare the legislative program, and draft measures for introduction into the legislature. A secretary, chosen by the members, appoints and supervises all employees of the legislature and has charge of "all service incidental to the work of legislation."

Closer relations between the governor and the legislature are established by placing the governor on the legislative council and by giving the chief executive and heads of departments seats in the legislature with the right to introduce bills, take part in debate, but without a vote. One-fifth of the members of the legislature may require the attendance of the governor before the legislature or a committee to answer inquiries with respect to the budget. By a two-thirds vote the legislature may remove or retire the governor from office, after permitting him an opportunity for defense. Provision is made to break deadlocks between the governor and the legislature. A measure rejected by the legislature may be referred to the people by order of the governor if one-third of the members voted for it upon final passage. Conversely, a measure vetoed by the governor and lacking support of two-thirds of the legislature for repassage may, by a majority vote, be referred to the people.

Executive power is vested in a governor elected by the voters for a term of four years. He is to appoint and remove the heads of such executive departments as may be established by law. His veto of legislation may be set aside by a two-thirds vote of the legislature. He is required to prepare the budget for submission to the legislature and may disapprove or reduce items in appropriation bills, subject to repassage by a two-thirds vote of the legislature. No provision is made for a lieutenant governor. An auditor, selected by majority vote of the legislature, conducts a continuous audit of departmental accounts and reports to the legislative council. The merit system is established for all appointments and promotions in the civil service of the state and of all civil divisions, including counties, cities, and villages.

Sections on the judiciary propose the establishment of a unified court of justice with departments for the performance of trial and appellate judicial functions. Judges are appointed by the governor for terms of ten years. The chief justice is the administrative head of the general court of justice. A judicial council is given power to make rules of pleading, practice, and procedure. Clerks of the courts are nominated by the chief justice and confirmed by the judicial council.

Other features of the Model State Constitution are a simplified bill of rights; the initiative and referendum on laws and constitutional amendments; home rule for cities and counties, with provision for consolidation of municipal and county functions; and a relatively simple method of amendment by legislative action and popular vote, by popular petition and vote, and by a constitutional convention called by popular vote resulting from legislative action or petition.

The Model State Constitution, said Professor W. B. Graves, was by no means perfect, and it had sometimes been severely criticized, but it represented the judgment "of some of the ablest students in the field of state government."[52] Professor

Howard White analyzed the relations between the governor and the legislature and predicted that the operation of the legislative council and the governor's cabinet would produce a conflict between the two agencies for leadership in the legislature.[53] He suggested also more frequent legislative sessions, and transfer to the administration of responsibility for legislative redistricting after each decennial census. Minor inconsistencies and possibilities of textual improvements were also pointed out by Professor White.[54]

Senator George W. Norris of Nebraska thought that the constitution contained "some remarkably good features," particularly the one-house legislature. But the constitution retained party control and that in his judgment was "the largest evil of every state government." He summarized his own plan for the reform of state government in the following paragraph:

> Why not go to the root of the matter—provide for a smaller legislature, giving them salary enough so that you will get the best talent the state affords and let them get their information first hand. Let them become experts. Pay them enough so they can devote all of their time to government, making a business institution of it. Eliminate partisanship entirely, and elect all of its members on a non-partisan ballot, taking it entirely and completely out of politics.[55]

In the academic field the Model State Constitution has received almost universal endorsement. Practically all texts on American and state government have made basic use of its provisions in the discussion of state government reorganization. Several texts on state government reprinted the complete document in the appendix, and thousands of reprints have been used for class discussion. Dr. W. F. Dodd characterized it as the "most important" of the numerous plans for the reorganization of state government.[56] Professor C. G. Haines and Mrs. B. M. Haines stated: "Though the provisions of this model constitution have not been adopted as a whole in any state, they furnish in convenient form some of the most important provisions which seem necessary in order to reorganize American state government."[57] Professor W. B. Munro wrote: "This model constitution has been widely discussed, but no state has adopted it as a whole, nor is any state likely to do so, for some of its provisions represent too radical a departure from the general trend of political development in the United States."[58] After a lengthy analysis of the provisions of the constitution, Professor A. N. Holcombe on the contrary said: "Radical though the innovations may seem to be, . . . they are not unprecedented, and, all in all, form a project which is in thorough harmony with the historical trend of American constitutional development."[59]

One can readily agree with Editor Howard P. Jones, in his note to the 1933 edition, in which he said: "The *Model State Constitution* sets the standard in its field and has had a wide influence over a period of twelve years on thinking with respect to problems of state constitutional law and the relations of state and local government." And Professor Holcombe admirably summarized the significance of the document in this statement: "The framing of the model state constitution will be amply justified, if attention is thereby directed to the problems of contemporary political practice which most require the thoughtful consideration of public-spirited citizens, and if their thinking is thereby turned into the channels most likely to lead to better government."[60]

A new Committee on State Government to revise the Model State Constitution was appointed by President C. A. Dykstra in 1939.[61] Professor W. Brooke Graves, Temple University, was chairman, and Wilbert L. Hindman, University of Southern California, was secretary of the committee.[62] Meetings of the committee were held at Indianapolis, with the League conference in November, 1939; at Washington, D. C. on December 27, 1939, in connection with the meeting of the American Political Science Association; at the League meeting in November, 1940; and at Chicago in December, 1940, with the annual meeting of the American Political Science Association. Approximately seventy-five consultants on particular subjects gave valuable assistance in the work of revision. Professor Edwin E. Witte of the University of Wisconsin contributed his technical skill to the improvement of the final draft of the fourth edition of the Model State Constitution which was issued in November, 1941.[63]

Greatly improved in form and arrangement and longer than previous editions, the fourth edition of the Model State Constitution incorporates a number of significant new developments in state government. The unicameral state legislature is made a "continuous body" during its two-year term, with regular sessions quarterly and special sessions to be called by the governor or by a majority vote of the legislative council. As an agency of the legislature the legislative council is continued and strengthened, with the governor no longer a member. A new provision is one permitting the legislature to delegate to the legislative council authority to supplement existing legislation by general orders, which do not become effective until published as provided by law. Committee procedure is improved by the requirement that each committee keep a journal of its proceedings as a public record, and that published notice one week in advance be given of all committee hearings, specifying all subjects to be considered.

The governor remains the only elective state administrative officer. Election for the four-year term is to be held in November of alternate odd numbered years. Heads of administrative departments are appointed by and may be removed by the governor. A new provision limits the number of administrative departments which the legislature may establish to twenty, exclusive of temporary commissions for special purposes. The number of departments may be reduced by the legislature through consolidation or otherwise. The governor, in order that his power of administration may be strengthened, is authorized to appoint an administrative manager to serve at his pleasure. Any or all of his administrative powers may be delegated by the governor to the administrative manager. Administrative aides to assist the governor and administrative manager may be provided by law,—all appointments to such positions to be under the merit system regulations. As a safeguard on executive action the constitution provides that "no executive order governing the work of the state or the administration of one or more departments, offices and agencies, shall become effective until published as provided by law."

A General Court of Justice to handle all judicial work of the state is established by the judiciary article of the constitution. The chief justice, elected by the voters of the state for a term of eight years, is presiding justice of the supreme court department and is executive head of the General Court of Justice. He appoints the judges of the various departments of the General Court of Justice from a list of three nominations for each vacancy submitted to him by the judicial council. Terms of judges are twelve years. After a judge has completed four years of his term the voters of the state or of the judicial district decide by ballot on the retention or removal of the judge. A judicial council, representing all parts of the judicial system, the legal profession and citizens, is given power to make and alter rules relating to pleading, practice, or procedure in the General Court of Justice. Such rules must be published before becoming effective.

Only a brief mention can be made of other features of the Model State Constitution. In the bill of rights citizens are guaranteed the right to organize and employees the right to bargain collectively. Election officers are to be appointed as determined by law, provided that selection must be made on the basis of merit and fitness to be determined by competitive examination, so far as practicable. Several restrictions and safeguards are added to prevent abuses of the initiative and referendum. The initiative cannot be used to make appropriations of public funds nor for the enactment of local or special legislation. Initiative measures cannot name a person as administrator of any agency to be established by the proposed law or constitutional amendment. Civil divisions of the state must use centralized purchasing, wherever practicable, and coöperative purchasing by two or more civil divisions may be authorized by law. Power of excess condemnation is given to the state and its civil divisions. Counties, cities, and other civil divisions must adopt an annual budget in such form as determined by law.

The merit system is continued for state and local employees, and the classification of positions according to duties and the establishment of salary ranges are made mandatory. Legislative and judicial employees must be selected in accordance with the merit provisions of the constitution. A department of civil service administers the personnel functions of the state and of such civil divisions as choose to come under its jurisdiction. Provision is to be made by law for personnel administration in civil divisions not electing to come under the state department and not establishing the merit system in a home rule charter. The article on public welfare seeks to confer constitutional powers upon the state to establish and maintain a complete program of public welfare services relating to education, health, public relief, inspection of welfare institutions, housing, conservation, and the development of the "natural beauty, historic associations, sightliness and physical good order of the state." In the article on constitutional revision the most significant additions are the provisions that a referendum on the calling of a convention must be submitted to the voters every twenty years, and for a preparatory commission to assemble data for the members of a constitutional convention.

Two new articles are added to the fourth edition of the Model State Constitution. A schedule is provided to facilitate the transition from the old constitution to the new. Recognition is given also to the emerging importance of intergovernmental relations. Authority is given to the legislature to establish effective coöperation of the state with the federal government and with the other states. Agreements for coöperative or joint administration of any function may be made by local units with the federal, state, or other local governmental divisions. Consolidation of local units or the establishment of coöperative enterprises on the local level may be facilitated and encouraged by legislation.

In 1946 the Committee on State Government, partly reorganized,[64] reexamined the 1941 document and made two changes. The minimum age for voting is reduced from twenty-one to eighteen years, and the provisions regarding the framing and adoption of home rule charters for cities and counties are shortened and simplified.

Chairman Graves, in the foreword to the partial revision of 1946 sums up the influence of the revised Constitution in this paragraph:

> Well ahead of common practice, in view of the backwardness of state constitutions generally, the high standards of the *Model State Constitution* have exerted a very considerable influence on thinking in connection with the improvement of state government. In all of the attempts at constitutional revision since the Fourth Edition was published, copies of it have been used by convention delegates or commission members as part of their background materials. In addition, it has been widely studied by citizen groups seeking to modernize the constitutions of their states.[65]

STATE ADMINISTRATIVE REORGANIZATION

In the field of administrative consolidation in state government the League has played a prominent role since 1919. In that year it published a supplement, "Administrative Consolidation in State Governments,"[66] by A. E. Buck of the New York Bureau of Municipal Research, and in 1920, "Administrative Reorganization in Illinois,"[67] by Professor J. M. Mathews of the University of Illinois. The latter study described the organization and operation of the Illinois state government under the civil administrative code adopted in 1917.

Mr. Buck's study discussed the general principles of reorganization and an analysis of the plans adopted in Illinois, Idaho, Nebraska, and Massachusetts, with a summary of plans proposed in other states. Demands for the supplement for general distribution and for class use in universities led to its revision in 1922 and issuance as a pamphlet in the League's technical series. Further revised editions were issued in 1924, 1928, and 1930. Thousands of copies were sent to governors, members of state legislatures, and local civic leaders everywhere throughout the nation.

In 1938 Mr. Buck completely rewrote the pamphlet and expanded it into a volume covering the experience of every state. In Part I he gave a résumé of the state reorganization movement, with a discussion of principles, methods, and results of administrative reorganization. Part II outlined the record of progress in each of the forty-eight states, with details of plans adopted and proposed. Describing the book as a "complete and scholarly compilation of essential information," Professor Graves said: ". . . this study should continue for some time to be the 'standard title' on the subject of state administrative reorganization." And Professor Harold M. Dorr, University of Michigan, declared that the study was a "manual or handbook . . . invaluable to students of government and laymen alike."[68]

The League's publications on the subject of administrative reorganization have exerted a profound influence on state government and have been used in practically all states in which plans for reorganization have been made. In texts and in academic circles they have been accepted as the basic references on the subject.[69]

COUNTY GOVERNMENT

The change in policy of the League to include state and county government was sponsored principally by Mr. Childs, who was interested in applying the short ballot principle to government on these levels. As early as 1913 he had advocated the county manager plan, and through his National Short Ballot Organization had led the movement for the simplification of county government.[70] "Ramshackle County Government," first published in the *Outlook*,[71] and later, April, 1921, separately reprinted as a pamphlet, became one of the most popular and influential of League publications. At the suggestion of Mr. Childs, H. S. Gilbertson, assistant secretary of the National Short Ballot Organization, prepared in 1917 *The County, The Dark Continent of American Politics*, which later was reprinted in the League's series of books. The same year saw the creation of the first Committee on County Government, with a large membership and with Otho G. Cartwright, White Plains, New York, as chairman. An informal conference of the committee was held at the annual meeting in 1917.[72]

By distribution of the pamphlet *Ramshackle County Government*, by correspondence, by articles in the *Review*, by coöperation in state conferences, and by building up a collection of literature, the League directed attention to the archaic character of county government. In 1925 two new pamphlets were widely distributed, *The County Manager Plan* by Richard S. Childs, and *A New Kind of County Government* by Herbert Quick.[73]

Ever-increasing inquiries as to the solution of the problems of county government led to the appointment, in May, 1929, of a Committee on County Government, under the chairmanship of Professor John A. Fairlie of the University of Illinois, and with Professor Paul W. Wager of the University of North Carolina, as secretary.[74] After more than a year's work in which meetings were held at Chicago in November, at New Orleans in December, 1929; and at New York in February, 1930, the committee drafted "A Model County Manager Law," which was published in 1930.[75] The committee did not think that its work was finished; the Model Law, in its opinion, was "the first practical step to be taken toward a solution." Admitting the difficulties in drafting such a law, the committee considered its law as a model only in the sense that it might "serve as a guide for those interested in improving county government in their states." The bill represented, said Editor Jones, "the best thought of the outstanding experts on county government in the country."

An introduction to the Model County Manager Law discusses classes of counties, legal status of the county, advantages of the county manager plan, jurisdiction of the manager, the short ballot, and presents a recommended organization chart for rural counties and one for urban-rural counties. The law itself makes no effort to include all phases of county government, but deals principally with the method of adoption of the charter; powers and duties of the county board; appointment, powers, and duties of the manager; preparation and submission of the budget; and the departments of finance, public works, public welfare, and education. A selected bibliography is included.

Chief merits of the plan are its provisions for a simple, responsible form of county government, commented Professor A. W. Bromage:

> In place of the existing assortment of elected officers in the typical county, it offers a chief executive, the manager, with administrative officers grouped under his unified command. It assures democratic government through the responsibility of the manager to the county board. The influence of this model is reflected in the optional county manager laws adopted in Montana in 1931 and in Virginia in 1932. Development of such a plan in American counties would revitalize county boards, and would center administration in a manager whom the board hired and might, if necessary, discharge.[76]

Remarkable interest throughout the nation in the improvement of local government and the realization by the League that its work in formulating the Model County Manager Law was only a beginning of this study led to the reorganization and enlargement of the Committee on County Government in the summer of 1931. Former Governor Frank O. Lowden of Illinois was honorary chairman, Professor John A. Fairlie, chairman, and Howard P. Jones, secretary.[77] Membership of the committee was representative of many states, different sections of the country, and various institutions and organizations—universities, research bureaus, rural organizations, official commissions, and state municipal leagues.[78]

Meetings of the committee were held at Buffalo, New York, in November, 1931; at Washington, D. C., in December, 1931; at Chicago, in May, 1932; at the University of Virginia, in July, 1932; at Detroit, in December, 1932; at Philadelphia, in December, 1933; and at Pittsburgh, in November, 1934. The complexity of the problem, the size of the committee, and the lack of funds for travel expenses made the work one of considerable difficulty.[79]

At the organization meeting of the committee it was agreed to study various aspects of county government before attempting to formulate a specific bill on the subject similar to the Model City Charter for municipal government. Subcommittees were appointed to consider constitutional provisions; coöperation, coördination or consolidation of counties; relation of the county to the state; form of local government; position of the township; financial provisions; and personnel administration. Decision was early reached to publish separate reports from time to time rather than to wait until the committee had reached its final conclusions on the whole problem.

The first report of the committee, "Constitutional Barriers to Improvements in County Government," by Howard P. Jones, was published as a supplement to the *Review* for August, 1932.[80] Mr. Jones discussed the constitutional obstacles which affected (1) the form of county government; (2) the area of government; (3) the functions of the county; (4) abolition of the county; and (5) improvements in administrative methods. His conclusion was that the provisions of the revised Model State Constitution furnished the most satisfactory solution of the problem.

The text of the recommendations of the Committee on County Government as to provisions of local government for the Model State Constitution was incorporated in the report. Subsequently these recommendations were accepted by the Committee on State Government and included in the revised edition of the Model State Constitution issued in March, 1933.[81]

"Principles of a Model County Government," by R. C. Atkinson of the Ohio Institute, the second report of the committee, was published as a supplement to the *Review* for September, 1933.[82] The plan proposed a county board of from five to nine members elected at large, preferably by the Hare System of proportional representation, with legislative and policy-determining duties. Appointment, removal, powers, and duties of the county manager were outlined. Other sections dealt with administrative departments and personnel administration. It was not the intent of the committee to present the detailed provisions of a bill or charter suitable for final enactment by any particular state or county. As remarked by its chairman, Professor Fairlie, in the foreword, "This statement presents the substantive provisions which should be embodied in a county government law or a county charter based on the recommended constitutional provisions." No consideration was given to the problem of county-state relations, although provision was made for the transfer of powers and functions between different local units.

The final report of the committee, "Recommendations on Township Government," was the work of Professor Arthur W. Bromage of the University of Michigan.[83] Government of the township as found in the Middle Atlantic and North Central states, excepting the New England townships, was studied. Objections to the township were presented and also the obstacles to township elimination. The committee found the township no longer a satisfactory unit for local administration and recommended its gradual elimination, suggesting methods by which this could be accomplished. Pending abolition of townships, immediate consolidation of townships in sparsely settled areas was suggested.

In May, 1934, a new department, "County Government," under the editorship of Professor Paul W. Wager, was established in the *Review*. The October, 1934, and February, 1939, issues of the *Review* were given over entirely to articles on county government.[84]

The American County—Patchwork of Boards, a pamphlet by Edward W. Weidner, was published by the League in 1946. It was also announced by Executive Secretary Alfred Willoughby in his report for 1946 that revisions of the Model County Manager Law and Principles of a Model County Government had been prepared by Dr. R. C. Atkinson in consultation with a group of authorities on county government. Further consultation, revision, and editing was set for 1947.[85]

Like the Model State Constitution, the publications on county government have been widely used as source material by text writers on American government and local government, and as supplementary text material in university courses in local government. Commenting on the report on township government, Secretary Jones said:

> The report has had a great deal of influence in crystallizing opinion in the country relative to the ultimate desirability of abolishing townships. Mean-

while, the previous publications of the committee continue to exert wide influence. The Model County Manager Law has been used as the basis of legislation in a number of states. Nebraska and Montana both adopted the model law with hardly a change and Douglas County, Nebraska, adopted the manager plan under the Nebraska enabling act on November 6. The report on Principles of a Model County Government has been in demand with the growth of county home rule.[86]

Municipal Reference Libraries

The 1908 conference of the League gave recognition to the growing importance of municipal reference libraries. Papers on the subject were read by Horace E. Flack, municipal reference librarian, Baltimore; and Charles McCarthy, legislative librarian, Madison, Wisconsin.[87] A Committee on Municipal Reference Libraries with Dr. Flack as chairman, was appointed in 1909 to report upon the feasibility and desirability of municipal reference libraries.[88] Letters of inquiry were sent to public libraries in all cities having a population of 50,000 or more. The committee also studied the organization, operation, and efficiency of existing legislative and municipal reference libraries. Its report submitted at the Buffalo conference in 1910 recommended the establishment of municipal reference libraries in all large cities, to be, as a general rule, under control of the public library, and situated in the city hall, where feasible. Head of the library should have had suitable training and should be chosen by a method which would insure merit and the elimination of political considerations. The library should be the agency for exchange of municipal documents; and its functions should be collection, compilation, and dissemination of information; aid in the drafting of ordinances; issuance of bulletins; and furnishing accurate information to the press.[89]

Before the 1911 meeting of the League, the committee was reconstituted and instructed to consider the question of municipal archives. In the committee's opinion the municipal reference library was the proper agency to preserve, classify, and index such archives. Its report to the Richmond conference, made by Chairman Flack, endorsed the report made the previous year and reviewed the movement for the establishment of municipal reference libraries during the past year, which it pronounced as "very successful." Attention was called to the need for a central municipal reference bureau which would serve all cities of the country and it was suggested that this might be undertaken by the Bureau of the Census or some other government department at Washington. Recommendation was made that the League take the necessary steps to make this proposal effective.[90]

At the Los Angeles meeting in 1912 the committee gave a summary of the progress of municipal reference libraries. Approval of the bill before the Congress for the creation of a national legislative reference bureau was favored, with the recommendation that the functions of the bureau should be expanded to include municipal reference work.

Further progress was reported by the committee to the Toronto meeting in 1913. New York, Chicago, Philadelphia, St. Louis, Portland (Oregon), Oakland, and Toronto had established municipal reference libraries. All except New York had followed the recommendations of the committee by placing the library under the control of the public library, with an office in the city hall. The committee stressed the importance of adequate appropriations, elimination of political interference, and scientific training for those in charge. Instead of preparing a new report or having the 1910 report reprinted, the committee had decided to use an article prepared by Professor Earl Crecraft of the School of Journalism of Columbia University. Mayors and public librarians in all the larger cities would be sent a reprint of the Crecraft article during the coming year.[91]

Establishment of municipal reference libraries in fourteen large cities, organized, almost without exception, along lines recommended by the committee, was reported to the 1914 meeting. The following year the committee called attention to the need of a central clearinghouse of municipal information and recommended that the League should bring to the attention of the Congress "the desirability of granting to the library of congress a special appropriation sufficient to enable it to establish a municipal reference division to serve as a central coöperating agency for the municipal reference libraries and similar organizations of the entire country."[92]

Secretary Woodruff informed the 1916 meeting that the committee had had a very active year and there had been much discussion as to whether a central clearinghouse of municipal material should be a governmental body or a commercial organization. Majority opinion of the committee favored making it a governmental function.[93]

At the spring meeting of the Council, 1919, the Committee on Municipal Information recommended through its chairman, Frederick Rex of Chicago, the establishment of a federal municipal bureau of information. The committee was asked to prepare a bill for submission to the Congress along the lines of its recommendation, and the report was referred to the Executive Committee with power to act.[94]

A committee of five members of the American Library Association under the chairmanship of Samuel H. Ranck, librarian of Grand Rapids, was appointed in 1916 to prepare library provisions for the revised Model City Charter.[95] Its report, including the proposed draft of the library section, was made to the League meeting in 1917. After critical discussion the report was referred to the Committee on Municipal Program.[96]

JUDICIAL ORGANIZATION

In 1911 a Committee on Municipal Courts was appointed to draft a model act for the use of legislators and publicists. Harry Olson, chief justice of the Municipal Court of Chicago, was chairman. He later became chairman of the board of directors of the American Judicature Society. Herbert Harley, secretary of the American Judicature Society, was secretary of the committee. Most of the members were connected with the Society.[97]

Through this joint committee, the League and the Society coöperated in the drafting of a model municipal court act. At the Toronto meeting of the League, 1913, Mr. Harley presented a paper, "The Model Municipal Court," which was in the nature of a preliminary report. He stated that the American Judicature Society had placed it first in a series of acts to be drafted in the interest of more efficient administration of justice. The formal report of the committee, comprising a legislative act with commentary, was published in the bulletins of the Society. An explanation and discussion of the principal features of the model act was prepared by Mr. Harley and incorporated in the League's volume, *A New Municipal Program.*[98]

In response to a number of inquiries as to the best method of selecting municipal judges, Secretary Russell Forbes in his annual report for 1929–1930 recommended that a study be made of the problem of appointive versus elective judiciary in state and local government. The secretary was later authorized by the Executive Committee to approach the American Judicature Society regarding a joint committee on this subject. A Committee on Selection of Judiciary, representing the League and the Society, was formed in 1931–1932 with Dean Justin Miller, Duke University Law School, as chairman, and Edward M. Martin, Chicago, as secretary.[99]

The primary objectives of the study were: (1) to survey the experience of the federal government and of the states employing different systems of selection, in order to make comparisons of the effect of diverse methods of selection on the efficiency of judicial administration; (2) to assemble and make available information which had hitherto been scattered and inaccessible; and (3) to point the way for further detailed studies. To attain these objectives the committee agreed upon the general policy of collecting existing information on the subject of judicial selection, tenure, and retirement, in the several jurisdictions; of stimulating research in this field through bar associations, research bureaus, law schools, and political science faculties; of formulating tentative basic principles; and of advancing the general interest in the subject by encouraging the publication of articles in the *National Municipal Review, Journal of the American Judicature Society, American Political Science Review,* and other journals.

For its research the committee estimated that a fund of $25,000 would be necessary. Mr. Martin did considerable research work, but the committee's investigation was seriously handicapped by lack of funds. Secretary Jones stated in his annual report for 1935–1936 that the committee had been inactive for several years because of lack of funds for research and publication.[100]

Federal-State-Local Relations

The principle of home rule for cities was incorporated in the first Municipal Program and in all later editions.[101] Home rule for cities and counties was provided in the Model State Constitution.[102] Discussions of home rule have been held at several annual conferences of the League, especially in 1924 and 1930. In his report for 1929–1930, Secretary Forbes said that in several states municipal home rule was a hope rather than a fact, and that the time seemed appropriate for the appointment of a committee to make a study of the situation and to formulate constitutional and statutory principles for adoption in the various states. The following year he reported that the personnel and work plans had been prepared for a Committee on Developments in Municipal Home Rule but appointments had not been made because funds for the necessary research work were lacking.[103]

In 1932 a series of articles, "What Municipal Home Rule Means Today," was published in the *Review*. Ten states with the widest experience under constitutional home rule grants—California, Minnesota, Michigan, Washington, Missouri, Ohio, Texas, Nebraska, Wisconsin, and New York—were discussed in successive issues.[104]

The League has not usually included federal affairs within its scope, but within the past thirty years, particularly since 1933, questions of federal-city relations have several times arisen.

At a meeting of the Council in the fall of 1917, E. T. Paxton of the University of Texas asked support for a bill introduced into the Congress by Senator Morris Sheppard of Texas, at the instance of Dr. Herman G. James of the University of Texas. The bill proposed to create a division of municipal research in the Bureau of the Census. In the discussion Secretary Woodruff stated that the subject had been considered several times in recent years and that a League committee had conferred with President Woodrow Wilson in 1914 on the matter. No action had been taken. A Committee on Federal Relations to Cities to consider the Sheppard bill was appointed by the Executive Committee in December, 1917.[105] Chairman W. B. Munro reported to the Council in 1918 that a majority of the committee was opposed to the bill chiefly because of the insufficiency of the appropriation provided. The committee was discharged and the Executive Committee was authorized to appoint a new committee on the subject.[106]

Efforts of the Committee on Municipal Reference Libraries to secure the establishment of a federal clearinghouse of municipal information have already been described.[107]

A Committee on Federal Aid to the States was appointed in 1927, with Professor Austin F. Macdonald of the University of Pennsylvania as chairman.[108] Professor Macdonald, an authority in this field, prepared the report, incorporating suggestions from the other members of the committee. The report summarized the history and growth of federal grants to the states, analyzed the operation of the principal laws, and presented a critical estimate of the system, with recommendations of the committee for changes.[109]

Examination of the programs of the annual meetings of the League for the past twenty-five years reveals that federal organization and functions have been discussed on several occasions: the national budget, 1919, 1922; Congress, 1922; and federal statistics with respect to municipalities, 1924.[110] Since 1933 increasing attention has been given to such subjects as the part of local government in recovery, federal aid to cities, social security and unemployment relief administration,[111] public housing, federal legislation to aid defaulting municipalities, and other matters. The significance of the federal-city relationship is also reflected in the pages of the *Review;* the index for 1935 and following years lists many articles under the heading, "Federal-State-Local Relations."

Summary

Revamping and improvement of the forms of local government has always been a major objective of the League. Within five years of its founding a Municipal Program had been formulated, the successive editions of which have incorporated the best in governmental organization and practice. To the impressive list of publications on the forms of municipal government there have been added studies on metropolitan government, state administrative reorganization, urban and state judiciary, and municipal reference libraries. A Model State Constitution and a Model County Manager Law have greatly influenced the structure of state and local government. The topic of federal-local relations, always recognized, has received greater emphasis within the past fifteen years.

A pioneer in the creation, adaptation, or placing in operation of new governmental forms and methods, the League has been leader in practically every movement designed to insure a more economical, efficient, and responsible local government.

VI

Making Democracy Work

The major objective of the League, in the opinion of Richard S. Childs, has always been the establishment of democratic and responsible local government.[1] It has sought to accomplish this by designing workable forms of government for cities, counties, and states.[2] But correct organization, while essential, is not enough to insure democracy. To succeed, it must rest upon a sound basis of local self-government. And this means that effective instruments of popular control must be provided; citizen interest must be stimulated; and active participation of informed citizens in the local government process must be secured.[3]

TOOLS OF POPULAR CONTROL

Since the Philadelphia conference the League has been vitally interested in the methods of getting capable people into office, of securing nonpartisanship in municipal affairs, and of establishing control of the people over their own local government. Such features as nominations, elections, registration for voting, proportional representation, preferential voting, initiative, referendum, recall, nonvoting, corrupt practices, short ballot, and the separation of local from state and national elections, have been the subject of investigation by many committees.

NOMINATIONS AND ELECTIONS

Sections of the first Municipal Program on electoral methods provided for separation of municipal from state and national elections, nomination by petition, personal registration, secrecy in voting, short ballot, and a blanket ballot with names of candidates alphabetically arranged under the title of the office. Direct legislation, minority or proportional representation in city elections, were not included as a part of the program, but these features might be established upon petition of the voters and a majority vote at an election.[4]

Primary election laws, direct primaries, and the Crawford County or direct primary system were the subjects of papers presented at the Milwaukee and Roches-

[1] For notes to chap. vi, see pp. 224–231.

ter meetings of the League in 1900 and 1901.[5] At the Boston meeting in 1902 a resolution was adopted authorizing the Executive Committee to appoint a Committee on Nomination Reform to study the problem and to report at the next annual meeting. Horace E. Deming, New York, was appointed chairman, and his associates were: John Davis, Detroit; George W. Guthrie, Pittsburgh; Ernest A. Hempstead, Meadville, Pennsylvania; L. E. Holden, Cleveland; Charles B. Spahr, New York; Amos Parker Wilder, Madison, Wisconsin; and Clinton Rogers Woodruff, Philadelphia.[6] Chairman Deming, at the 1903 meeting, outlined the fundamental principles involved in the committee's work in an address, "The Meaning and Importance of Nomination Reform."[7] Further analysis of the problem and elaboration of the principles involved were presented to the 1904 meeting in seven papers by members of the committee.[8] The committee also submitted as a part of its report a draft of a proposed municipal nominating law, based upon and adapted to New York conditions. According to its provisions, nominations for municipal elective office could be made only by nominating elections or by petition.[9]

A revised draft of the proposed nominating law was presented to the 1905 conference as part of the final report of the committee. Papers by Mr. Deming and Secretary Woodruff and three studies of political organizations and primary legislation in New York, Pennsylvania, and Minnesota concluded the formal report. The recommendations of the committee were approved and adopted by the annual meeting and the report was referred to the Executive Committee with power to act.[10]

Additional studies of primary legislation and its operation in two states, Wisconsin and New Jersey, were presented to the Atlantic City meeting in 1906.[11]

Discussion of electoral reform was continued at the 1907 meeting with three papers presented dealing with the desirability of excluding the influence of national parties and issues in local elections and with means of doing so. To continue the League's consideration of this subject the Council authorized the appointment of a Committee on Electoral Reform. To this committee was referred the material on nomination reform and it was instructed to consider also questions of registration; form of the ballot; casting, counting, and return of the vote; and the initiative, referendum, and recall. Mr. Deming was again chairman, and other members included Richard H. Dana, Cambridge; Stiles P. Jones, Minneapolis; John C. Rose, Baltimore; Samuel E. Sparling, University of Wisconsin; Thomas Raeburn White and Clinton Rogers Woodruff, Philadelphia.[12]

At the annual meetings, 1908–1910, problems of electoral reform were discussed in several papers and in round table sessions: the initiative, referendum, recall, short ballot, elimination of national party designations from municipal ballots, publicity and regulation of campaign funds, preferential voting, and direct primaries.[13] No formal reports were submitted by the committee, which, during this period, underwent several reorganizations. At the Toronto meeting, 1913, the committee was discontinued and its work transferred to the new Committee on Municipal Program.[14]

The policy of nonpartisanship in municipal elections, enunciated in the first program, was reiterated in the New Municipal Program. As already described, the Model City Charter provided for the separation of municipal from state and national elections, nomination by petition, election by proportional representation on a nonpartisan ballot, the short ballot, and the initiative, referendum, and recall. Proportional representation, the initiative, referendum, and recall were supported by a majority of committee members. Election of the council by the preferential ballot was given in the appendix to the Model City Charter as an alternative method of election.[15]

A feature of the Springfield meeting, 1916, was the discussion of political parties in city government. The question of nonpartisanship in municipal affairs was re-examined in the light of recent experience, and from new standpoints. Actual experiences with nonpartisanship in Canadian cities, and in New York, Boston, and Pittsburgh, were related by League members.[16] Professor Charles A. Beard of Columbia University introduced an interesting discussion when he said:

> ... I am prepared to defend the thesis that non-partisanship has not worked, does not work, and will not work in any major city in the United States. We have plenty of non-partisan election laws designed to smash party organizations. We also have direct primary laws designed to take nominations out of the hands of party leaders. I think these laws have in many instances put a wholesome fear in the minds of political leaders, but I do not believe that they have permanently reduced the power of the expert political minority that manages public affairs.[17]

In the summer of 1920 the Council voted to create a Committee on Electoral Reform to draft a model election law.[18] Professor Ralph S. Boots of the University of Nebraska served as secretary of the committee.[19] A comprehensive examination of the presidential primary at work with proposals of reform, prepared by Dr. Boots, was published in September, 1920.[20]

The best attended session at the annual meeting in Indianapolis in 1920 was the dinner discussion on the topic, "The Fate of the Direct Primary." This was the subject of the presidential address of Charles E. Hughes. Professor Charles E. Merriam of the University of Chicago spoke on the subject, "Recent Tendencies in Primary Election Systems." Report of the Committee on Electoral Reform was given by its secretary, Dr. Boots.[21]

The final report of the committee was published in December, 1921. In the introduction the committee said:

> Purity and accuracy in elections are essentials of popular government. But purity and accuracy in actual practice are in many parts of the country only attained to a degree, and nowhere is there satisfactory freedom from suspicion of dishonesty and error. We do not have properly conducted elections. Scandals are constantly occurring to shock the public conscience, but the vast majority of frauds and errors are never revealed.

Recommendations were presented regarding registration of voters, election officers, conduct of elections, and suggestions were made for a modified direct primary. The committee said the proposals regarding the direct primary were submitted not as recommendations but as subject for discussion. It was not generally agreed that its proposals were an improvement over the direct primary system employed throughout the country, though many felt that the suggestions made would insure democratic control over party nominations and also preserve party leadership and party responsibility. "The committee believe that these are desirable ends but are not confident, as a body, that the means here outlined will attain these ends."[22]

Three sections of the Model State Constitution dealt with suffrage and elections. These outlined the qualifications for voting and provided that the legislature must establish a system of absentee voting. Elsewhere in the constitution provision was made for the election of legislators by the system of proportional representation with the single transferable vote, and for the use of the initiative and referendum on laws and constitutional amendments.[23]

In 1924 a Committee on Non-Voting in Municipalities was organized in cooperation with the National Association of Civic Secretaries.[24] Trends in voting since 1912 were to be studied. Statistics from about forty cities covering a period of twelve to fifteen years were collected and tables were compiled. For secretary the committee had first Evelyn B. Parker and later Edna Trull, both of Columbia University. The Council meeting in November, 1925, was informed that the findings of the committee were negative in character, but that the study would be continued and a report made later.[25]

Secretary Harold W. Dodds stated to a Council meeting in April, 1926, that Professor Joseph P. Harris of the University of Wisconsin was making a study of registration systems throughout the United States under a fellowship granted by the Social Science Research Council, and that Dr. Harris was willing to become secretary of a League committee on the subject.[26] A Committee on Election Administration was appointed with Professor Charles E. Merriam as chairman, and Dr. Harris as secretary.[27] The report of the committee was published in January, 1927. Part I discussed the need of registration improvement and described existing systems as "inconvenient to the voter, expensive in operation and ineffective in preventing fraudulent voting." Part II analyzed present systems of registration and their operation. In Part III were outlined the specifications for a model registration system, based on the best features of the most successful laws. Comments were made on each specification and the suggestions were in such form as to be easily adaptable to the election requirements of any state.[28]

During 1928–1929 Dr. Harris continued his field study of election administration as a member of the staff of the Institute for Government Research of Washington, D. C., and prepared the draft of a Model Election Administration System for the Committee on Election Administration.[29] The final report of the committee was published in September, 1930. Commenting on the need for election reform the committee said: "There is probably no phase of public administration which is today so badly handled as the conduct of elections. Every election contest brings to light gross inaccuracies, irregularities, uncertainty, slipshod practices, and a disregard of the election statutes. In many communities the elections are marked by frauds." Specifications for a model election system were discussed and a Model Election Administration Code was presented in Part IV.[30] The committee said that the present report included the results of experience since 1921, when the Committee on Electoral Reform published its findings and recommendations. It hoped that its proposals would be as influential on legislation as the earlier report on a model registration system had proved.

In the foreword to the second edition of the Model Registration System, issued in February, 1931, the effectiveness of the document was summarized as follows: "Since this report was issued in 1927, registration laws based wholly or in part on these recommendations have been enacted in California, Iowa, Kentucky, Michigan, Ohio, and Wisconsin. Active movements to secure laws on permanent registration are now (1931) on foot in Illinois, Indiana, Missouri, New York, Pennsylvania, and Washington." Use of the Model Election Administration System as a basis for the revision of election laws in Pennsylvania, Missouri, Washington, Indiana, Illinois, Michigan, Wisconsin, and New York, was mentioned by Secretary Russell Forbes in his report to the annual meetings in 1930, 1931, and 1932.[31] Both the Model Registration System and the Model Election Administration System are standard references in texts on municipal, county, and state government, and on political parties and elections.[32]

A third edition of the Model Registration System was prepared in 1939 for the Committee on Election Administration[33] by its secretary, Professor Harris, then of the University of California. Commenting on the progress made by permanent registration since the first report of the committee in 1927, Secretary Howard P. Jones said:

> In 1927 few large cities had permanent registration; now very few large cities still use the older forms. Twelve states have adopted permanent registration laws along the lines recommended by the committee: Wisconsin, Iowa, California, Kentucky, Michigan, Indiana, Ohio, Illinois, Missouri, Pennsylvania, New Jersey and Washington. In addition, permanent registration is also in use in one form or another, in twenty-two other states. In November 1938, the voters of New York State approved a constitutional amendment permitting permanent registration, and legislation to give effect to the amendment is now pending.[34]

Creation of a committee to prepare a model corrupt practices law for use by local governments was suggested by the Secretary of the League in his annual report for 1929–1930. Mr. Forbes commented on the need for uniformity in this field and for closer regulation of campaign expenditures. Such a law, he said, would supplement the Model Registration System and the Model Election Administration System and would constitute another important phase of the League's campaign to improve election machinery and methods. Personnel for such a committee was suggested, together with a proposed work program and a budget of $10,000. He regretfully reported in 1930–1931, and again in 1931–1932, that the committee had not been appointed because of lack of funds for research.[35]

PROPORTIONAL REPRESENTATION

All League committees drafting model programs for city, county, and state government have endorsed proportional representation as a method of election for the legislative body. The first Municipal Program did not incorporate proportional representation as an integral part of the Municipal Corporations Act, but it did provide that it might be established by (1) submission of the proposal by the council and approval by popular vote, or (2) by petition of the voters approved at an election.[36] Election of the council by the Hare method of proportional representation was preferred by a substantial majority of the members of the second Committee on Municipal Program and was written into the text of the Model City Charter. Use of the preferential ballot as an alternative method was included in the appendix to the charter.[37]

In the third edition of the Model City Charter the Committee on New Municipal Program again approved election of the council by proportional representation. Clinton Rogers Woodruff and Delos F. Wilcox voted against its inclusion as an integral part of the charter but favored it as an alternative plan of municipal elections. New rules for counting the ballots, prepared by the Proportional Representation League on the basis of experience in four cities, were adopted.[38] Two systems of election of the council were recommended by the committee in the fourth and fifth editions of the Model City Charter: (1) proportional representation, and (2) nonpartisan election at large. Proportional representation was favored by a majority of the members, but as an alternative the committee recommended the nonpartisan election-at-large system. New rules for counting the ballots under proportional representation were incorporated.[39]

The Committee on State Government likewise approved proportional representation with the single transferable vote as the method of election of legislators under the Model State Constitution. No change has been recommended in this feature in any of the subsequent editions of that important document.[40] For the election of members of the county board the Committee on County Government chose the Hare system of proportional representation but included majority election-at-large as an alternative plan.[41]

Thus the League had accepted the principle of proportional representation as a fundamental and necessary part of its program of reform for municipal, county, and state government. For some time the Proportional Representation League, organized in 1893, had been advocating the manager plan along with proportional representation. Both organizations supported the Cincinnati plan of city government as the ideal system, combining the manager plan, proportional representation, and the citizens' organization for good government. Since 1929 joint annual meetings of the two Leagues had been held.

With such similarity of purposes and points of view the possibility of a union seemed to hold advantages for both groups. At the annual meeting of the National Municipal League at Buffalo, 1931, the proposed merger, suggested by the Proportional Representation League, was discussed and referred to the Council with power to act. The Council gave the Executive Committee authority to work out some form of closer relationship between the two assocciations.[42]

Following the Buffalo meeting the secretaries of the two Leagues prepared a statement setting forth in detail the plans for the combination of staffs, with the advantages and disadvantages to both organizations. The Executive Committee of the National Municipal League, on December 4, 1931, endorsed the merger plan, but voted to conduct a mail poll of the Council before final adoption. Trustees of the Proportional Representation League, on December 22, 1931, accepted the proposal with certain suggested amendments. Secretary Forbes reported to the Executive Committee on February 19, 1932, that a majority of the replies received from Council members were favorable. After further discussion the Executive Committee approved the plan for consolidation, including the changes desired by the trustees of the Proportional Representation League.[43]

Under the terms of the merger effective May 1, 1932, there was to be added to the secretariat of the National Municipal League the staff of the Proportional Representation League: George H. Hallett, Jr., who became assistant secretary in 1919 and executive secretary in 1926; Walter J. Millard, field secretary; and Elsie S. Parker, assistant secretary. Quarters were to be provided in the National Municipal League office; the membership list of the Proportional Representation League would be incorporated into that of the National Municipal League; work of both organizations was to be carried on in the name of whatever organization might seem to be most appropriate in each case; the *National Municipal Review* would carry the information formerly printed in the *Proportional Representation Review*; a proportional representation committee, with Mr. Hallett as secretary, would be appointed; and the secretary of the National Municipal League would exercise the same financial responsibility for the new activities and personnel as for other League activities and keep new expenditures for proportional representation from outrunning a justifiable proportion of the National Municipal League's budget.[44]

The Proportional Representation League has continued in existence, holding its annual meeting with that of the League. Its trustees are still officially responsible for the League's work, but its activities are conducted as a part of the program of the National Municipal League.[45] Supervision is furnished by the Proportional Representation Committee.[46] Beginning with June, 1932, the *Review* has carried a proportional representation department, edited by Mr. Hallett. A summary of proportional representation activities of the League is given in the report of the secretary to each annual meeting. Wide distribution is given to the literature on the subject.[47]

INITIATIVE, REFERENDUM, AND RECALL

Direct legislation was not included in the first Municipal Program, but provision was made that it could be established by vote of the people on a proposal submitted by the council or by petition of the voters. There was no mention of the recall.[48] In the interval between the first and second programs, League interest in direct legislation and the recall continued; the subject was discussed at several annual meetings and in the *Review*.[49] The New Municipal Program contained sections on the initiative, referendum, and recall inserted by a majority vote of the committee. A note to the recall sections stated that they were not applicable when proportional representation was used but should be substituted when a charter provided some other method of election.[50] The third and fourth editions of the Model City Charter included the initiative, referendum, and recall. Dr. Wilcox objected to the presence of the recall in the 1927 edition, believing that under proportional representation the use of the recall was impracticable. Mr. Woodruff disagreed with the action of the committee in 1927 and in 1933 in incorporating the initiative and referendum in the charter. In the fourth edition, 1933, the committee inserted a note stating that it did not recommend the recall when proportional representation was used for the election of the council, but did intend that the recall provisions should be used by cities employing a different method of election. No mention is made of the recall in the fifth edition of the charter in 1941.[51]

League committees have also approved the initiative and referendum for state and county government. There was no provision for the recall in the Model State Constitution. Members of the county board were subject to recall, when a four-year term was used. However, the Committee on County Government thought that under proportional representation (its preferred system of nomination and election) with a two-year term, the recall was by no means essential.[52]

Equity, a quarterly magazine, edited and published since the 'nineties by Charles Fremont Taylor of Philadelphia, was primarily concerned with promotion of the initiative, referendum, and recall. Dr. Taylor was also interested in the League's broader program of improvements in municipal and state government, and agreed in 1919 to consolidate *Equity* with the *Review.* The League promised to appoint a committee to carry on systematic observation of the operation of the initiative, referendum, and recall.[53]

Announcing the merger of the two magazines, the *Review* editorially said:

> In this issue we consolidate with *Equity,* the happy little quarterly which Charles Fremont Taylor has for over twenty years issued as his personal organ from a quiet little office in Philadelphia. Primarily *Equity* was devoted with passionate faith to the initiative, referendum and recall, and Dr. Taylor has been the faithful librarian, historian and fact-gatherer of that movement. He never appeared in the field or fought campaigns and his research was mainly conducted by patient correspondence but every fight on these issues drew heavily upon his stock of ammunition and often on his funds. His was a modest and gentle flame but unwaveringly steady.[54]

Carrying out the arrangement with Dr. Taylor the League has gathered annually all information obtainable regarding the operation of the initiative, referendum, and recall in the United States.[55]

SHORT BALLOT

Mr. Childs is the father of the short ballot principle. With Woodrow Wilson he organized, in 1909, the National Short Ballot Organization.[56] Through the *Short Ballot Bulletin* and other publications the idea of the short ballot was spread.[57]

With the expansion of the League's work to include state and county government and with the publication of the *Review* as a monthly it was decided to amalgamate the National Short Ballot Organization with the League and the *Short Ballot Bulletin* with the *Review.* This was completed in May, 1920.[58]

The short ballot principle, from the beginning, has been one of the fundamental features of the League's program. It was incorporated in the first Municipal Program, in all subsequent editions of the Model City Charter, and in the Model State

Constitution, the Model County Manager Law, and other publications on state and county government. The League, then, is the leader of the movement to apply the short ballot principle to state, county, and municipal government. Mr. Childs' pamphlet, *The Short Ballot*, 1921, has been through many editions and has become a standard reference on this subject.

Exact statistical information about adoptions of the short ballot principle is lacking, but it is possible to point out its wide acceptance in hundreds of commission and city-manager cities, in a score of reorganized states, and in a few counties with the manager plan. "The short ballot idea," said Secretary Forbes, "is . . . one of the most significant contributions of the twentieth century to American political science."[59] And elsewhere it was claimed that the short ballot principle had been endorsed by practically all American writers on government and was being taught in the political science classes of all colleges and universities.[60]

CITIZENSHIP TRAINING IN COLLEGES AND SCHOOLS

That steady and substantial improvement in municipal government must depend to a great extent upon the education of coming generations was early realized. Since 1900 a number of important committees have studied and made reports on instruction in municipal government in universities, colleges, high schools, and elementary schools. Civic work among college men has been promoted and essay prizes have been offered to high school and college students to stimulate interest in municipal affairs.

INSTRUCTION IN MUNICIPAL GOVERNMENT IN COLLEGES

At the Milwaukee conference, 1900, a resolution was adopted authorizing the chairman of the Executive Committee to appoint a committee to ascertain the extent of instruction in municipal government offered in colleges and universities, and to bring to the attention of college authorities the necessity for more extended instruction in the subject. President Thomas M. Drown of Lehigh University was made chairman, and Dr. William H. Allen of the University of Pennsylvania secretary, of the Committee on Instruction in Municipal Government in American Colleges.[61] Two reports of the committee, with a long series of illustrative papers, formed a leading topic of discussion at meetings of the League in 1901, 1902, and 1903. Outlines, syllabi, lists of texts, and reference books were published, and also a list of lecturers available for lectures singly or in courses. Two thousand copies of the first report of the committee did not satisfy the demand. "Its generous reception indicated that it was meeting a need, and from the committee's correspondence we are persuaded that it has proved helpful and stimulating." A number of institutions added courses in municipal government and several professorships on the subject were established.[62]

Professor Leo S. Rowe of the University of Pennsylvania read a paper, "University and Collegiate Research in Municipal Government" at the 1904 meeting. He stressed the advantages of bringing students into direct contact with public affairs and suggested that this might be done by having each student in the regular course in municipal government report on some phase of governmental activity.

A Committee on Coördination of University and Collegiate Instruction in Municipal Government, composed of college and university teachers, was appointed with Professor Rowe as chairman.[63] In its report to the meeting in 1905 the committee stated that it had decided to suggest topics for investigation in all institutions giving special attention to the study of municipal government. For 1904–1905 the topic selected was, "The Relation of the Municipality to the Street Railway Service;" for 1905–1906, "The Relation of the Municipality to the Gas and Electric Light Service;" and for 1906–1907, "The Relation of the Municipality to the Water Supply." To the 1906 meeting the committee reported that its topic had also been made the subject for the William H. Baldwin Prize. It was felt that the plan had passed the experimental stage and that other institutions offering little work in municipal government should be asked to coöperate.[64]

The results of an elaborate inquiry into the status of instruction in municipal government in the universities and colleges of the United States were reported to the 1908 meeting by the chairman of the committee, Professor W. B. Munro. Data collected were tabulated and presented in the appendix to the report. The committee noted a marked development in special courses within the past ten or fifteen years, the popularity of instruction in municipal government with students, the lack of approach to uniformity in methods of instruction, and the concentration of attention mainly on American cities. "The results of the inquiry have been distinctly encouraging and show that the outlook is more promising than ever." The purpose of the committee had been to secure coöperation among teachers of municipal government and such coördination of instruction in the subject as was practicable. "It has not been the committee's aim to advocate any definite system or method of instruction in municipal government, much less to carry on a propaganda for any political principles." It hoped that through the mutual interchange of views between instructors and the collection and dissemination of data, the efficiency of college instruction might be increased.[65]

Under the auspices of the committee, round table conferences on methods of instruction in municipal government were held in connection with the annual meetings of the American Political Science Association at Richmond, Virginia, in December, 1908, and at New York, in December, 1909.[66]

A new survey of instruction in municipal government was made by the committee in 1912. Replies from one hundred and seventy-two institutions indicated that instruction in municipal government was being offered in sixty-four universities and colleges as compared with forty-six in 1908. One hundred and eighteen schools (about one hundred in 1908) gave some attention to municipal government in the general political science course. As in 1908, the committee reported no uniformity in methods of instruction, and concentration, for the most part, on the study of American city government. Some contact with actual problems of administration was afforded by fifty-five institutions. Many instructors in municipal government stated their requirements for offering improved training and made specific suggestions how the League could be of further service. Professor Munro concluded the report with a description of the work of the bureau for research in municipal government at Harvard University.[67]

During 1916 the committee conducted another survey. Data from one hundred and sixty-two replies enabled the committee to say in summary:

> The amount of independent instruction in municipal government has greatly increased [95 institutions] and to all appearances is likely to increase still further. The methods of instruction have greatly improved. The equipment for teaching the subject is far better than it has been, and the establishment of research bureaus, reference libraries and similar workshops of study [46 universities] has helped to make the teaching of municipal government more effective than ever before. Finally there is the effort, in spite of great and obvious difficulties, to bring the postgraduate students into actual touch with municipal affairs by having them serve for a time at least in some piece of constructive public work. Putting all these things together we have had notable progress during the last four or five years.[68]

Instruction in municipal administration was the subject of discussion at one of the sessions of the annual meeting in 1916. Participants, including Professors W. B. Munro of Harvard, Everett Kimball of Smith, E. A. Cottrell of Wellesley, and O. C. Hormell of Bowdoin, discussed the place of municipal government in the college curriculum, and methods of teaching their students.[69]

For several years no further reports on the teaching of municipal government were made. At the annual meeting in 1927 one round table discussed the topic "Improving College Courses in Municipal Government." A resolution was passed by the round table calling upon the League to organize a committee to study and appraise the effectiveness of present college courses in municipal government. A preliminary Committee on Teaching Municipal Government in Colleges and Universities was appointed by the Executive Committee in August, 1928, with Professor William Anderson of the University of Minnesota as chairman.[70] The committee was asked to confine its program for the present to the formulation of the objectives of courses in this subject. Its report to the annual meeting in 1928 recommended the appointment of a smaller permanent committee. As organized in 1929, the Committee on Teaching Municipal Government was composed of the following: H. W. Dodds, Editor of the *Review*, chairman; Joseph D. McGoldrick, Columbia University, secretary; John A. Fairlie, University of Illinois; Clyde L. King, University of Pennsylvania; Murray Seasongood, Cincinnati; and Stephen B. Story, Rochester, New York.[71]

Several possibilities were considered by the committee. One was that it should prepare a standard examination, open to students of all colleges, with appropriate prizes for winners. Another was a study of various methods currently employed by teachers, with an appraisal of the merits of these methods, and the preparation of small handbooks to place in the hands of instructors.

Further discussion of the subject occurred in the Executive Committee in 1931 and 1932. President Murray Seasongood thought there was an opportunity for coöperation with the American Political Science Association. At a subsequent meeting Secretary Forbes told of the possibility of coöperating with the political scientists in the publication of a manual on teaching municipal government which the Subcommittee on Political Education of the Committee on Policy of the American Political Science Association had under way. The Executive Committee voted that such a manual should be published by the League as one of its regular publications.[72] Professor Munro, a member of the Committee on Policy, prepared for the Policy Committee, a report, "Instruction in Political Science in Colleges and Universities."[73]

INTERCOLLEGIATE CIVIC WORK

"The College Man in Public Affairs" was the title of a paper by Professor Harry A. Garfield of Princeton University read at the annual meeting in 1905. This meeting authorized the appointment of a Committee on Work Among College Men, with Travis H. Whitney of New York as chairman.[74] The purpose of the committee was to create among college students a deeper interest in municipal affairs and to direct their attention to the important public work to be done by college men, especially along the lines of creating sound public opinion. In 1906 the annual meeting listened to an address, "Work Among College Men," by William S. Moorhead, president of the Yale City Government Club, and also president of the Intercollegiate League of Civic Clubs, in which the speaker described the organization and work of the two groups.[75]

Nine years later representatives of the Intercollegiate Civic League[76] and the New York City Club conferred with the Executive Committee regarding the transfer of the activities and good will of the Intercollegiate Civic League to the National Municipal League. Since funds for the remainder of the academic year were still available, the executive committee agreed to appoint an Intercollegiate Civic Committee to continue the work of the Intercollegiate Civic League, with Wayne D. Heydecker, New York, as secretary. In 1916 the Executive Committee reported to the Council that the intercollegiate division had been functioning under the secretaryship of Arthur Evans Wood, formerly professor at Reed College and now a Harrison Fellow at the University of Pennsylvania. Special subscriptions maintained the division and it was not a charge upon the funds of the League. Meetings of the intercollegiate division were held in New York in April, 1916; in Springfield, Massachusetts, in November, 1916 (with the League) ; and in New York in April, 1917.[77] During the next four years only a few scattered references to this activity appear in the League's records. Evidently it was absorbed into the general program of the League.[78]

PRIZES

As a means of stimulating interest in local affairs on the part of students in universities, colleges, and high schools, the League, through the generosity of some of its leading supporters, has offered several prizes for the best essay on some phase of local government. Oldest and best known of such prizes is the William H. Baldwin Prize, established in 1905 by Mrs. George H. Burnham, Jr. of Philadelphia to perpetuate the memory of the civic work of William H. Baldwin, Jr. The announcement of the prize in 1929 said: "It is the intention of the donor to commemorate a man who achieved rapid success in the business world (at 33 years of age he was president of the Long Island Railroad) without sacrificing in any way his high ideals of fairness, humanity and good will in business. A hard-working man, dying at the early age of 41, he yet found time to render large public service."[79] After the death of Mrs. Burnham in 1931, the contribution for the annual prize was continued by her family.[80]

Competition for this prize of one hundred dollars for the best essay on a subject connected with state or municipal government is open to undergraduate students registered in a regular course in any college or university in the United States offering direct instruction in state or municipal government. Announcements regarding the contest, including subjects, conditions, and other details, are widely distributed among colleges and universities. Award of the prize is made by a board of judges selected by the Executive Committee, and a notice is published in the *Review*.[81] From 1918–1935 Professor E. A. Cottrell of Stanford University served as chairman of the Committee on Prizes.

A high school prize, established in 1910, the gift of Mrs. Charles Richardson of Philadelphia, wife of one of the vice-presidents of the League, was continued through 1916 by the generous coöperation of a number of prominent women supporters of the League. Two prizes of thirty dollars and twenty dollars were offered for the best essays by high school students on a municipal subject.[82]

In commemoration of the victory for good government in their city, certain Cincinnati members of the League, in 1911, contributed five hundred seventeen dollars to establish an annual prize of twenty dollars, to be known as the Cincinnati Prize. Competition was open to any student in the University of Cincinnati and the essays were required to deal with some aspect of municipal government or civic life in Cincinnati. There was no award of this prize in 1916 or thereafter.[83]

Meyer Lissner, member of the Council from Los Angeles, established in 1914 a League prize of one hundred dollars for the best essay on the subject, "The Best Charter for Los Angeles." Competition was open to students of Occidental College, University of Southern California, and to students in the last two years of high school.[84]

The Morton Denison Hull Prize was established in 1914 through a gift of Morton D. Hull of Chicago, who had always been keenly interested in the promotion of original thought and research in the problems of government. An annual award of two hundred fifty dollars for the best essay on a subject connected with municipal government was made available to postgraduate students registered and resident in any college or university in the United States offering distinct postgraduate courses in municipal government. Lack of entries for several years caused the League to offer the prize biennially; the announcement for 1925–1926, the last one available, listed the award as five hundred dollars.[85]

In 1914 friends of Reed College, Portland, Oregon, contributed to the League a fund of six hundred dollars for the establishment of the Portland Prize. Income from the fund has been awarded annually since 1914 as a prize to the undergraduate student in Reed College presenting the best essay on some phase of municipal government.[86]

Supplementing its radio series in 1933 on the topic, "The Crisis in Municipal Finance," the League offered two scholarships of one hundred dollars each to senior high school and to college students for an essay on the subject, "My Town— What Can I Do to Boost Its Credit?" Funds for the scholarships were donated by Morris Tremaine, comptroller of New York State and Frank H. Morse of Lehman Brothers, New York. The winning essays were published in the *Review*.[87]

TEACHING MUNICIPAL GOVERNMENT IN THE PUBLIC SCHOOLS

The activities of League committees, above described, dealt with only one phase of this problem, instruction in institutions of higher learning. To carry on the work in secondary and elementary schools, the League meeting in April, 1903, authorized the appointment of a Committee on Instruction in Municipal Government in American Educational Institutions. Dr. William H. Maxwell, superintendent of schools of New York, was chosen as chairman; and James J. Sheppard, principal of the High School of Commerce, New York, as secretary, of a large committee of leading educators of the country.[88] Five subcommittees were organized: history of instruction in municipal government, literature, high school program, elementary school program, and school-city and other forms of pupil government. Twelve hundred copies of a questionnaire were sent out in November, 1903, to teachers and school officials, and a hundred and twenty replies were received. A tentative program for the teaching of municipal government and of civics in the elementary school was presented to the Chicago meeting in 1904. Papers were also prepared on student self-government and the school-city as a form of student government. The final report of the committee to the New York meeting in 1905 included the report of subcommittees on the elementary school program, high school program, the school-city, and on the literature of instruction in municipal government.[89]

For the purpose of testing the conclusions reached by the Maxwell Committee and to coördinate instruction in secondary and elementary schools, a new Committee on Instruction in Municipal Government in Elementary and High Schools was authorized by the Executive Committee in April, 1905. Professor James J. Sheppard, New York, who had served as secretary of the Maxwell Committee, was appointed chairman.[90] Under the direction of Professor Sheppard the course outlined for high schools by the Maxwell Committee was adopted in the New York High School of Commerce. The committee reported the results of this experiment at the Cincinnati meeting in 1909, and there was a thorough discussion of the problem of teaching civics in elementary and high schools.[91]

To consider the reports and recommendations of four former committees, to study the results of many experiments in civic education, and to ponder the larger conception of citizenship for which the League had stood from the beginning, a new Committee on Civic Education was formed in 1910. Arthur W. Dunn, former educational director of the Philadelphia City Club, and then secretary of the Public Education Association of New York was chairman.[92] Suggestions for a program of constructive activity for the League in this field were made in the report of the committee to the Toronto meeting in 1913. Closer coöperation with the National Bureau of Education, state and local educational officials, and professional teachers' organizations was recommended. The report concluded with a recommendation that the League establish a department for the promotion of civic education with an advisory committee and a secretary. Approval of this last suggestion was given by the Council and Executive Committee. It was agreed to underwrite a portion of the salary of Mr. Dunn, who arranged to give his entire time as secretary of the committee. Maurice Fels of Philadelphia was chosen as chairman of the committee.[93] Several pamphlets were issued and active work was begun in establishing relations with school authorities. Describing its procedure, the committee said: "The central feature of the plan of work is to make available to every school, or other agency interested in civic education, the best thought and experience found anywhere. This involves a careful study of the best that is now done in any place, arriving at fundamental principles, formulating such methods as will be most sane and economic, and then propagating them through printed bulletins and by personal visits of the secretary and others."[94]

The coöperation of the United States Bureau of Education was secured, and Mr. Dunn was appointed a collaborator in the Bureau and specialist in civic education. In announcing the Bureau's new work Commissioner P. P. Claxton said that in the larger sense all education was really education for citizenship; citizenship training was coextensive with effective education in general; and the final justification of public taxation for public education lay in the training of young people for citizenship. In its report to the 1914 meeting the committee stated that the affiliation with the Bureau of Education was the most important result of its work. Inability of the committee to raise sufficient funds for its program led to the resignation of Secretary Dunn in 1915. The Executive Committee decided not to continue the work.[95]

In 1919 the Executive Committee authorized the creation of a new Committee on Civic Education. Professor Edgar Dawson of Hunter College, New York, who had been given a year's leave of absence to make a study of the teaching of government in secondary schools, was made chairman of the committee and also field representative on civic education for the League. Other members of the committee were: John A. Lapp, Columbus, Ohio; Raymond Moley, Cleveland; J. Lynn Barnard, Philadelphia; John L. S. Tildsley, New York; and Clinton Rogers Woodruff, Philadelphia. The League published in 1923 and distributed gratis to teachers several thousand copies of a pamphlet entitled *Outlines of Responsible Government,* designed as supplementary reading for texts in civics. Editor-in-charge was Professor Dawson, and chapters on the short ballot, the city manager plan, the budget, and essentials of a state constitution were prepared by Richard S. Childs, A. R. Hatton, Luther Gulick, and Edgar Dawson, in collaboration in each case with an experienced high school teacher of civics. The foreword stated that the League was "seeking the coöperation of teachers in an effort to bring to the attention of the rising citizen those principles of organization which have passed beyond the stage of hypothesis."[96]

CIVIC EDUCATION BY RADIO

A significant experiment in adult civic education was begun, in 1932, by the Committee on Civic Education by Radio of the National Advisory Council on Radio in Education and the American Political Science Association. Dr. T. H. Reed, chairman of the League's Committee on Citizens' Councils for Constructive Economy and of the Committee on Policy of the American Political Science Association, was chairman of the Committee on Civic Education by Radio. Time for the weekly evening broadcasts over a nation-wide network in the series, "You and Your Government," was donated by the National Broadcasting Company, and outstanding educators, public officials, and publicists participated in the programs. It was the purpose of the committee to design programs presenting the results of the scientific study of government and politics in popular form to appeal to the mass of adult citizens. Round table discussions, interviews, and addresses were employed, with Professor Reed introducing many of the programs.[97]

From 1933 to 1936 eight series in these broadcasts were sponsored by the League in coöperation with the Committee on Civic Education by Radio and the American Political Science Association.[98] Broadcasts in several series were given in coöperation with the programs of the Committee on Citizens' Councils for Constructive Economy and the National Pay-Your-Taxes Campaign.[99] At the Providence meeting of the Council it was decided to discontinue the radio programs after February, 1936.[100]

All of the eight series of broadcasts were sold by the League in bound volumes, and more than 50,000 printed copies of the individual broadcasts were distributed. Many broadcasts were printed in the *Review* and in the official publications of other national organizations, and much of the material was used for rebroadcast purposes. Secretary Jones, in his annual report for 1935–1936, commented: "They have attracted extensive editorial comment in the nation's press, and have been enthusiastically received by civic organizations, schools and colleges, study groups, and individuals." In 1935 the "You and Your Government" radio programs received the award of the Women's National Radio Committee for the best non-commercial and nonmusical program on the air.[101]

Citizen Organization and Action

Itself a citizen organization for the promotion of better state and local government, the League has always been interested in local citizens' organizations for governmental improvement. It will be the purpose of this section to describe the work of the League in developing methods of citizen participation in political activity, the organization and work of Citizens' Councils for Constructive Economy, the National Pay-Your-Taxes Campaign, and the recent campaign on education for democracy.

ORGANIZATION FOR POLITICAL ACTIVITY

During the first ten years of League history there were many discussions at the annual meetings of the efforts of local citizens' groups to secure the nomination and election of honest men to public office and to promote the League's program for civic betterment. The contributions to reform by municipal leagues, good government clubs, commercial organizations, citizens' unions, municipal political parties, and other voluntary and temporary groups were described by many who had participated in such movements. In his reports to the annual conferences, Secretary Woodruff chronicled the advance of municipal reform and the part played by citizen associations affiliated with the League.[102]

Militant political work for better city government was discussed at the Chicago meeting in 1904 at a session under the auspices of the City Club. The secretary of the Citizens' Union of New York, John J. Murphy, debated with George E. Cole, founder of the Municipal Voters' League of Chicago, as to the best policy to be followed by civic organizations.[103] Two methods of active participation in municipal elections had been developed in different cities: independent nominations by separate municipal parties, employed by the Citizens' Union of New York, in Philadelphia and Cincinnati; and the endorsement of the best candidates nominated by the national parties, a plan followed by the municipal voters' leagues of Chicago, Detroit, Buffalo, Milwaukee, Minneapolis, and St. Paul. Further debate and exchange of experiences by delegates from scores of cities in round table sessions at the League conferences of 1906, 1908, and 1909, failed to bring agreement as to the most effective method of citizen activity for good city government.[104] At the 1909 conference there was discussion of such problems as what offices should be attacked; what constructive work could be done between campaigns; and what was to be the part of progressive groups working entirely within the organization of one of the regular parties, such as the Brooklyn Young Republicans Club.[105]

On invitation of Secretary Woodruff there was held in connection with the conference at Buffalo in 1910 a meeting of secretaries of civic associations. Members discussed the purpose, basis of membership, and methods to be used by local civic associations. As a result of the meeting a Civic Secretaries Committee of the League was formed for the purpose of considering questions of organization and methods of work of civic associations. In coöperation with the League, members of the committee sought to promote generally the interests of city clubs, voters' leagues, and other groups in the field of civic organization.[106] A conference of civic secretaries was a feature of each annual meeting of the League. At the 1917 meeting the name of the organization was changed from the Civic Secretaries Committee to the Civic Secretaries Association. Close relations with the League have always been maintained and the National Association of Civic Secretaries, since its establishment, has held its annual meetings in conjunction with those of the League.[107]

On motion of A. Leo Weil of Pittsburgh the Council, at its Toronto meeting in 1913, voted to request the Executive Committee to appoint a committee to prepare a plan of nonpartisan organization suitable for adoption by communities interested in good municipal government. Separate political organizations to conduct campaigns for civic improvement had been formed in many cities. Few such groups had been able to continue without coming under the control of the regular party organizations. The problem was to devise a plan which would so far as possible avoid the pitfalls into which similar organizations heretofore had fallen. A Committee on Political Methods was subsequently appointed, with Mr. Weil as chairman.[108] This committee made a preliminary report to the Baltimore meeting in 1914. It did not present a definite plan of political organization but expressed hope of doing so at the next meeting. Continued from year to year until 1917, the committee never presented a final report.[109]

In the spring of 1926 the Council discussed the part which citizens' associations could play in the selection of better men for local offices. The Secretary was instructed to take up with the Association of Civic Secretaries the question of a study of the organization, methods, and results of leading civic associations.[110] However, it was not until 1929 that a Committee on Organized Citizens' Participation in City Government was appointed to prepare a report on the history, organization, methods, accomplishments, and the future of organized citizen groups. Carl H. Pforzheimer, treasurer of the League, was chairman of the committee, and W. P. Lovett, secretary of the Detroit Citizens' League, was secretary.[111] Considerable information from various sources was collected by the League secretariat. Elma L. Greenwood, a graduate student of Syracuse University and later a member of the staff of the Philadelphia League of Women Voters, undertook the compilation of the data and the preparation of a tentative report for the committee. Acting Secretary Jones reported in 1933 that Parts I and II of the report had been revised by Miss Greenwood in accordance with the suggestions and criticisms of the committee members, and that Part III was in manuscript form. "The report, when completed, will be a very comprehensive piece of work and will make a sizeable volume. Its publication must be postponed until funds can be secured for the purpose."[112]

In 1929 steps were taken by the Secretary of the League to organize a committee to prepare a report which would summarize the best methods for organizing and conducting a city manager campaign, and which would show how to organize a permanent charter committee to acquaint voters with progress accomplished and to defend the plan against organized attacks. A Committee on Citizens' Charter Organization was formed with Henry Bentley, president of the Cincinnati City Charter Committee, as chairman, and Emily Kneubuhl, executive secretary of the National Federation of Business and Professional Women's Clubs, New York, as secretary.[113] The report of the committee, published by the League in 1934, described the organization, financing, and methods of work employed by the City Charter Committee of Cincinnati.[114] Because Cincinnati had been able, through the efforts of this effective organization of citizens, to maintain good city government for a period of ten years, it was chosen for this study. "The success obtained in Cincinnati," said the committee, "has shown that the way to improve municipal administration is to improve the method of citizen organization."[115]

The topic of citizen organization, education, and action has had a prominent place on the program at practically every meeting of the League and coöperating organizations within the past fifteen years. At the Indianapolis meeting, 1939, a Committee on Campaign Manual was organized to prepare a campaign manual for use by local citizens' organizations. A subcommittee to assemble material was appointed at the first meeting of the committee.[116]

CITIZENS' COUNCILS FOR CONSTRUCTIVE ECONOMY

Early in 1932 J. W. Esterline, member of the Council from Indianapolis, urged the League to assume leadership in the movement for the improvement of government and the reduction of expenditures in state and local government through the organization of strong citizen groups in each state. This proposal was fully discussed by the Executive Committee in February and by the Council in May, and a Committee on Constructive Economy in Government was appointed.[117] Under the chairmanship of Professor Reed, the committee was given the task of formulating a plan for constructive economy in government, which would not impair services vital to the public welfare.[118] A summary of the report of the committee was given on November 15, 1932, by Professor A. R. Hatton over the nation-wide network of the National Broadcasting Company, in the "You and Your Government" Series.[119]

On invitation of the President of the United States a conference of citizens selected by national organizations representing agriculture, business, government, education, and public welfare, was held in Washington, D. C., January 5, 1933, to consider the crisis in education. One outcome of the meeting was the suggestion that citizens' councils, broadly representative of all interests, should be established in every community and charged with the responsibility of directing the movement for economy in government into constructive channels, without the impairment of essential social and cultural services. Immediate interest in the proposal was shown by scores of national organizations. Meetings of representatives of some eighty organizations in New York, Chicago, and Washington, D. C., resulted in the appointment of an executive committee to develop a work program and plans for the organization of a national committee on citizens' councils. The League was invited to act as the clearinghouse or secretariat of this movement. Approval of this proposal was given by the Executive Committee and Council, and President Seasongood appointed a Committee on Citizens' Councils for Constructive Economy, including the members of the League's Committee on Constructive Economy and representatives of fifty-six coöperating national organizations.[120] Professor Reed was appointed chairman, and Howard P. Jones, secretary, of the executive committee of this larger committee.[121]

The committee conducted an intensive campaign, made possible through a grant of $10,000 from the Carnegie Corporation, for more than a year, beginning in April, 1933. Four pamphlets, describing the objectives of citizens' councils, methods of organizing them, accounts of work done, and suggestions of possible programs, were published and thousands of copies were distributed.[122] For six months a Citizens' Councils News Bulletin was sent to all citizens' councils and to a mailing list of 225 magazines. Reprints of articles in other publications, sample constitutions, and mimeographed reports of the work of thirty-two citizens' councils were also distributed.[123] News releases were sent to 2,057 newspapers and 225 magazines. Addresses on citizens' councils were made in eighteen cities in twelve states by the director or other representatives from the League office. A national conference of citizens' councils was held in connection with the annual meeting of the League in 1933, and regional meetings of delegates of local citizens' councils were held in various parts of the country. Four series in the "You and Your Government" broadcasts were sponsored by the League.[124] Printed copies of the broadcasts were distributed in bound volumes and also as individual copies. All broadcasts were designed to stimulate interest in citizens' councils and to help in the solution of their local problems.

As a result of these efforts, Secretary Jones was able to report to the annual meeting in 1934 that citizens' councils existed in thirty-three states and that three state-wide councils had been organized. Seven hundred and twenty-five communities had been directly reached by the committee's program.[125] Each group was autonomous, formulated its own program, and devised the methods for carrying it out.

At the same meeting the round table on citizen action passed a resolution requesting the appointment of a committee representing the citizens' councils and the League to devise a plan for a national federation of local citizens' councils. Dr. P. P. Womer of Washburn College headed the committee which, during the year, prepared a plan for a national federation of citizens' councils to be designated The Citizens' Council Section of the National Municipal League.[126] A Citizens' Council Board of nine members, the chairman and two others to be appointed annually by the Council of the League, was to have control of the federation. Approval of the plan was voted by the Council of the League and by delegates from citizens' councils at the annual League meeting in 1935.[127] Dr. Womer was appointed chairman of the executive board, and Frank C. Moore, Kenmore, New York, and Robert M. Goodrich, Providence, were chosen by the Council to serve with him.

During 1935–1936 a pamphlet, *Making Democracy Work—The Citizens' Council Plan*, was issued. This commented on the history of the plan, the character and work of local groups, and contained directions on how to form a council, and a proposed constitution. At the 1936 meeting the Council of the League voted to merge the citizens' council movement with the regular program of the League. This was done because improvement in economic conditions had led to a shift in emphasis of the citizens' councils from combating harmful reduction of expenditures to a more positive program of governmental improvement in line with the League's normal activities.[128]

In the summer of 1939 Secretary Jones announced that the citizens' council plan was being reorganized, given a larger significance, and more closely integrated with the program of the League in a National Federation of Citizens' Organizations. Arrangements had been made for Dr. Womer to spend full time in the field promoting the organization of local citizen groups.[129] Two new pamphlets had been prepared for use in the campaign for the establishment of citizens' councils.[130] To report significant activities of citizen groups a new department, "Citizen Action," was inaugurated in the January, 1940, issue of the *Review*.[131]

PAY-YOUR-TAXES CAMPAIGN

In May, 1933, the Council authorized the Secretary to launch an educational campaign on a nation-wide scale to restore municipal credit by stimulating current and delinquent tax collections. The "tax striker" menace threatened the continuance of governmental service in many communities. Investment bankers and officials of commercial and savings banks organized a National Pay-Your-Taxes Campaign Committee, with Sanders Shank, Jr., editor of the *Bond Buyer*, as secretary. Slightly more than five thousand dollars was raised by this group and the League was asked to manage the campaign, because of its leadership in the citizens' council movement. Direction of the program was placed under the Committee on Citizens' Councils for Constructive Economy, with Dr. Reed as chairman.[132]

Thus organized and financed the national campaign was carried on intensively for two years along four main lines. (1) Newspaper and magazine publicity. More than 25,000 copies of various publications including a campaign manual, a publicity handbook, information bulletins, current tax problems series[133] promotion leaflets, together with numerous reprints, press releases, and mimeographed articles, were distributed to interested officials and citizens.[134] Of great importance was the document, "A Model Real Property Tax Collection Law," drafted by a League committee.[135] A new department of the *Review*, "Taxation and Government," dealing with problems of tax delinquency and other financial matters, was begun in January, 1934, and has been continued as a regular feature of the magazine. (2) Stimulation of local Pay-Your-Taxes Campaigns. Hundreds of cities organized local tax-paying campaigns in response to suggestions of the National Committee and in some instances the committee undertook the preliminary organization work. Citizens' councils frequently assumed responsibility for the campaign. (3) Coöperation with other national organizations. Many national organizations associated with the League in the citizens' council movement, gave aid by informing their members of the importance of the campaign. A significant result of the coöperation of the banking and investment groups was their education in the value of the League's constructive program for the improvement of local government. (4) Radio broadcasts. Speakers on the weekly broadcasts in the four radio series sponsored by the League in 1933–1934 stressed the Pay-Your-Taxes Campaign.[136] From June to September, 1935, fifteen broadcasts on the topic, "Taxation for Prosperity," popularized the idea of taxes as payments for service.

Summarizing the results of the two years' campaign, Mr. Shanks said:

> The campaign of the National Pay Your Taxes Campaign Committee has achieved results far exceeding the expectations of even the more optimistic members of the committee. Two years ago when the committee was organized, the situation was so critical none dared to predict how far the collapse of municipal credit would go. Today, not only have tax collections picked up to an extent that delinquent taxes are a serious problem in but a relatively few municipalities, but the market for municipal bonds is the best in the history of governmental finance. Your committee does not, of course, take credit for all of this. It does, however, claim to have played a very vital part in turning the tide at the critical time and to have altered citizen psychology in many sections of the country from the negative "tax strike" attitude to the positive constructive realization of the importance of preserving municipal services and municipal credit.[137]

COÖPERATION OF UNIVERSITIES AND CIVIC ORGANIZATIONS

In 1937, after the voters of New York State had approved the calling of a constitutional convention to meet in the spring of 1938, the New York State Committee of the League[138] appointed a Special Committee on the New York State Constitution. The committee consisted of the presidents or administrative heads of forty-seven New York State colleges, universities, and normal schools, and representatives of thirteen state-wide citizens' organizations. S. Howard Evans of the Payne Fund, New York City, was chairman of the committee. The objective of the committee was to promote public understanding of the important problems before the convention and to explain and analyze for the voters the amendments submitted by the convention.[139]

Under the plan worked out by the committee each participating college served as a regional center of information, including fact-finding about constitutional issues, distribution of literature, and supplying speakers for forums. A faculty member in each institution was assigned to this activity. Responsibility of each of the state-wide citizen groups was to encourage the coöperation of their members with the regional educational institutions and to sponsor widespread discussion of the facts.[140]

The results of the new technique for informing voters on the constitutional issues were highly successful. At the general election in November, 1938, New York State citizens voted on nine constitutional amendments "with an intelligence and discrimination astonishing to the experts."

The success of the technique employed by the New York State Committee convinced the officers of the League that it should be tried on a national scale. Arrangements were made with the Payne Fund to release part of the time of Mr. Evans to direct the new project on education for democracy.[141] Invitations to participate in a Conference on American Self-Government were sent to some six hundred college and university heads and to national citizens' organizations, in the name of a sponsoring committee of university presidents, headed by President C. A. Dykstra of the University of Wisconsin, who was then president of the League.

Two hundred and eight colleges and universities and thirty national citizens' organizations accepted the League's invitation to a Conference on American Self-Government at Indiana University, May 13–14, 1940. More than one hundred college presidents, professors, and observers from citizen groups spent two days in planning a program of coöperation between universities and local civic organizations. Chairman Dykstra and Director Evans led discussion of some forty projects which had been submitted in response to the League's request.

The final outcome of the conference was the adoption of the report of a Committee on Findings and Recommendations, of which Professor James K. Pollock of the University of Michigan was chairman. The League was requested to act as a national clearinghouse to correlate the efforts of educational institutions and civic groups engaged in coöperative programs for increasing the effectiveness of self-government. The conference recommended that the League should appoint a small permanent committee to direct the work.

After enumerating several important projects for coöperative effort, the conference agreed that an effective attack upon any problem involved three separate functions: (1) research to secure basic facts for discussion; (2) public discussion to test the facts and to enable people to form convictions about them; and (3) citizen action to give effect to programs developed by fact-finding and discussion. The first function, essentially one of scholarship, was the responsibility of colleges and universities. Discussion, the second function, was the responsibility of citizens' organizations. Translation into action of the programs of civic and educational agencies must await the completion of the other two functions. The objective of all fact-finding and discussion should always be the formulation of a program which would make possible effective participation of citizens.[142]

The holding of this conference at Indiana University was not the first instance of coöperation between the League and that institution. In the fall of 1939 the League and Indiana University joined in establishing on the university campus a research project on the relation of the citizen to his government. Conditions in Indiana were to be studied and the coöperation of local civic organizations was contemplated. Dr. Roy V. Peel of New York University secured a leave of absence to direct the program and was given the title of Director of Research for the League. He was appointed professor in the department of government of the university and director of the Institute of Politics. Research studies in progress include such subjects as election costs, state legislation, campaign funds, electoral behavior, citizen organizations, and Negroes in appointive and elective office.[143]

In his report to the 1941 Conference Secretary Jones referred to the national celebration of "Citizenship Day" during the past two years and stated that many educators and civic leaders had urged the League to assume general leadership of this movement in order to develop a constructive program of training for young citizens. Funds to support such a program had been requested of five foundations. He also previewed briefly the League's efforts to improve citizen training in the schools and suggested that the League should seek the coöperation of other organizations in setting up a committee to investigate the extent and effectiveness of instruction in local government and citizenship in the primary grades, secondary schools, and colleges and universities.[144] A meeting of the Executive Committee of the League, January 20, 1944, discussed this problem and it was decided to investigate the desirability of reconstituting a committee on citizen education and training.[145]

Dr. P. P. Womer, who had served as chairman of the Citizenship Committee of the League since 1939, found it necessary in 1946 to relinquish this activity because of ill-health. The Council of the League, at the annual meeting in 1946, adopted a resolution of thanks to Dr. Womer for his unselfish services.[146]

Education for citizenship was again stressed by Executive Secretary Willoughby in his report for 1946. Leaders in many fields look to the League for guidance in formulating a practical plan of education of young and old in democratic citizenship, which would include teaching materials, training of civic leaders, and dissemination of civic information to the general public through newspapers, magazines, forums, radio, and films. "We have recently been in conference with leaders in education in radio and films. These new media are bound to play an increasingly powerful role in shaping the future minds and conduct of our citizens."[147]

SUMMARY

The problem of electoral reform has had much study by the League since the first Municipal Program was formulated. Through its model laws on registration and election administration it has exerted a great influence on legislation and administrative practice. Consolidation with the Short Ballot Organization and the Proportional Representation League has made the League the principal national sponsor of these reforms. Direct legislation has long been a part of its program.

Since 1900 the training of young people in the duties and responsibilities of citizenship has been a primary interest of the League. Many committees have studied and reported on methods to expand and improve collegiate and school programs and methods of instruction in local government, to secure the coöperation of teachers and the interest of students. Through the intercollegiate division, through prizes offered to university and high school students, through distribution of its literature in college classes, the League has sought to provide the fundamentals of a program for useful citizenship.

Nor has the adult citizen been neglected. The radio has been effectively used to acquaint the people with the problems of government and their relation thereto. In the field of citizen organization, participation, and action the League has sought to develop a satisfactory plan of local citizen organization and has, in recent years, assumed the leadership of the citizens' council movement and of a new education program designed to increase the effectiveness of democratic government through coöperation of educational institutions and local civic agencies.

VII

Higher Administrative Standards

WHEN THE First National Conference for Good City Government assembled in Philadelphia in 1894, the urgent municipal problems were largely those relating to the organization, powers, and duties of cities, their relationship to the state, and the struggle to wrest local government from the spoilsmen. The League's pioneer work in formulating its Municipal Program and its efforts to secure workable forms and democratic control of local government have been described in the preceding chapters.

Shortly after the turn of the century insistent problems of administration demanded more attention. The bureau of municipal research idea, beginning in New York in 1906, spread rapidly to the larger cities of the country. Uniform accounting and statistics, budgeting, centralized purchasing, auditing and financial control, assessment and collection of taxes, special assessments, excess condemnation, regulation of public utilities, planning and zoning, personnel, liquor control, municipal reporting, and measurement standards of government activities,—all these and others like them presented technical questions of administration which challenged the League and other organizations interested in higher administrative standards to seek and to formulate solutions.

Dr. W. F. Willoughby, assistant director of the Bureau of the Census, made a plea to the 1910 conference that the League should assume responsibility for the formulation of administrative principles, practices, and procedures.[1] As we shall see, the League had already begun such studies in several fields. Commenting on a statement of the Schenectady Bureau of Municipal Research, which had characterized the League as "the grandfather of municipal research," Secretary Howard P. Jones, in 1936, said:

> Certainly our relationship with municipal research is a very close one. The League's job has been to initiate, develop and publicize plans and methods for operating local government more efficiently. This has been done largely through the coöperation of research men throughout the country who are glad

---

[1] For notes to chap. vii, see pp. 232–241.

to give others the benefit of their studies. The National Municipal League has served as the focal point to bring together the best in municipal research and the National Municipal Review and other League publications have put this into a form enabling its use to the advantage of communities everywhere.[2]

It will be the purpose of this chapter to outline the League's program for administrative efficiency as formulated by its committees and promoted by the staff. This will include also a history of the Municipal Administration Service and the Consultant Service, with an analysis of their relation to the League. The coöperation of the League with the governmental research group and other organizations interested in specific aspects of administration will also receive attention.

GOVERNMENT PERSONNEL

From the beginning the merit system has been a fundamental principle of the League's program and has been included in all of its model charters, laws, and constitutions. At the Philadelphia conference, Carl Schurz, president of the National Civil Service Reform League, addressed the delegates on the subject, "The Relation of Civil Service Reform to Municipal Reform."[3] Other leading civil service reformers were also interested in municipal improvement—Dorman B. Eaton, Charles J. Bonaparte, Everett P. Wheeler, William Dudley Foulke, Richard Henry Dana, and George McAneny. Mr. Bonaparte and Mr. Foulke were presidents of the League during the period, 1903–1915. The call for the First National Conference for Good City Government was signed by many men prominent in the civil service reform movement. On several occasions the League and the National Civil Service Reform League coöperated in forming a joint committee to study some problem of personnel administration.

In 1908 Professor A. Lawrence Lowell of Harvard University pointed out to the League meeting the importance of permanent experts in municipal government and outlined the relationship of the expert and the layman in the conduct of municipal affairs.[4] Three years later a Committee on the Selection and Retention of Experts in City Government was created as a joint enterprise of the League and the National Civil Service Reform League. Clinton Rogers Woodruff, Philadelphia, was chairman, and other members included: Horace E. Deming, Elliot H. Goodwin, New York; Richard Henry Dana, Cambridge; William Dudley Foulke, Richmond, Indiana; Stiles P. Jones, Minneapolis; and Robert Catherwood, Chicago. Arthur Dexter Brigham of Harvard University was employed to assist the committee in gathering pertinent information. Mr. Dana made a preliminary report for the committee at the 1911 League meeting in Richmond, Virginia.[5]

Civil service problems had a prominent place on the program of the 1912 meeting in Los Angeles. President Foulke's address, "Expert City Management," emphasized the necessity of engaging experts in order to secure efficient municipal government. Elliot H. Goodwin, secretary of the National Civil Service Reform League, read a paper, "The Need for an Adequate Civil Service Law." The final report of the joint committee recommended that policy-determining officials should be directly responsible to the people and should hold office at their pleasure. "On the other hand, operating officials carrying out the policies so determined should hold office during continued efficiency and good conduct, and should be experts of education, training, experience and executive ability, and selected and promoted under civil service rules of a kind to determine these qualifications."[6]

To continue the work of the joint committee a new Committee on Experts was authorized at the Toronto meeting, 1913. Since the Committee on Municipal Program had appointed a subcommittee on administrative civil service, which would probably cover the same ground, the appointment of the committee was deferred until the Committee on Municipal Program had completed its work.[7]

The Executive Committee reported to the Baltimore convention of 1914 that, at the invitation of the joint committee of the American Political Science Association and the American Economic Association, a Committee on Training for Municipal Service, consisting of R. S. Childs, New York; John A. Fairlie, University of Illinois; and Secretary Woodruff, had been appointed to coöperate with the two organizations.

A feature of the same meeting was a civil service exhibit presented by the Women's Auxiliary of the Massachusetts Civil Service Reform Association and the Chicago and Philadelphia civil service commissions. Training for public service was the subject for one of the sessions of the meeting held at Springfield, Massachusetts, in 1916. The following year at Detroit the Society for Training for Public Service joined with the League and other organizations in holding the Twenty-fifth National Conference for Good Government. Meantime the *Review* chronicled the progress of municipal civil service and took up various personnel problems, such as standardization of salaries, pensions, and methods of removal.[8]

President Lawson Purdy's address to the 1917 meeting dealt with the pressing problem of municipal pensions. Appointment of a Committee on Civil Service and Efficiency was authorized by the Council at the same meeting. Its membership included: William G. Rice, Albany, New York, chairman; E. O. Griffenhagen, Chicago; Don C. Sowers, Akron, Ohio; Lawson Purdy, Darwin R. James, New York. With the same membership the committee was continued for 1919–1920, under the title Civil Service Efficiency and Municipal Pensions.[9] Enlarged to include representatives of the National Civil Service Reform League, the committee was reorganized by the Council and Executive Committee in 1920 as the Committee on Pensions.[10]

Paul Studenski, director of the Bureau of State Research of the New Jersey State Chamber of Commerce, acted as secretary and prepared the report entitled, "Pensions in Public Employment," which was published in April, 1922. It set forth the main defects of existing pension systems, discussed the principles of a correct system, and described seven satisfactory systems in operation and several sound penion bills before legislative bodies. In minority statements Albert de Roode objected to the contributory principle, and Mr. Purdy presented an alternative pension plan for government employees.[11] In his annual report Secretary Harold W. Dodds said in reference to the study: ". . . a difficult and neglected subject on which this is the only publication of importance."[12]

The question of appointing a committee on labor unions consisting of municipal employees was discussed by the Council in December, 1919, and referred to the

Executive Committee.[13] At the annual meeting in 1920, the right of government employees to organize and strike was discussed by Luther C. Steward, president of the National Federation of Federal Employees, and Albert S. Faught of Philadelphia. The next step in civil service reform, a civil service commission with the full function of employment management, was outlined by Dr. W. E. Mosher of the National Institute of Public Administration.[14]

During 1922 a Special Committee on Civil Service was appointed with the following personnel: Henry S. Dennison, Framingham, Massachusetts, chairman; W. E. Mosher, New York, secretary; Wm. C. Beyer, Philadelphia; Morris B. Lambie, University of Minnesota; John Steven, Albany, New York; Whiting Williams, Cleveland. Charles P. Messick, Trenton, New Jersey, was originally a member of the committee but resigned because of disagreement over the nature of the report.

An abstract of the committee report was presented to the Philadelphia meeting in 1922 by Dr. Mosher. The report was referred to the Council with power to act.[15] One hundred copies were printed for distribution to the Council and members, and a digest of the report was published in the *Review*.[16] Sharp differences of opinion over the recommendations of the committee developed, and the Council decided at its meeting in March, 1923, that the report should be referred to the committee for such revisions as it might desire to make and then it should be published in the *Review*, with articles and comments pro and con. This procedure, the Council believed, would insure full and intelligent discussion by the League membership before the next annual meeting. President Henry M. Waite emphasized the fact that the League and the Council had taken no action on this report; that it was not published as being sanctioned by the League but simply to place the findings before the membership.[17]

The committee report, "Employment Management in Municipal Civil Service," was published in August, 1923, together with brief explanatory and critical articles by Leonard D. White, Alfred Bettman, Clyde L. Seavey, Henry M. Waite, Robert Moses, Frank O. Lowden, Robert Catherwood, George C. Sikes, Henry T. Hunt, Allen M. Ruggles, Charles S. Shaughnessy, Clinton Rogers Woodruff, Fred Telford, and William Dudley Foulke. Chapter I discussed the present status of the municipal civil service, with the general conclusion that cities were not handling their personnel problems in an effective manner. Chapter II analyzed employment methods in private enterprise with a view to their applicability to the public service. Positive recommendations for a new public employment policy were outlined in Chapter III. These included: (1) centralized employment control through a single civil service commissioner selected by competitive examination, with a salary equal to that of department heads of similar responsibility; (2) adequate appropriations to carry out a complete personnel program; and (3) personnel committees, chosen in equal parts from the supervisory and administrative officials and from the rank and file of the employees.[18]

Final action on the report was taken at the League meeting in 1923, in the form of a resolution expressing agreement with the committee's recommendations for enlarged powers and adequate appropriations for the personnel agency and for appointment of civil service commissioners on the basis of fitness and experience and not of political acceptability. "As to other provisions of the report the views of the members of this League are diverse."[19]

In April, 1923, the *Review* announced that the League and the National Civil Service Reform League had undertaken a joint survey on the effects of veteran preference in state and municipal civil service. "It is a particularly difficult subject upon which to gather fact information, but it is hoped that we shall have something definite to report in the near future."

During the discussion of the work of the Special Committee on Civil Service, Mayo Fesler of Chicago suggested that other organizations—National Civil Service Reform League, Governmental Research Conference, and the National Assembly of Civil Service Commissioners—be invited by the League to name representatives to a joint committee to report upon the composition, method of selection, and functions of the civil service commission.[20] The Bureau of Public Personnel Administration joined with the four organizations in forming the Conference Committee on the Merit System. Henry M. Waite, New York, and Secretary Dodds were designated by the League as committee members; Mr. Waite acting as chairman of the joint committee. After several meetings in 1924 and 1925 the committee agreed upon its final report, which was published in book form by the League. The report discussed the membership, selection, form of organization, and functions of the public personnel agency. Unable to agree upon the form of organization of the personnel agency, the committee included descriptions of six principal types, existing or proposed, with a discussion of advantages and disadvantages of each. A model law for a state or city employment commission was included in the appendix.[21] In the same year the League published a study of the salaries of municipal employees in relation to the increasing cost of living.[22]

Ten years elapsed before the League joined with other groups in the organization of a committee to draft a model personnel law. In the meantime the *Review* continued its interest in problems of personnel and several supplements on the subject were issued.[23] During 1932 the Executive Committee and the Council discussed the matter of closer coöperation, and perhaps merger, of the League and the National Civil Service Reform League, but no definite plan was formulated.[24]

In March, 1935, Secretary Jones proposed to the Executive Committee that a committee be created to draft a model state personnel law. This suggestion was approved and the president was authorized to appoint a Personnel Committee which might work with other groups.[25] It was found that the National Civil Service Reform League and the Civil Service Assembly of the United States and Canada had appointed similar committees and that the membership of the three committees somewhat overlapped. Coöperation was desirable to prevent the issuance of three model laws, and therefore a meeting of the representatives of the personnel committees of the three organizations was held in Chicago in March, 1938, and general agreement was reached on the provisions of the model law. The conference instructed its presiding officer, Professor Leonard D. White of the University of Chicago, to appoint a drafting committee, and he designated G. Lyle Belsley, H. Eliot Kaplan, and Howard P. Jones.[26]

Early in 1939 a *Draft of a State Civil Service Law* was issued jointly by the League and the National Civil Service Reform League. Acknowledgment was made in the foreword of the collaboration of the Civil Service Assembly of the United States and Canada and of other organizations interested in public personnel administration. It was also stated in the foreword that "While it is not intended as a counsel of perfection, it is generally adaptable to the needs of any state, and even to those of a county or city, with such modifications as may be necessary to fit it into the existing constitutional and statutory framework of government. It will encourage uniformity of such laws." Adoption of its principles by several current state legislatures was announced in April, 1939.

Three organizations, the National Civil Service League, the Civil Service Assembly of the United States and Canada, and the National Municipal League, prepared and published in 1946 *A Model State Civil Service Law*, which superseded the 1939 draft.

A Fiscal Program

Problems of taxation, excess condemnation, revenues, special assessments, collection of taxes, accounting, budgets, and purchasing, have engaged the attention of the League since its organization.

MUNICIPAL TAXATION

At the Chicago meeting in 1904 Lawson Purdy of New York read a paper on municipal taxation and also introduced a resolution requesting the Executive Committee to appoint a Committee on Municipal Taxation to report on necessary and desirable changes in the tax laws and constitutional provisions of the various states.[27] To the 1905 meeting Chairman Purdy reported that the principal work of the committee during the past year had been the selection of an advisory committee of persons from the different states.[28] The final report of the committee in 1907 recommended home rule in taxation, in accordance with the Municipal Program, and the separation of state and local taxation.[29] Accompanying the report were a number of supplementary papers dealing with different aspects of the general subject: taxation of state and municipal bonds, of public service corporations, of savings banks, of life insurance, of railways; outline of a model system of state and local taxation; exemption of money and credits from taxation; the general property tax; substitutes for the personal property tax; and the effectiveness of taxation.[30]

EXCESS CONDEMNATION

An outgrowth of the Committee on Municipal Taxation was the appointment in 1910 of a Committee on Taxation of Benefits Caused by the Growth of Cities and Excess Condemnation.[31] Its progress report to the 1911 meeting indicated that it had confined its work almost exclusively to a study of excess condemnation in the United States and Europe. Data had also been collected from cities on the financing of street improvements and parks by special assessments.[32] The conclusions of the committee presented to the 1912 meeting stressed the fact that a city was entitled to powers which would enable it to secure "the fullest use of city land and the greatest possible freedom in adjusting its streets, parks and transit systems to the needs of city life. . . . " Herbert S. Swan, a member of the committee, had gathered from foreign countries much material on excess condemnation which was being edited for publication in the "National Municipal League Series."[33] Members of the committee concurring in the conclusions were Robert S. Binkerd, chairman, Lawson Purdy, Edward M. Bassett, Nelson P. Lewis, Herbert S. Swan, New York.[34]

SOURCES OF REVENUE

By action of the Council at the Los Angeles conference in 1912 the Committee on Taxation of Benefits and Excess Condemnation was discharged and a Committee on New Sources of Municipal Revenue was created. A few years later the word "New" was dropped from the title of the committee.[35] With several reorganizations of personnel the committee continued in existence for more than ten years and issued a number of important reports and documents. A brief preliminary report was submitted to the 1915 meeting.[36] In its report to the meeting the following year the committee noted the trend in taxation away from the general property tax and toward income taxes; condemned the amateurish assessment methods of real property used in most cities; recommended a light increment tax and the wide use of special assessments; considered business, habitation, and salary taxes as useful substitutes for the income tax; approved a light tax on intangibles as suitable for cities desiring "a short step from the old general property tax system"; opposed licenses for revenue, poll taxes, and tax limitations where elected officials were directly responsible; and favored "restrictions on debt incurred for nonproductive purposes and the imposition of full charges for special privileges."[37]

In 1919 the committee published a report, "The Assessment of Real Estate," by Lawson Purdy of New York. This study discussed the best type of administrative organization, and described the forms, methods, and procedures used in assessing real estate. The foreword by Chairman Robert M. Haig explained: "The document is not intended to be a complete manual of technical procedure in this field, but nevertheless, in it the technician will find a general guide and a number of references to sources where details may be found. It is rather a nontechnical statement of Mr. Purdy's general conclusions arrived at after a long period of experience as a practical tax administrator."[38]

"New Revenues for City Government" was the title of the report of the committee in 1922, dealing with six important problems of municipal taxation. Regarding the relation of state and local taxation the committee believed that the model tax system of the National Tax Association contained satisfactory provisions, and urged that an adequate share of revenues collected by the states through personal and business income taxes should be allocated to the cities. Further extension of special business, occupational, and license taxes, and the municipal retail sales tax, was considered undesirable. Special assessments as a means of financing public improvements and the levying of taxes upon signboards had the committee's approval, but it did not believe in tax limits. In conclusion the committee listed ten essentials of a good system of property assessment.[39]

A more detailed report, "Special Assessments," was published the following month. It was based upon data prepared for the committee by Clarence E. Ridley and William A. Bassett of the National Institute of Public Administration, and William C. Ormond, president of the New York City Board of Assessors. Distribution of costs, and methods of assessing improvements for streets, sewers, parks, and public utilities were described.[40] The report was reprinted immediately as one of the technical pamphlets of the League; a second edition was issued in 1923 and a third in 1929. Foreign recognition was given by its translation into Japanese in 1923.

Supplementing its earlier studies the committee issued in 1923 a report entitled, "Minor Highway Privileges as a Source of City Revenue," based on material prepared by Mabel Newcomer of Vassar College. Charges made by a number of cities for vaults and tunnels, spur tracks and sidings, vendors' stands, street signs and awnings, pipes and conduits, and storage building material, were analyzed and methods of administration described. The conclusion of the committee was that minor highway privileges were at the present time a neglected source of municipal revenue. Charges for such privileges should be developed extensively.[41]

MODEL BOND LAW

In 1919 the Council authorized the creation of a Committee on a Model Municipal Indebtedness Law. This committee prepared a tentative draft of a model bond law, but it never prepared a final report.[42] At the request of the Governmental Research Conference the committee was reorganized in 1924 under the chairmanship of Carl H. Pforzheimer, New York.[43] C. E. Rightor and John S. Rae of Detroit acted as secretaries and prepared tentative drafts of the law in accordance with the wishes of the committee.[44] In 1927 the report of the Committee on Municipal Borrowings was issued under the title, *A Model Bond Law*. The committee said that the lack of uniform and standard procedure among the states had made it seem advisable to prepare a model law as a guide to state legislatures wishing to enact state-wide bond legislation.[45]

Response to the issuance of the Model Bond Law was immediate and favorable. Metropolitan newspapers and the financial press gave it favorable comment and requests for copies were received from bond attorneys, bond dealers, legislative committees, and bill draftsmen in all parts of the United States. Provisions similar to those of the Model Bond Law were incorporated into the laws of Massachusetts, New Jersey, Ohio, North Carolina, Michigan, and Minnesota. The Minnesota law of 1927 followed very closely the League's recommendations.[46] A second edition of the document was issued in 1929 for use of legislatures meeting that year.

MODEL SPECIAL ASSESSMENTS LAW

On recommendation of Secretary Russell Forbes the Executive Committee, in December, 1931, authorized the appointment of a Committee on a Model Special Assessments Law to formulate a model state law for application to local government.[47] President Murray Seasongood appointed the committee with Carl H. Pforzheimer, New York, as chairman, and C. E. Rightor, Detroit, as secretary.[48] A preliminary report of the committee was made in July, 1932, which included the comments of the members on the model law of the Investment Bankers' Association of America and the tentative draft of the report of the United States Chamber of Commerce. Work of the committee was delayed because of lack of funds, and for this reason it was reported as inactive in 1935 and 1936.[49]

MODEL REAL PROPERTY TAX COLLECTION LAW

A precipitate drop in the percentage of collection of local real property taxes from 1930 to 1933 and the consequent disastrous effects on local government finance led the League, in 1934, to appoint a Committee on a Model Tax Collection Law. Arnold Frye, New York, was chairman and C. Rudolf Peterson, New York, was secretary.[50] After a study of the most effective state laws the committee prepared its report, "A Model Real Property Tax Collection Law," which was published in 1935.[51] It proved to be a very useful document in the Pay-Your-Taxes Campaign, and Secretary Jones said in 1935: "From the wide demand, it was evident it filled a real need."[52]

OTHER PUBLICATIONS

In the field of taxation and finance a number of other publications of the League deserve notice. A tabulation of the tax rates of cities in the United States with more than 30,000 population has been published annually in the *Review* since 1922. C. E. Rightor of the Detroit Bureau of Governmental Research prepared the material from 1922 to 1935 and Rosina K. Mohaupt of the same organization made the compilations from 1936 to 1944. The same individuals also compiled from 1923 to 1943, for annual publication in the *Review*, the bonded debt of cities with a population of more than 30,000. In 1927 a series of articles dealing with the trend of expenditures for federal, state, county, and municipal governments, and for public education, public works, and police service was published in the *Review* under the title, "Are We Spending Too Much for Government?" Since January, 1934, the *Review* has carried a section on, "Taxation and Finance." Three issues of the *Review* in recent years have been entirely on the subject of municipal debt and one on the real estate tax limitation.[53] One should also note in this connection the financial sections of the Model City Charter and the Model State Constitution, the broadcasts in the radio series, and the literature used in the Pay-Your-Taxes Campaign,[54] as well as some of the publications of the Municipal Administration Service and the Consultant Service.[55]

UNIFORM ACCOUNTING AND STATISTICS

The meeting of 1896 heard a paper by Frederick W. Holls of New York on the subject, "State Boards of Municipal Control."[56] In 1898 the preliminary report of the Committee on Municipal Program contained strong arguments in support of its recommendations for uniform municipal bookkeeping and for the audit of municipal accounts by a state officer.[57] Accompanying the final report of this committee to the 1899 meeting were seven papers discussing the financial provisions of the Municipal Program.[58]

In one of three papers on the subject of uniform municipal accounting presented to the 1900 meeting, M. N. Baker of New York, associate editor of *Engineering News,* suggested that the League appoint a committee to coöperate with similar committees from other organizations in a study of uniform municipal accounting and statistics. Following the presentation of the three papers a resolution was adopted authorizing the chairman of the Executive Committee to appoint a committee to investigate and to report to the League such methods or systems of municipal accounting and collection of municipal statistics as it might find to be most desirable.[59] Accordingly a Committee on Uniform Municipal Accounting and Statistics was appointed early in 1901, with Dr. Edward M. Hartwell of Boston, as chairman, and Dr. Milo R. Maltbie, New York, as secretary.[60]

During the following eight years the reports of this committee and the papers presented at the annual meetings in elaboration of its principles constitute a contribution as significant in its field as the work of the earlier Committee on Municipal Program. Including five reports of the committee, twenty-seven papers on the subject were published in the annual volumes of *Proceedings* from 1901 to 1908. Several of them were separately reprinted and circulated. Nearly all of these papers were prepared by members of the committee.[61] As reconstituted and enlarged in 1904 the committee consisted of eighteen persons.[62] It was finally discharged by the Executive Committee in November, 1908.[63]

Describing the general scope of its work in its fifth report, the committee said that its activities had been designed

> ... (1) to stimulate discussion of the theoretical and practical aspects of uniform municipal accounting not only by the National Municipal League, but by other assocations devoted to municipal interests or the public welfare; (2) to promote the devising and publishing of forms and schedules suitable for securing uniform reports of financial statistics; (3) to test the usefulness and practicability of such forms and schedules through the re-statement of the figures contained in the financial reports of a number of leading cities; (4) to win recognition for its views and recommendations and to secure trial of its schedules by enlisting the support and cooperation of influential city, state and national officials; (5) to render aid to citizens' associations and city officials who were seeking to introduce modern systems of accounting or improved forms of financial reports.[64]

The classification of payments and receipts recommended by the committee was adopted, with minor changes, by the Bureau of the Census and made the basis of its annual volume of statistics of cities. The League's schedules as enlarged, improved, and standardized by the Bureau, were adopted by hundreds of cities.[65] Under instructions from the League much work was done to incorporate the papers and reports of the committee into a volume on uniform municipal accounting. A subcommittee, consisting of Horace E. Deming, chairman, M. N. Baker, F. A. Cleveland, Dr. Hartwell, and Secretary Woodruff was chosen to supervise its preparation,[66] but it was never completed and published by the League.[67]

On several other occasions the question of municipal accounting, expenditures, and statistics was discussed by the Council and Executive Committee, and committees were authorized. However, records of the appointment and reports of these committees are lacking and the inference is that they were not organized. After discussing a letter from Dr. F. A. Cleveland, the Council, in 1916, authorized the appointment of a Committee on the Classification of Municipal Expenditures to serve jointly with a similar committee of the City Managers' Association.[68] In 1919 a Committee on Statistical Information for Municipalities was authorized.[69] The annual business meeting in 1921 adopted a resolution calling for the appointment of a committee to investigate and report upon the best method of taking municipal statistics and gathering information on municipal government.[70] A Committee on Municipal Statistics, to include representatives of the Governmental Research Conference, was authorized in 1924 for the purpose of bringing to the attention of the Bureau of the Census means of improving statistics published by the Bureau.[71] Secretary Jones, in 1936, suggested to the Executive Committee the appointment of a committee to study and make recommendations regarding the reports of the Bureau of the Census on financial statistics of states and cities.[72] This committee was merged with the National Committee on Municipal Accounting, created in 1934, and composed of representatives of leading national associations of professional accountants, public officials, and citizen groups. A. E. Buck, New York, was the League's representative on the committee. Each organization with a member on the national committee also appointed an advisory committee.[73]

BUDGETS AND ACCOUNTING

In continuation of the work of the earlier Committee on Uniform Municipal Accounting and Statistics the Executive Committee appointed in 1909 a Committee on City Finances and Budgets, under the chairmanship of George Burnham, Jr. of Philadelphia. Three papers discussing the subjects of municipal budgets and expenditures, the budget of the District of Columbia, and the work of the Boston Finance Commission were presented to the 1909 meeting of the League.[74] The 1910 meeting heard a preliminary report by the chairman of the Committee on City Finances and Budgets and three papers discussing municipal accounts, budgets, and statistics.[75] Of the three papers one was by Dr. W. F. Willoughby, Washington, D. C., on "The Correlation of Financial and Physical Statistics of Cities." In December, 1910, the business committee appointed a Committee on a Program for the Improvement of Methods of Municipal Administration, with Dr. Willoughby as chairman.[76]

Mr. Burnham briefly reported progress to the meeting in 1911. He stated that two members of the committee, F. A. Cleveland and Harvey S. Chase, had been appointed by President Taft as members of the Commission on Economy and Efficiency. Dr. Willoughby was also a member of the President's commission. Three papers on various aspects of municipal finance were presented.[77] At the same meeting the Executive Committee discontinued the Committee on City Finances and Budgets and the Committee on a Program for the Improvement of Methods of Municipal Administration and created a new Committee on City Finances and Efficiency.[78] Two papers on municipal budgeting and accounting were read to the meeting in 1912.[79] Chairman Burnham's recommendation to this meeting that the Committee on City Finances and Efficiency be discharged and that there be appointed two new committees, one on sources of municipal revenue and another on budget making and accounting, was accepted by the Council.[80]

The fundamental principles of municipal budget making were outlined in the preliminary report of the Committee on Municipal Budgets and Accounting to the meeting in 1913.[81] Further reports were made to the meetings in 1914 and 1915.[82] The final report of the committee, giving the requirements of a model budget, was presented to the 1916 meeting in the form of proposed amendments to the financial sections of the Model City Charter. These financial provisions, as prepared by the Committee on Municipal Program, had already been incorporated in the charter; therefore it was decided to print the report of the Committee on Municipal Budgets and Accounting in an appendix to the Model City Charter.[83]

During the next nine years progress of municipal budgets and accounts and of state budget making was discussed in the *Review,* by two experts on the subject, C. E. Rightor, director of the Dayton Bureau of Municipal Research, and A. E. Buck of the New York Bureau of Municipal Research. There was also debate and discussion over the budget amendment of the Maryland constitution, the executive versus the legislative budget, the budget in the Model State Constitution, and the federal budget and accounting law of 1921.[84]

In 1925 announcement was made of the establishment of a "National Municipal League Monograph Series" dealing with the technical aspects of local government and administration. The first in the series was *Municipal Budgets and Budget Making,* by A. E. Buck. This practical handbook of sound budget practice brought favorable comment from budget officials throughout the country. A conference on budget practice, called by the League for April, 1926, in New York, was attended by twenty budget officers and experts of state and municipal governments and research bureaus. Mr. Buck was selected as chairman to continue the discussion of improved budget methods in the *Review.*

During the preparation of the Model Bond Law it seemed desirable that a companion model municipal budget law should be prepared to complete a program of sound municipal financing. Accordingly the Council, early in 1927, agreed to organize a Committee on a Model Municipal Budget Law with Carl H. Pforzheimer, New York, as chairman, and C. E. Rightor, Detroit, as secretary.[85] At the 1927 meeting, held jointly with the Governmental Research Conference, a session was held for discussion of the proposed model law.[86] "A Model Municipal Budget Law," prepared by the committee, was published in 1928. The law covered the essential steps in the preparation, adoption, and execution of the budget. It was drawn in form for enactment by the state legislature and was intended to be applicable to all local subdivisions of the state.[87] Secretary Forbes reported that the document had been widely praised by newspapers, magazines, and budget experts, and would undoubtedly have great influence upon future budget legislation.[88]

CENTRALIZED PURCHASING

Matters of efficiency and centralization in city purchasing were early considered in the pages of the *Review.*[89] In 1920 A. E. Buck analyzed the purchasing organization and methods of state governments in an article entitled, "The Coming of Centralized Purchasing in State Government."[90] Centralized purchasing in city manager cities was surveyed in 1924 by Russell Forbes, research secretary of the National

Association of Purchasing Agents.[91] Mr. Forbes became secretary of the League in 1928 and was soon called upon as a consultant in drafting state and local purchasing laws. During 1930–1931 he assisted in the drafting of state purchasing laws adopted by Maine and North Carolina, and in drafting an optional law for Ohio counties; this, however, failed of passage in the 1931 legislature. Following a survey he recommended central purchasing for Newark, New Jersey. He also supervised a survey of purchasing methods of Chicago and gave assistance in drafting a new purchasing ordinance.[92] Several of his books and pamphlets on centralized purchasing, though not published by the League, have been distributed through its office.[93]

MODEL FISCAL LEGISLATION

As has been noted, the League's program for the improvement of fiscal legislation and procedure, including the Model Bond Law, Model Municipal Budget Law, and Model Real Property Tax Collection Law, had wide acceptance and influence on state and local financial practice. The economic depression of the 'thirties contributed much to the knowledge of officials and students of the whole problem of local taxation, credit, and fiscal control. With this knowledge and under the necessity of revising its model financial laws, the League decided in 1937 to organize a committee to draft a comprehensive program of local fiscal legislation, including assessment of property, collection of taxes, custody of funds, and control over expenditures. Plans were made for the raising of funds to support a three-year program, with a paid secretary, draftsman, and other assistance. It was proposed to give the first year to designing and drafting the model fiscal program and the second and third years to promotional work for its adoption.

A large Committee on a Program of Model Fiscal Legislation for Local Governments, consisting of public officials, investment bankers, bond attorneys, university professors, governmental researchers, and representatives of organizations of public officials, was formed under the chairmanship of Arnold Frye of New York.[94] Meetings of the committee were held in 1937, 1938, and 1940 in connection with the annual League conferences. After part of the necessary funds had been raised, preliminary work on the committee's program was begun in the fall of 1938. The committee coöperated with the Committee on Revision of the Model City Charter in working out the finance provisions of the fifth edition of the Model City Charter. In 1946 a *Model Accrual Budget Law* was published. This was announced as the first of a series of model laws which would include a model cash basis budget law, a model bond law, and a model real property tax collection law.[95]

PLANNING AND ZONING

The interest of the League in popularizing city planning began about 1913. In that year the *Review* started the publication of articles and notes on city planning, including an annual review of American city plan reports. Charles Mulford Robinson, Rochester, New York, prepared these reviews until 1917 and thereafter, through 1925, they were prepared by Theodora Kimball of Cambridge.[96] At the time of the publication of the Municipal Program in 1900 the term city planning was practically unknown in this country, and hence does not appear in that document. However, in the Model City Charter, 1916, provision was made for a city planning board, and the revised editions of the charter in 1927, 1933, and 1941 contained sections on city planning and zoning.[97]

Three books in the "National Municipal League Series" treated various aspects of the problem: Graham R. Taylor, *Satellite Cities* (1915); John Nolen, *City Planning* (1916); and Charles S. Bird, Jr., *Town Planning for Small Communities* (1917). In addition, the League has published a number of pamphlets and supplements on this subject.[98] Court decisions on zoning were reported in the *Review* and general inquiries from the public were handled through the League office.

Cordial relations have been maintained with other organizations in this field. In 1919 a joint Committee on City Planning, to include representatives of the League, the American Civic Association and the City Planning Institute, was authorized by the Council but was never organized.[99] Secretary Dodds reported to the meeting in 1920 that the National Conference on City Planning had made the *Review* its official organ, though there was no arrangement for joint membership.[100] Along with other organizations, the League in 1921 designated a representative, Nelson P. Lewis of New York, on the Advisory Committee on Zoning appointed by Secretary of Commerce Herbert Hoover.[101] Lawson Purdy and Harold S. Buttenheim have been presidents of national planning groups. At several annual meetings planning groups have joined in the program, the Massachusetts Federation of Planning Bodies in 1916; Ohio State Conference on City Planning in 1930; the American City Planning Institute, American Institute of Park Executives, National Council for Protection of Roadside Beauty, and District of Columbia Commission, George Washington Bicentennial, in 1932.

With the American Civic Association especially close relations have existed. Joint meetings of the two organizations were held in 1907, 1908, 1909, 1921, and 1932. President J. Horace McFarland of the American Civic Association was a vice-president of the League from 1912 to 1928. Secretary Woodruff served as first vice-president of the American Civic Association from 1904 to 1909, and there were other instances of overlapping of the officers of the two groups. Merger of the League and the Association was discussed by the Executive Committee of the League in 1908 and a committee was authorized to confer with the Association regarding the proposed consolidation.[102] Twelve years later the meeting of the League in 1920 approved the action of its officers in making the *Review* the official organ of the American Civic Association and permitting members of that body to subscribe to the *Review* for $2.50 per year, with no membership privileges in the League. Overlapping councils of the two groups were chosen and it was agreed to hold a joint convention in 1921. The Association continued to maintain its offices in Washington, D. C. Change of the name of the *Review* to represent the new interests was taken under consideration by the Council of the League.[103]

After a year of operation of these coöperative arrangements the governing councils of the Association and the League met jointly in New York to consider further steps. It was the sense of the meeting that it was highly desirable to reduce overlapping and to bring about a consolidation as soon as possible. However, it was agreed that further amalgamation of the two organizations was not feasible at this time. The coöperative arrangements regarding subscriptions to the *Review* were to remain in effect, and the *Review* was to continue publication of items of interest to the American Civic Association. Joint subscriptions were discontinued in 1927. Occasional notes were published until 1925.[104]

In 1937 the League collaborated with several national planning groups—the American City Planning Institute, the American Society of Planning Officials, the American Civic and Planning Association—in organizing a National City Planning Exhibit, which was opened in New York under the auspices of the Young Men's Board of Trade of New York.[105]

Beginning with the May, 1938, issue the *Review* inaugurated a new department, "Planning—Including Zoning and Housing," to be edited by Alfred Bettman, chairman of the City Planning Commission of Cincinnati, and Walter Blucher, executive director of the American Society of Planning Officials, Chicago,[106] but after a few months the department was discontinued.

PUBLIC UTILITIES

At the Minneapolis meeting, 1894, Professor Edward W. Bemis of the University of Chicago read a paper entitled, "Some Essentials of Good City Government in the Way of Granting Franchises."[107] Thus began a discussion of franchises and other public utility problems, a subject which has had an important place on conference programs and has been the object of investigations by several League committees. From 1894 to 1910 no less than forty-two separate conference papers dealt with franchises; municipal ownership; street railways; rates, accounting, taxation, regulation, and control of public utility corporations.[108]

The first Municipal Program applied the principle of municipal home rule to public utility matters and conferred complete freedom upon the city to determine its public utility policy.[109] Appointment of a special Committee on the Relation of Public Service Corporations to Municipalities was authorized by the meeting of the League in 1905.[110] Horace E. Deming, New York, was chosen chairman and authorized to prepare a list of names for submission to the business committee. Chairman Deming reported to the Executive Committee in 1909 that little active work had been done by the committee because of the existence of a similar committee appointed by the National Civic Federation.[111]

In the summer of 1910 a new Committee on Franchises was appointed, with Robert Treat Paine of Boston as chairman. This committee, in a preliminary report to the Buffalo conference, 1910, reviewed briefly the principles relating to franchises contained in the first Municipal Program and the papers presented at subsequent meetings of the League. It recommended the appointment of a larger committee to continue the investigation,[112] and such a committee was authorized by the Executive Committee at the same conference.[113]

A subcommittee of the Committee on Franchises, consisting of Delos F. Wilcox, New York, and James W. S. Peters of Kansas City, Missouri, presented to the meeting in 1911 an outline of a model street railway franchise.[114] Both members also read papers at Los Angeles the following year; Dr. Wilcox discussed the Chicago and Cleveland street railway settlements, and Mr. Peters' paper dealt with a suggested sliding scale of dividends for street railways. Two California officials discussed the pros and cons of state versus municipal regulation of public utilities.[115]

At Toronto in 1913, the full committee submitted a report in which the growing movement for exclusive state control of public utilities was discussed in relation to the principle of municipal home rule as championed by the League. The conclusion of the committee was that the public interest would be best served by a policy of coöperation of local and state authorities rather than by exclusive control by either jurisdiction. Other franchise problems—the control and financing of extensions, duration of franchises, amortization of investment, and resettlement of outstanding franchises—were also briefly discussed in the report.[116] The conclusions regarding state and local coöperation had been strengthened by further study, the committee reported to the 1914 meeting. It also stressed the importance to cities of a permanent, continuous, municipal organization for public utility problems, regardless of whether local control or state control was the norm.[117] In 1915 the report of the Committee on Franchises was printed in the appendix to the report of the Committee on Municipal Program.[118] After discussion, the annual meeting voted to refer the franchise provisions to the Committee on Municipal Program.[119]

The New Municipal Program of 1916 contained provisions for home rule for cities in public utility matters. General principles regarding the public utility and franchise policy to be followed by a city were incorporated in the Model City Charter.[120] Dr. Wilcox prepared the article, "The Franchise Policy of the New Municipal Program," which was published with the charter.[121]

Report of the committee to the 1916 meeting was on the timely subject of "Public Regulation of Wages, Hours and Conditions of Labor of the Employes of Public Service Corporations." Interest of the League in this subject was stimulated by the request, made in 1915 by the Consumers' League, for consideration by the National Municipal League of the questions of the eight-hour day and the minimum wage in connection with public utility franchises. The threat of a strike of national railway employees in 1916, the passage of the federal eight-hour law, and actual strikes of local transportation workers in New York City contributed to the public interest in this problem. The report recognized the three parties to labor disputes in public utilities, the employees, the public service corporations, and the public, and followed this with an analysis of the means possessed by the respective parties for protecting their interests. Regarding the right of employees of public service corporations to strike, the committee concluded that the public interest in the continuous operation of many utilities, such as local transit and telephone systems, was sufficient to warrant the curtailment of the use of the strike weapon. As a matter of justice to the employees it then followed that it was the obligation of the state to guarantee protection of their legitimate interests in wages, hours of labor, and conditions of work. The remainder of the report discussed the methods to be used in establishing public control of employer-employee relations in public service corporations.[122]

In its 1917 report the committee reviewed recent developments in the public utility field affecting franchise policies and municipal ownership. Chairman Wilcox and his colleagues reiterated their belief in municipal home rule and regarded "the adoption of the policy of exclusive state control as a menace to the integrity of municipal government." The essential principles of municipal policy and coöperation between state and local agencies in public utility regulation were outlined in the following recommendations:

(1) That every state remove the handicaps from municipal ownership by clearing away legal and financial obstacles, so far as they are now embedded in constitutional and statutory law.

(2) That every state provide expert administrative agencies for the regulation and control of public utilities. These agencies should have full jurisdiction over interurban services and over local services where the local authorities are unwilling or unable to exercise local control. They should have limited jurisdiction wherever the local authorities are in a position to exercise the full normal functions of municipal government, and should even have jurisdiction with respect to accounting and reports in the case of utilities owned and operated by municipalities.

(3) That every city where public utilities are operated primarily as local services definitely recognize these services as public functions and set in motion at once the financial machinery necessary to bring about the municipalization of public utility investments at the earliest practicable moment.

(4) That every such city, pending the municipalization of its utilities, recognize the necessity of giving security to public utility investments and to a fair rate of return thereon, and to that end assume as a municipal burden the ultimate financial risks of public utility enterprises and insist upon receiving the benefits naturally accruing from this policy in the form of a lowered cost of capital.

(5) That every city definitely adopt the policy of securing public utility service to the consumers either at cost, or at fixed rates not in excess of cost with subsidies from taxation whenever needed for the maintenance of the service at the rates fixed.

(6) That every large city provide itself with expert administrative agencies for the continuous study of local public utility problems. . . ."[123]

The 1918 meeting of the League was held in New York in conjunction with the War Time Economy Conference. Dr. Wilcox reported for the Committee on Franchises and W. L. Ransom, counsel for Public Service Commission Number 1 of New York City, read a paper entitled "A New Deal on the Franchise Question."[124] A conference on American Reconstruction Problems called by the League at Rochester, New York, November, 1918, adopted a resolution calling for the appointment of a committee to study the problem of public ownership and operation of the national systems of communication and transportation as a part of the program of national reconstruction, particularly as it affected the welfare of the people of cities. The following month the Executive Committee discussed the resolution and appointed a Committee on Public Ownership and Operation of Utilities. In April, 1919, President Purdy reported to the Council that the problem would be considered by the Committee on Franchises.[125]

Street railway problems held the attention of the Committee on Franchises during the postwar period, 1919–1921. The *Review* published a series of articles, under the title, "Fate of the Five-Cent Fare," describing the situation in Montreal, Boston, Chicago, Toledo, San Francisco, Toronto, Detroit, Indianapolis, Minneapolis, Pittsburgh, Seattle, and Philadelphia.[126] "A Correct Public Policy Toward the Street Railway Problem" was the title of the report of the Committee on Public Utilities[127] submitted to the Cleveland meeting in 1919. Emphasis was placed upon the critical situation of local street railways; the public utility policy of the League from 1900 to date was sketched; and a specific program of work necessary for the establishment of a definite, constructive street railway policy was outlined. Municipal ownership and operation seemed to the committee the ultimate solution. "Street railway transportation is a public function; it cannot be put upon a permanently sound basis until the organized community has prepared itself to perform the function."[128] Four papers on the street railway problem presented at the 1920 meeting were printed as a separate pamphlet in 1921 under the title, "Service At Cost for Street Railways: A Symposium."[129]

During 1921–1922 the *Review* published a series of articles by John Bauer, public utility consultant of New York, under the title, "Deadlock in Public Utility Regulation," and in 1925 a series, "Chief Elements of Controversy in Public Utility Rate Making," by the same author.[130] *Depreciation in Public Utilities*, by Delos F. Wilcox, was published in 1925 as one of the "Monograph Series." From 1926 to 1932 a "Public Utilities" department of the *Review* was edited by Dr. Bauer. In announcing the establishment of the new department the *Review* said:

> The purpose of this new department is to discuss and promote the public aspects of the whole utility problem; to help establish a clearer economic and technical understanding of the industries involved and bring about more definite policies and methods of conserving the public interest. The department will be devoted to all public aspects of utility organization, operation and control. As to regulation, it will discuss principles and policies, causes of controversy, court decisions, legislative remedies, methods and machinery of control. It will constantly seek to bring out the essential facts, clarify the issues and consolidate sound public views for effective regulation. It will have no bias toward public ownership.
>
> In most of these matters, there are honest differences in point of view. The department will endeavor to give sincere consideration to all disinterested and intelligent opinion. This is the only way by which progress can be made.[131]

No further reports were made by the Committee on Public Utilities after 1920. League interest in the question continued, however, as subsequent publications have indicated. Several times since 1920 the Council and Executive Committee have considered proposals to expand the public utility service of the League. In 1921 and again in 1935 Dr. Bauer suggested a plan for organizing in the League or in the Consultant Service a public utility consulting service for cities. Officials of the League discussed in 1932 the request of Dr. Bauer that the League should name an official representative on the governing committee of the American Public Utilities Bureau. Decision in each instance was unfavorable to the suggestions.[132]

Similarly with reference to a proposal to endow a department in the *Review* in memory of Delos F. Wilcox, who died in 1928, opinion was divided and the project was permitted to lapse.[133]

Early in 1927 the Council authorized the appointment of a Public Utilities Committee. The Executive Committee decided that it should be organized with an impartial person not closely identified with utility subjects as chairman and that it should consider general economic and ethical phases of the problem. Apparently the committee was never organized.[134] Secretary Forbes, in 1932, recommended to the Executive Committee the appointment of a committee to draft a model law for public utility regulation, and suggested its personnel. The Executive Committee favored the creation of such a committee provided funds could be secured to support its work.[135]

OTHER ADMINISTRATIVE PROBLEMS

Brief attention should be given to a number of other questions which the League has studied during its long history. For the development of most of the administrative problems now to be discussed—police, health and sanitation, liquor control, recreation, housing, social security, public works, education—separate national organizations, citizen and professional, exist. On all of these subjects, however, the League has published reports, usually the result of committee investigation undertaken independently or in coöperation with other organizations.

POLICE

The first discussion of police matters at a League conference occurred in 1906 when Dr. Edward M. Hartwell of Boston presented a paper entitled, "The Police Question."[136] At the same meeting the Executive Committee appointed Dr. Hartwell and Secretary Woodruff a subcommittee to prepare and secure reports on the police problem.[137] Two papers on the subject were read to the 1909 meeting, followed by a lively discussion. Organization of police forces was the topic of a paper and a luncheon discussion at the 1910 meeting.[138] Appointment of a Committee on Police was authorized by the Executive Committee at this meeting.[139] The chairman of the Executive Committee reported to the 1911 meeting that Professor Frank J. Goodnow of Columbia University was chairman of the committee, that the investigation was just beginning, and that it would continue for several years.[140] In 1912 the personnel of the committee was as follows: Howard S. Gans, chairman, Henry de Forest Baldwin, New York; Richard Sylvester, Washington, D.C.; Harvey N. Shepard, Boston; William B. Munro, Harvard University.[141] League records reveal no formal reports by this committee.

HEALTH AND SANITATION

At the Cleveland conference in 1895 Dr. John S. Billings, deputy surgeon-general of the United States, read a paper, "Good City Government from the Standpoint of the Physician and Sanitarian."[142] Ten years later the subject, "Civics and Sanitation," was discussed by Dr. Thomas Darlington, health commissioner of New York City.[143] An all-day session at the 1907 meeting, held jointly with the American

Civic Association, heard seven speakers discuss municipal health and sanitation. Appointment of a Committee on Municipal Health and Sanitation was authorized to study methods of promoting coöperation between national, state, and local governments regarding municipal sanitation, the committee to work with a similar committee of the American Civic Association, should one be appointed.[144] Members of the committee contributed papers to the meetings in 1908 and 1909; and in 1910 Chairman M. N. Baker reported on city and state boards of health and the proposed federal department of health.[145] Other phases were discussed at the meetings in 1911 and 1912.[146] The committee was discontinued in 1914.[147]

Public health matters have received frequent attention in the *Review*. During 1924–1925 Dr. Carl E. McCombs of the National Institute of Public Administration edited a department in the magazine under the title, "Public Health Notes."[148]

LIQUOR CONTROL

The relation of the city to the liquor problem was discussed at annual meetings in 1908 and 1910.[149] A Committee on the Liquor Problem was authorized by the Executive Committee in November, 1910.[150] The committee first gave its attention to the licensing question and presented reports to the meetings of 1911, 1913, and 1914. There was also collaboration with the American Section of the International Committee for the Scientific Study of the Alcohol Question, through John Koren, who served as secretary of the League's committee and of the American Section.[151] Because of the times the committee reported in 1914 that its activities had been suspended; and by action of the Executive Committee in December, 1914, it was discontinued.[152]

Another committee on the liquor problem was not appointed for nineteen years. A session of the 1933 meeting on the topic, "Government Control of Liquor" adopted a resolution calling upon the League to appoint a committee to study the problem. A Committee on Liquor Control Legislation was accordingly appointed with Frank O. Lowden, Oregon, Illinois, as chairman, and Luther Gulick, New York, as secretary.[153] The committee's first report, issued in 1934, discussed the principles governing liquor control legislation and presented the draft of a Model State Alcohol Control Act, based upon the Fosdick-Scott report, *Toward Liquor Control*.[154] Professor Paul Studenski of New York University prepared the second report for the committee, "Liquor Taxes and the Bootlegger." The conclusion of the committee was that ". . . the combined federal and state taxes on hard liquor and on imported beverages are so high under existing conditions as to increase immensely the difficulty of suppressing the illegal alcohol trade." Consequently it recommended reduction in the tax levies.[155]

Secretary Jones reported in 1936 that fifteen states had adopted the Model State Alcohol Control Act, in whole or in part.[156]

SCHOOLS AS CIVIC CENTERS

At the 1909 meeting Edward J. Ward, supervisor of social centers under the Board of Education of Rochester, New York, described Rochester's experiment in using the public school building as a social center and civic club house. Subsequently a

Committee on School Extension was appointed with Mr. Ward as chairman.[157] Papers by members of the committee, presented at the 1910 meeting, were later consolidated into a volume in the "National Municipal League Series."[158] The committee was discontinued in 1911.

IMMIGRATION

Grace Abbott of Hull House, Chicago, director of the League for the Protection of Immigrants, discussed at the 1909 meeting the immigrant problem in relation to municipal government and in 1910 the education of immigrants in American citizenship.[159] Appointment of a Committee on Immigration was authorized by the Executive Committee in November, 1914, and it continued in existence for two years. In its report to the 1915 meeting the committee reviewed the progress of the campaign for the Americanization of the immigrant population.[160]

FOOD SUPPLY

The Toronto meeting, 1913, authorized the appointment of a Committee on the Cost of Living, whose title was later changed to Committee on the Relation of the City to Its Food Supply.[161] Reports of the committee to the meetings in 1914, 1915, and 1916 were issued separately by the League. The committee was discharged following its report to the 1916 meeting.[162]

RECREATION

In 1921 the League published an illustrated supplement, "State Parks," by Harold A. Caparn, landscape architect of New York.[163] A decade later the Committee on Play and Recreation Administration prepared a report, "Standards of Play and Recreation Administration."[164] The report outlined the administrative principles involved and recommended definite division of responsibility between city governments and school systems in control of parks and playgrounds.[165]

SOCIAL SECURITY

Issues of the *Review* for March and April, 1936, were concerned entirely with different aspects of the problem of social security.[166] These articles were reprinted the same year as a separate pamphlet, *Social Security*, edited by Dr. Joseph P. Harris, director of research for the Committee on Public Administration of the Social Science Research Council. Through these and other articles in the *Review* the relationship of the federal Social Security Act to local government was emphasized.[167]

HOUSING

As early as 1909 League attention was drawn to the problem of building codes in a conference paper by Lawrence Veiller of New York.[168] Since 1912 the *Review* has printed many articles on housing conditions in cities, and on government and private developments in housing during the First World War and afterwards. In 1931 the Executive Committee agreed that a committee should be created to report on the relationship of cities to the housing problem, but there is no record of its appointment.[169] Several pamphlets on the subject have been published in recent years.[170]

PUBLIC WORKS

A new department, "Items on Municipal Engineering," edited by William A. Bassett of the National Institute of Public Administration was inaugurated in the *Review* in 1923 and was continued through 1925.[171] The meeting in 1933 adopted a resolution asking the League to appoint a committee to draft a model law for the advance planning of public works. President Seasongood announced the appointment of a Committee on Public Works early in 1934, but the committee has not formulated a report.[172]

ADMINISTRATIVE CODE

Secretary Forbes in 1928 recommended that the Executive Committee appoint a committee to prepare a model administrative code designed to supplement the Model City Charter.[173] Approval was given by the Executive Committee and President Richard S. Childs in 1930 appointed a Committee on Model Administrative Code.[174] Emmett L. Bennett, of Cincinnati, prepared a tentative draft of *A Model Municipal Administrative Code*, which was considered at several meetings of the committee. Funds for publication have not been available and the report remains in mimeographed form.[175]

MUNICIPAL REPORTING

The Executive Committee in December, 1917, authorized the appointment of a Committee on Uniform City Reports. Two years later Lent D. Upson, Detroit, chairman, presented the tentative report of the committee to the Council and its recommendations were approved.[176] In 1927 Clarence E. Ridley was appointed review editor for municipal reports for the *Review*. For eleven years Dr. Ridley's articles, "Appraising Municipal Reports," were a feature of the annual volumes of the *Review*.

A National Committee on Municipal Reporting was organized in January, 1929, on the initiative of the League. Other organizations represented in its personnel were the Governmental Research Association, International City Managers' Association, and the American Municipal Association. C. O. Sherrill of Cincinnati was chosen as chairman, C. E. Ridley, Chicago, as vice-chairman, and Wylie Kilpatrick, Trenton, New Jersey, as executive secretary. Professor Herman C. Beyle of Syracuse University and Dr. Ridley represented the League on the joint committee. A large advisory council, drawn from various fields of administration, assisted the committee in its work.

Supported by a grant from the Spelman Fund the committee conducted a two-year study of municipal reporting. Its conclusions were incorporated in a monograph, *Public Reporting*, published by the Municipal Administration Service in 1931.[177] Wide distribution of the document was given by the League, the *American City*, and several state leagues of municipalities. Secretary Forbes estimated that almost 45,000 individuals had been reached by these circulation methods.[178]

With the assistance of a grant from the Columbia Foundation of San Francisco, the League in 1941 established a Municipal Reporting Consultant Service for

California under the direction of Miriam Roher, formerly a member of the League's editorial staff. The Service was designed to offer to public agencies and civic organizations advice and help in preparing annual reports, newspaper articles, leaflets, radio programs, and other material. Before war conditions caused its discontinuance in August, 1942, the Service had prepared reports for Berkeley and for the civilian defense activities of Oakland and San Francisco.[179]

MEASUREMENT STANDARDS

The establishment of standards for measuring the efficiency of municipal services has long interested the League. In 1912 the *Review* published an article, "Efficiency Standards in Municipal Management," by Jesse D. Burks, director of the Bureau of Municipal Research in Philadelphia.[180] Since then a number of articles on the subject have appeared in the League's journal.[181] Secretary Dodds in 1927 undertook the preparation of a pamphlet on standards of municipal administration, each chapter to be written by a specialist or committee on such topics as general administration, public welfare, police, fire, public health, planning and zoning, parks and recreation, and public works.[182] The next year a National Committee on Municipal Standards was created, with representatives of the League, International City Managers' Association, American Municipal Association, and Governmental Research Association. Charles A. Beard, New Milford, Connecticut; A. E. Buck, New York; and H. M. Waite, Cincinnati, represented the League on the joint committee. Officers of the committee were: H. M. Waite, chairman; Charles A. Beard, vice-chairman; and Clarence E. Ridley, Chicago, secretary.[183]

A tentative report, *Units of Measurement for Street Cleaning, Refuse Removal and Disposal,* was prepared by Dr. Ridley and published in 1929.[184] Funds to support the work of the committee for a three-year period were granted in 1929 by the Julius Rosenwald Fund and the Local Community Research Fund of the University of Chicago. Donald C. Stone, assistant director of the Committee on Uniform Crime Records of the International Association of Chiefs of Police, was employed in January, 1930, as full-time director of the work.[185] The committee coöperated with the Committee on Uniform Street Sanitation Records of the International Association of Street Sanitation Officials and with the Committee on Uniform Crime Records of the International Association of Chiefs of Police.[186] Since 1930 the work has been carried on principally by the International City Managers' Association.[187]

MUNICIPAL ADMINISTRATION SERVICE

A new agency for municipal improvement, the Bureau of Municipal Research, was established in New York in 1906. The municipal research idea spread rapidly and the League early invited its leaders to discuss the new movement at the annual convention. In 1908 Dr. William H. Allen and Rufus E. Miles of the New York bureau discussed the methods and achievements of their organization,[188] and in 1909 Mr. Miles reviewed the growth of the municipal research movement during the past four years. The first volumes of the *Review* contained several articles on research and reference bureaus.[189]

Mention has already been made of the paper by Dr. Willoughby at the 1910 conference in which he suggested that the League should assume the leadership in the formulation of a program for the improvement of the business organization and administration of cities.[190] In the discussion which followed this paper, Dr. Allen urged that the League should take immediate steps to establish a fund of sufficient size and under such conditions as would permit the organization of a central bureau which might act as a general clearinghouse for information relating to municipal administration and also as a center of research into all subjects related to municipal government and methods of administration.[191] A Committee on a Program for the Improvement of Methods of Municipal Administration, with Dr. Willoughby as chairman, was appointed but was discontinued in 1911.[192]

Informal sessions of representatives of a number of research organizations were held in connection with the meetings of the League in 1914 and 1915. At the 1916 meeting the conference on municipal research formed a temporary organization, The Association of Governmental Research Agencies, and elected an executive committee. A permanent organization, the Governmental Research Conference, was formed by the representatives of nineteen governmental research agencies of the United States and Canada in attendance at the meeting of the League in 1917.[193]

Sixteen times since 1917 the annual meetings of the League and of the Governmental Research Conference have been held jointly, and in other ways coöperation between the two organizations has been close.[194] Governmental researchers have served on many important League committees, contributing technical information and much hard work. From the time of removal of its headquarters to New York in 1920 until 1939 the League occupied offices adjacent to the New York Bureau of Municipal Research. Beginning in 1921 each volume of the *Review* has carried notes on the activities of the Governmental Research Conference. Several joint committees of the two organizations have been established. Russell Forbes, who became secretary of the League in 1928, served as secretary-treasurer of the Governmental Research Association from 1926 to 1931. Since 1926 Mr. Forbes had been the director of the Municipal Administration Service, a joint enterprise of the League and the Association, which will now be described.

Formation of a national organization to promote the bureau movement, to formulate a national research program, and to give technical assistance and advice to local bureaus, was discussed in the early meetings of the Governmental Research Conference. Between 1919 and 1924 definite proposals were submitted by Jesse D. Burks, St. Louis Bureau of Municipal Research; C. P. Herbert, St. Paul Bureau of Municipal Research; L. D. Upson, Detroit Bureau of Governmental Research; and R. E. Miles of the Ohio Institute. None of the plans could be carried out because of lack of finances. In 1922 Professor Charles E. Merriam of the University of Chicago, in discussing the organization of municipal research, commented on the lack of coördination of the many studies of municipal problems and emphasized the need for an "adequate central clearinghouse for interchange of information, and for mature analysis and interpretation of all the various types of data collected."[195]

During 1923–1924 Secretary Dodds assumed the leadership in the movement to establish a central clearinghouse for the governmental research field under the joint supervision of the League and the Governmental Research Conference. Approval of the project was given by the executive committees of both organizations and plans for the organization and financing of the new research agency were formulated.[196] At the 1924 meeting the Council authorized the appointment of a committee of seven to prepare a program of enlarged activity for the League, the membership to include leaders of the Governmental Research Conference who were interested in the establishment of a national bureau of governmental research. President Frank L. Polk appointed on the Committee on Expansion the following: Henry M. Waite, West New York, New Jersey, chairman; R. E. Miles, Columbus, Ohio; Lent D. Upson, Detroit; Charles A. Beard, Luther Gulick, Richard S. Childs, New York; and Thomas H. Reed, University of Michigan.[197]

After thorough consideration of plans worked out by two subcommittees, the committee prepared and submitted to the Laura Spelman Rockefeller Memorial in April, 1926, a request for a grant of $15,000 per year for a period of three years for the purpose of establishing, in coöperation with the Governmental Research Conference, an administrative research department. In May, 1926, an appropriation was made by that agency to the League of the sum of $15,000 for each of three years, beginning September 1, 1926. In announcing the organization of the new service, Editor Dodds pointed out that the League's usefulness would be greatly increased by extending to the administrative field the service which it had been rendering in the field of structure and organization of government.

Commencing on October 1, 1926, the new department, under the title of Municipal Administration Service, operated in connection with the League office for a period of six and one-half years. Originally a governing committee of three members of the League and three members of the Governmental Research Conference, with the president of the League acting as ex officio chairman, supervised the work. In 1929 three members were named to serve on the governing committee by the International City Managers' Association, and in 1930 a similar arrangement was made with the American Municipal Association. Presidents Frank L. Polk, Richard S. Childs, New York; Murray Seasongood, Cincinnati; and Harold S. Buttenheim, Harold W. Dodds, New York; and Henry M. Waite, Cincinnati, represented the League on the governing committee during the time the Municipal Administration Service was functioning in New York. George H. McCaffrey, Boston, the first director, resigned on January 1, 1927, and was succeeded by Russell Forbes, New York, who continued as director until the removal of the Service to Chicago. Esther A. Crandall, Milwaukee, served as librarian until August, 1929, and her successors were E. K. Ostrow and Edna Trull, New York. Welles A. Gray, University of Kansas, was assistant director from 1928 to 1930 and was followed by Frederick L. Bird of New York.[198]

Five distinct activities were carried on by the Municipal Administration Service. (1) Promotion and conduct of research in the application of sound administrative methods to government, by furnishing an opportunity for the publication of reports and by applying constructive criticism in their preparation and editing.

(2) Publication of technical pamphlets, as well as statistical and other data on public administration. Thirty monographs on administrative problems, incorporating the best techniques developed in practice and through research, were published. Abstracts of noteworthy research reports made by research bureaus were mimeographed, and a statistical series presented figures on important phases of administration in some of the larger cities. Publications were widely distributed among public officials and also furnished to contributing and sustaining members of the League and to members of the Governmental Research Association.[199] (3) Conduct of an inquiry service on best methods of administration for the benefit of public officials, research bureaus, chambers of commerce, and interested citizens, many of whose inquiries required a large amount of original research by the staff. (4) Maintenance of a research library of publications and materials on municipal administration. This library served as depository of all publications issued by research bureaus. From April, 1929, to November, 1932, the librarian edited a section in the *Review,* giving brief reviews of reports and pamphlets received. (5) Acting as secretariat of the Governmental Research Association. From 1926 until November, 1931, the director of the Service served as the secretary-treasurer of the Governmental Research Association, and edited a department, "Governmental Research Association Notes," in each issue of the *Review* during that period.[200]

When the original Spelman fund grant expired in 1929, a renewal was sought and obtained to May, 1932. Under the terms of the renewed grant it was necessary for the Municipal Administration Service to secure contributions from other sources to match in part the Spelman appropriation. Contributions from the organizations represented on the governing committee were relied upon to match Spelman funds until May 1, 1932, and after that to continue the Service on a limited basis. During 1931–1932 the director and governing committee carried on negotiations with the Brookings Institution of Washington, D. C., which had made a tentative proposal to move the Municipal Administration Service to Washington and to make it an integral part of the Brookings Institution. The proposal involved enlarging the enterprise into a public administration service to cover the fields of national, state, county, and municipal administration, with the retention of the existing governing committee in an advisory capacity.

These plans were never consummated because of lack of funds. Instead, on the invitation of Louis Brownlow, director of the Public Administration Clearing House, the Municipal Administration Service was moved to Chicago in the spring of 1933. The name was changed to Public Administration Service, and Charles S. Ascher, assistant director of the Public Administration Clearing House, became director of the Publications Division and Donald C. Stone, director of the Consulting and Research Division. Secretary Jones represented the League on the governing board composed of the directors or the secretaries of these groups: Public Administration Clearing House, American Public Welfare Association, American Municipal Association, United States Conference of Mayors, Municipal Finance Officers' Association, Governmental Research Association, International City Managers' Association, and American Legislators' Association.[201]

In response to a critical situation in which thousands of local and state governmental units found themselves in financial difficulties, the Council and Executive Committee approved in November, 1933, arrangements to establish the financial Consultant Service for local governments in distress. The League announced that it was prepared to assist state and local governments through this Service by making financial studies, refunding plans, administrative surveys, drafting charters, and providing legislative counsel. The League was also prepared to cooperate in improving local financial conditions by assisting in the organization of a Pay-Your-Taxes Campaign and by recommendation of more efficient methods of tax collection.

An advisory committee, consisting of Harold S. Buttenheim, chairman, and Richard S. Childs, Frank H. Morse, Carl H. Pforzheimer, Laurence A. Tanzer, New York, was appointed to have general direction of the Service. Professor Thomas H. Reed of the University of Michigan, one of the foremost authorities in the country in the field of local government and administration, was selected as director. Dr. Reed had had a long record of experience with both the theory and the practice of government. In California he had served as secretary to Governor Hiram Johnson, as city manager of San Jose, and as professor of municipal government in the University of California. He was the author of numerous books and treatises on government. An authority on metropolitan government, he had served as consultant to consolidation commissions in Pittsburgh, St. Louis, and Oakland, California. At the time of his appointment as director Dr. Reed was chairman of the Committee on Policy of the American Political Science Association, of the Committee on Civic Education by Radio of the National Advisory Council on Radio in Education, and of the League's Committee on Citizens' Councils for Constructive Economy.[202]

A contract between the League and Dr. Reed was signed for a five-year period, beginning January 1, 1934. According to its terms the League assumed no responsibility for the conduct of any survey, for the findings of the director, or for the financial soundness of a municipality. It was not liable financially in any way and was not to use its general funds for the work, but agreed to supply the Consultant Service with office space and with incidental clerical assistance in its promotion. Salaries of the director, his assistants, and other expenses were to be paid from fees collected for service to contracting cities. After payment of all expenses, any excess was to be divided between the League and the director, 75 per cent to the League and 25 per cent to the director. During the life of the contract the director agreed not to engage in similar work independently.[203]

Despite the protest of a Chicago firm of consultants against the policy of the League in entering this field, the Executive Committee and the advisory committee decided that in the League's history there was ample precedent for the Service and voted its continuance.[204] During the five-year period the Consultant Service conducted more than twenty-five studies for cities, counties, and citizen groups in New York, New Jersey, Connecticut, Massachusetts, Maine, Pennsylvania, Ohio,

Georgia, and Florida.[205] In most instances a financial and administrative survey was made, sometimes accompanied by a refunding plan. City and county consolidation was studied in Jacksonville, Florida; in Brookline, Massachusetts, the survey was of park and recreation activities. For Essex County, New Jersey, a history of twenty years of government in the county was prepared. In Nassau County, New York, following the survey, the Consultant Service drafted the county charter, which went into effect on January 1, 1938. New Bedford, Massachusetts, employed the Service to make a charter study. The Atlanta, Georgia, report covered all functions of the city and county governments and also the city and county school systems.[206] Many of the reports were made available for distribution by the League.[207]

Dr. Reed accepted a position as director of studies for the National Republican Program Committee and resigned as director of the Service on June 1, 1938. Thereupon the Executive Committee appointed Secretary Jones as director to carry on the work in hand and to report possibilities for continuation and expansion of the Service to a special advisory committee composed of Frank H. Morse, chairman, Frederick L. Bird, Harold S. Buttenheim, Arnold Frye, John S. Linen, Carl H. Pforzheimer, New York. Secretary Jones reported to the Council in November, 1938, that the apparent need for a service to work primarily with citizens' groups had convinced the advisory committee that the Service should be continued.[208] A summary of the financial relationship between the League and the Consultant Service to June 1, 1938, revealed a total income to the League of slightly more than five thousand dollars.[209]

Since 1938 the Consultant Service has conducted surveys of Bar Harbor, Maine; White Plains and Rome, New York; Passaic, New Jersey; Wallingford, Connecticut; Augusta, Georgia; Cincinnati; the Cleveland Metropolitan Area; Wicomico County, Maryland; Richmond County, Georgia, and of other communities.[210]

SUMMARY

That good city government is dependent not only upon improved organization but also upon sound administration was early realized by the League. Important sections of the first Municipal Program dealt with taxes, assessments, indebtedness, accounting, civil service, and franchises. On these problems and many others, the League has organized research committees and has published significant reports and model laws. Successive editions of the Model City Charter have incorporated the best administrative practices. Through the Municipal Administration Service and the Consultant Service the League has initiated and developed plans and methods for the more efficient operation of local government.

As a citizen organization the League has effectively coöperated with the governmental research group and other associations in the field of public administration. Its task is to translate the results of research by experts into popular form and then, through all the media of education, to promote the acceptance of the program through citizen action.

VIII

Education and Promotion

THE WORK of the League falls logically into two parts. First is the development of a program for better local government. In previous chapters outlining this program we have seen that most of the research and technical work for the League is done by volunteer committees, carefully selected and representative of the best academic and practical thought in the country on each specific subject. "When our committee reports are published," said Secretary Russell Forbes, "they are then the basis for education and promotion. The promotion of our principles with legislators and city councils is one of our most important tasks. . . ."[1] This is the second phase of the League's activities.

By what methods is this promotion accomplished? Not by political action, it can be positively stated. The League is a nonpartisan organization; the constitution states that it "shall have no connection with local, state or national political parties or political party issues as such."[2] It does not enter local campaigns supporting or opposing specific candidates for office, nor does it seek appointment of its members to public posts. It is not a lobbying organization. It has never engaged in personalities or muckraking.

From the beginning the League has relied upon an educational program to accomplish its objectives. Improvement in municipal government, said President James C. Carter, would be attained "not by going into partisan politics, but by arousing a public sentiment which would demand better officials and better government."[3] One of the objects of the League, as stated in the constitution, is to "develop a sound public opinion on questions of government. . ."[4] And President Harold W. Dodds once said that the long-term program of the League was "the education of a nation in civic standards and administrative proficiency."[5]

One is, therefore, naturally interested in the character of the League's educational and promotional work. Has the League an aggressive, militant promotional policy? In its long history, has there been any change in its educational methods? The Council in November, 1917, disclosed at some length the question whether the

---

[1] For notes to chap. viii, see pp. 241–245.

League should be more active in promoting its principles.[6] On the following day the annual meeting continued the discussion and authorized the appointment of a Survey Committee to study the League's organization and activities.[7] This committee reported in 1918: "The League has for the most part maintained the conservative attitude of a scientific society or an academy of learning in the domain of municipal reform, studying causes and remedies in an impartial and critical spirit, and attempting to establish by common consent an orthodoxy of reform among the leading intellectual spirits in the municipal field." The committee believed that the League would fail of its highest usefulness if it did not "promptly assume the role of militant and aggressive leadership in the advocacy of these well established political principles and doctrines." In its opinion, the League should become "a vigorous leader and advocate, rather than a passive observer and critic," and should organize a "program of frank and vigorous pamphleteering and propaganda...."[8]

Shortly after the adoption of a number of the Survey Committee's recommendations several changes in policies occurred. Headquarters of the League were moved from Philadelphia to New York, and a more active campaign of pamphleteering in the fields of city, county, and state government was begun. A field director and charter draftsman was employed. Closer relations were established with a number of national civic organizations and other groups. Campaigns for the city manager form of government, for state administrative reorganization, for the short ballot, and for improvements in county government were pushed with greater vigor. Speakers on various subjects were furnished; material was prepared for the press; numerous inquiries were answered; and assistance furnished to college classes, charter committees, campaign committees, and civic organizations. A number of technical supplements and campaign pamphlets was issued.[9]

Besides the promotional methods above mentioned, in 1929 a publicity department was established in charge of a trained newspaper man, and during the depression of the 'thirties, the radio was effectively used to promote the League's program and to help in the Citizens' Councils and Pay-Your-Taxes campaigns.

PUBLICATIONS

Chief among the educational agencies of the League are publications. These include the *National Municipal Review*, "Books and Pamphlets," "Campaign Pamphlets," the "National Municipal League Series" of books, the "National Municipal League Monograph Series," *Proceedings* of the annual conferences for good city government and of the League, addresses in the Radio Series, "You and Your Government," and books and pamphlets of a miscellaneous nature. To this list should also be added the publications of the Municipal Administration Service and the Consultant Service.

"NATIONAL MUNICIPAL REVIEW"

Establishment of a journal for the League or the adoption of some existing publication as its official organ was discussed at the first meeting of the Board of Delegates in May, 1894, and the question was considered at many subsequent meetings of League officials. In 1911 the League approved the report of a special committee recommending the publication of a magazine and the first number of the *Review* was issued in January, 1912.[10] For five years (1912–1916) it was issued quarterly; it was published bimonthly from January, 1917, through March, 1919; and from May, 1919, it became a monthly. Three national journals have been consolidated with the *Review;* namely, *Equity* (1919), the *Short Ballot Bulletin* (1920), and the *Proportional Representation Review* (1932).

Editing the *Review* has been the responsibility of the secretary, except for the period, 1928–1933, when secretarial and editorial duties were separated.[11] Assistance to the editor has been given, at various times, by associate and assistant editors, department editors, review editors, contributing editors, and an advisory editorial board or council.[12]

The *Review* records monthly, through its major articles and departments, the progress of improvements in municipal, county, and state government. Articles are contributed by academic men, professional researchers, public officials, editors, civic leaders, and laymen. No payments are made for such articles. Naturally most of the material deals with local government in the United States, although significant developments in European and Latin American countries are not neglected. Many series of articles on important aspects of local government have been published.[13] In 1919 the practice of giving over an entire issue of the magazine to a special problem was begun, and during 1921–1922, as an economy measure, several committee reports and technical pamphlets were published in the regular issues of the *Review.*[14]

Shorter articles in the form of notes and comments are found in the different departments. At various times the *Review* has carried departments on judicial decisions, public utilities, municipal engineering, public health, headlines, contributors in review, national defense and the cities, the local front, and notes regarding the activities of the Governmental Research Association, American Civic Association, City Managers' Association, National Conference on City Planning, Civic Secretaries Association, and American Municipal Association. Present departments, including date of estabilshment, are: "Books in Review" (1912); "Editorial Comment" (1919); "The League's Business" (1920); "Letters to the Editor" (1935); "News in Review," including the following sections: "City, State and Nation" (1912), "County and Township" (1934), "Taxation and Finance" (1934), "Proportional Representation" (1932), "Citizen Action" (1940); "Local Affairs Abroad" (1925), and "Researcher's Digest" (1939).

The editorial and business office of the magazine is that of the League in New York; publication office is in Worcester, Massachusetts. Copyright for the magazine is held by the League. Contents of the *Review* are indexed in Public Affairs Information Service, International Index to Periodicals, Index to Legal Periodicals, and Engineering Index Service. The *Review* is used by the League to advertise its own publications and those of several organizations in allied fields. Attempts to increase the sale of advertising space in the magazine have not been successful.

The Survey Committee made a number of recommendations regarding the *Review.* These included employment of an editorial secretary; making it a monthly;

the use of editorials, illustrations, and more attractive subject titles; a change of typography and paper; and a different name.[15] Improvements in the journal during the past twenty-five years have been along the lines recommended by the committee. Within the last fifteen years several changes in cover design, color, and make-up have added to the attractiveness of the magazine. A slight reduction in the size of the *Review* was made, beginning January, 1939.

Suggestions for a new name for the journal have been made on numerous occasions.[16] The Survey Committee commented: "Successful circulating managers tell us that the name 'National Municipal Review' is a handicap and that it makes little initial appeal to the mind of the layman. They say that the word 'municipal' suggests unwelcome public duties, struggling civic leagues, city hall technicalities, and a sense of effort."[17] Among the titles proposed have been: "Government," "American Government," "Civics," "Democracy," "Local Government," "Constructive Democracy," "Government in America," "American Civic Journal," "Civic Affairs," "Civic Preview," "Public Affairs," "National Civic Review," "American Citizenship," "Civic Progress," "Review of Public Affairs," and "Democracy in America." The principal arguments for the change in name are that the title does not reflect the present character of the magazine nor indicate the scope of the expanded program of the League in the fields of county and state government.[18] However, no agreement on a new name has been reached by the officers of the League.

Other proposals for increasing the effectiveness of the magazine have been considered by the Council, the Executive Committee, and the editorial staff at different times. The most important of these suggestions have been: reduction in the subscription price; engagement of a full-time editor; employment of state and municipal reporters; a larger free list of newspaper editors; a combination with other magazines in the same field; more revenue from advertising; discontinuance of the book review department; publication of articles which could be syndicated for use in state municipal league journals; payment for specially prepared articles by noted writers; more attention to problems of smaller cities, to certain social problems, and to the romance of the movement for better government; and popularizing the *Review* to enlarge the scope of its reading public. A two-day session of League officers in 1931, at which the work program was critically examined, reached the conclusion that efforts should be made to improve the present editorial policy of the *Review* rather than to take the more drastic step of adopting a totally new one.[19]

What is the purpose of the *Review*, how is it used in the League's educational work, and how effective is it as a promotional organ? The principal purpose of the magazine is to furnish a monthly chronicle of progress in local and state government. It ascertains the facts and publishes articles on important problems facing public officials and others interested in governmental improvement. Many important research studies by League committees and technical pamphlets are published as supplements. Announcements of items of interest to members, election of officers, committee appointments, dates and programs of annual meetings, are published, usually on "The League's Business" page.

In announcing to the meeting in 1911 the decision to establish the *Review*, the chairman of the Executive Committee said, "It is not designed that it shall be the organ of the League in the sense of representing any particular propaganda; it is to be the medium of discussion from every point of view, a genuinely national journal."[20] The Survey Committee recommended a policy of "militant and aggressive leadership" in advocacy of the League's principles and doctrines,[21] and Richard S. Childs, in 1919, enthusiastically announced that henceforth the League would "propagate and proselyte," and "lobby" for the enactment of its program. The *Review* would have editorials and opinions, and would become "less of a 'review' and more of a crusader."[22] Since 1920 the magazine has been used to promote the League's program, namely, city manager plan, improved county government, short ballot, state administrative reorganization, proportional representation, citizen education and action, and other reforms. Many of the articles are designed to show that the adoption of these reforms would bring about economies and improved service. But the other side of the question is not ignored; for example, it is admitted that the city manager plan has not been successful in all cities. Both sides of many controversial questions are given.

Copies of the *Review* go to all members and subscribers,—the academic group, public officials, editors, governmental researchers, civic leaders, and laymen. As stated by the Survey Committee, "The men who buy and read the *Review* are the serious, responsible, progressive and farseeing leaders of political thought in their respective communities."[23] In many college and university classes in political science the *Review* is required reading,[24] and practically every text and monograph on government and administration draws heavily for material upon its articles and supplements. Scores of unsolicited endorsements are annually received in the League office. Secretary Harold W. Dodds accurately characterized the publication as "the indispensable newspaper of the political reformers and political scientists carrying material that is to be found in no other publication. . . . It is closely read by a large section of its subscribers as their sole professional publication and its influence upon them is authoritative and rarely questioned. By reason of the *Review* and our pamphlets a local reformer . . . can quote the whole experience of the country in support of his projects and bring to the debates, legislative hearings and platform committees abundant evidence to support his pleas."

BOOKS AND PAMPHLETS

At a Council meeting in 1915 Mr. Childs suggested the publication of certain articles of permanent value as supplements to the *Review*.[25] In September, 1919, the first supplement to the magazine was issued. As explained by Mr. Childs, "Our typical 'Technical Pamphlet' undertakes to tell the whole story of one reform proposal, the need for it, the advantage of it, all the trials of it and their working and the ideals to which it should measure up. . . ."[26] All committee reports since 1920, with a few exceptions, have been published as supplements. Included among the books and pamphlets are the Model City Charter, Model State Constitution, other model laws, publications on proportional representation, state reorganization, city management, housing, social security, and several special numbers of the *Review*.[27]

Copies go to all of the membership and an extra supply is used for sales purposes and for legislative promotion. They are widely used in college classes and accepted as authoritative by authors. Several have been translated into foreign languages. Some have proved to be very popular, running through several editions. The Model Laws above all have much affected legislation and administrative practice.

Campaign pamphlets.—Although a number of pamphlets and leaflets have been issued since 1894, the Survey Committee was convinced that much more "pamphleteering" must be done in promoting the League's program. A League without pamphlets was like an army without small arms. Furnishing information to local officials and civic organizations would do much to facilitate the acceptance of the League's ideas.[28]

Since 1920 more than a half-dozen small pamphlets have been issued, first as the "Pocket Civic Series" and later under the title "Campaign Pamphlets."[29] Concise, authoritative accounts, written in nontechnical language by the League staff, have been prepared on the short ballot, city manager plan, county manager plan, and other subjects. Hundreds of thousands of copies have been sold at bulk rates or distributed free to students, civic organizations, and interested individuals. Their most effective use is as campaign literature distributed in large quantities a few weeks before a local election turning on the acceptance or rejection of some governmental reform.

Beginning in January, 1938, the League has published a series of pamphlets under the title, "Democracy in the Modern World." These have contained short "success stories" of manager cities, with incidental mention of other aspects of the League's program. Considerable quantities were distributed in communities where there were movements to adopt or abandon the manager plan, and to local chambers of commerce, civic leagues, and banks.[30]

National Municipal League series.—In 1906 the Executive Committee adopted a resolution providing for the publication of a "National Municipal League Series." The League was to assume editorial responsibility but no financial obligations.[31] The purpose of the series was to publish papers read before the League and other material on various subjects.[32] Fourteen books in the series were published by D. Appleton and Company from 1911 to 1919.[33] These books were advertised by the League as "constructive handbooks on fundamental problems which confront those engaged in municipal affairs, by authors of established authority. Invaluable not merely to municipal administrators, but to students, teachers, and all public-spirited citizens." While the books were being published frequently in the series they were of great influence in the League's education work. A few are still standard works and their sale has continued to the present time. The series was officially discontinued in 1930.[34]

National Municipal League monograph series.—This series was inaugurated in 1925 with the intention "to deal in a practical and helpful manner with the technical phases of local government and administration. It is hoped thereby to present in book form material which must now be gleaned from a number of books and magazines or which, because of its specialized nature, lends itself to treatment in brief compass." Five monographs were published between 1925 and 1930 dealing with budget making, depreciation in public utilities, the merit system, the President's removal power, and public borrowing.[35] The book on the merit system was the report of a joint committee and proved to be a popular seller. Other monographs also have had considerable influence.

Proceedings of the Annual Conference for Good City Government.—From 1894 to 1910 seventeen volumes containing the proceedings of the conference for good city government and the annual meeting of the League were issued. Under the editorship of Secretary Clinton Rogers Woodruff the principal papers delivered at the annual meetings, with discussion, banquet speeches, list of officers and committees, were published in the *Proceedings*. These volumes constituted the most important publications of the League during this period. "While never attaining more than a limited circulation, the *Proceedings* reach those who read and digest and apply. Thus they have an influence more extended and potent than many more widely circulated books."[36] With the decision to publish a journal, issuance of the annual *Proceedings* was discontinued after 1910.

Other publications.—In addition to the regular publications just described, the League has issued a number of other books, monographs, addresses, pamphlets, and leaflets. Several books are not included in the series of books and monographs, such as *A Municipal Program*; R. T. Crane, *Loose-Leaf Digest of City Manager Charters*; *The Government of Metropolitan Areas*; G. H. Hallett, Jr., *Proportional Representation—The Key to Democracy*; A. E. Buck, *The Reorganization of State Governments in the United States*; and *Model Laws* prepared by League committees. Although not published by the League, about a dozen books on important governmental problems and several reprints of articles and addresses by League officers have been distributed through its office.

Handbooks.—Two of these were published, in 1904, and in 1914, giving information regarding League meetings, publications, constitution, officers, committees, and members. While Mr. Woodruff was secretary, a "Clipping Sheet" was distributed to newspapers. Eight volumes of addresses delivered in the radio series, "You and Your Government," were published and distributed by the League. Numerous leaflets and folders descriptive of League organization, methods, and activities, have been issued for use in membership and financial campaigns. Mention should also be made of articles and committee reports separately printed or reprinted from the *Proceedings* or the *Review*. Reports and monographs of the Municipal Administration Service, the Consultant Service, and of the Citizens' Councils and Pay-Your-Taxes campaigns should also be included in this list.[37]

DISTRIBUTION OF PUBLICATIONS

In the *Review* for November, 1927, it was stated that in the past three years more than 100,000 pamphlets had been distributed free on an education basis or at cost price in answer to requests. Orders had come from every state and from thirty foreign countries. Regarding the influence of this educational work the comment was this:

> Hundreds of high school and college students, coming voters, through use
> of our pamphlets have learned the principles of government which we advo-

cate. City, county and state officials have consulted our books and reports; a steady inpouring of 250 to 450 inquiries a month have been answered. Newspaper editorials have called attention to the principles advocated in selected pamphlets, portions of other pamphlets have been reprinted in weeklies, monthlies and dailies, and not infrequently we receive requests for permission to publish entire documents. All recently published readings on governmental questions for use as college textbooks include League publications.

During the next thirteen years more than 356,000 regular publications were distributed. These figures do not include the following: Individual radio broadcasts, 123,000; radio programs, 1,225,000; Citizens' Councils pamphlets, 27,000; Pay-Your-Taxes campaign, 25,000; Democracy Series, 206,000; *What's in the Proposed Constitution?*, 22,500. Distribution of League publications, which had declined during the war period, increased to a total of 102,604 in 1948, the largest in the League's history.[38]

The League has always attempted to make its publication program self-supporting through sales. Most of the time it has been compelled to finance publications from its general fund. Within recent years a small publication revolving fund has been accumulated.

Publicity Methods

Publications play a major part in the League's educational campaign. Other media of information have also been successfully used: radio, newspaper and magazine publicity, speeches, offering of prizes, answering inquiries, and circulation of letters and literature in membership promotion.

NEWSPAPER PUBLICITY

About 1906 a "clipping sheet" service was inaugurated. Editorials, news items, short quotations, extracts from papers read before the League, were sent in printed form, and at various intervals, to newspapers. In 1908 the chairman of the Executive Committee, Horace E. Deming, reported that the service was producing "most marked results."[39]

Grace R. Howe, assistant secretary, had charge of the detailed work in publicity and membership campaigns from 1920 to 1929. Her records show that three press releases were sent out during 1924–1925 and 7,864 during 1924–1927. In 1927 Secretary Dodds reported increased attention to League publications by other journals and newspapers. "It takes the form for the most part of partial or complete reprinting of letters, pamphlets, committee reports and articles appearing in the *Review*. The attention received from the financial press, the metropolitan newspapers and other governmental periodicals is particularly gratifying."[40]

At the suggestion of President Childs a public relations department was established in the League office in February, 1929, to report progress in local government and the activities and accomplishments of the League. Howard P. Jones, former newspaper editor and graduate student in municipal government, was appointed to head the new service. The response from newspaper editors was immediate and encouraging. Secretary Forbes stated the next year that the work of the League was receiving more widespread newspaper and magazine mention than at any time during the past fifteen years. He continued: "It seems undeniable that our public relations work has helped greatly in arousing public interest in all parts of the country in the general question of municipal reform."[41]

About 1,500 newspapers are now on the mailing list for League material. Through constant checking the list has been reduced to those newspapers which have shown by their editorial policy, character of news printed, or otherwise, that they are interested in such material. One or two releases a week go to a large number of newspapers, and special releases for particular areas are sent out daily. Feature articles are also prepared for magazines and Sunday supplements. Approximately 200 civic organizations receive certain releases. The syndicated editorial series, developed by Mr. Jones, has not been employed in recent years.

Every release is a factual statement based on articles or news notes in the *Review*, committee reports, and developments in local government as noted in newspapers and magazines. The city manager plan and the movement to improve county government are the subjects most frequently discussed. The National Conference on Government receives the most publicity during the year. This conference is covered not only by the local press but by the principal national news agencies, the Associated Press, United Press, International News Service, and Canadian Press. Little use is made of cartoons in publicity because of expense of production and lack of a staff artist.

The best friends of the League among newspapers, judged by use of its material and general attitude toward improvement of local government, are the Scripps-Howard chain, the Gannett newspapers, the Central Press Association, and Consolidated News Press. All national news agencies, as mentioned above, give special attention to the annual conference on government. New York City newspapers are particularly interested in items on the financial aspects of local government. Newspaper opposition to the League's program is seldom found, although an occasional criticism of the organization is voiced by newspapers during local campaigns for the city manager plan.

Articles are prepared for such magazines as *Survey Graphic, American City, Public Management, Christian Science Monitor, Independent Woman, Wall St. Journal, American Bankers' Association Journal*, and many others. Recently cooperation has been given to such national magazines as *Life, Time, Fortune*, and *Reader's Digest* in their search for test communities to be used as illustrations of progress in government. In this manner the accomplishments of several manager cities were given publicity in 1938. The League seeks no credit for this aid.

In offering to editors an informational service dealing with progress in state and local government the League has emphasized that it has nothing to sell except better government. No attempt is made to get publicity for the League as an organization, although every mention of its work brings inquiries for information. Frequently a release is keyed to some name so as to enable a check on its use. A conservative publicity policy is followed; the question of whether material should be sent is considered almost entirely from the standpoint of the newspaper editor himself. It is the purpose of the League to coöperate with newspapers and magazines in communities where there are reform movements. As Secretary Howard P. Jones said: "The enlarged publicity program has not been directed at newspaper space for the National Municipal League or city manager plan, but rather to encourage an *entente cordiale* with editors of newspapers and magazines, to show them that our purpose is to educate, and to help them with their own problems of governmental subject matter."[42]

Accurate methods of measuring the use and effectiveness of League publicity are not available. However, according to Secretary Jones, the success of the League's new policy "is proved by the large amount of editorial and columnist comment that our news releases have inspired; by the use of our releases by some of the largest newspapers in the country. . . and by requests often made by newspapers and wire services for specific releases or information."[43]

OTHER MEDIA

Speakers' bureau.—Secretary Woodruff spoke in explanation of the League's program on as many occasions as his busy schedule would permit. Since 1920 Secretary Dodds, his successors in that office, and members of the staff, have made numerous addresses on city and county manager government, centralized purchasing, improved election methods, and other aspects of the League's work. Professor A. R. Hatton and Walter J. Millard, field representatives of the League, spoke often and effectively on the city manager plan and proportional representation before civic clubs, luncheon clubs, women's organizations, and other groups. All of the presidents of the League have contributed much of their valuable time to this activity. A list of speakers is kept in the League office and many engagements are filled by these volunteer friends of reform. Unfortunately the League's budget does not permit payment of even a speaker's expenses.[44]

Information service.—An unspectacular but important service of the League is the answering of hundreds of inquiries monthly from interested citizens, officials, and civic groups. Sending a form letter or a publication will answer many inquiries, but others require special investigation and individual reply. The secretariat believes that the service, although time-consuming, is worth while.

Membership promotion.—Members of an organization may be considered as a source of financial support and also as a channel through which principles are promoted. In this latter sense membership promotion work deserves to be mentioned here. It is conducted by the staff principally by letters and distribution of literature. The general publicity program of the League, the annual convention, and answering inquiries are contributing factors.

Prizes.—Reference has already been made to the essay prizes offered to college and high school students.[45] Announcements about the prizes are made through the *Review* and by wide circulation of notices among colleges and universities. In this way publicity is given to the general program of the League and student interest in the organization is stimulated.

Radio and motion pictures.—In an article in the *Review* in 1922, Mr. Woodruff discussed the place of motion pictures in education for democracy. He foresaw in their use unlimited possibilities for dramatizing the great issues and ideas of modern civic life.[46] At the Council meeting in Chicago in February, 1931, Professor Charles E. Merriam of the University of Chicago suggested that films prepared by the League could be sold to universities and colleges for classroom use. Employment of the radio in connection with the League's program was discussed, and there was agreement that a wider use of the radio was desirable.[47] The question of expense alone prevented the immediate use of these media. How the League co-operated from 1933 to 1936 in the program of civic education with the Committee on Civic Education by Radio of the National Advisory Council on Radio in Education and the American Political Science Association has already been described.[48]

During 1938 the Executive Committee and Council discussed the question of co-operation with radio and motion picture groups in utilizing these media of education "for popular dramatic treatment of the values of democracy and ways of making it work." President C. A. Dykstra suggested the appointment of a committee including representatives of the League and leaders in the motion picture and radio fields, to study the problem. It was agreed that such a committee should be formed, but to date it has not been appointed.[49]

NATURE OF LEAGUE'S APPEAL

Has municipal reform been considered a moral or an economic question, a positive or a negative force? Is the League's appeal emotional or intellectual? How have leading reformers viewed the League's work, as a struggle for efficiency and economy or as a crusade for democracy in local government? Where has the emphasis fallen in the educational program, on political and structural improvements in local government, or upon the development of higher administrative standards?

Many of the men prominent in the formation of the League and in guiding its course during its earlier years looked upon municipal reform as a moral question and considered it to be the patriotic duty of all people of high ideals to enlist in the movement. President Carter said: "These men and women ... who had patriotic feelings and patriotic emotions in their breasts set themselves to work to see if they could not do something to bring order out of this chaos; to see if they could not do something to purify the government of our cities."[50] Charles Joseph Bonaparte, who succeeded Mr. Carter as president of the League, stated his belief that the question of good government in cities was "essentially a moral and only incidentally a political one...."[51] Secretary Woodruff hopefully recorded the growth of "civic patriotism" and the movement toward "righteousness and progress." Commenting on religious activity in behalf of better government, Mr. Woodruff declared that the problem was essentially a moral one.[52] The great work of the League, in the opinion of A. Leo Weil of Pittsburgh, has been "the creation and stimulation ... of high municipal ideals." Speaking at the same meeting William Dudley Foulke, of Richmond, Indiana, found the true measure of a city's excellence "in the development of the manhood of its citizens—the development of character."[53]

In early meetings of the League it was often affirmed that good city government was dependent not so much on good forms as upon good men, and also that a good citizenship was absolutely essential. A few typical quotations will illustrate. "The first essential for good city government is good citizenship" (Charles Richardson). ". . . that good government depends for its very existence upon good men, is the fundamental basis of municipal reform" (Clinton Rogers Woodruff). "To have a good city government in the United States we must, first of all, and before all else, have good citizens" (Charles J. Bonaparte). All, however, agreed that the evils of bad laws and charters were greatly mitigated when good men occupied the offices.[54]

A circular letter of 1911 from Secretary Woodruff inviting the coöperation of the clergy pointed out that apart from its economic and political aspects, the question of municipal government had a distinctly moral side. Promotion of a "general and intelligent moral development" was one of the principal objectives of the League. "From its organization the League has sounded the moral note, and has sought by spoken word and printed page to arouse the conscience of the American people to the gravity and importance of the municipal problems."

Emphasis on the moral aspects of reform declined with the passing of the early reform leaders, many of whom had been prominent in other moral crusades, such as civil service reform. During the past twenty-five years more attention has been given to the problem of developing a more efficient, more practical, and less costly form of government. An occasional circular to prospective members has called attention to the economies resulting from the League's work for efficient government. "It is no exaggeration to say that millions of dollars in taxes have been saved by the more efficient governmental methods developed by the League." But the League has not placed major emphasis upon the economic benefits to individuals through support of its program. Indeed, during the depression of the 'thirties, when a hysteria of indiscriminate tax slashing seized public officials, the League led a national movement to halt destructive economy in local government.[55]

The League was organized by men and women who had for years been fighting bosses and spoilsmen in their local communities. Early meetings concentrated attention upon the bad conditions of municipal government, with an analysis of causes and possible remedies. In this respect the work of the League during its formative years may be characterized as negative, as a fight against political bosses and machines and an effort to get better officials in public positions. However, it was soon realized that a positive, constructive program was necessary. The Louisville meeting in 1897 saw the appointment of a committee to draft a Municipal Program. This program and the work of other committees has already been described.[56] Today little emphasis is given to the slogan "Turn the Rascals Out." There is a realization that many public officials are doing the best they can under the circumstances, and that much more is to be gained by coöperation with them in installing better forms and techniques than by attacking them. In city manager campaigns, where advice is sought from the League, it counsels emphasis on the merits of the new plan and not upon personalities. League publicity stresses the positive benefits to be derived from adoption of its program. Of course, in proposing a program, the League is bound to point out that evils must be eradicated before they can be replaced by a sound system. In that sense the activity of the League is both negative and positive.

League officials frankly admit that their work has little emotional or dramatic appeal. Secretary Woodruff once declared that progress was neither "spectacular" nor "sensational," but "slow and sure and observable only in the final results."[57] In an article, "Drastic Proposals for a New National Municipal League," which was written anonymously "By Some of our 'Best Minds,' " this conclusion was reached:

> Civic work of this scientific-propagandist character is an acquired taste. It has no heart appeal and few friends with money. If we would cut out the science and make a lurid one-sided appeal for the direct primary, for example, in headlong disregard for any inconvenient facts, we would draw supporters and funds, but a sober revelation of the facts pro and con with technical proposals for correction of certain basic evils is too cold-blooded a process for most people![58]

Secretary Dodds acknowledged that funds must come from those of "unusual civic insight, who recognize that our appeal is not emotional or dramatic." In advertising the *Review* a 1927 circular stated, "Municipal betterment is not as spectacular as a burning ship nor as dramatic as a Belasco play. It isn't light work and it isn't light reading." And Secretary Forbes spoke of the difficulty of financing this type of work "which has little heart interest, and which appeals solely to the logic and the pocketbook of citizens."[59] An examination of letters used in membership campaigns reveals that the appeal is made to "public-spirited," "forward-looking," "intelligent," and "civic-minded" citizens interested in good government to join an organization which is worthy of their support because of its long record of accomplishments in the field of state and local government. Furthermore, it is argued that the informational service to members is of itself worth more than the cost of the membership.

Because its program is broad, including many specific reforms, the appeal of the League for support is necessarily general. As has been indicated, those interested in propaganda for a single reform will not give funds because the League is too scientific and impartial in its attitude. One League official insists that any appeal for funds must be based on an appeal to the feelings of those people who already share in a zest for the reform of local government.

Improvements in both the political and administrative aspects of local government are stressed in League publicity, but approximately three-fourths of its efforts are directed to improving the structure of local government through the city manager plan, county manager plan, short ballot, proportional representation, and other reforms. It must be noted, however, that changes in structure are naturally followed by improvement in administrative techniques. For example, the change to the city manager form usually brings with it not only the short ballot and nonpartisan ballot, but also important administrative improvements such as centralized purchasing, scientific assessment methods, sound budgeting procedure, and good personnel administration.

The educational policy of the League is directed toward assisting communities in working out their problems in a democratic way. It takes the position that what a community wants to do represents the democratic point of view, in which the

League is fundamentally interested. Horace E. Deming, chairman of the Committee on Municipal Program, insisted that the League's efforts must be directed "toward making city government a genuine representative democracy." Analyzing the provisions of the Municipal Program he concluded that a city under it was a "representative democracy." "The people are the government," he said.[60] To Mr. Childs the objective of the League's program has always been democracy. Its proposals for reform—city manager plan, short ballot, proportional representation, initiative, referendum, and recall—should be preached "in terms of a high crusade for liberty" and "couched in terms of democracy." He has little regard for such arguments as "lower taxes," "business-like government," or "efficiency." He is confident that it is possible to design "a government that will automatically and perforce be a democracy."[61]

Has the name of the League been a help or a hindrance to its work? The question of a change of name has been discussed at many meetings of the Council and Executive Committee. With the expansion of its program to include state and county government and with the absorption of other reform organizations have come suggestions that a new title be adopted. On behalf of a change in the organization's name it is contended that it is not a league and that the scope of its work is broader than municipal government. New names suggested have been: American Municipal League, American Governmental League, American League for Responsible Government, Academy of Democracy, and Academy of Politics. It has also been proposed that the term, institute, should be included in the title.[62]

ASSISTANCE TO LOCAL CITIZEN ASSOCIATIONS

Several forms of aid to local citizens groups through information service, a speakers' bureau, and distribution of literature, have been described. Mention should also be made here of the Consultant Service, which conducts financial and administrative surveys of local government, and the clearinghouse work performed for citizens' Councils.[63]

The Survey Committee thought that an important service of the League should be the furnishing of advisers to local civic organizations. "It should be equipped to send its representative to every constitutional convention and before every charter commission having under consideration improvements in which the League is interested."[64] In accordance with this recommendation a field director was added to the staff in 1920. Professor A. R. Hatton of Western Reserve University, who had been field representative of the National Short Ballot Organization since 1917, was appointed.[65] In 1921 Walter J. Millard, field secretary of the American Proportional Representation League, was added to the staff on a part-time basis.[66]

During the period, 1920–1925, Dr. Hatton was very active as charter consultant and speaker for the League. He drafted optional charter bills, city-county consolidation bills, and was called into consultation at local expense regarding charter drafting in a score of cities. He was the draftsman for the Cleveland city manager charter of 1924, and he and Mr. Millard had a leading part in the campaign for its adoption. Between 1917 and 1922 he gave assistance to constitutional conventions in Massachusetts, Illinois, and Louisiana.[67]

Secretaries Dodds, Forbes, Jones, and Willoughby aided in drafting charters, optional charter bills, home rule amendments, enabling legislation for city and county manager government, and bills for improved election and registration methods. Mr. Forbes prepared several state laws on purchasing. Frederick L. Bird, assistant director of the Municipal Administration Service, was frequently called in by communities as a consultant on public utilities. State reorganization bills for Arizona and Tennessee were written by A. E. Buck of the New York Bureau of Municipal Research, acting as a representative of the League. Secretary Dodds made several visits to Nicaragua as adviser on election and registration methods and he also was on General Pershing's staff as technical adviser in the Tacna-Arica arbitration (1925–1926) between Chile and Peru.

The League has published many model laws and charters setting forth its principles in a form available for adoption, but the organization does not lobby in local and state legislatures for passage of legislation based on its principles. At the request of an executive officer, a legislative committee, or a local civic group, the League will send literature, a representative to appear at hearings, and will assist in drafting legislation. It does not sponsor such legislation; it leaves that to local groups who are sufficiently interested in the League's program to make it their own. Friends at state capitals, or in other places, frequently notify the staff of the introduction of bills and ask that literature be sent. Some publications, for example, those on administrative reorganization, have been sent to members of all state legislatures. But the League is not a national pressure group introducing the same legislation in every state and lobbying for its adoption. Its publications are the result of careful research, representing the consensus on the particular subject. Its publicity policy aims to bring these principles before as wide an audience as possible. Consultation and advice will be given on request, but the League's work stops short of the point of political action.

Since, 1920 much of the effort of the League has been spent in promoting the city and county manager plans. In cities where manager campaigns are in progress or contemplated, the League furnishes information on the experience and campaign methods of other communities, provides literature at cost to be used in the education of voters, and suggests persons qualified as speakers or campaign advisers to be employed by the local group. Advice on campaign techniques is given to many community leaders and officials either in their cities or when they visit the League office. At the request of local groups assistance is given in the drafting of charters. Sometimes this is done by mail, and a whole charter or important parts of it will be sent to the secretariat for analysis and comment.

The League does not participate as an organization in local charter campaigns. It serves as a clearinghouse for information and seeks governmental betterment by long-range education. It is nonpartisan and tries to be scientific in its approach. The city manager plan, for example, is advocated because the League believes that it is the best form of government for cities. Should a better form of city government be developed, League officials say that that is what they would advocate.

A pertinent question may be asked here: could the League perform its work more effectively if it had local and state chapters? This problem is discussed elsewhere but brief mention of it here is appropriate.[68] Establishment of local chapters has several times been considered by the Council and Executive Committee.[69] In 1930 a Committee on Local Branches[70] recommended to the annual meeting that the League should not become a federated organization with local chapters. It recommended the creation of local membership councils to be built around the present local membership and those who later become members of the League.[71]

In his report for 1937–1938 Secretary Jones spoke of the importance of effective local and state organizations in promoting the League's principles, and said that he had been studying "the problem of knitting established organizations more closely to the League." He outlined the efforts being made, with the coöperation of J. W. Esterline, to establish in Indiana local branches or local civic organizations closely affiliated with the League, to function eventually under the supervision of a State Council of the League. Suggestions had been made that the League should serve as a clearinghouse for the activities and accomplishments of local civic groups and should assist in the formation of new civic organizations, possibly through the services of an organization adviser. Financial details had not been worked out, he said, but the need was obvious for closer coördination of League activity with state and local associations.[72]

A larger budget would permit the employment of field agents for consultation and assistance to local groups and would also permit the office staff to spend more time in the field in observing governmental conditions. "It is next to impossible," said Secretary Jones, "adequately to serve local organizations struggling with technical local problems from a desk in New York. Field work is essential."[73] Mr. Childs once described the League as "a manufacturing plant with a good quality and small quantity of civic output—and no selling force on the road. . . ."[74]

During 1938–1939, as a result of the funds made available by Mrs. Nellie S. Childs, the League was able to expand its field staff. Dr. P. P. Womer, former president of Washburn College and chairman of the Citizens' Council Committee of the League, arranged to serve full time in the field promoting the citizens' council movement. Dr. Roy V. Peel of New York University was appointed director of research for the League and was put in charge of a research program on the relation of the citizen to his government, undertaken jointly by the League and Indiana University. Elwood N. Thompson was added to the staff as a full-time field representative. S. Howard Evans was released by the Payne Fund to become director of the education project.[75]

Relations with Civic Organizations and Other Groups

Within the past fifty years, hundreds of organizations have been formed to bring about improvement in public administration on all levels of government, national, state, and local. Some are essentially citizen groups existing for the promotion of reforms such as the merit system, proportional representation, the short ballot, direct legislation, or the physical improvement of cities. Such an organization is the League with a broad program of reform which it seeks to translate into practice by an educational campaign. Governmental researchers and other technical workers are organized into national associations, and there are scores of organizations of public officials.[76] Of municipal reform groups in general Professor W. B. Munro has said: "The overlapping of effort among them is notorious. At times they are extremely jealous of one another. . . . Often there is every reason why two organizations should unite into one, thus saving both time and money—but they rarely do it." Reformers "should find some means of ensuring better team play among themselves."[77]

What have been the relations of the League with other civic associations, with professional governmental workers, and with organizations of public officials? Have such groups shown coöperation with the League's program, or hostility toward it, or just neutrality? Has the League absorbed any other reform associations, and what progress has been made toward amalgamation or federation of national civic agencies? What success has the League had in enlisting the support of women's organizations, labor unions, and business bodies?

We have previously noted that the *Review* has served as the official organ of the American Civic Association, the National Conference on City Planning, the Governmental Research Conference, the City Managers' Association, and the Civic Secretaries Association.[78] There has been overlapping of membership and of officers between the League and the National Civil Service Reform League; they have set up joint committees, and shared a general community of interest. Scores of civic and professional organizations have appointed members to serve on League committees, such as the American Judicature Society, the American Library Association, the Honest Ballot Association, the National League of Women Voters, the Public Administration Clearing House, the Brookings Institution, the Institute of Public Administration, and many others. The League has sent its secretary, other officials, or a committee to represent it at the annual conferences of many allied organizations or to speak before them.

Two organizations, the National Association of Civic Secretaries and the Governmental Research Association, sprang from the informal meetings of these technical workers at the annual League conferences. Since their formation both groups have maintained close working relations with the parent body.[79] The question has often been asked why these organizations separated from the League. Apparently it was their wish to have an association concentrated on their more specialized, technical interests. In other fields such as city planning, the development of organizations has been along the same general lines.

The civic awakening of the 'nineties, which saw the birth of the League, was also responsible for the creation of numerous other organizations in the municipal field. Some of them, such as the League of American Municipalities, the American Society for Municipal Improvements, and leagues of municipalities in different states, were composed of public officials and represented primarily the official point of view in municipal affairs. City managers formed an association in 1914, and today nearly a score of professional associations of public officials (the "1313" group), have headquarters in Chicago.[80] Coöperation of the League and the International City Managers' Association, especially since 1929, has been elsewhere described.[81] For three years, 1930–1932, the American Legislators' Association joined with the League in the National Conference on Government. Representatives of the public officials' associations have served on many League committees and made numerous addresses at annual conferences. Several organizations, along with the League, sponsored the Municipal Administration Service, and appointed members to the supervisory board. Louis Brownlow, director of the Public Administration Clearing House, has served as vice-president of the League and as a member of the editorial council for the *Review*. Mr. Brownlow has assumed responsibility for financing several conferences of League members and representatives of the Chicago group for the discussion of important governmental problems. His wide knowledge of public administration and his leadership in the official organizations have made his advice and assistance to the League invaluable.

In his reports to the annual conferences Secretary Woodruff noted the growth and work of associations of municipal officials in various states. He was authorized by the Executive Committee in 1908 to inquire into the question of closer affiliation of state leagues of municipalities with the League.[82] At Los Angeles in 1912, H. A. Mason, secretary of the League of California Municipalities, read a paper describing the work of his organization.[83] A Committee on State Municipal Leagues, appointed by the Council at this meeting to study the problem of affiliation, suggested a conference of secretaries of state municipal leagues in connection with the annual meeting of the League.[84] Upon invitation of the secretary such conferences were held with the League in 1914, 1917, and 1918. The 1917 meeting resulted in the formation of a Conference of State Leagues of Municipalities.[85]

A permanent national organization of state municipal leagues was formed in 1924 under the title of American Municipal Association. Its third convention was held at St. Louis in 1926 in conjunction with the League's meeting.[86] In January, 1929, the *Review* announced the inauguration of a new department, "American Municipal Association Notes," to be edited by the secretary of the Association. However, such notes were published in only two issues of the *Review*.[87] The Association has joined with the League and other organizations in appointing representatives to committees on reporting and on standards of measurement, and also to the governing committee of the Municipal Administration Service.[88]

Some observers have wondered why the League has not enlisted the state municipal leagues as local branches and secured more members among city officials. There are several plausible explanations. Official opinion as to the causes of bad city government and remedies for it, often honestly differs from that of citizen reform agencies. Many public officials consider the League a militant reform organization and are alienated by its vigorous endorsement of the city manager plan. Furthermore, their tenure of office is short; there is a high percentage of turnover; and many local officials lack a national or even a state-wide point of view.

Cordial and substantial coöperation has been given to the League by university and college professors of social science, particularly the political scientists. They have worked hard and often on many committees. A number have served as members of the Council and two recent presidents of the League, H. W. Dodds and C. A. Dykstra, are political scientists who also know the problem of administering great universities. Secretary Woodruff was a frequent lecturer on university campuses and Secretaries Dodds, Forbes, and Jones, while serving the League, have held part-time teaching posts in neighboring universities. Reference has been made to the work of League committees on the teaching of municipal government, to the use of the *Review* and other publications by college classes and by authors of textbooks on local government, and to League prizes and the activities of the intercollegiate division.[89] For several of the annual conferences universities have acted as one of the local hosts.[90]

At the 1917 meeting the Council discussed the question of closer relations with the American Political Science Association, and there were suggestions of joint meetings and even consolidation of the two organizations.[91] A joint meeting with the American Political Science Association was arranged in 1919 for the discussion of the Model State Constitution, and round tables on instruction methods were conducted under the auspices of the League's committee at the Association's meetings in 1908 and 1909. Coöperation of the two organizations in the radio series, "You and Your Government," has elsewhere been described.[92] At the meeting in Philadelphia in 1922, the American Academy of Political and Social Science broke its tradition of a generation and joined the League in two evening sessions. The 1918 meeting of the League was held in conjunction with the Conference on War Time Economy called by the Academy of Political Science of New York and the New York Bureau of Municipal Research.

Credit should be given here to the support which has been extended to the League by two magazines, the *American City* and the *Engineering News-Record*, covering in part the same field as the *Review*. H. S. Buttenheim, editor of the *American City*, has been a member of the Executive Committee and is one of the League's best friends. M. N. Baker, associate editor of the *Engineering News-Record*, was for many years a member of the Council and Executive Committee and three times a member of the Committee on Municipal Program.

Annually the League answers inquiries from scores of foreign countries and sends its literature to them. The Executive Committee in 1913 voted to affiliate with the International Municipal League, an organization sponsored by W. D. Lighthall, honorary secretary of the Union of Canadian Municipalities, and designed to bring municipal organizations in Canada, America, and Europe into a closer communication.[93] In the same year the meeting of the National Municipal League was held in Toronto, the only conference ever held outside the United States. The League is one of the organizations represented on the American Committee for the International Union of Local Authorities and has participated through official delegates at several meetings of the International Union held in foreign countries.[94] In 1925 the League arranged for specialists to prepare a series of fifteen articles on American municipal government; these were sent to the German Union of Municipalities and published in two special editions of its journals for distribution to all cities belonging to the International Union of Cities.[95]

The problem of the federation or amalgamation of national civic agencies has been before the League on a number of occasions. In 1901 the annual meeting voted to refer to the Executive Committee the question of the federation of the League with the League of American Municipalities, the American Society of Municipal Improvements, and other national bodies dealing with municipal problems.[96]

Further consideration of the federation of civic societies was continued at the 1903 League conference through papers and discussion by J. Horace McFarland, president of the American League for Civic Improvement; Charles Carroll Brown, former vice-president of the American Society for Municipal Improvements; Charles Mulford Robinson, secretary of the American Park and Outdoor Art Association; and Charles Richardson of the League's Executive Committee. A resolution was adopted approving the idea of a civic alliance and authorizing the Executive Committee to arrange for the League's coöperation. Next year Secretary Woodruff reported that an Alliance of Civic Organizations had been formed with the League, League of American Municipalities, American Park and Outdoor Art Association, American League for Civic Improvement, Architectural League, and the Eastern Conference of Public Education Associations as members. Three members of the League were appointed to serve as trustees of the Alliance.[97] In 1907 the Executive Committee had before it a report, submitted by its Massachusetts members, which suggested consolidation, federation, or coöperation with other national societies in the field.[98]

Multiplication of civic agencies continued to be a subject of discussion at League meetings. In his review for 1914 Mr. Woodruff argued that there was need for "one big organization of all the officials dealing with municipal problems" and expressed the hope that the conference of city managers to be held in December would take steps along these lines. J. Lionberger Davis of St. Louis wrote in the *Review* for 1915 an article entitled "The Danger in a Multitude of Organizations."[99] A luncheon session at the 1916 meeting on the subject of the coördination or amalgamation of civic forces heard H. S. Gilbertson, secretary of the National Short Ballot Organization, deplore the "present multiplicity of organizations" as the "greatest sort of impediment to our civic movements." He proposed that the League, the National Civil Service Reform League, the National Voters League, and the Short Ballot Organization unite in a new organization, capable of making "a big appeal to the imagination of the people." Raymond B. Fosdick of New York, in discussing Mr. Gilbertson's paper, thought that amalgamation of a number of separate national organizations would be extremely difficult. He believed also

> . . . that progress is not achieved in the fashion that Mr. Gilbertson implies. Reform is never accepted wholesale. Civic ideals never advance in a uniform line. A little progress in this direction is followed by a little progress in another direction, or from another angle. These advances are irregular, sometimes irrational, often without relation to each other, but by and by we find that the whole line has gradually moved forward. The result has been achieved not by a mighty drive but by a series of petty skirmishes. The methods by which human society changes its form may not be scientific but they have to be given pretty weighty consideration.

He suggested greater coördination of civic agencies in getting their ideas before the public. "Why should not all our many organizations club together to support a common selling agency or clearinghouse, whose business it would be to take the well established results of study and investigation, and by temperate, sure-footed, and dignified publicity put them before the entire country?"[100]

In 1917 the Council debated the question of the combination of several separate civic organizations but reached no agreement.[101] One of the questions submitted to the membership by the Survey Committee was this: "Would the effectiveness of the closely allied reform movements in these various fields be promoted by coördinating them under one association with a new name?" A majority of those who replied were doubtful or opposed to the proposal. Several suggested a federation of agencies and a general annual conference similar to the National Conference of Charities and Correction or the American Association for the Advancement of Science."[102]

After the League expanded its scope to include state and county government and developed a more aggressive promotional policy, there began a period of consolidation with other national organizations devoted to specific reforms. The absorption of *Equity* in 1919 was followed in 1920 by the consolidation with the Short Ballot Organization and the one-year union with the American Civic Association in 1921. The Proportional Representation League merged with the League in 1932. At various times suggestions have been made that the National Civil Service Reform League, the American Civic Association, and the National Popular Government League combine with the National Municipal League into a single reform organization. In 1932 the Council discussed the question of calling a meeting of representatives of a number of civic and research agencies for the purpose of consultation on their respective programs.[103] It should be noted here that since 1929 the annual meeting of the League, known as the National Conference on Government, has been held with the coöperation of several other national organizations.

Turning now to business, labor, and women's organizations, let us examine their attitude toward the League's program. At the 1897 meeting two papers on the businessman and municipal reform were read: "Commercial Organizations and Municipal Reform," by Ryerson Ritchie, secretary of the Cleveland Chamber of Commerce, and "The Business Man in Municipal Politics," by Franklin Mac-Veagh of Chicago. Eleven years later H. D. W. English, formerly president of the Pittsburgh Chamber of Commerce and chairman of the Pittsburgh Civic Commission, read a paper entitled, "The Function of Business Bodies in Improving Civic Conditions."[104] A Committee to Invite the Co-operation of Business Bodies reported to the 1901 meeting that eighteen organizations were already affiliated with the League, ten bodies had accepted the invitation for affiliated membership, and several other organizations had the matter under consideration.[105] Attention was called by the committee to the admirable work done by some of the leading commercial associations such as the Merchants' Associations of New York and San Francisco, the Cleveland Chamber of Commerce, the Ohio State Board of Commerce, the Scranton Board of Trade, and the Pittsburgh Chamber of Commerce.[106] In his annual reviews of municipal conditions Secretary Woodruff commented on the civic activities of commercial associations and the increasing interest of business men in municipal problems.[107]

The League has always had among its members hundreds of businessmen interested in municipal reform as a national as well as a local problem. During the economic depression of the 'thirties, banking and financial interests became conscious of the fact that good municipal administration meant good municipal credit. With hundreds of municipalities in default, they gave financial support to the League's national campaign for constructive economy and for the payment of taxes.[108] After the immediate crisis was past, the League organized a committee to study local government finance, with a number of financial leaders included in its membership.[109] It is a distinct gain to the League to have secured the interest of these groups.

One student believes municipal reform has relied too strongly on the middle and upper classes for support and has "never had a solid basis in mass support." In campaigns for the adoption of the city manager plan much of "labor's stock suspicion of newfangled municipal machinery" could be dissipated by more emphasis upon better municipal services and less upon the lowering of taxes. With the correct appeal, labor's interest in the improvement of local government could be secured, as the support given by organized labor to the new charter in New York City in 1936 demonstrated.[110]

In the past, labor has, generally speaking, supported parts of the League's program such as the manager plan, proportional representation, and the initiative, referendum, and recall. Statements of labor leaders regarding the benefits of the manager plan have been printed in *The Story of the City Manager Plan* and other League publications. In 1923 a staff correspondent of the *Portland Press Herald* visited fifty-three manager cities and came to the conclusion that organized labor approved the city manager plan of government.[111] Within recent years some labor organizations in Chicago, Philadelphia, Battle Creek, and other cities have shown antagonism to the manager plan.[112] Their objections stressed the point that labor would have inadequate representation on the council, that the plan would be used to the disadvantage of labor, and that it centralizes too much power in the manager. Complications arise from the split in the national labor groups and from the fact that labor, in order to secure its gains, has allied itself in some cities with the dominant political machine. Steps have been taken by the League to gather incontrovertible evidence as to labor's benefits under the manager plan in order to convince labor unions of the error of their position. Secretary Jones reported in 1938: "Closer relations are being developed with labor groups to provide greater opportunity for their members to understand the important developments in local government and their significance to wage earners."[113]

Women formed no small part of the attendance at the sessions of the Philadelphia conference in January, 1894, and they read papers there and at many later meetings of the League. In his annual reviews of municipal progress, Secretary Woodruff noted the growing interest of women in municipal reform and their contribution to it. An Auxiliary Committee of Women, formed in 1907, reported to the meeting of that year that its work had been tentative and its purpose was to find out what could be done with other women's organizations already in the field.[114] The first woman member of the Council, Mrs. Charles Farwell Edson of Los Angeles, was elected at the 1912 meeting.[115] Since then women have held important offices in the League and have been represented on many committees. In 1915 *Woman's Work in Municipalities,* by Mary Ritter Beard, was published in the "National Municipal League Series."

The 1912 conferences of the League and the General Federation of Women's Clubs were held in California, the former in Los Angeles and the latter in San Francisco. Secretary Woodruff attended the Federation meeting and later suggested to the Council at Los Angeles closer affiliation with the women's organization. A Committee on Relations with the General Federation of Women's Clubs made a tentative report to the 1914 meeting which was referred to the Executive Committee.[116] In another organization of women, the National League of Women Voters, the League has had a powerful ally. Mr. Childs, in 1921, welcomed "this fresh new civic army of women, an organized army, armed abundantly with enthusiasm and well aware of the enemy—and looking for ammunition."[117] Committee reports and other publications of the League have furnished the ammunition for many legislative battles waged by the national, state, and local divisions of this dynamic organization. Two officers of the League, Belle Sherwin of Cleveland, and Marguerite M. Wells of Minneapolis, have served as presidents of the National League of Women Voters.[118]

"As Others See Us"

It will be interesting to see how the municipal reformers have described themselves and also how others have viewed the reformers. By League officers and speakers, members of the organization are represented as optimistic, earnest, persistent, patriotic, and unselfish workers. President Carter denied that the League was composed of "mere theorists" or "perfectionists." "We are not cranks gathered together for argument of a fad; we are business men and professional men, regularly engaged in the ordinary pursuits of life, who happen to feel very gravely concerned over what we conceive to be, and which all will agree to be, the very low and degraded condition of our city government."[119] The League was organized, said Vice-President Richardson, "by men of the highest ideals, the purest motives, the truest civic patriotism."[120] Editor Woodruff was impressed by the earnestness of the participants in the annual meetings:

> The meetings of the League are never largely attended: but the delegates who do attend are present because of their deep and abiding interest in its work. They are the leaders of the movement in their respective localities. They come full of the subject, full of a keen desire to help and to be helped. Consequently the discussions are of a high order. There is no spread eagleism, no self-glorification, but always a sincere desire to know the truth and follow it.[121]

Mr. Childs contributed the following description of himself and his fellow reformers to the *Review* for July, 1927, under the title, "The Reformer":

> A reformer is one who sets forth cheerfully toward sure defeat. His serene persistence against stone walls invites derision from those who have never been touched by his religion and do not know what fun it is. He never seems victorious, for if he were visibly winning, he would forthwith cease to be dubbed 'reformer.' It is his peculiar function to embrace the hopeless cause when it can win no other friends and when its obvious futility repels that thick-necked, practical, timorous type of citizen to whom the outward appearance of success is so dear.

Has the League any outstanding, persistent critic? Are there any distinct foci of opposition to its program? Careful inquiries have revealed none. Mr. Childs says: "There [is] ... no organized opposition except inertia and political self-interest."[122] A few minor criticisms were discovered.

Two years after the organization of the League a monthly magazine, *City Government*, began publication; it was concerned with the practical aspects of municipal affairs. In announcing a national conference of mayors and councilmen to be held in the fall of 1897, the editor noted the "existence of the large and very talkative National Municipal League," and continued: "If clergymen, college professors, and doctors of law and medicine assemble from all parts of the country once a year for the purpose of advancing their theoretical plans for better municipal government, why not have a meeting of experienced city officials for the interchange of their practical views and absolute knowledge?" The annual conferences of the League have not been productive of practical results principally because of the fact that "the reformers, well meaning as they may be, have shown a disposition to criticize and destroy rather than a disposition to devise and construct." Municipal reform could best be handled by those with actual experience in city affairs, thought this journal.[123]

Secretary Woodruff, six years later, took cognizance of this antagonism but said, "... this feeling has long since passed away and those who were responsible for this hostile feeling have been replaced by those who believe that the largest measure of coöperation on the part of all concerned is essential to the elevation of American city life."[124] Some public officials today, it is true, still regard the League as a reform organization and are critical of its support of the city manager plan.

Most of the newspaper attacks upon the League have come as a result of its advocacy of the manager plan. A few examples will illustrate the character of this criticism. A Maine editor saw in the League's publicity for the manager plan "a deeply hidden purpose," and a newspaper in another state, after mentioning the League as the proponent of the plan, said: "Stripped of its camouflage, the manager form of city government is the phantasy of a set of pestiferous folks who always want to reform somebody." League officials were advised to turn attention to the reform of government at the national capital before attempting to "inflict their advice upon this part of the country."[125] Pointing out that Walter J. Millard had once worked as a Socialist organizer and lecturer, an Iowa critic wanted to know if the city manager plan was part of "The Socialist Challenge?"[126] The League was described by a former New Jersey mayor as "lurking behind the scenes" in its attempt to foist city management upon the public, and was derided as consisting of "one office man, two speakers and field men, and three stenographers."[127]

Opponents of the city manager charter in Charleston, South Carolina, made the amusing charge that the League was really a syndicate representing the manufacturers of materials used by cities and its purpose was to place its sales representatives in cities as city managers in order to obtain a monopoly of orders for city supplies. From an Iowa newspaper came the statement that League efforts on behalf of the manager plan were "for those who are or may want to become managers at princely salaries and at the expense of the innocent taxpayers."[128]

As a climax to this fantastic type of political attack, the following is quoted from a recall petition against the city council in Dallas, Texas:

> (Because) the said Councilmen, and each of them, and their appointee the said City Manager Edy, are operating the affairs of the City of Dallas under direct instructions and policies emanating from a trust-controlled organization known as the National Municipal League, . . . and which said "League" was organized, is financed and controlled by Wall Street trusts, and is purposed to inveigle the people of the towns and cities of the United States, by falsehoods and traitorous propaganda, into installing this corporate, imperialistic "City Manager" system, or "King's Agent" government, in all the towns and cities of the country.[129]

For every criticism noted, scores of unsolicited endorsements of the League and the *Review* are annually received in the secretary's office. These come from chambers of commerce, leagues of women voters, newspaper editors, public officials, college professors, librarians, governmental researchers, civic secretaries, League members, and interested citizens. A few have come from local officials and students abroad.

Leading newspapers have testified to the constructive work of the League. An editorial in the New York *Independent* said: "Altogether the League has been carrying on a group of activities of the highest usefulness to the cities of the country. It has been earnest in advocating higher standards and effective in suggesting ways and means for improvement." The Philadelphia *Public Ledger* wrote: "One of the most potent factors in arousing the people and stimulating public interest in municipal affairs has been the National Municipal League." *Every Evening* of Wilmington thought that the League had done "more for the betterment of municipal administration than any other agency of this character which now exists, or ever did exist, in this country." It concluded: "The direct influence of this League upon the practical operation of municipal government in this country has been surprising."[130] Welcoming the first issue of the *Review*, the editor of the Portland (Oregon) *Telegram*, commented: "The work that the National Municipal League has been doing these past 10 years needs no advertisement at anybody's hands. It has been a most powerful factor in arousing the intelligence and the conscience of the country to the call for better municipal conditions; and more than any other agency has directed public attention to the methods by which those improved conditions could be brought about."[131]

Writers on municipal, county, and state government are unanimous in their appreciation of the League's contribution to local government progress. Dr. W. F. Dodd wrote in 1922: "For current information regarding local government the *National Municipal Review* is indispensable."[132] In the same year Professor K. H. Porter invited the attention of students "to the splendid articles appearing regularly in the *National Municipal Review*."[133] Professor T. H. Reed declared: "The development of the municipal reform movement in this country can be best traced in the *Proceedings of the National Conferences for Good City Government*, for the period from 1894 to 1911, and in the *National Municipal Review*, from 1911 to the present."[134] Elsewhere Professor Reed designated the League as "the most influential organization in the field of municipal reform."[135] "The National Municipal League, for example," said Professor A. F. Macdonald, "has been responsible for important studies covering almost every phase of city government and administration. . . . *The National Municipal Review* . . . contains a wealth of information concerning municipal activities and problems."[136] Professor J. M. Gaus referred to the League as "the pioneer organization in the field of municipal reform with a policy of militancy. . . ."[137]

Professor W. B. Munro gives an entire chapter to municipal reform and reformers. After discussing different types of reformers, he makes the comment that they form national organizations to promote the "betterment of conditions in all American cities," and continued with this evaluation of the League:

> The outstanding organization of this type is the National Municipal League, a body which has existed for more than thirty years, during all of which it has contributed materially to the enlightenment of opinion on municipal affairs. Its membership is drawn largely from the two upper groups of municipal reformers, and more especially from that portion of the citizenship which, while not holding public office, is disposed to keep a close and intelligent eye upon those who do. The League has not sponsored any single reform or group of reforms. It has lent a hand to every project that looked both practicable and promising. It has been a clearing house for information and ideas. Its chief service has been the dissemination of knowledge concerning the facts of municipal government.[138]

A fitting conclusion to these comments of academic writers is the following tribute by Professor William Anderson:

> Among national non-professional organizations the *National Municipal League* easily outranks all others in importance. Founded only thirty years ago (1894), and never composed of many thousand members, it has nevertheless been the head and front of the advancing column, and a principal focal point for the dissemination of municipal information and the promotion of municipal reform throughout the United States. It has chosen to represent the great body of informed citizens and students rather than the politician and office holder as such, and it has been sufficiently catholic in its views to refuse to be the tool of any one interest or to stake its existence upon any one reform proposal. It is, in fact, the reform programme of this league, first adopted in 1900 and then revised and reaffirmed in 1916, which furnishes most of the material for this chapter. This programme covers most of the important phases of the municipal problem in America today. The *National Municipal Review* and other publications of the League are our principal sources of information upon the progress of municipal reform in all its branches.[139]

SUMMARY

To secure the adoption of its program the League carries on a constant campaign of citizen education. The chief instruments in this work are its publications, newspaper publicity, speakers' bureau, information service, and provision of assistance to local civic groups. All of these are used in the campaign to attain democratic, efficient local government. In all educational work emphasis is placed first on the positive benefits to follow through adoption of the League's program.

Within the last fifteen years the League has expanded its publicity program, employing modern methods in the hands of trained people. At no time in its history have the League's activities been brought before a larger audience and with greater effectiveness. Careful attention has been given to the attractiveness of League publications and a distinct improvement can be noted.

With other associations in the public administration field the League has successfully coöperated in many joint enterprises. It has been the parent body for the civic secretaries and governmental research group. Amalgamation or federation with other groups has made a little progress. Business and financial interests and women's organizations have accorded the League generous support, and efforts are being made to convince organized labor of its stake in improved local government.

Since the League is not a lobbying, muckraking organization, and does not engage in political campaigns, it has escaped violent attack, though an occasional criticism of its activities is heard. Newspapers, publicists, and academic writers are practically unanimous in their praise of the League as a national citizens' organization working for the betterment of local government.

IX

Problems of the League

THUS FAR we have been concerned primarily with the League's program, what it is, how it is formulated, and by what methods it is promoted. Other important problems remain to be discussed: how is the League organized for its work; who supplies the leadership in direction and strategy; what is its financial condition and prospects; what is the program and policy for the future?

ORGANIZATION

In describing the government of the League it will be our purpose to determine (1) whether the constitution reflects the present organization and condition of the League, (2) whether the League is a federal or integrated group, (3) whether local branches would be desirable, (4) whether the name should be changed and headquarters removed from New York, and (5) finally, whether the present organization is suitable to the needs of the League and, if not, what changes are required to facilitate its present and future programs.

OFFICERS

According to the Constitution the officers ot the League are a president, a first vice-president, a second vice-president, not more than twenty-five regional and honorary vice-presidents, a treasurer, and a secretary. Nominations for president and vice-presidents, and members of the Council are made by a nominating committee appointed by the president and election is ratified by the members at the annual meeting. The Council annually appoints the secretary and the treasurer. Provision is also made in the constitution for an Executive Committee and for the appointment of committees for the investigation of special subjects.[1] Several other officials, not mentioned in the constitution, and the office staff complete the League's organization.

Thirteen persons have served as president of the League.[2] To mention the names of James C. Carter, Charles J. Bonaparte, William D. Foulke, Lawson Purdy,

---
[1] For notes to chap. ix, see pp. 245–248.

[173]

Charles E. Hughes, Henry M. Waite, Frank L. Polk, Richard S. Childs, Murray Seasongood, Harold W. Dodds, Clarence A. Dykstra, John G. Winant, and Charles Edison is to furnish proof of the distinguished character of the leadership it has enjoyed.

James C. Carter (1827–1905) of New York was elected the first president of the League in 1894 and served until 1903. Upon his retirement in 1903 he was elected honorary president, a position which he held until his death in 1905. A great jurist and author on legal subjects, he was a founder of the New York Bar Association and five times its president, president of the American Bar Association, and counsel for the United States in the Behring Sea Arbitration. Association with the city's attorneys in the Tweed case interested him in municipal reform; he served on a commission named by Governor Tilden to devise an improved form of government for the cities of New York State and later as a member of the Constitutional Commission.[3] As the first president of the New York City Club he had a leading part in calling at Philadelphia the National Conference for Good City Government and in organizing the League.[4]

Charles J. Bonaparte (1851–1921) of Baltimore was president from 1903 to 1910. Jurist, administrator (a member of President Theodore Roosevelt's cabinet), orator, publicist, and philanthropist, he was always a leader in the movement for governmental reform. One of the founders of the National Civil Service Reform League, he spent a lifetime in that cause.[5] A speaker at the Philadelphia conference, he became first chairman of the Executive Committee, a position which he held until his election as president in 1903. Upon his retirement from that office in 1910 he was elected vice-president, a post in which he continued until his death.[6]

The third president, from 1910 to 1915, was William D. Foulke (1848–1935) of Richmond, Indiana. Like his predecessor in the office, Mr. Foulke had a long and vigorous career in public service, his main interests being civil service reform and municipal government. For fifty years he was a consistent worker for the merit system, serving on the United States Civil Service Commission under President Theodore Roosevelt and as president of the National Civil Service Reform League, 1923–1924.[7] Mr. Foulke was chairman of the Committee on Municipal Program, which prepared in 1916 the revision of the Model City Charter of 1899.[8] After his retirement from the office of president, Mr. Foulke continued his interest in the League, serving as a member of the Council, 1915–1920, and as vice-president, 1920–1923.[9]

Succeeding Mr. Foulke as fourth president was Lawson Purdy of New York, 1915–1919. An expert in taxation, Mr. Purdy was secretary of the New York Tax Reform Association, 1896–1906, and president of the Department of Taxes and Assessments of New York City, 1906–1917. His other public interests were housing and building laws, city planning, and social welfare. In all of these fields he held important posts including the vice-chairmanship of the New York Commission on Building Districts and Restrictions, 1915–1916 and the office of general director of the Charities Organization Society of New York, 1918–1933.[10]

Charles E. Hughes (1862–1948) of New York was the fifth president, 1919–1921. Counsel for important investigating committees of the New York Legislature, governor of New York for two terms, associate justice and subsequently chief justice (1930–1941) of the United States Supreme Court, Republican nominee for the Presidency in 1916, leader of the American Bar, Mr. Hughes was, as the *Review* said, the best prepared of all public men "to coöperate in our enterprises by an accumulation of matured convictions based on experience as governor of our most populous state."[11] He resigned when appointed Secretary of State by President Harding.[12] While president, Mr. Hughes took special interest in state government and direct primary reform.

Following the resignation of Mr. Hughes, the Council elected Henry M. Waite (1869–1944) of New York as sixth president. He served for the period, 1921–1923. A distinguished civil engineer in private and public positions, Mr. Waite was the first city manager of Dayton, Ohio, from 1914 to 1918.[13] Long a worker in the civic field, he had been chairman of the Executive Committee for two terms, proving himself, as the *Review* said, "an invaluable friend and counsellor."

The annual meeting of 1923 elected as seventh president Frank L. Polk (1871–1943) of New York, whose term extended until 1927. Mr. Polk was well known for his services in the State Department and as head of the American Delegation to the Peace Conference at Paris in 1919. In New York City he had been president of the Civil Service Commission, corporation counsel, and a member of the New York Charter Commission, 1922–1923. For a number of years he had been treasurer of the New York Bureau of Municipal Research.[14]

From 1927 to 1931, Richard S. Childs of New York directed the affairs of the League as its eighth president. While building a successful business career, Mr. Childs has found time to be a leader in practically every reform movement in city and state government for the last forty years. With Woodrow Wilson he initiated the short ballot idea in 1909 and became its principal promoter. He is the "father" of the city manager plan.[15] For more than thirty years Mr. Childs has been most active in League affairs, serving as chairman of its finance committee for most of the period. Since his retirement as president in 1931 he has been chairman of the Council.[16]

Turning to the Middle West for its next leader the League chose as its ninth President, Murray Seasongood of Cincinnati, who guided the organization during the trying period, 1931–1934. Possessing a national reputation as a lawyer and a public official, Mr. Seasongood is also widely known as an author and lecturer on local government problems. He was one of the leaders of the reform group in Cincinnati and served for two terms as mayor (1926–1930) under the new manager charter. In addition to pursuing a busy professional career, he has been a part-time professor of law at the University of Cincinnati and a member and officer of many important public bodies and private associations.[17]

A former League secretary and editor of the *Review* became the tenth president when Harold W. Dodds of Princeton, New Jersey, was chosen at the 1934 meeting for a three-year term. Dr. Dodds was secretary of the League, 1920–1928, and editor of the *Review*, 1920–1933. An authority on municipal government, Dr. Dodds also achieved an international reputation as an expert on electoral methods and plebiscites, serving as adviser in several Latin American countries. He became lecturer in politics at Princeton University in 1925, professor of politics in 1927, and president of Princeton University in 1933.[18] Since his resignation as editor in 1933, Dr. Dodds continued as chairman of the editorial council of the *Review* for many years.

Clarence A. Dykstra (1883–1950) formerly president of the University of Wisconsin and later provost of the University of California, Los Angeles, became the eleventh president in 1937. Dr. Dykstra had combined in a successful career university teaching and administration, civic work, and municipal administration. He had been on the political science faculty at Ohio State University, at the University of Kansas, and at the University of California, Los Angeles; he had served as secretary of civic leagues and city clubs in Cleveland, Chicago, and Los Angeles; commissioner and director of personnel in the Los Angeles Department of Water and Power. From 1930–1937, he was city manager of Cincinnati. Under his management Cincinnati acquired the reputation of being the best governed city in the United States. During World War II, he was first director of Selective Service and chairman of the National Defense Mediation Board. In 1945 he returned to university life in Los Angeles as stated above.[19]

John G. Winant (1889–1947) of Concord, New Hampshire, twelfth president of the League, was elected at the annual meeting in 1940. Mr. Winant's distinguished career in state, national, and international affairs included service in the New Hampshire house of representatives and senate, as an officer in World War I, governor of New Hampshire, first chairman of the Social Security Board, and director of the International Labor Office at Geneva. In February, 1941, President Roosevelt appointed him United States Ambassador to Great Britain. He resigned this post in the spring of 1946 to become United States member of the Economic and Social Council of the United Nations. A liberal in politics, Mr. Winant was always interested principally in problems of social reform.[20]

At the annual meeting in November, 1946, the League chose as its thirteenth president Charles Edison of West Orange, New Jersey. Mr. Edison is president of Thomas A. Edison, Inc., and has had a long career of public service, serving as assistant secretary and secretary of the Navy. While governor of New Jersey, 1941–1944, he gained national attention through his fight against political bossism in his state and through his leadership of the nonpartisan movement of 1944 for a modern state constitution.[21]

It has been noted that in the first twenty-five years the League had but four presidents. The Survey Committee recommended changes in the office at intervals of two or three years and believed that this policy would "broaden the League's influence, create a new interest in its conferences, and bring into its councils and activities many other men of influence and ability."[22] Beginning in 1919 the policy of more frequent rotation of the presidency has been observed; the League has had nine presidents since that year.

Only five persons have served as secretary of the League. Clinton Rogers Woodruff (1868–1948) of Philadelphia, the first secretary, held the office from 1894 to 1920. Upon his retirement in 1920, Mr. Woodruff was elected honorary secretary of the organization. Mr. Woodruff became secretary of the Municipal League of

Philadelphia in 1891, was a member of the committee of arrangements for the Philadelphia Conference, acted as secretary of the meeting, and was elected secretary of the League at the first meeting held in New York City in May, 1894. In addition to performing secretarial duties, Mr. Woodruff edited the annual volumes of *Proceedings*, the *Review*, the books in the League series, and contributed scores of articles to magazines. Besides working for the League and other civic organizations, Mr. Woodruff found time for a law practice, for religious and social service work, and for holding important public offices. For two terms he was a member of the Pennsylvania Legislature; president of the Board of Personal Registration Commissioners of Philadelphia, 1906–1916 and 1919–1920; president of the Philadelphia Civil Service Commission, 1920–1924; special assistant city solicitor, 1924; director of public welfare for the City of Philadelphia, 1932–1936; and a trustee of the Free Library from 1908 to his death.[23]

At the meeting at Cleveland, December 29, 1919, the members of the League presented to their retiring secretary a gift bearing the following inscription:

As every institution is but the lengthened shadow of a man so the *National Municipal League* hereby gratefully acknowledges that it is but another name for

CLINTON ROGERS WOODRUFF

who has been for twenty-five years its devoted secretary, its organizing genius, its motive force, its guiding spirit.

He found the *National Municipal League* a mere project; he leaves it the central force of American civics. He found municipal reform a feeble aspiration; he leaves it the foremost achievement of modern democracy.[24]

On April 1, 1920, Harold W. Dodds of Cleveland became the second secretary of the League. Dr. Dodds graduated from the Grove City (Pennsylvania) College in 1909 and received the A.M. degree from Princeton University in 1914 and the Ph.D. degree from the University of Pennsylvania in 1917. He was instructor in economics at Purdue University, 1914–1916, and during 1917–1919 he served as executive secretary for the United States Food Administration in Pennsylvania. At the time of his appointment as secretary to the League he was assistant professor of political science at Western Reserve University.[25]

Upon the resignation of Secretary Dodds, effective July 1, 1928, the Executive Committee chose as his successor Russell Forbes of New York. After college graduation Dr. Forbes spent several years in chamber of commerce work. In 1922 he enrolled in the Training School for the Public Service of the National Institute of Public Administration. From 1923–1926 he was research secretary of the National Association of Purchasing Agents in charge of the field of government purchasing. At the time of his appointment he had been lecturer in municipal government at New York University for two years and director of the Municipal Administration Service since 1927. After his resignation in 1933 he became commissioner of purchase of New York City, and professor and director of the division of research in public administration at the New York University.[26]

Howard P. Jones joined the staff in 1929 as director of public relations and was elected secretary in 1933. Following several years of newspaper experience as reporter and editor, Mr. Jones did graduate work in political science at the University of Michigan and at Columbia University. He was instructor in journalism at the University of Michigan for two years; professor in the Columbia University School of Journalism, 1934–1939. Governor Lehman appointed Mr. Jones a member of the New York State Civil Service Commission in 1939, and arrangements were made for him to give one-half of his time to the League.

Mr. Jones resigned from the Civil Service Commission in January, 1943, to accept appointment as deputy comptroller of the State of New York in charge of the Division of Municipal Affairs. He was called to active duty as a major in the Military Government Division of the United States Army in the summer of 1943. The Executive Committee granted him a leave of absence as secretary for the duration of the war. Serving overseas with Military Government since 1943, he advanced to the rank of colonel before reverting to civilian status. In 1948 he received a permanent appointment in the United States diplomatic service.[27]

The present secretary, Alfred Willoughby, received his academic training at the University of Wisconsin and at Columbia University. With twenty years of experience in newspaper reporting, editing, and advertising, he was appointed assistant secretary of the League in 1937 and editorial writer for the *Review* in 1938. His title was changed in 1940 to executive secretary and he became acting editor of the *Review* in 1942. When Secretary Jones was granted a leave of absence in 1943 for the duration of the war, Mr. Willoughby was authorized to act in his stead during such absence. At the Nashville conference of the League, November 12, 1947, the Council appointed Mr. Willoughby secretary of the League and editor of the *Review*.[28]

The Survey Committee found that Mr. Woodruff performed the dual functions of secretary of the League and editor of the *Review*. This combination of executive and editorial work seemed to the committee too heavy for one individual, and accordingly it recommended the separation of the two duties and the employment of an editorial and research secretary.[29] Nevertheless, except for the period, 1928–1933, both executive and editorial duties have been performed by the secretary.[30]

Since 1894 only five persons have served as treasurer of the League. Elected treasurer at the first meeting in May, 1894, R. Fulton Cutting (1852–1934) of New York resigned on December 22, 1894. An officer or director in numerous corporations, Mr. Cutting was prominently associated with social, educational, and political movements in New York City. He was a founder of the New York Bureau of Municipal Research and an active member of the Charities Organization Society, Citizens' Union, and City Club.[31] His successor, George Burnham, Jr. (1849–1924) of Philadelphia, served from 1894 to 1919. When he resigned in the spring of 1919, Mr. Childs wrote in the *Review:*

> For over twenty years the quiet, helpful, genial presence of Mr. Burnham has graced the conferences of the National Municipal League. He commonly read no papers, made no speeches,—he was the treasurer. His own bookkeeper kept our accounts, at no cost to us. When the bottom of the treasury was bare,

the pay-roll money still came unfailingly. When his loans became large, he called them gifts and we started afresh. And finally this spring he volunteered thus to erase $3,000 of our war deficit in order to be allowed to resign.

The facts are themselves his tribute.[32]

After his retirement as treasurer, Mr. Burnham continued as a member of the Council and as vice-president.

To fill out the unexpired term of Mr. Burnham, the Council appointed Raymond V. Ingersoll (1875–1940) of Brooklyn, who served from April 1, 1919, until the annual meeting in December, 1919.[33] A practicing attorney, Mr. Ingersoll had served as city magistrate, campaign manager for the Committee of One Hundred in the New York City campaign of 1909, park commissioner of Brooklyn, and secretary of the City Club of New York.[34]

Frank A. Vanderlip (1864–1937) of New York, noted banker and formerly assistant secretary of the United States Treasury, was elected treasurer of the League in December, 1919, and served for two years. At the time of his election, it was stated in the *Review* that he "has not only had very broad experiences as a banker, but has held public office in two national administrations and has always kept closely in touch with important public questions."[35]

At a meeting of the Council on December 12, 1921, Carl H. Pforzheimer of Harrison, New York, was elected treasurer. Banker, patron of education and the arts, philanthropist, and collector of rare books and original manuscripts, Mr. Pforzheimer's interest in government "has come through active efforts for business-like practices in the administration of the city in which he lives."[36] Mr. Pforzheimer has taken an active interest in the League's work, particularly in the field of financial administration, and has been a generous contributor to the treasury.

In addition to those mentioned, the officers and staff of the League now include: George H. Gallup, Princeton, N. J., vice-president; J. W. Clise, Seattle, vice-president; George H. Hallett, Jr., associate secretary; John E. Bebout, assistant secretary; William Collins, chairman finance committee; and Elsie S. Parker, assistant editor of the *Review*.[37] Richard S. Childs, chairman of the Council, has been a volunteer unpaid member of the staff since his retirement from business in October, 1947.

COUNCIL AND EXECUTIVE COMMITTEE

General supervision of the affairs of the League, direction of its policies, and control of its property is vested in the Council. In many matters the Executive Committee acts for the Council.

Under the constitution and by-laws of 1894 the management of the League was placed in the hands of a Board of Delegates chosen by the member associations, and an Executive Committee, chosen annually by the Board. Growth in size of this Executive Committee led in 1904 to the creation of a small Business Committee, to which was transferred many of the powers of the Executive Committee *ad interim*. At the annual meeting in 1911 the constitution was amended to create the Council and Executive Committee, the former Executive Committee becoming the Council and the Business Committee taking over the name of the Executive Committee.[38]

The thirty members of the Council serve for three years, ten members being elected at each annual meeting. A member may not succeed himself until one year has elapsed. The retiring president of the League automatically becomes a life member of the council. Whether the president shall be chairman of the Council is optional. The organization of the Council involves the appointment of its chairman and six other members to serve as an Executive Committee for the ensuing year. Authority is given to this Executive Committee to select its own chairman. Between meetings of the Council and subject to its approval, the Executive Committee supervises the administrative work of the League.[39]

In selecting members of the Council an attempt is made to have all sections of the country represented, but it has been difficult to secure adequate representation from the southern states. Before 1912 there were no women on the Council, but since that time several women have usually been included in the membership each year. Ideal qualifications for councilors are real interest in the work of the League and a willingness to participate actively in the direction of its affairs. Entire success has not always been achieved in securing persons with these qualifications; in fact, there have been instances of the election of individuals who were not even members of the League.

For many years the Council held two meetings annually, one in the spring, usually in New York, and another in the fall along with the annual conference. Since 1930 there has been a tendency to hold fewer spring meetings; from 1930–1939, fourteen meetings were held, only three of which were in the spring. During the same period the Executive Committee held twenty-three sessions, all in New York. Attendance at Council meetings rarely includes more than one-third of the membership. The Executive Committee has a better record of attendance; to this no doubt its small membership and the fact that it is composed almost exclusively of members resident in New York or near-by cities, greatly contributes.

More frequent changes in the personnel of the Council and of the Executive Committee were suggested by the Survey Committee in 1918. Revision of the constitution the next year provided for the election of one-third of the Council membership at each annual meeting. The Survey Committee also questioned the wisdom of the policy of confining membership on the Executive Committee to persons resident in New York or Philadelphia. It concluded that the Executive Committee was "the real governing body of the League" and that Council activity amounted to little more than the ratification of the decisions of this Committee.[40] On the whole, procedure of the two bodies since 1918 seems to confirm this.

Some members believe that the influence and activity of the Council should be strengthened, and that it should be made the real directing body of the organization. At present, certain of its members individually, perhaps a dozen, rather than the body as a whole, appear to exert what influence the Council possesses. Its most active members are usually included in the membership of the Executive Committee. More careful selection of members would give greater vigor to the Council, and if the League had sufficient funds to pay the traveling expenses of members to meetings, improvement in attendance and activity would certainly result.

Since the conclusion of the war there has been an impressive increase in the attendance of officers and Council members at meetings and in their active participation in the affairs of the League.

COMMITTEES

No standing committees are provided for in the constitution. A nominating committee of five members must be appointed by the president at least ninety days before the annual meeting. All committees are appointed by the president, subject to confirmation by the Council or Executive Committee. The constitution stipulates: "No committee shall incur any indebtedness, make any expenditures, or represent the League in advocacy of or opposition to any project or issue, without the specific approval of the Council or Executive Committee, or such confirmation as may be clearly granted under general powers delegated to that committee by the Council."

The size of committees varies; a membership of seven, or even more, being common. Several important committees in recent years have acted jointly with committees from other national organizations, for example, that on Municipal Standards and Municipal Reporting.[41] These two committees and the Committee on Metropolitan Government were financed by special grants from foundations. Expenses of most committees are handled through the League's regular budget. Occasionally a committee is fortunate enough to secure as its secretary a professor who holds a research fellowship or someone with special training for investigation of a particular problem. Coördination of the work of committees is effected through the secretary's office, which furnishes clerical and stenographic services and edits and publishes each committee's final report.

Much of the important work of the League is done through its volunteer, unpaid committees. Some would say that the influence of the League is the influence of its committees. Experience has demonstrated the soundness of the committee system. A certain unevenness and lack of continuity may sometimes result, but this is offset by many obvious advantages. They bring together the best academic and practical thought on a special subject; they provide technical service which the League could never hire; they do work which the central office staff could not perform; they stimulate the interest of many people in the League's general program. A larger budget would permit great improvement in committee work by making possible the payment of the traveling expenses of members to meetings, by providing more research and secretarial assistance and better coördination through the central office, and by insuring prompt publication of reports.[42]

ANNUAL MEETING

Fifty annual meetings have been held by the League.[43] Nearly all have met in eastern and mid-western cities, with a few in the upper South, one on the Pacific Coast, and one in Canada. The constitution requires the meeting to be held in November, unless otherwise directed by the Council or Executive Committee. Conference periods have ranged from two to five days; since 1914 the trend has been definitely toward a three-day program.

From 1894 to 1910 the annual meetings were designated as Conferences for Good City Government. Since 1929 the meeting has been called the National Conference on Government. Many national organizations of civic workers, governmental researchers, and public officials have joined with the League in sponsoring these. The National Association of Civic Secretaries, Governmental Research Association, and Proportional Representation League have been the most regular in coöperation. The International City Managers' Association, the American Legislators' Association, the American Civic Association, the American Political Science Association, the American Municipal Association, and some others, have at times participated in these national conferences.

Attendance at annual conferences has varied according to the location of the city, interest in the program, and other factors. The Survey Committee found the best attendance in eastern cities and estimated that the non-local representation averaged about 150. "Fifty per cent of this number are the professionals who come practically every year. The attendance of city officials, except city managers whose association meets concurrently, has been exceedingly small."[44] In 1931 Secretary Forbes estimated that of an average attendance of 300, seventy-five would be governmental researchers, seventy-five university and college professors, thirty or forty public officials, and the rest laymen interested in government. Attendance at conferences held since the end of the war has markedly increased; approximately 700 people were present at the Boston Conference in 1948.

Professor Thomas H. Reed, active in League affairs for many years, commented in 1934 on the changed character of the annual conferences as follows:

> In the organization's earlier years, these meetings were attended largely by prominent citizens whose interest in municipal affairs, though vigorous, was unprofessional. They read papers to one another on the duties of citizenship, the evils of partisanship, the essentials of primary reform, and so on. Today these meetings are attended almost exclusively by highly trained and salaried specialists—employees of research organizations, secretaries of civic organizations, city planners, university professors, and city officials. The programs are devoted largely to rather technical discussions of financial procedure, traffic regulation, government of metropolitan areas, and related subjects. The prominent citizens continue to finance the forces of municipal reform, but the problems have become too specialized for them to take more than a minor part in the discussions.[45]

The chief purpose of the annual conference is to provide a means for the interchange of ideas and for a review of the year's work. Mr. Woodruff's address on municipal conditions and the progress of reform constituted a feature of the annual meetings for twenty-five years. The *Secretary's Report*, an annual inventory of progress, is now mimeographed for distribution at the conference. Meetings of the Council, Executive Committee, and other committees are held. Frequently the selection of the convention city and the nature of the program are arranged so as to influence local or regional conditions. The National Conference on Government has become well established as a real focus of news interest; more publicity is secured by the annual convention than by any other phase of the League's work. One League official, emphasizing the importance of the annual meeting, said that without it there would not be a League.

Thirty years ago the Survey Committee pointed out that the distance from convention centers at which many members lived and the heavy travel expenses involved in long journeys militated against a large attendance at the National Conference. It suggested, therefore, a number of regional conferences each year in addition to the National Conference,—these to be sponsored by the League along with local and regional civic groups and organizations of city officials. Such meetings would be of value to the regions and afford excellent opportunities for extending the influence of the League.[46] On several occasions the Council and Executive Committee have discussed this problem and there has been no disagreement as to the value of such a plan. Without funds for a larger field staff it has not been feasible, until recently, to put these suggestions into effect.[47]

As part of its expanded field service the League inaugurated in 1940 a new program of regional conferences on citizenship and government with conferences held at Atlanta and Minneapolis in February, and at Dallas in March. The League also coöperated with the Massachusetts Federation of Taxpayers' Associations in a one-day conference in March at Worcester on proportional representation and the council-manager plan. These conferences, jointly sponsored by the League and local civic organizations, "(1) opened up new territory for the development of the League's program; (2) brought to representatives of key citizens' groups in 15 states a concrete picture of the way to solve current governmental problems; (3) spread the story of accomplishments through the press and thus further widened the reach of the meetings."[48]

LOCAL ASSOCIATIONS

The League was originally "composed of associations formed in cities of the United States, and having as an object the improvement of municipal government."[49] Member associations chose representatives to the managing Board of Delegates and all voting was by associations. Individuals might be admitted as associate members but without the right to vote or act for the League in any way.[50]

In 1911 the constitution was amended to provide for individual as well as association membership.[51] The provision for association membership was omitted from the constitution as amended by the meeting in 1919.[52] Any individual interested in the objects of the League is eligible for membership. Five classes of membership are established by the Constitution: active, with dues of $5 per year; sustaining, at $10; contributing, at $25 or upward; patrons, at $100 or upward; and honorary life members, who are exempt from payment of dues. Members are enrolled from twenty-four foreign countries. Total membership on November 1, 1948, was 2,565. In the last four years membership has increased 40 per cent, with a net gain of almost 400 members in 1948 alone.[53]

The constitution, as amended in 1919, provides that, with the approval of the Council, members of the League may establish "affiliated or subsidiary associations" to promote some specific reform. Permission is granted to use the League's name as part of their name, but no action or resolution of a local group shall bind the League unless Council approval is given. Affiliation with the League may be dissolved at any time by the Council.[54]

Only three local branches of the League have been established since 1920. A state-wide committee under the name of the New Jersey Chapter of the League was organized in 1921 to promote manager government in New Jersey. In 1936 a New York State Committee of the League was organized. It has held a number of meetings to consider problems of state legislation. Through a special subcommittee on the New York State constitution an educational campaign was conducted to promote public understanding of the important issues before the convention.[55] It later issued under the League's name a summary and analysis of the amendments submitted by the New York State Constitutional Convention.[56] During the convention in Toledo in 1936 a decision was reached by a number of local citizens to form a chapter of the League in the City of Toledo.[57]

On a number of occasions the Council and Executive Committee have considered changing the unified organization of the League into a federated organization with local chapters.[58] A Committee on Local Branches,[59] after reviewing carefully the arguments for and against local branches, reported to the 1930 meeting against the advisability of the League becoming at that time a federation of local chapters. It recommended as an alternative plan the creation of local membership councils to be built around the present local membership of the League and those who may later become members. Such an informal group, without a budget, could help in promoting the League's program, securing new members, stimulating financial support; it could also serve as a liaison agency between the League and local reform groups. Eventually it might "supply the leadership and serve as a stimulus for the promotion of a permanent militant local reform movement, either through the formation of a new organization which thereafter would function independently, or through the activity of some existing body."[60]

The constitutional name of the organization, indicating that it is a federation of local associations, has not been in harmony with the facts for over thirty years. This situation constitutes one of the most powerful arguments for a change in the official name. Although many new names have been suggested, none has received the approval of the governing bodies of the League.[61]

Proposals to incorporate the League had been discussed by the Executive Committee and the Council at several meetings since 1905.[62] A motion to incorporate under the laws of New York was approved at a meeting of the League held in New York City on September 18, 1923. The certificate of incorporation, dated October 23, 1923, stated that the League was "an association, having no capital stock and not organized for pecuniary profit. . . ."

HEADQUARTERS

For the first twenty-six years headquarters of the League were maintained in Philadelphia. The Survey Committee found the offices very much congested and recommended more commodious quarters.[63] In July, 1920, headquarters were established in New York City, where they have since remained.[64] Location in New

York has several advantages. It has afforded opportunity for close coöperation with the New York Bureau of Municipal Research, with its successor, the Institute of Public Administration, and with other groups. Many influential members live in the community, and important financial contributions have come from New York citizens and institutions. On the other hand, it is argued that the New York location means heavy traveling expenses for the large majority of the membership and makes it difficult to secure a representative attendance at Council and Executive Committee meetings. League principles have had more ready acceptance in the West and Middle West than in the East, it is pointed out. In the South there seems to be some suspicion of an organization centering in New York City, home of Wall Street and Tammany Hall. Some Council members have encountered criticism of the general tendency toward New York domination of organizations.

Within the past seventeen years several proposals to move the headquarters from New York have been considered. In 1931, when negotiations were under way to move the Municipal Administration Service to the national capital and to integrate it with the Brookings Institution, an invitation was extended to the League to move to one of the Institution's buildings in Washington.[65] Among the reasons urged for the transfer were that it would make possible close coöperation with the organizations in the "Brookings Community," would make available the resources of the Library of Congress, put the League in close touch with federal agencies serving cities, and enable the League to do more intensive work in and receive more support from the South. Opposing arguments were that Washington has no local self-government and that the League would be overshadowed by national affairs. The plans for the removal of the Service to Washington were never consummated.

Location in the Middle West has several times been debated. Removal to Chicago and affiliation with the public officials' organizations there has been suggested.[66] During 1938–1939, the Council and Executive Committee discussed other locations in New York City, in the Chicago area, and also the proposal of Indiana University for an affiliation with the League, with headquarters at Bloomington or Indianapolis. The necessity of moving the offices, because of the demolition of the building at 309 East Thirty-fourth Street, forced an immediate decision. Advantages and disadvantages of an institutional affiliation and a mid-western location were thoroughly explored at the Council meeting in Columbus. A majority of those present doubted the wisdom of too close an affiliation with any university and favored a location in the Chicago area, but not with the "1313" group. It was voted that a committee should be appointed to investigate the ultimate possibilities of financial support in the Chicago area and opportunities for transfer to that city.[67] The immediate problem of location was solved by the removal of the offices to 299 Broadway, New York City, on August 1, 1939.[68]

FINANCE

We are interested here in the amount and sources of income, in the methods which have been used to finance the League, and in the subject of budgeting and auditing of funds and other fiscal practices. Finally, the adequacy and stability of income and the problem of increased financial support will receive our attention.

SOURCES OF INCOME

At the first annual meeting of the Board of Delegates held at Cleveland, May, 1895, Treasurer Burnham reported receipts totaling $676.78.[69] In 1900 he stated that the average annual income for the five-year period had been about $2,380; membership dues amounted to an average of $1,400 per year and the remainder was derived from contributions and sales of publications.[70] The Survey Committee listed total receipts for the ten-year period, 1908–1917, showing an income of $10,135.13 in 1908 and $20,804.26 in 1917. Gross income during the last five years of the period averaged approximately $18,000 annually. The bulk of the income, the Committee found, came from membership dues and special contributions. An average of about $10,000 a year for the ten-year period had been derived from membership dues, and special contributions of from $25 to $500 had brought in an average annual amount of $5,000. Approximately 50 per cent of the total income was credited to membership dues and 25 per cent to contributions. Income from sale of publications, royalties on books, interest, and other minor items, accounted for the additional receipts of the organization.[71]

A report prepared for the officers and members of the Council in 1935 presented comparative data on receipts classified by sources for the fiscal years 1926 and 1930–1934.[72] The following table was incorporated in the report to show the total income in each year and the percentage of the total assigned to contributions, dues, sale of publications, and miscellaneous.

Year (ending Dec. 31)	Total Income	Contributions	Dues	Sale of Publications	Misc.
	Amount	Per Cent	Per Cent	Per Cent	Per Cent
1926	$32,381	54	32	12	2
1930	$45,326	63	28	7	2
1931	$50,562	60	29	9	2
1932	$39,117	63	31	5	1
1933	$27,339	52	41	6	1
1934	$39,396	58	27	10	5

Commenting on the significance of the data on income, the report called attention to these facts: (1) Receipts from membership dues have been the most stable, fluctuating only a few thousand dollars from year to year. (2) Drastic decreases in the amount of contributions have been accompanied uniformly by a deep slump in total income, showing the key position of this item. (3) Sale of publications has been playing a gradually improving part in the total picture since 1932. (4) A breakdown of the Miscellaneous Revenues . . . indicates that sale of advertising is the chief factor responsible for the heavier position of this item in 1926 and 1930–1931. For the four-year period, 1936–1939, income averaged $44,651 per year.[73]

Average annual income for the ten-year period, 1937–1946, was about $38,000. Of this amount 25 per cent came from membership dues, 5 per cent from sale of publications, and the remainder from contributions.[74] Income for each of the years, 1947 and 1948, was twice the annual income during the war years.

The League receives no income from endowment funds.[75] Nor have quotas ever been levied upon local associations. The original constitution provided that there should be no dues or assessments, and that no association should be liable for any sums except such as it might, from time to time, voluntarily agree to contribute.[76] Several grants have been made by foundations for a specific project, for example, the gift of $10,000 by the Russell Sage Foundation in 1925 for the metropolitan government study, the contribution of the Laura Spelman Rockefeller Memorial for the support of the Municipal Administration Service, and the grant of $10,000 by the Carnegie Corporation in 1933 for Citizens' Councils' work, as already noted.[77] In 1938 a gift of $25,000 a year for three years by Mrs. Nellie S. Childs made possible a significant expansion of the program of the League.[78]

During the last fifteen years the leading individual contributors to the League have been: Mrs. Nellie S. Childs, Richard S. Childs, Carl H. Pforzheimer, Murray Seasongood, John D. Rockefeller, Jr., Henry L. Shattuck, James W. Clise, George H. Gallup, George Arents, and Harrison S. Hires. Among foundations and corporations the most consistent supporters have been: C. F. Taylor Trust, Julius Rosenwald Fund, Economic and General Foundation, Davison Fund, New York Foundation, Thomas A. Edison, Inc., Carl and Lilly Pforzheimer Foundation, Lawson Purdy Fund, and Allied Stores Corporation.

METHODS OF RAISING FUNDS

As indicated, the major part of income has been derived from contributions and membership dues, which are deductible for United States income tax purposes. From the beginning, however, the League's activities have never been supported entirely from the dues of members. It has always been necessary to secure additional contributions to finance the program, and this problem has been the constant responsibility of League officials.[79] Several times the League has declined to employ professional canvassers as money raisers.[80] A finance committee has functioned at times in the raising of funds. This is not a regular standing committee, however, and its activities have usually been those of a few energetic members. Employment of a financial secretary and the formation of membership councils have frequently been discussed by the Council and Executive Committee, but lack of funds has prevented effective use of these agencies. The idea of securing contributions on a joint or coöperative basis with cognate organizations has not been favored by the governing committees.[81]

Too much of the burden of securing contributions falls upon the secretary and staff. This is an embarrassment to the staff and takes valuable time away from promotional activities. Their efforts must then be supplemented by assistance from members of the Council and officers of the League. In reviewing the financial history of the League certain individuals deserve special mention for their faithful and consistent support. At the head of this list is Richard S. Childs, the principal financial backer during the past twenty-five years. George Burnham, Jr., treasurer for nearly twenty-five years, and Carl H. Pforzheimer, treasurer since 1921, have been generous supporters. Louis Brownlow and Murray Seasongood showed their helpfulness on many occasions in time of need. Several friends in Cincinnati, H. M. Waite, Henry Bentley, Ralph Holterhoff, and C. O. Sherrill, raised several thousand dollars in 1930, at a time when the League faced a serious deficit. The Cincinnati City Charter Committee made a substantial contribution in 1932. The trustees of the Taylor Trust—Thomas Raeburn White, Samuel S. Fels, and C. G. Hoag—were a mainstay in the difficult financial period of the 'thirties. Special acknowledgment is also due to Frank H. Morse, to the Rosenwald fund, and to the Economic and General Foundation for their support in this period.[82] President Edison and William Collins are leaders in the financing program which was inaugurated in 1947.

The League has never been able to afford a membership and financial secretary and consequently the work of membership promotion has fallen upon the regular staff, usually upon the assistant secretary. Practically all of the work is done by letter. From 1920–1929, under the capable direction of Assistant Secretary G. R. Howe, the publications of the League—the *Review*, a reprint, or a pamphlet—were used to solicit memberships. Such material was sent to a selected group interested in that particular subject, together with an invitation to membership. As Secretary Dodds said in his report for 1926–1927: "It is necessary to carry on a constant campaign for new members. Of late years this has been made a part of the general educational work. People join the League because of interest in some subject of which we treat. Our free distribution of literature is to carefully selected lists of persons who are most apt to make use of it. Such persons also prove to be those among whom new members are most likely to be found." Also: "During the past three years an increasing number of professional people have joined. Prior to that time the majority of new members were moved by a more or less philanthropic purpose. Of late years the reason for joining appears to be a special technical interest in the subjects with which we deal."[83]

Within the past fifteen years more emphasis has been given to the general program of the League, with the point stressed that the League is worthy of support because of the work it is doing to promote democratic, efficient local government.[84] Many officers and members have coöperated by preparing lists of prospective members and by signing letters of invitation on their own personal stationery; these have been supplemented by letters from the secretariat.[85]

The Council of the League, meeting in Philadelphia in November, 1946, heard Executive Secretary Willoughby outline the urgent demand for the League's services and voted that the budget should be increased and that a specific plan of financing should be developed.[86] A plan for a larger budget was the principal subject of discussion at the meeting of the Executive Committee in New York later in the same month. It was agreed that the League had never conducted an adequate organized promotion; a campaign to raise at least $100,000 from previously untapped sources should be organized; there should be continuous follow-up and promotion; and a new type of promotional literature was needed.[87]

With a grant of $12,000 from the C. F. Taylor Trust of Philadelphia to support the first year of the plan, work on the financing program was started in February, 1947, by the League staff with the assistance of a consultant on finance. A brochure was prepared stating the League's goals for 1947 as (1) a material increase in the number of contributors, and (2) a budget of $110,000. The detailed plan to meet the League's present and future financial needs included these points: (1) at least one large pace-setting gift; (2) increased support from members of the Council; (3) appointment of a finance committee chairman; (4) initial solicitation in the New York area; (5) then solicitation in ten to fifteen selected cities; (6) further organization in fifteen to twenty-five other cities, and mail solicitation to increase ordinary membership; and (7) eventual support of the League by a large number of comparatively small gifts.[88]

A meeting of the Executive Committee, May 23, 1947, resulted in general agreement on the financing plan. Members pledged subscriptions and coöperation in securing contributors. President Edison was authorized to appoint a chairman and members of a finance committee.

William Collins of Yonkers, New York, accepted the chairmanship of the finance committee. Dividing the country into thirteen regions, Mr. Collins, aided by President Edison, other officers and members, and the headquarters staff, enlisted the coöperation of business and professional leaders in the financing and membership program. Income from contributions more than doubled in 1947. To the 1948 annual meeting of the League Mr. Collins reported a continued upward trend of memberships and contributions and the recruitment of additional allies for the financing program in different parts of the country.[89]

CONTROL OVER EXPENDITURES

Supervision and control of finances is vested by the constitution in the Council and Executive Committee. Subject to the approval of the Council, the Executive Committee is authorized, when the Council is not in session, to act for it "in all matters relating to the raising and expenditure of necessary funds; ... the annual audit of accounts, and the general management and prosecution of the work of the League." Committees of the League may not incur any indebtedness nor make any expenditures without authorization by the Council or Executive Committee. Article IX provides that no "disbursements of the funds of the League shall be made unless they shall have been approved and ordered by the Council or Executive Committee. All checks shall be signed by the Secretary and countersigned by the Treasurer, provided, however, that under disbursements authorized by the Council or Executive Committee, the Treasurer at his option may draw blanket checks in favor of the Secretary, to be disbursed in turn through checks signed by the Secretary."[90]

The budget for the fiscal year, January 1 to December 31, is prepared by the secretary and adopted by the Council at the annual meeting of the League. An annual audit is made by a firm of certified public accountants. League funds are kept on deposit at the New York Trust Company. Funds for specific purposes now include the Publications Revolving Fund, Committee on a Model Fiscal Program, and the Lawson Purdy Fund.

THE PROBLEM OF FINANCE

For more than a half century the League has struggled to improve local government with an inadequate and uncertain income. The League was born in a period of financial stress and its finances have gone up and down with the general levels of business prosperity. Ironically enough, in periods of economic instability, when its funds were low, the League has been confronted with its greatest opportunity for assistance to local government. During the last depression the League gained new strength from the support of banking and financial leaders who became convinced that good municipal credit must be based on good municipal administration.[91]

Surveying the decade of the 'thirties, we may say that during the first five years of the period, the League had a desperate fight to maintain its existence. Drastic economies and curtailment of staff and services were necessary. Only through the support of a few loyal officers and friends was the organization able to continue. By 1936 the financial condition of the League had improved and Secretary Jones was able to report to the 1937 meeting that "the financial problems of this past year have been those of financing a broader program rather than those involved in keeping our heads above water."[92] The gift by Mrs. Nellie S. Childs in 1938 permitted a much needed expansion of League activities, but presently war conditions compelled the League to operate with a reduced budget. In the post war period, however, there has been a most gratifying improvement in League finances.

In 1918 the Survey Committee recommended that additional revenue of $10,000 annually be raised to cover the cost of expanded services of the League. It suggested several possible means of securing the added revenue: (1) a campaign for at least one thousand new members; (2) a plan whereby cities and towns could receive the League's informational service through payment of an annual contribution; and (3) arrangements for local civic organizations to become affiliated with the League, receiving its informational service, speakers, and publications in return for an annual membership fee.[93]

Proposals for additional expenditures of $103,000 for enlargement of the work of the League were prepared in 1921 "By Some of Our 'Best Minds'" and printed in the *Review*. The article concluded: "Hence, we wait on funds!" but did not indicate how the funds were to be raised. Consolidation of the League and the American Civic Association would give an income of about $50,000 a year. To this should be added $100,000 for the financing of new projects and services.[94]

Files in the Secretary's office contain many memoranda outlining the financial needs of the League. From a study of these and other data it is conservative to say that the League needs 10,000 members and an additional budget of $100,000 to $150,000 per year.

This raises the problem of how the additional funds are to be secured. Prospects of endowment are remote. Affiliation with a university might afford some stability of income, but would, according to some Council members, have definite disadvantages. Large grants from foundations are possible, though past experience is none too encouraging. The possibilities of consolidation of agencies in the same general field have already been explored.[95] Seemingly, then, the League must continue to rely upon its traditional supports, membership dues and contributions. Income from sale of publications and from miscellaneous sources may contribute a small part to an expanded budget, but it is clear that subscriptions from individuals and foundations must continue to furnish the core of League revenues.

The scope of the League's activities are thus always limited by the condition of the treasury. There is no more important problem for the organization than that of securing and maintaining an adequate and stable income. The problem of finance is sometimes critical, at other times serious, and always a challenge.

PROGRAM AND POLICY

SURVEYS

Three times in its history the League has paused to take inventory and to make an audit of operations. During the annual meeting in 1917 the Council discussed at length the activities and program of the League.[96] The following day the meeting adopted a resolution authorizing the president to appoint a committee of five members, each from a different city, to

> ... examine into the records of the League, to analyze its contributions and subscription list, to inquire into its activities, to consider the possibility of increasing its income, extending its field of effort and perfecting a closer coordination of its work with other associations in closely allied fields of effort and to make a full report of its findings at the next annual meeting.[97]

Mayo Fesler of Cleveland was appointed chairman and the other members of the Survey Committee were: W. B. Munro, Harvard University; Richard S. Childs, New York; L. D. Upson, Detroit; and George C. Sikes, Chicago. This committee made a very careful study of the League's activities and submitted a report to the annual meeting in New York in June, 1918. Its eleven recommendations were approved and referred to the Council for adoption as soon as possible.[98]

Although some of these suggestions have already been mentioned, they will be given here as a whole. As approved, they were:

(1) The personnel of the Council and of the Executive Committee should be more frequently changed.

(2) Committees of the League should be given greater assistance and encouragement in their work, by supplying them with investigational service, and publishing their reports.

(3) Separate and more commodious offices should be provided for the League's secretary and assistants.

(4) An editorial and research secretary should be appointed to whom will be assigned all the editorial duties now performed by the executive secretary.

(5) The *Review* should be changed:

    a. By making it a monthly instead of a bi-monthly magazine.

    b. By improving its typographical appearance.

    c. By changing its name.

    d. By popularizing the reading matter contained in it.

(6) A committee on publications should again be appointed to give closer and more critical supervision to the editing of the volumes printed in the National Municipal [sic] series books.

(7) A special committee on annual conference should be appointed to work out a plan governing the arrangements to be made between the League and local committees for the holding of the annual conference.

(8) Regional conferences might be arranged by the League in co-operation with local civic and commercial associations.

(9) The League should develop its informational service by printing and distributing pamphlets and other reports, and become a vigorous leader and advocate of governmental reforms, not a passive observer and critic.

(10) An annual budget should be prepared and the League's accounting methods improved.

(11) Plans should be developed for increasing the membership and raising an additional income of, at least, $10,000 to meet the cost of the proposed increased service.[99]

A number of these recommendations were acted upon by the Council and Executive Committee. Others, though not adopted, remain, in the opinion of some League officers, germane to the present problems of the organization.

Before the annual meeting at Chicago in 1921, there was published in the *Review* an article, "Drastic Proposals for a New National Municipal League," from the pen of an anonymous author calling himself "Some of Our 'Best Minds.' "[100] The article was a plea for a better factual basis for the work of the League. Having outlined the expanded activities of the League during the past two years, the article pointed out what could be done with an additional $100,000. Among the proposals for an enlarged program were the following: (1) putting more people into touch with modern political reform principles and progress, by (a) employment of a trained editor for the *Review* and a field reporter, (b) a revival of the newspaper clipping sheet service to supply the press with news and facts on political reform, (c) organization of state chapters to consist of informal organizations with no local dues or paid staff, (d) a series of popular pamphlets, for wide circulation and for use in civics classes and college courses; (2) extension of the technical pamphlet series and a new pamphlet series of studies in municipal administration; (3) employment of three field secretaries and three campaign secretaries; (4) research in the problems of democracy through small grants to college professors of political science and postgraduate students; and (5) an allowance for committee secretaries.

A meeting of the Council held during the annual convention of 1930 decided to hold a two-day conference for consideration of the work program and future policy of the League.[101] This conference was held at Chicago, February 21–22, 1931. The agenda for the meeting, prepared by President Childs, called for a survey of "all work of the League: its present condition, character of membership, finances, its influence or its lack of influence, and what we would do with more money." Secretary Forbes reported on the budget and the activities of his office, and submitted pertinent data as to membership and legislative promotion. He presented also a table showing the work of the League analyzed by functions, subjects, and methods.

Committees on the *Review,* membership promotion, appeals to individuals and foundations for contributions, and public relations work and legislative promotion of League principles, were appointed to review these phases of the present work program. Meantime the meeting took up discussion of the real function of the League. "Is it to be a militant reform organization, or a scientific research body, or a combination of both?" It was the consensus of opinion that there could be no separation of the dual functions of the League.

Discussion of the report of the committee on the *Review* resulted in the conclusion that improvement of the present policy of the magazine should be attempted rather than adoption of a new editorial policy. The committee on membership promotion agreed that membership dues should never be considered as a means of financing the work of the League, but that reliance must be placed on contributions to meet the expenses of the secretariat. Membership would grow as the result of a vigorous policy and a dynamic organization. Establishment of membership councils and prompt employment of a membership agent were urged.

Mr. Childs, in reporting for the committee on appeals to individuals and organizations for contributions, said that it seemed rather well established that the League could not depend upon support from foundations for its general educational work; he thought it might reasonably hope to receive help from foundations to finance specific research projects. That the public relations work had greatly broadened the influence of the League was the conviction of the committee on public relations work and legislative promotion of League principles. Several new methods were suggested, including a speakers' bureau, more public addresses by members of the staff and lay members, and more observation of actual governmental conditions by members of the central office. In the ensuing discussion wider use of the radio was advocated and suggestion was also made that moving pictures and talking pictures should be used.

On the second day of the conference, it was voted to change the fiscal year, which began April 1, to coincide with the calendar year. Authorization was given to the Executive Committee to employ a financial secretary and to the president to appoint a finance committee. Once again there was discussion of changing the name of the organization but no decision was reached. Broadening the scope of the League to include the problems of housing, unemployment, and taxation, was urged. The need for a clarification of the programs of the League and eight other organizations in the general field of municipal government was pointed out. One member commented on the failure of the League to "tap the research resources of universities."

After this two-day discussion of officers, the first in League history, the meeting reached the general conclusion that the work of the League was being administered efficiently and that needed improvements would be found in an expansion of its present policies rather than in a drastic change in policy.[102]

An analysis of these three major surveys indicates that the problems confronting the League are not new, but are recurrent. Many of the suggestions have been adopted, but lack of funds has prevented the League from taking full advantage of several important proposals for expansion.

In any organization like the League differences of opinion as to scope, methods, program, and policy inevitably occur. Discussion usually brings about a compromise. We intend here to review briefly some of the conflicts of opinion and to see whether any fundamental division exists as to scope and program.

As already noted, the League in 1916–1917 voted to expand its scope to include state and county affairs.[103] This decision was opposed by some members, who thought that the League should confine itself strictly to the municipal field, where many problems remained to be solved. Others were willing to consider county and state problems only so far as they directly touched municipal affairs.[104] Among some opponents of the new program there was talk of forming another association devoted exclusively to the municipal field. Criticism of the program of the 1922 annual meeting because of extensive attention to federal problems resulted in the appointment of a committee by the president to report "upon the relative attention which should be given at future meetings of the organization to municipal affairs on one hand, and to state and national affairs on the other."[105]

Removal of headquarters to New York in 1920, popularization of the *Review*, and the change in the status of the League from that of a "scientific society or an academy of learning in the domain of municipal reform," into an organization with a militant, aggressive policy of promotion, were not accomplished without objections in some circles of League membership. The merger of the Proportional Representation League with the League in 1932 was voted by the Council, but not unanimously.[106] A protest was made by some Chicago members to the sponsoring of the Consultant Service by the League. Proposals for the removal of headquarters to Chicago or elsewhere in the Middle West have evoked differences of opinion in the Council and Executive Committee and no decision has been reached. Research committees are not always in complete agreement on reports and an occasional dissent is recorded.

These differences of thought are only normal for any citizen organization and reveal no fundamental cleavage in League ranks. There exists no old or young guard, no left, right, or center factions. Annual business sessions and meetings of the Council and Executive Committee are harmonious. About the only criticism of the League now heard is that it should do more work, provided funds could be secured.

SUMMARY

A review of problems of organization, finance, program and policy, reveals no crisis in the affairs of the organization. On the whole, the basic organization is sound, though certain improvements could be made. Distinguished people have served as officers and the secretariat has always been in capable hands. No serious divisions of opinion exist among members and officials as to the scope, methods, policy, or future program of the League. The problem of finance is, as it has always been, the principal factor in determining the scope and effectiveness of the League's program. A long-range solution to this problem is urgently needed.

X

Summary and Conclusions

THE THREE DECADES following the close of the Civil War have been called the "Dark Ages" of American municipal development.[1] Checks and balances, legislative meddling, and the lack of standardized forms of organization, resulted in a complicated structure of local government, full of confusion and irresponsibility. Systematic information regarding municipal affairs was scant, and there was a lamentable failure on the part of the citizens and the press to provide leadership in improving conditions. Boss and machine rule were further facilitated by the feeling of strong partisanship, the spoils system, the mass of ignorant voters, and by a cumbersome system of nominations and elections. Adequate safeguards for popular control and aids for scientific administration were nonexistent. Enormous expenditures to provide services for rapidly expanding cities and the development of public utilities and public works on a large scale furnished a fertile field for exploitation by predatory politicians.

Professor W. B. Munro says: "They were the days when our cities, in point of consistent maladministration, had none elsewhere to rival them. Tweed Rings, Gas Rings, County Rings and other plunderbunds reigned unashamed. In municipal misgovernment America led the world."[2] Professor T. H. Reed records that, despite machine government, cities had increased in population, had grown economically, and had developed in culture. Progress had also been made toward standards of municipal service. But his general conclusion is ". . . in 1888 our city governments were burdened with debt, and sodden with corruption and inefficiency."[3] Many were shocked by the indictment of James Bryce in 1888 that municipal government was a "conspicuous failure," but no informed person could deny the accuracy of the observation.

These disgraceful conditions did not go entirely unchallenged. Citizen indignation and action helped to drive the Tweed Ring from power and started movements in many cities to oust the politicians and elect better men to public office. Through the grand jury and the local prosecutor, through publication of the records of candidates and office-holders, through endorsement and sometimes nomination of

[1] For notes to chap. x, see p. 248.

[195]

candidates, and always by a campaign of civic education, the reformers struggled to improve municipal government. A few temporary groups were formed in the 'seventies; more numbers and permanency were secured in the 'eighties. By the early 'nineties municipal reform had attained the status of a national movement and the need for a union of civic groups in many states into a national league or federation was recognized almost simultaneously by reformers in different parts of the country.

Under a call issued jointly by the Municipal League of Philadelphia and the City Club of New York, and endorsed by leading citizens in many communities, there was convened in Philadelphia in January, 1894, the First National Conference for Good City Government. Out of this Conference came the demand for a permanent national organization of the municipal reform forces. A second meeting in New York City in May, 1894, resulted in the creation of the National Municipal League.

Since that time the League has given its attention to the study of city government, and later to county and state government, and has developed and promoted a comprehensive program for the reform of local government. The most important elements of this program are the activities in behalf of charter reform, improved forms of governmental organization, democratic local government, and higher standards and better methods of administration.

After a few years spent in general discussion of municipal conditions, the League adopted in 1899 a municipal program, popularly referred to as the first Model City Charter. Revised in 1916, 1927, 1933, and 1941, the successive editions constituted a "progressive redefinition of the minimum goal. . . ." Providing a strong mayor type of municipal executive in 1899 and adopting the council manager plan in the 1916 and later revisions, the drafts of the Model City Charter have "foreshadowed and crystallized significant tendencies in American municipal organization."⁴ The charters were notable also for many other progressive features including home rule; the short ballot; the merit system; the initiative, referendum, and recall; proportional representation; nonparisanship in municipal affairs; separation of legislative and administrative functions; administration by experts; integration in administration; and provisions relating to nominations and elections; financial and personnel administration; city planning, zoning, and slum clearance; public utilities; and condemnation of property and special assessments.

The League studied the commission form of government but never completely endorsed it. Instead, the Committee on Municipal Program incorporated the council manager plan in the 1916 draft of the Model City Charter. League support of the manager plan has been vigorous and many of its important publications have been on this subject. Recognition of the metropolitan problem resulted in a survey by a committee and the publication in 1930 of a significant volume on the government of metropolitan areas. The coöperation of librarians was secured for a study of municipal reference libraries, which extended over a period of years. Some attention has been given to the problem of municipal court organization and that of the selection of judges, but, on the whole, the League has left consideration of these problems to other national organizations. Expansion of the scope of League activities to include state and county government came in 1917. Its best known publication in this field is the Model State Constitution, but also notable are the studies of state administrative reorganization, the Model County Manger Law, and other reports. The emergence of the federal government as a factor in local affairs has been appreciated by the League, and within the last fifteen years increasing attention has been given to the problem of federal-local relations.

If democratic government is to survive locally, it must be correctly organized, subject to control by an intelligent and well-informed citizenry, and efficiently administered. This is the firm conviction of the League. Accordingly, it has devised workable forms of local government, and has made a major part of its program popular control of government through improved registration, nomination, and election procedure; the short ballot; proportional representation; direct legislation, and the recall. Its Model Registration System and Model Election Administration System take their place alongside the other well-known model laws. A long campaign has been waged to extend and improve instruction in local government in colleges and schools and to provide education in the fundamentals of citizenship. Plans for citizen organization and participation in local affairs have been prepared, and leadership has been assumed of the Citizens' Council movement and the promotion of coöperative work among universities and local civic associations. Citizen education, citizen control, and citizen organization and participation,—these are the absolute requisites of effective self-government.

Improvement of administrative organization and methods has been a constant objective of the League. Through committee studies and through coöperation with research bureaus and national organizations it has sought to develop higher administrative standards in regard to personnel, finance and taxation, planning and zoning, public utilities, and other municipal functions. A Model Municipal Budget Law, Model Bond Law, Model Real Property Tax Collection Law, Model Liquor Control Law, and other publications are a part of the League's contribution in this field. Through the Municipal Administration Service and the Consultant Service sound administrative methods in local government have been devised and promoted.

After the program of the League has been formulated it must be translated into legislation and administrative practice. Promotion of its principles of better government is accomplished through a campaign of education, including distribution of publications, newspaper publicity, speakers' bureau, information service, membership promotion, prizes, the radio, and assistance to local citizen groups. Coöperation of other national civic associations, governmental researchers, public officials, university professors, and of women, labor, and business groups, has been sought, and on the whole, has been secured. Without an emotional or dramatic appeal, League publicity has of late given relatively less attention to the political regeneration of cities, and has emphasized constructive efforts to create and maintain a more workable, democratic, and efficient local government. Avoiding muckraking, lobbying, and participation in local political campaigns, the League has escaped organized opposition. An occasional criticism is buried under the almost unanimous favorable comments of individuals, newspapers, and writers on local government.

In reviewing the history of the League, one is impressed with the high quality of its leadership and with the number and character of people it has been able to enlist in its service as volunteer officers; as members of the Council, the Executive Committee, and special investigating committees; and as speakers, contributors to the *Review* and other publications, and participants in its conferences. The League, like all similar organizations, has had to give attention periodically to matters of organization, finance, and policy. Differences of opinion have usually been settled without serious difficulty and today no conflict for control of the organization and its policies exists. The problem of adequate financial support has been, and is, the major problem of the League.

II

Surveying the development of urban government since 1890 the National Resources Committee concluded that it had become "one of the Nation's major industries," with a growth comparable to that in private business and industry. With over a million and a quarter employees and with expeditures in 1932 about four billion dollars (trebled since 1915), with the number of cities and the size of the urban population increasing threefold since 1890, city government in 1940 had assumed "an increasingly significant role in the Nation's economy."

Municipal services have grown rapidly, and in some fields, as water supply and electricity, there has been a tendency toward municipal ownership. Structurally, the most significant trend has been toward a strong single executive of the mayor type or the popular city manager form.

Urban governments have experimented with and made widespread use of such administrative creations as executive budgets, municipal reference libraries, neighborhood health centers, unit cost accounting, central purchasing, central registration, and public reporting. They have pioneered with some of the country's most dramatic mechanical devices and scientific techniques, including traffic signal lights, police radio broadcasts, sewage-treatment processes, epidemiology, lie detectors, voting machines, and parking meters.

Merit selection has been displacing spoils in municipal employment; the technician and expert are no longer strangers at the city hall. Except in a few large cities, the old boss and machine system of politics is extinct. Organizations of municipal employees have multiplied and municipal officials and cities have been joined in state and national professional associations. Intermunicipal arrangements for services have increased, and coöperation between cities and between the federal government and the cities is a significant development. Intergovernmental relationships, municipal finance, the legal powers of the city, and the government of metropolitan areas, constitute unsolved problems of urban government.[5]

Civic associations have increased in number and influence, citizen-supported research agencies have coöperated to improve administrative methods, and business, labor, women, the churches and other groups have recognized the growing importance of the city hall.[6] Newspapers, the radio, and motion pictures have been employed to stimulate increased citizen interest in government. The literature of local government is voluminous; instruction in city, county, and state government is now found in practically every college and secondary school. Democratic local government has been facilitated through the development and perfection of devices for popular control.

Observers are unanimous in the opinion that city government in the past fifty years has greatly improved. James Bryce, in 1921, in reevaluating municipal government, spoke of the reforms in city government and of the remarkable growth of the manager plan.[7] Professor Munro calls the years, 1895–1925 the "Civic Renaissance," which witnessed "an almost unbelievable improvement all along the line."[8] The conclusion of Professor Reed is that "formidable progress" has been made. "On the whole, city politics today is a better game than in 1888. Elections are more honest; graft, with the one exception of police graft, is diminished in significance; the various municipal services have attained a technical perfection undreamed of in the earlier period."[9] And Professor William Anderson writes that the records show that "city government in America today is much more honest, efficient, and democratic than it was a generation or two ago."[10]

Many factors have influenced this improvement. The authorities just quoted agree in giving first mention to the municipal reformers and their followers, the independent voters. Among other facts and events exercising strong influence for the better on municipal government should be mentioned the rapid spread of secondary education, the practical removal of public utility politics in many cities through the establishment of state regulation, and the coming of woman suffrage. Scientific discovery and the increasingly technical character of administration have made notable contributions to progress. Local research agencies and professional organizations of public officials in cities and states are responsible for many betterments. National organizations, some lay, and others professional and official, have had a leading part in the reform movement.[11]

III

In this half-century of municipal reform, what has been the role of the League? What has been its contribution to the reform of local government? How can its influence be measured?[12]

In 1910 the League published a pamphlet attempting to answer these questions. It admitted that ordinary standards of measurement would not apply. "One cannot weigh it. One cannot measure it with a yardstick. One cannot count it up. One cannot photograph it. How then is one to determine whether it has any influence, and if it has, how far-reaching and how wholesome it is?"[13] With this introduction, it proceeded to set forth certain factors which it deemed evidence of influence: the number and character of its membership; and testimonials from those who had sought the services of the League, from newspapers, publicists, and professors.

A practical way to measure the effectiveness of the League's work is to examine, over a long period of time, the list of adoptions of various reforms advocated by it,—the city manager plan, improved budget procedure, reorganization of state administration, new forms of county government, modern election procedure, among others. To this should be added the development of interest in better government as evidenced by movements to adopt new forms and methods. To Richard S. Childs success is measured by the number of city manager adoptions.

Accepting this method of evaluation as sound, we can agree with the following statement of Secretary Howard P. Jones:

> The National Municipal League, since its establishment in 1894, has led the way in the development and promotion of principles of better government. Its Model City Charter (first drafted in 1899) has probably exerted more influence upon the structure, organization and administration of city government than any other one document. Today, 466 cities are operating under the form of government—the council manager plan—prescribed by that charter. Similarly, the other model documents of the League have had extensive influence. The Model State Constitution has been accepted as established doctrine and is used extensively in colleges and universities as well as by state commissions concerned in constitutional revision. It is interesting to note, for instance, that the unicameral state legislature—under which Nebraska is operating for the first time this year—was included as a proposal in the Model State Constitution fourteen years ago. The Model Budget Law, the Model Bond Law, and more recently, the Model Tax Collection Law, have had wide influence upon state statutes and municipal practice throughout the country.[14]

The League does not claim credit for inventing or designing all of the improvements which it has sponsored. It has, however, through the research of its committees and staff, developed and put into usable form new governmental ideas and devices, and then promoted their widespread adoption by a campaign of education. In the words of Secretary Jones: "The League more and more is acting as the liaison agent between the experts who develop new and improved methods of government and the public which must understand them before they can be adopted."[15]

An impartial appraisal of the League may be found in the writings of professional students of municipal government. Without exception, they place it first among national citizen organizations engaged in civic reform. They refer to the League as the pioneer, as the outstanding, the most important, and the most influential organization in the movement for better city government.[16] It has been called a "civic army," a "civic clinic," a "national clearinghouse on governmental subjects," a "reservoir of facts and information," and "an established medium for disseminating information on government." Secretary Clinton Rogers Woodruff once said of the League: "It represents the interest of citizens in the solution of the municipal problem. It is at once a reviewing body, a clearing-house for ideas and experiences, a propagandizing influence and a maker of programs."[17]

The National Municipal League is a school of thought that stabilizes reform along sound and practical lines; it represents the consensus of opinion of thinking people as to what local government should be. It has been and is the heart of the municipal reform movement in the United States.

Appendices

APPENDIX A

CALL FOR THE CONFERENCE AND
ENDORSEMENT[1]

THE MUNICIPAL LEAGUE OF
PHILADELPHIA

Philadelphia, December 29, 1893

Dear Sir—The MUNICIPAL LEAGUE of Philadelphia, with the cooperation of the CITY CLUB of New York, has decided to issue a call for a NATIONAL CONFERENCE FOR GOOD CITY GOVERNMENT, to be held in Philadelphia on the 25th and 26th days of January, 1894.

The Principal objects of the Conference will be to determine, so far as is possible by inquiry and debate, the best means for stimulating and increasing the rapidly growing demand for honest and intelligent government in American cities, and to discuss the best methods for combining and organizing the friends of Reform so that their united strength may be made effective.

The programme for the papers and discussions, as at present outlined (subject to possible changes), is as follows:

First.—A brief summary of existing conditions in different cities, and a description of Municipal Government and Municipal Officials as they ought to be.

Second.—Methods for obtaining better Government without resorting to the nomination or support of independent candidates.

Third.—Methods that involve the nomination or support of independent candidates.

Further details will be mailed hereafter to those proposing to attend.

You are respectfully invited to be present at the meetings and to take part in the discussions. It is believed that by attending this Conference, those who realize the vast importance of the problems to be discussed will accomplish much in arousing public interest, in raising the popular standards of political morality, and in securing for the advocates of Municipal Reform that feeling of brotherhood and co-operation and that unity of action and methods, which will multiply their strength and enthusiasm, and inspire the people with the hope and confidence essential to final success.

If you are an officer of any association of voters, which has for one of its objects the improvement of Municipal Government or the proper management of City affairs, we shall be greatly obliged if you will at once do whatever may be necessary to extend this invitation to such organization, and procure the appointment of delegates to attend the Conference. It is our desire to have copies of this letter sent to the secretaries of all associations of a kindred character in the United States, but there may be many whose addresses are unknown to us, and we shall, therefore, be very glad to receive any that you can furnish.

[1] *Proceedings of the Philadelphia Conference* (1894), pp. 46–48.

[201]

An early response is specially requested, as our time for preparation is brief. Letters may be directed to the Corresponding Secretary of the League—Clinton Rogers Woodruff, 514 Walnut Street, Philadelphia, Pa.

Very respectfully,

Charles Richardson,
Stuart Wood,
George Burnham, Jr.,
S. D. McConnell,
Edmund J. James,
William I. Nichols,
Joseph G. Rosengarten,
Francis B. Reeves,
W. M. Salter,
Herbert Welsh,
Clinton Rogers Woodruff,
Thomas Martindale,
George Gluyas Mercer,
R. Francis Wood,

Committee of Arrangements

Edmond Kelley,
John Harsen Rhoades,
R. Fulton Cutting,

*Committee of City Club
of New York*

We desire to express our cordial approval of the call issued by the Municipal League of Philadelphia for a National Conference for Good City Government, to be held in Philadelphia on the 25th and 26th days of January, 1894. Appreciating the vital importance, as well as the difficult nature, of the problems to be discussed, we sincerely hope that those who have given particular attention to such subjects will make special efforts to attend the Conference.

James C. Carter, President of the City Club of New York.
Edmond Kelly, Secretary of the City Club of New York.
Charles Francis Adams, Boston.
Theo. Roosevelt, Washington, D. C.
Richard H. Dana, Boston.
Charles J. Bonaparte, Baltimore, Md.
Henry C. Lea, Philadelphia.
Charles A. Schieren, Brooklyn.
Chas. Eliot Norton, Cambridge, Mass.

George W. Childs, Philadelphia.
Gamaliel Bradford, Boston.
Moorfield Storey, Boston.
R. W. Gilder, New York.
Carl Schurz, New York.
Charles W. Eliot, Cambridge, Mass.
Abram S. Hewitt, New York.
Lyman J. Gage, Chicago.
Wayne MacVeagh, Philadelphia.
Washington Gladden, Columbus, O.
Daniel C. Gilman, Baltimore, Md.
Lyman Abbott, New York.
Richard T. Ely, Madison, Wis.
Matthew Hale, Albany, N. Y.
L. Clarke Davis, Philadelphia.
R. Fulton Cutting, New York.
Horace White, New York.
William G. Low, Brooklyn.
Edward M. Shepard, Brooklyn.
John Field, Philadelphia.
Fred. Law Olmstead, Brookline, Mass.
Philip C. Garrett, Philadelphia.
Samuel B. Capen, Boston.
Isaac Sharpless, Haverford Coll., Pa.
Ansley Wilcox, Buffalo, N. Y.
Finley Acker, Philadelphia.
Edward Cary, Brooklyn.
John B. Garrett, Philadelphia.
Joel J. Baily, Philadelphia.
J. Andrews Harris, Philadelphia.
Joseph Krauskopf, Philadelphia.
Edwin D. Mead, Boston.
Charles C. Harrison, Philadelphia.
Isaac J. Wistar, Philadelphia.
Everett P. Wheeler, New York.
Jacob F. Miller, New York.
Seth Sprague Terry, New York.
Samuel H. Ordway, New York.
James S. Whitney, Philadelphia.
Franklin MacVeagh, Chicago.
R. C. McMurtrie, Philadelphia.
Joseph S. Harris, Philadelphia.
Marshall Field, Chicago.
Hervert Lee Harding, Boston.
Causten Browne, Boston.
E. P. Allinson, Philadelphia.
Alexander Brown, Philadelphia.
Francis A. Walker, Boston.
Edward E. Hale, Boston.
John R. Procter, Washington, D. C.
Edwin L. Godkin, New York.
Wendell P. Garrison, New York.
William Potts, New York.
W. Harris Roome, New York.
H. B. Adams, John Hopkins Univ.
Wm. J. Gaynor, Brooklyn.
Sylvester Baxter, Boston.
Hampton L. Carson, Philadelphia.

Theodore M. Etting, Philadelphia.
Ellis D. Williams, Philadelphia.
O. W. Whitaker, Philadelphia.
W. W. Frazier, Philadelphia.
W. Dudley Foulke, Richmond, Ind.
H. La Barre Jayne, Philadelphia.
John H. Converse, Philadelphia.
Wm. P. Henszey, Philadelphia.
Horace E. Deming, New York.
Anson Phelps Stokes, New York.
Alfred Bishop Mason, New York.
A. R. MacDonough, New York.
Chas. R. Codman, Barnstable, Mass.
George Burnham, Philadelphia.
J. Rodman Paul, Philadelphia.
James E. Rhoads, Bryn Mawr.
E. W. Clark, Philadelphia.
William Pepper, Philadelphia.
S. Davis Page, Philadelphia.
Albert Shaw, New York.
Dorman B. Eaton, New York.

APPENDIX B

CONSTITUTION OF THE NATIONAL MUNICIPAL LEAGUE[1]

ARTICLE I

Name

The name of this association shall be The National Municipal League.

ARTICLE II

Objects

1. Its objects shall be: First: To multiply the number, harmonize the methods, and combine the forces of those who are interested in more effective city, county, state, and national government.

Second: To promote the thorough investigation and discussion of the conditions and methods of the organization and administration of government, and of the methods of selecting and appointing public officials.

Third: To develop a sound public opinion on questions of government by furnishing data for public information and discussion, by the publication of the proceedings of the League's meetings, reports of committees, and other papers, pamphlets, books, and periodicals bearing upon the subject of government.

2. The League shall have no connection with local, state or national political parties or political party issues as such.

ARTICLE III

Membership

1. The membership of the League shall be composed of individuals interested in the objects of the League as stated in Article II.

2. Any person approved by the Council or by its authorized representative and qualified as herein provided may become a member of the League. The amount paid for dues shall include a subscription for one year to any periodical issued by the League. Any membership may be cancelled by a three-fourths vote at any meeting of the League, or by the Council for the non-payment of dues.

3. Five classes of membership are hereby established.

    a. Active members whose dues shall be $5.00 per annum

    b. Sustaining members whose dues shall be $10 per annum

    c. Contributing members whose dues shall be $25.00 or upward

    d. Patrons whose dues shall be $100 or upward

    e. Honorary life members who shall be exempt from payment of dues. Such members may be elected by the League or the Board, but not more than two such members may be elected during any one year.

[1] Adopted at Annual Meeting, Washington, D. C., September 20, 1932.

ARTICLE IV

Council and Officers

1. The government of the League, the direction of its work, and the control of its property shall be vested in a Council consisting of thirty members elected for a term of three years, ten to be elected each year. The President may or may not be chairman of the Council.[1]

2. The officers of the League shall be a President, a First Vice-President, a Second Vice-President and not more than twenty-five Regional and Honorary Vice-Presidents, a Treasurer and a Secretary. The President and the Vice-Presidents shall be elected at the annual meeting by the members of the League. The Secretary and Treasurer shall be appointed annually by the Council.

3. The Secretary shall have charge of the publications, records and correspondence of the League; shall be Secretary to all committees unless otherwise provided by the Council; shall supervise the work of all employes of the League; and shall perform such other duties incident to the office as shall be required by the Council. His salary shall be fixed annually by the Council.[2]

ARTICLE V

Committees

1. Immediately upon the election and organization of the Council, it shall appoint its chairman and six other members to be an Executive Committee for the current year. The Executive Committee shall select its own chairman. Subject always to the approval of the Council, the Executive Committee shall in the interim between meetings of the Council act for it in all matters relating to the raising and expenditure of necessary funds; the approval of appointments and direction of committees; the appointment of employes; the annual audit

of accounts, and the general mangement and prosecution of the work of the League.

2. The President shall, subject to confirmation by the Council or Executive Committee, appoint all committees of the League. No committee shall incur any indebtedness, make any expenditures, or represent the League in advocacy of or opposition to any project or issue, without the specific approval of the Council or Executive Committee, or such confirmation as may be clearly granted under general powers delegated to that committee by the Council.

ARTICLE VI

Elections and Referenda

1. Nominations. At least ninety days before the annual meeting, a nominating commmittee consisting of five members, shall be appointed by the President. At least thirty days before the annual meeting, the committee shall place ten members in nomination for membership on the Council, one member for President, one member for First Vice-President, one member for Second Vice-President and not more than twenty-five members for Honorary and Regional Vice-Presidents. Such nominations shall be published to the membership of the League at least thirty days before the annual meeting in the League's publication, or by mail. Such publication shall invite additional nominations from members of the League. Such additional nomina-

---

[1] The membership voted at the 1937 annual meeting at Rochester, New York, that this section should be interpreted also as providing that the retiring president of the League should automatically become a life member of the council.

[2] It was also voted at the Rochester meeting that this section should be interpreted as empowering the secretary also to serve as director of the League, and that the word "employes" should be interpreted to include members of the staff.

tions may be made at the annual meeting, at which the election shall take place.

2. Referenda Provisions shall be made by the Council for the submission to the members by mail for approval or disapproval, of recommendations of the Council or any committee of the League on any question of organization policy.

ARTICLE VII

Subsidiary Organizations

Members of the League, with the consent and approval of the Council, may form affiliated or subsidiary associations for promoting more effectively a special improvement or reform in which they are interested. Such associations may, subject to the approval of the Council, adopt their own rules and regulations. They may use the name of the League as a part of their name; but no action or resolution of any such association shall be binding upon or expressive of the sense of the League unless approved by the Council. Any such affiliation with the League may at any time be dissolved by the Council.

ARTICLE VIII

Meetings

1. Unless otherwise directed by the Council or the Executive Committee, the annual meeting of the League shall be held in November of each year. Special meetings of the League may be called at any time by the President, or the Council, or the Executive Committee.

2. A meeting of the Council shall be held in connection with each annual meeting of the League. Other meetings of the Council and Executive Committee, and meetings of all other committees, shall be held when called by their respective chairmen or by the President or Secretary of the League.

3. Reasonable notice shall be given of all meetings.

4. At meetings of the League those present, and at meetings of the Council, ten members, and at meetings of committees a majority of the members, shall constitute a quorum. But whenever a quorum is lacking, the action of the majority of those present may be validated by the written approval of a sufficient number of the absentees to make up the deficiency.

ARTICLE IX

Liabilities and Disbursements

No disbursements of the funds of the League shall be made unless they shall have been approved and ordered by the Council or Executive Committee. All checks shall be signed by the Secretary and countersigned by the Treasurer, provided, however, that under disbursements authorized by the Council or Executive Committee, the Treasurer at his option may draw blanket checks in favor of the Secretary, to be disbursed in turn through checks signed by the Secretary.

ARTICLE X

By-Laws

The Council may adopt such by-laws, not inconsistent with the provisions of this constitution, as shall be deemed necessary for the government of the League and the direction and control of its activities.

ARTICLE XI

Amendments

Amendments to this constitution may be adopted by a majority vote at any meeting of the League provided a notice of the proposed change shall have been published to the members in the League's publication, or by mail, not less than thirty days before such meeting.

1. No Council member shall be eligible to succeed himself without a lapse of one year.[1]

Lawson Purdy	1915–1919
Charles E. Hughes	1919–1921
Henry M. Waite	1921–1923
Frank L. Polk	1923–1927
Richard S. Childs	1927–

APPENDIX C

OFFICERS OF THE LEAGUE, 1894–1948

PRESIDENTS

James C. Carter	1894–1903
Charles J. Bonaparte	1903–1910
William D. Foulke	1910–1915
Lawson Purdy	1915–1919
Charles E. Hughes	1919–1921
Henry M. Waite	1921–1923
Frank L. Polk	1923–1927
Richard S. Childs	1927–1931
Murray Seasongood	1931–1934
Harold W. Dodds	1934–1937
Clarence A. Dykstra	1937–1940
John G. Winant	1940–1946
Charles Edison	1946–

HONORARY PRESIDENT

| James C. Carter | 1903–1905 |

SECRETARIES

Clinton Rogers Woodruff	1894–1920
Harold W. Dodds	1920–1928
Russell Forbes	1928–1933
Howard P. Jones	1933–1947
Alfred Willoughby	1947–

TREASURERS

R. Fulton Cutting	1894–1894
George Burnham, Jr.	1894–1919
Raymond V. Ingersoll	1919–1919
Frank A. Vanderlip	1919–1921
Carl H. Pforzheimer	1921–

CHAIRMEN OF THE COUNCIL[2]

Charles J. Bonaparte	1894–1903
Horace E. Deming	1903–1910
Albert B. Hart	1910–1911
William D. Foulke	1911–1915

APPENDIX D

OFFICERS AND COUNCIL OF THE LEAGUE, 1949

Charles Edison, West Orange, N. J.,
President
George H. Gallup, Princeton, N. J.,
Vice-President
James W. Clise, Seattle,
Vice-President
Carl H. Pforzheimer, New York,
Treasurer
Alfred Willoughby, New York,
Secretary

COUNCIL

Richard S. Childs, New York, Chairman
William Anderson, Minneapolis
Frederick E. Baker, Seattle
James L. Beebe, Los Angeles
Frederick L. Bird, New York
Albert D. Cash, Cincinnati
William Collins, Yonkers, N. Y.
L. P. Cookingham, Kansas City, Mo.
Philip H. Cornick, Yonkers, N. Y.
James A. Cunningham, Chicago
Harold W. Dodds, Princeton, N. J.
C. A. Dykstra, Los Angeles
Herbert Emmerich, Chicago
B. H. Faulkner, Montclair, N. J.
Clarence Francis, Bronxville, N. Y.
Max E. Friedmann, Milwaukee
Arnold Frye, New York
Lloyd E. Graybiel, San Francisco
Lloyd Hale, Minneapolis
Harrison S. Hires, Berwyn, Pa.
Robert W. Johnson, New Brunswick, N. J.

---

[1] Adopted, Baltimore, November, 1938.
[2] Designated as the Executive Committee from 1894 to 1911.

Mrs. Siegel W. Judd, Grand Rapids
John S. Linen, New York
Mrs. Virgil Loeb, St. Louis
Mrs. Thomas H. Mahony, Boston
Joseph D. McGoldrick, New York
D. K. Pfeffer, New York
Ed. P. Phillips, Richmond
Walter M. Phillips, Philadelphia
Lawson Purdy, New York
Harry W. Schacter, Louisville
Murray Seasongood, Cincinnati
Henry L. Shattuck, Boston

HONORARY VICE-PRESIDENTS

H. L. Brittain, Toronto, Ont.
Henry Bruere, New York
Charles C. Burlingham, New York
Harold S. Buttenheim, New York
Harry Woodburn Chase, New York
Rev. Edward Dowling, S. J., St. Louis
John N. Edy, Houston, Texas
Samuel S. Fels, Philadelphia
Russell Forbes, Tampa
Robert C. Henrickson, Woodbury, N. J.
Ralph B. Maltby, Bronxville, N. Y.
Seabury C. Mastick, Pleasantville, N. Y.
C. E. Merriam, Chicago
Frank H. Morse, New York
Stratford Lee Morton, St. Louis
Anne M. Mumford, Los Angeles
W. B. Munro, Pasadena, Calif.
William J. Pape, Waterbury
Mrs. F. Louis Slade, New York
Harold E. Stassen, Philadelphia
Charles P. Taft, Cincinnati
Lent D. Upson, Detroit
Wilson W. Wyatt, Louisville

APPENDIX E

The League's Honor Roll

The *Review* for April, 1929, presented the League's Honor Roll: a list of persons and organizations that had been members of the League for twenty-five years or longer. The following note was appended: "The National Municipal League has been unusually fortunate in having a large body of members who continue their support from year to year. We take pleasure, therefore, in reprinting below the names of those who have held membership continuously for more than twenty-five years. Some have been members ever since the League was organized in 1894. This list includes many who have stood in the forefront of every movement for municipal reform which has been waged during the last quarter century." The compilation was made from the membership records and was not guaranteed as to completeness. No similar roll has been issued since 1929.

William P. Bancroft, Wilmington, Del.
Mrs. George Burnham, Jr., Kintore,
Berwyn, Pa.
George F. Canfield, New York, N. Y.
Harvey S. Chase, Boston, Mass.
Chicago Civic Federation
C. M. Clark, Philadelphia, Pa.
Harry C. Clark, Providence, R. I.
R. Fulton Cutting, New York, N. Y.
Robert W. DeForest, New York, N. Y.
Horace E. Deming, New York, N. Y.
A. H. Devers, Portland, Ore.
George Eastman, Rochester, N. Y.
John A. Fairlie, Urbana, Ill.
Samuel S. Fels, Philadelphia, Pa.
F. W. Lyman, Minneapolis, Minn.
George R. Lyman, Pasadena, Calif.
V. Everett Macy, New York, N. Y.
George W. Marston, San Diego, Calif.
Miss Ida M. Mason, Boston, Mass.
Samuel Mather, Cleveland, Ohio
Stanley McCormick, Chicago, Ill.
Hon. Vance McCormick, Harrisburg,
Pa.
J. Horace McFarland, Harrisburg, Pa.
Adelbert Moot, Buffalo, N. Y.
New York Citizens Union
New York Tax Reform Association
Frederick Law Olmsted, Jr., Brookline,
Mass.

Robert Treat Paine, Boston, Mass.
Edward A. Filene, Boston, Mass.
Professor Irving Fisher, New Haven, Conn.
Hon. William Dudley Foulke, Richmond, Ind.
Thomas H. Franklin, San Antonio, Texas
A. S. Frissell, New York, N. Y.
Harry A. Garfield, Williamstown, Mass.
William Gemmell, Providence, R. I.
F. J. Goodnow, Baltimore, Md.
Professor Albert Bushnell Hart, Widener Library, Cambridge, Mass.
Charles M. Higgins, Brooklyn, N. Y.
William V. Kellen, Cohasset, Mass.
Clarence H. Kelsey, New York, N. Y.
Arthur H. Lea, Philadelphia, Pa.
Joseph Lee, Boston, Mass.
Eugene Levering, Baltimore, Md.
Los Angeles Municipal League
William G. Low, New York, N. Y.
Dr. A. Lawrence Lowell, Harvard University, Cambridge, Mass.

Frank Lyman, New York, N. Y.
Lawson Purdy, New York, N. Y.
George H. Putnam, New York, N. Y.
Alfred G. Scattergood, Awbury, Germantown, Philadelphia, Pa.
Benjamin F. Seaver, Brooklyn, N. Y.
Professor Edwin R. A. Seligman, Columbia University, New York, N. Y.
Henry D. Sharpe, Providence, R. I.
Dr. Albert Shaw, New York, N. Y.
James Speyer, New York, N. Y.
Fred W. Squires, New York, N. Y.
Hon. Charles W. Stage, Cleveland, Ohio
Samuel Thorne, Jr., New York, N. Y.
Twentieth Century Club, Boston, Mass.
Cornelius Vanderbilt, New York, N. Y.
Richard Welling, New York, N. Y.
George Wigglesworth, Boston, Mass.
Rev. D. D. Wood, Washington, D. C.
Clinton Rogers Woodruff, Philadelphia, Pa.
George Woodward, M. D., Philadelphia, Pa.

Notes

Notes to Chapter I

[1] C. A. Beard, *Contemporary American History, 1877–1913* (1923), p. 28.

[2] A. M. Schlesinger, *The Rise of the City, 1878–1898* (1933), p. 387.

[3] *The Education of Henry Adams* (1918), p. 355.

[4] U. S. Bureau of the Census, *Fifteenth Census of the United States* (1930), pp. 9, 14; C. M. Kneier, *City Government in the United States* (1934), p. 2; W. B. Munro, *The Government of American Cities* (4th ed.; 1926), p. 31.

[5] A. F. Macdonald, *American City Government and Administration* (rev. ed.; 1936), p. 26.

[6] Munro, *op. cit.*, p. 32.

[7] T. H. Reed, *Municipal Government in the United States* (rev. ed.; 1934), p. 115; C. W. Patton, *The Battle for Municipal Reform* (1940), chap. i.

[8] Reed, *op. cit.*, p. 122.

[9] Schlesinger, *op. cit.*, p. 194.

[10] James Bryce, *The American Commonwealth* (1888), II, chap. lxxxviii.

[11] C. C. Regier, *The Era of the Muckrakers* (1932), chap. iii. This chapter discusses the periodical literature of "The Restless Eighteen-Nineties."

[12] Schlesinger, *op. cit.*, p. 182.

[13] *Ibid.*, p. 183.

[14] *Poole's Index to Periodical Literature* (rev. ed.; 1891). See also "Bibliography of Municipal Government and Reform," *Proceedings of the National Conference for Good City Government*
Held at Philadelphia January 25 and 26, 1894, pp. 341–381 (hereafter cited as *Proceedings of the Philadelphia Conference*); and R. C. Brooks, "A Bibliography of Municipal Administration and City Conditions," *Municipal Affairs*, I (1897).

[15] Reed, *op. cit.*, p. 122.

[16] A number of published studies related to particular cities. See E. S. Griffith, *The Modern Development of City Government in the United Kingdom and the United States*, II (1927), pp. 638–641.

[17] Among these were: A. R. Conkling, *City Government in the United States* (1895); T. C. Devlin, *Municipal Reform in the United States* (1896); D. B. Eaton, *The Government of Municipalities* (1899); F. J. Goodnow, *Comparative Administrative Law* (1893), *Municipal Problems* (1897), *Municipal Home Rule* (1895); W. H. Tolman, *Municipal Reform Movements in the United States* (1895); A. F. Weber, *The Growth of Cities in the Nineteenth Century* (1899); D. F. Wilcox, *The Study of City Government* (1897); J. F. Dillon, *Treatise on the Law of Municipal Corporations* (1872).

[18] *Report of the Commission to Devise a Plan for the Government of Cities in the State of New York* (Tilden Commission, 1877); *Testimony Taken before the Senate Committee on Cities Pursuant to Resolution Adopted January 20, 1890* (Fassett Committee, 1891), 5 vols.; *Report and Proceedings of the*

Senate Committee to Investigate the Police Department of the City of New York (Lexow Committee, 1895), 5 vols. For excerpts from these reports and for memorials from citizen reform organizations, see T. H. Reed and Paul Webbink, *Documents Illustrative of American Municipal Government* (1926), pp. 114–130, 141–155, 226–232.

[19] J. M. Gaus, *A Study of Research in Public Administration* (mimeo., 1930), p. 8.

[20] Schlesinger, *op. cit.*, p. 202.

[21] *Ibid.*, p. 213.

[22] C. E. Merriam, *American Political Ideas* (1923), p. 373. For a particularly informative discussion of this period, see Anna Haddow, *Political Science in American Colleges and Universities, 1636–1900* (1939), chaps. xi-xiii.

[23] Merriam, *op. cit.*, p. 375.

[24] *Proceedings of the Rochester Conference for Good City Government* (1901), p. 226 (hereafter cited as *Proceedings*, with year of conference).

[25] Merriam, *op. cit.*, p. 374; Haddow, *op. cit.*, p. 255.

[26] Among these were: *American Economic Review* (1885); *American Historical Review* (1895); *American Journal of Sociology* (1895). The *Political Science Quarterly* (1886) and the *Annals* (1890) were published by Columbia University and the University of Pennsylvania, respectively.

[27] Albert Lepawsky, "Development of Urban Government," *Urban Government* (Volume I of the *Supplementary Report of the Urbanism Committee to the National Resources Committee*, 1939), pp. 42–43.

[28] E. A. Greenlaw, "Office of Mayor in the United States," *Municipal Affairs*, III (1899), pp. 33–60.

[29] J. A. Fairlie, *Municipal Administration* (1901), p. 87.

[30] Lepawsky, *op. cit.*, p. 39.

[31] Fairlie, *op. cit.*, pp. 87–88, 92–93, 99.

[32] Kneier, *op. cit.*, p. 70.

[33] Fairlie, *op. cit.*, p. 92.

[34] *Ibid.*, pp. 92–93.

[35] *Ibid.*, p. 97.

[36] Greenlaw, *op. cit.*, p. 55.

[37] W. B. Munro, "Municipal Government," *Encyclopedia of the Social Sciences*, XI (1933), p. 113.

[38] Lepawsky, *op. cit.*, p. 41.

[39] William Anderson, *American City Government* (1925), p 298.

[40] Lepawsky, *op. cit.*, p. 40.

[41] Macdonald, *op. cit.*, pp. 300–302; Reed, *op. cit.*, p. 124; Kneier, *op. cit.*, pp. 223–225.

[42] F. L. Bird and F. M. Ryan, *The Recall of Public Officers* (1930), p. 3; W. B. Munro, ed., *The Initiative, Referendum and Recall* (1912).

[43] L. D. White, *Trends in Public Administration* (1933), pp. 245–246; Lepawsky, *op. cit.*, p. 47.

[44] White, *op. cit.*, pp. 219–221.

[45] *Ibid.*, pp. 218–219.

[46] *Ibid.*, p. 222.

[47] *Ibid.*, pp. 311–316.

[48] *Ibid.*, pp. 325–328. See also Gaus, *op. cit.*, chap. v.

[49] H. D. Smith and G. C. S. Benson, "Associations of Cities and of Municipal Officials," *Urban Government* (Volume I of the *Supplementary Report of the Urbanism Committee to the National Resources Committee*, 1939), pp. 182–184.

[50] Bryce, *op. cit.*, I, 608.

[51] A. D. White, "The Government of American Cities," *Forum*, X (1890), pp. 357–372.

[52] J. H. Dougherty, "Seth Low's Service in Behalf of Non-Partisan City Government," *National Municipal Review*, VI (1917), pp. 210–216 (hereafter cited as *Review*).

[53] Patton, *op. cit.*, p. 69.

[54] Reed, *op. cit.*, chap. viii. See also C. E. Merriam and H. F. Gosnell, *The American Party System* (rev. ed.; 1929), chaps. iv-vii.

⁵⁵ Patton, *op. cit.*, chap. ii. For a description of many of the leading political bosses of the day, see Harold Zink, *City Bosses in the United States* (1930).

⁵⁶ Bryce, *op. cit.*, II, chap. lxxxviii; Reed, *op. cit.*, pp. 113–114; Zink, *op. cit.*, Pt. II, chap. iii; M. R. Werner, *Tammany Hall* (1928).

⁵⁷ Bryce, *op. cit.*, II, chap. lxxxix; Reed, *op. cit.*, p. 114; Schlesinger, *op. cit.*, p. 391; Zink, *op. cit.*, Pt. II, chap. ix.

⁵⁸ Schlesinger, *op. cit.*, pp. 389–390.

NOTES TO CHAPTER II

¹ T. H. Reed, *Municipal Government in the United States* (rev. ed.; 1934), p. 117.

² *Ibid.*, p. 119; W. D. P. Bliss, ed., *The Encyclopedia of Social Reform*, (1897), pp. 907–910; C. W. Patton, *The Battle for Municipal Reform* (1940), chap. iii.

³ W. H. Tolman, *Municipal Reform Movements in the United States* (1895); *Proceedings of the Philadelphia Conference* (1894), pp. 303–340; *Annals of the American Academy of Political and Social Science*, XXV (1905), pp. 359–401 (hereafter cited as *Annals*); *Constitutions and By-Laws of Leading Municipal Reform Organizations* (National Municipal League, Pamphlet No. 4, 1895); *Review of Reviews*, XI (1895), pp. 415–427; S. B. Capen, "The Boston Municipal League," *American Journal of Politics*, V (1894), pp. 1–13; Herbert Welsh, "Municipal Leagues and Good Government Clubs," *Proceedings*, 1894–1895, pp. 146–153; Patton, *op. cit.*, chap. iv.

⁴ Tolman, *op. cit.*, pp. 47–133.

⁵ *Ibid.*, p. 70.

⁶ *Ibid.*, pp. 77, 79.

⁷ Reed, *op. cit.*, pp. 120–121; Tolman, *op. cit.*, pp. 47–133.

⁸ *Ibid.*

⁹ *Proceedings of the Philadelphia Conference* (1894), pp. 103–110, 315–318, 324–326; Tolman, *op. cit.*, pp. 70–71, 91–96; *Annals*, XXV (1905), pp. 374–376; *Constitutions and By-Laws of Leading Municipal Reform Organizations* (1895), pp. 12–17.

¹⁰ *Proceedings of the Philadelphia Conference* (1894), pp. 332–334; Tolman, *op. cit.*, pp. 115–116; *Annals*, XXV (1905), p. 181; *Constitutions and By-Laws of Leading Municipal Reform Organizations* (1895), pp. 4–11; A. B. Woodford, "The Municipal League of Philadelphia," *Social Economist*, II (1892), pp. 366–369. See also articles by C. R. Woodruff, *Harper's Weekly*, XXXVIII (Oct. 27, 1894), p. 1019; *American Journal of Politics*, V (1894), pp. 287–294; *American Journal of Sociology*, XI (1905–1906), pp. 336–358.

¹¹ *Proceedings of the Philadelphia Conference* (1894), pp. 323, 329, 330; *Proceedings*, 1897, pp. 118–128, 133–144.

¹² Cf. A. W. Small, "Civic Federation of Chicago," *Proceedings*, 1894–1895, pp. 474–481; Tolman, *op. cit.*, pp. 137–163.

¹³ A typical illustration was the Municipal Reform Association of Cincinnati, established in 1883. It disbanded in 1886 and was revived in 1888 for just one campaign.

¹⁴ Bliss, *op. cit.*, p. 907.

¹⁵ *Proceedings of the Philadelphia Conference* (1894), pp. 135–143, 177–185; *Proceedings*, 1894–1895, pp. 482–491, 500–523; 1896, pp. 275–281; 1897, pp. 261–267; 1898, pp. 272–273; Tolman, *op. cit.*, pp. 100, 167–219.

¹⁶ Tolman, *op. cit.*, *passim*; W. G. Low, "Results Obtained by Voluntary and

Temporary Movements," *Proceedings,*
1894–1895, pp. 136–145.

[17] Reed, *op. cit.,* p. 117.

[18] *Ibid.,* p. 120.

[19] F. P. Prichard, "The Study of the
Science of Municipal Government,"
Annals, II (Jan., 1892), p. 23.

[20] Herbert Welsh, "A Definite Step
Toward Municipal Reform," *Forum,*
XVII (1894), p. 182.

[21] See p. 201.

[22] See p. 202.

[23] See pp. 202–203.

[24] Organizations represented by delegates were: Municipal League of Philadelphia; City Club of New York; Good Government Clubs A, B, C, D, E, New York; Civil Service Reform Association, New York; Baltimore Reform League; Baltimore Tax-Payers' Association; Citizens' Reform Movement of Baltimore; Union League Club of Chicago; Real Estate Board of Chicago; Citizens' Association of Boston; Civil Service Reform Association of Cambridge, Mass.; Advance Club of Providence, R.I.; Board of Trade of Minneapolis; Municipal League of Milwaukee; Library Hall Association of Cambridge; Massachusetts Reform Club, Boston; American Institute of Civics; Jefferson Club, New Orleans; Good Government Club, Yonkers, N.Y.; Chadwick Civic Club, New York; Citizens' League of Camden; Board of Trade of Reading; Presbyterian Ministers' Association of Philadephia; Temple Congress of Philadelphia; Public Opinion Club of Philadelphia.

[25] Welsh, *op. cit.,* p. 182.

[26] See p. 201.

[27] Among those who participated prominently in the discussions and in the organization of the Conference were: James C. Carter, Edmond Kelly, Carl Schurz, Horace E. Deming, W. Harris Roome, Alfred Bishop Mason, Rev. W. S. Rainsford, and R. W. Gilder,

New York; Charles J. Bonaparte, Baltimore; Franklin MacVeagh, William A. Gates, Chicago; Rev. Washington Gladden, Columbus, Ohio; John A. Butler, Milwaukee; Rev. J. H. Ecob, Albany; Theodore Roosevelt, Washington, D.C.; Mayor Charles A. Schieren, William G. Low, Brooklyn; George G. Wright, Cambridge, Mass.; Professor Leo S. Rowe, University of Pennsylvania; Moorfield Storey, Samuel B. Capen, Edwin D. Mead, Sylvester Baxter, Boston; George Burnham, Jr., Clinton Rogers Woodruff, George Gluyas Mercer, Mrs. Mary E. Mumford, George S. Graham, John Field, Herbert Welsh, Francis B. Reeves, James M. Beck, Mayor Edwin S. Stuart, Charles Richardson, Philadelphia.

[28] *Proceedings of the Philadelphia Conference* (1894), pp. 299, 84–85, 133, 137, 185, 244, 262, 71, 284.

[29] *Ibid.,* pp. 18, 30, 38, 39.

[30] LVIII (1894), p. 76.

[31] IV (1893–1894), p. 854.

[32] XLIX (1894), pp. 208–209.

[33] January 27, 1894. For additional comment on the Conference, see *Harper's Weekly,* XXXVIII, Pt. I (1894), p. 79; *American Journal of Politics,* V (1894), p. 329; *Independent,* XLVI, Pt. I (1894), p. 166.

[34] *Proceedings of the Philadelphia Conference,* IV (1894).

[35] Welsh, *op. cit.,* p. 184.

[36] *Annals,* IV (1893–1894), p. 854.

[37] Herbert Welsh, "The Movement For Good City Government," *American Journal of Politics,* V (1894), pp. 67–75.

[38] *Annual Report of the Secretary Read at the Annual Meeting of the Club, 2nd April, 1894,* pp. 10–12.

[39] *Ibid.*

[40] Letter from James W. Pryor to Herbert Welsh, April 5, 1894.

[41] Associations represented by delegates were: City Club of New York;

Municipal League of Philadelphia; Council of Confederated Good Government Clubs, New York; Boston Municipal League; Baltimore Reform League; Citizens' Reform Movement of Baltimore; Advance Club of Providence; National Civil Service Reform League; Municipal League of Milwaukee; Good Government Club of Yonkers; Citizens' Association of Albany; Good Government Club of Troy; City Club of Hartford; Municipal Reform Club of Syracuse; Pittsburgh Patriotic Guild. The last six organizations were admitted to membership at the meeting. (*Minutes of the First Meeting of the Board of Delegates of the National Municipal League Held at New York, May 28, 29, 1894*) (hereafter cited as *Minutes of Board of Delegates*).

[42] *Ibid.*
[43] *Ibid.*
[44] *Ibid.*
[45] *Minutes of Executive Committee of the National Civil Service Reform League,* Nov. 16, 1893.
[46] *Minutes of Board of Delegates.*
[47] *Ibid.*
[48] *Minutes of Executive Committee,* May 29, 1894.
[49] *New York Times,* May 29, 30, 1894.
[50] *Proceedings of the Philadelphia Conference* (1894), pp. 303–305.
[51] *Minutes of Board of Delegates.*
[52] See pp. 179–181.
[53] *Proceedings,* 1894–1895, p. 37.
[54] *Ibid.,* p. 23.
[55] *Ibid.,* p. 53. See also *Outlook,* L (1894), p. 1080.
[56] *Annals,* VI (1895), pp. 166–167. Papers were read describing municipal conditions in Cincinnati, Columbus, Pittsburgh, Allegheny, Buffalo, Jersey City, Washington, D.C., Indianapolis, Detroit, Louisville, Chattanooga, New Orleans, Omaha, Denver, Portland, Seattle, and San Francisco.
[57] LI (1895), p. 769.

[58] *Proceedings,* 1894–1895, pp. 213, 221, 231, 237.
[59] *Ibid.,* pp. 183, 185.
[60] *Ibid.,* pp. 218, 219, 239.
[61] *Ibid.,* pp. 226–227.
[62] *Ibid.,* pp. 304–305, 306, 310; *American Magazine of Civics,* VII (1895), pp. 66–73.
[63] LI (1895), pp. 969–970. See also *American Magazine of Civics,* VII (1895), pp. 167–171.
[64] *Proceedings,* 1896, *passim; Annals,* VIII (1896), pp. 188–190. See also *Outlook, LIII* (1896), pp. 715, 888–889. *American Magazine of Civics,* VIII (1896), pp. 656–657.
[65] *Proceedings,* 1896, pp. 62–74.
[66] *Ibid.,* 1897, pp. 129–132. See also *Outlook,* LVI (1897), p. 148; *Municipal Affairs,* II (1898), pp. 136–139; *Annals,* X (1897), p. 121; *Engineering News,* XXXIX (1898), p. 427; *Harper's Weekly,* XLI, Pt. I (1897), p. 510; *Review of Reviews,* XV (1897), p. 651.
[67] *Proceedings,* 1897, pp. 6–11, 37–39.
[68] See chap. iii.
[69] *Proceedings,* 1897, pp. 33, 45–62.
[70] *Ibid.,* 1894–1895, p. 310. The pamphlets were: No. 1, *City Government and the Churches,* by C. F. Dole; *What a Private Citizen Can Do for Good City Government,* by Charles Richardson (1894); No. 2, *Address to the Public,* by C. J. Bonaparte; *Constitution and By-Laws of the National Municipal League* (1894); No. 3, *The Relation of Civil Service Reform to Municipal Reform,* by Carl Schurz (1894); No. 4, *Constitutions and By-Laws of Leading Municipal Reform Organizations* (1895).
[71] *Minutes of Executive Committee,* Oct. 6, 1894; Dec. 20, 1895; May 8, 1896; May 7, 1897.
[72] *Proceedings,* 1896, p. 71.
[73] *Annals,* VI (1895), pp. 166–167.
[74] *Proceedings,* 1894–1895, p. 310.
[75] Patton, *op. cit.,* p. 34.

NOTES TO CHAPTER III

[1] *Municipal Problems* (1897), p. 18; *Harper's Weekly*, XLI, Pt. I (1897), p. 510.

[2] *Proceedings*, 1897, pp. 6–11, 37.

[3] *Minutes of Executive Committee*, May 7, 1897.

[4] *Who's Who in America*, IV (1906–1907), pp. 461–462; *Proceedings of the Philadelphia Conference* (1894), p. 48; *Review*, XIX (1930), p. 451.

[5] *Harper's Weekly*, XLIII (1899), p. 1219; *Political Science Quarterly*, XVIII (1903), p. 49; *Proceedings*, 1898, p. 2.

[6] LX (1898), p. 894.

[7] J. A. Fairlie, *Municipal Administration* (1901), p. 423.

[8] *Proceedings*, 1898, pp. 1–15.

[9] *Ibid.*, pp. 16–100.

[10] Professor Goodnow's paper was discussed by C. S. Palmer of Kansas City, Mo.; E. J. McDermott of Louisville; and J. A. Butler, president of the Municipal League of Milwaukee. Josiah Quincy, mayor of Boston; Dr. D. F. Wilcox of Cleveland; and N. F. Hawley, secretary of the Minneapolis Charter Commission, read papers in discussion of the article by Dr. Shaw. The three commentators on Mr. Richardson's paper were S. M. Jones, mayor of Toledo; L. B. Swift of Indianapolis; and E. W. Bemis of the Agricultural College, Manhattan, Kan. (*Proceedings*, 1898, pp. 152–173, 186–206, 220–248).

[11] *Proceedings*, 1898, pp. 153, 181, 198, 205.

[12] *Ibid.*, p. 215. For additional comment on the Indianapolis Conference, see *Outlook*, LX (1898), pp. 894–895; *Engineering News*, XLI (1899), p. 292; and *Annals*, XIII (1899), pp. 267–269.

[13] *Proceedings*, 1899, p. 6.

[14] *Ibid.*, pp. 51–86, 96–123.

[15] "A General View of the New Municipal Program," by J. A. Butler; "The Work of the Ohio Municipal Code Commission," by Edward Kibler; and "The Work of the Ohio Commission," by E. J. Blandin all in *Proceedings*, 1899, pp. 87–95, 188–206.

[16] *Proceedings*, 1899, pp. 216–249.

[17] *Ibid.*, pp. 35–36, 42.

[18] *Ibid.*, pp. 45–47. Cf. *Annals*, XV (1900), pp. 122–126; *City Government*, VII (1899), pp. 130, 140–142; *Harper's Weekly*, XLIII (1899), p. 1219; *Engineering News*, XLII (1899), pp. 343–344.

[19] Popularly referred to as the first Model City Charter, though it was not so designated by the League. Hereafter 1899 will be given as the date of adoption of the first Model City Charter and 1900 as the date of publication of the first Municipal Program.

[20] *A Municipal Program, Report of a Committee of the National Municipal League, adopted by the League, November 17, 1899, Together with Explanatory and other Papers* (1900). (Hereafter cited under title *A Municipal Program*.)

[21] Several papers on charter reform presented at earlier conferences of the League should be read in this connection: E. J. James, "The Elements of a Model Charter for American Cities," *Proceedings*, 1894–1895, pp. 154–173; H. W. Williams, "Reform of Our Municipal Councils," S. B. Capen, "Shall We Have One or Two Legislative Chambers?," J. A. Butler, "A Single or a Double Council?" and J. W. Pryor, "Should Municipal Legislators Receive a Salary?," all in *Proceedings*, 1896, pp. 236–266; F. J. Goodnow, "The Powers of Municipal Corporations," H. E. Deming, "The Legislature in State and City—1797–1897," and F. M. Loomis, "The Exclusion of Partisan Politics from Municipal Affairs: the Democratic-European Method," in *Proceedings*, 1897, pp. 63–74, 89–117.

[22] C. R. Woodruff, "An American Municipal Program," *Political Science Quarterly*, XVIII (1903), pp. 50, 54–55; D. F. Wilcox, *The American City: A Problem in Democracy* (1904), pp. 335–336.

[23] This analysis is based entirely on the volume, *A Municipal Program*.

[24] See pp. 35–37.

[25] See pp. 36–37.

[26] See p. 33.

[27] See p. 35.

[28] A footnote thus explains the attitude of the committee: "The Committee is of the opinion that the local schools should be under local control subject to a State supervision which compels the local standard to be fully equal to the State standard, and that so far and so rapidly as practicable this result should be accomplished. The Committee is aware, however, that there is a great diversity of practice in the different States, and that on account of the deep popular interest in education there is no branch of the public administration which on the whole has been so successful. It has therefore seemed best to leave the elaboration of the provisions of the draft relative to education to be made in accordance with the local conditions of each particular State."

[29] Woodruff, *op. cit.*, p. 50.

[30] *A Municipal Program*, pp. 153, 36–58.

[31] H. E. Deming, "A Municipal Program," *Annals*, XVII (1901), p. 441.

[32] *A Municipal Program*, pp. 173, 134–136, 157–158, 166, 231, 236; Woodruff, *op. cit.*, p. 53.

[33] *A Municipal Program*, pp. 82–87, 130–138, 163, 170, 232; Wilcox, *op. cit.*, pp. 332–333.

[34] *A Municipal Program*, p. 54.

[35] *Ibid.*, pp. 144–5, 164–6, 225–239.

[36] J. F. Dillon, *Commentaries on the Law of Municipal Corporations* (5th ed. rev.; (1911), Vol. I, 61.

[37] *A Municipal Program*, pp. 160, 235, 141; *Annals*, XIII (1899), pp. 267–269; Woodruff, *op. cit.*, pp. 51–52; Fairlie, *op. cit.*, p. 426; H. E. Deming, *The Government of American Cities* (1909), pp. 205–208. A second edition of the Municipal Program was printed in Deming's book, pp. 239–304.

[38] *A Municipal Program*, pp. 70, 62.

[39] *Ibid.*, pp. 67, 88–128, 162–163, 170, 232, 238; Woodruff, *op. cit.*, p. 53; Deming, *op. cit.*, pp. 219–233; A. R. Foote, *Powers of Municipalities* (1898).

[40] *A Municipal Program*, p. 74.

[41] *Ibid.*, pp. 75–76, 43–48, 159, 234.

[42] *Ibid.*, pp. 79, 80, 83, 154–155, 167–168, 234; Woodruff, *op. cit.*, pp. 55–56.

[43] *A Municipal Program*, pp. 169–170.

[44] Deming, *op. cit.*, p. 212.

[45] *A Municipal Program*, pp. 169, 25, 28–29, 81, 140, 154.

[46] *Ibid.*, 233–234, 168. See also Deming, *op. cit.*, pp. 210–217; Charles Richardson, "Does the New Municipal Program Confer Dangerous Powers on the Mayor?," *Proceedings*, 1900, pp. 119–126.

[47] Woodruff, *op. cit.*, p. 56; *A Municipal Program*, pp. 155, 159, 233.

[48] *A Municipal Program*, pp. 155, 165, 237; Deming, *op. cit.*, pp. 209, 218–219, 236–237. See also W. D. Foulke, "Proportional Representation and Municipal Reform," *Proceedings*, 1898, pp. 135–142, and "Representation of Different City Interests in the Council," *Proceedings*, 1900, pp. 147–156.

[49] *A Municipal Program*, pp. 81, 165, 170–171, 230–237.

[50] *Proceedings*, 1898, pp. 227–231; 1900, pp. 136–146.

[51] *A Municipal Program*, p. 239.

[52] H. E. Deming, "A Municipal Program," *Annals*, XVII (1901), pp. 435; *The Government of American Cities*, pp. 203–237.

[53] *A Municipal Program*, p. 156.

[54] *Proceedings*, 1898, pp. 2–3.

[55] *A Municipal Program*, pp. 59–62; Woodruff, *op. cit.*, pp. 47–58; Deming, *The Government of American Cities*, p. 216; J. A. Butler, "Some Essential Features of the New Municipal Program," *Proceedings*, 1900, pp. 94–96.

[56] Fairlie, *op. cit.*, pp. 426, 431.

[57] *A Municipal Program*, pp. 26–34, 158, 170; Deming, "A Municipal Program," *Annals*, XVII (1901), pp. 431–443; *Proceedings*, 1900, pp. 95–96; Woodruff, *op. cit.*, pp. 47–58; Fairlie, *op. cit.*, pp. 426–427.

[58] *A Municipal Program*, pp. 160, 167, 168; Fairlie, *op. cit.*, pp. 426–427; Woodruff, *op. cit.*, p. 52.

[59] *Proceedings*, 1900, pp. 96, 262–265.

[60] *Municipal Affairs*, IV (1900), pp. 236–238.

[61] For comments on the Program, see *New York Times*, Feb. 24, 1900; *Brooklyn Daily Eagle*, Mar. 6, 1900; *Washington Post*, Mar. 12, 1900; *Hartford Courant*, Mar. 5, 1900; *Providence Journal*, Mar. 11, 1900; *Detroit Free Press*, Mar. 17, 1900; *Chicago Record*, Mar. 17, 1900; *Chicago Evening Post*, Mar. 12, 1900; *Minneapolis Journal*, Mar. 17, 1900; *Morning Oregonian*, Mar. 18, 1900; *Review of Reviews*, XXI (1900), p. 632; *City Government* (Troy, N.Y.), May, 1900.

[62] *Municipal Affairs*, IV (1900), p. 238.

[63] XV (1900), p. 330. Professor Durand later set forth his theory of the complete control of the council over municipal government. (*Political Science Quarterly*, XV (1900)), pp. 426–451, 675–709.

[64] *Municipal Affairs*, III (1899), pp. 3–17.

[65] See pp. 42, 43.

[66] Wilcox, *op. cit.*, p. 307.

[67] J. A. Fairlie, *Essays in Municipal Administration* (1908), p. 15; *Municipal Administration* (1901), pp. 427–431.

[68] *Essays in Municipal Administration* (1908), p. 20.

[69] Quoted in leaflet, *National Municipal League's Work for Charter Reform* (New Series No. 8, 1909), pp. 6–7.

[70] XL (1898), p. 345.

[71] XLII (1899), p. 336. See also M. N. Baker, *Municipal Engineering and Sanitation* (1901), p. 236.

[72] Wilcox, *op. cit.*, p. 404.

[73] Cf. *National Municipal League's Work for Charter Reform* (1909).

[74] *Proceedings*, 1904, p. 189.

[75] *Ibid.*, 1908, p. 214.

[76] *Ibid.*, 1910, p. 210.

[77] *A Municipal Program*, p. 88.

NOTES TO CHAPTER IV

[1] *Review*, IV (1915), pp. 13–25 V (1916), pp. 12–23 XXII (1933), pp. 593–595.

[2] See chaps. v, vi, vii.

[3] *Minutes of Executive Committee*, Nov. 26, 1912; June 12, 1913; *Minutes of Council*, April 25, 1913; *Review*, II (1913), pp. 289, 561; *Handbook of the National Municipal League*, 1914, p. 4. (Hereafter cited as *Handbook*, with date.)

[4] G. W. Guthrie had been appointed ambassador to Japan; Professor F. J. Goodnow had gone to China to draft a new constitution for that country; Professor L. S. Rowe was a member of the Panama Canal Commission; and H. E. Deming and Charles Richardson were unable to serve because of ill-health.

[5] *Minutes of Council*, Nov. 12, 1913.

[6] M. N. Baker, Montclair, N. J.; Richard S. Childs, Delos F. Wilcox, New York; John A. Fairlie, University of Illinois; Mayo Fesler, Cleveland; A. R.

Hatton, Western Reserve University; Herman G. James, University of Texas; A. Lawrence Lowell, William B. Munro, Harvard University; Robert T. Paine, Boston; Clinton Rogers Woodruff, Philadelphia. *A New Municipal Program* (1919), pp. vii, viii, 21–22, 302.

[7] *Review,* IV (1915), pp. 190.

[8] *Tentative drafts of the sections ... as prepared by the Committee on Municipal Program ... and presented at the Twentieth annual meeting of the National Municipal League* (Dec. 1, 1914).

[9] *Model City Charter and Municipal Home Rule* (June 15, 1915).

[10] *Municipal Home Rule and a Model City Charter* (3d ed.; Nov. 15, 1915).

[11] *Review,* V (1916), pp. 187–190, 180–183; H. A. Stone, D. K. Price, K. H. Stone, *City Manager Government in the United States* (1940), pp. 4, 13, 16, 20.

[12] *A Model City Charter and Municipal Home Rule* (Jan. 15, 1916).

[13] Files of Clinton Rogers Woodruff.

[14] *Review,* V (1916), p. 190.

[15] *Minutes of Council,* April 19, 1916.

[16] *A Model City Charter and Municipal Home Rule as prepared by the Committee on Municipal Program of the National Municipal League* (Final ed.; Mar. 15, 1916).

[17] *A New Municipal Program,* p. 24.

[18] Files of Clinton Rogers Woodruff.

[19] *A New Municipal Program,* p. 24.

[20] *Minutes of Council,* Nov. 23, 1916.

[21] *Ibid.,* Nov. 21, 1917. The report of the committee on the library section of the Model City Charter was made to the League meeting in Detroit, and was referred to the Committee on Municipal Program. (See p. 90.)

[22] *Minutes of Executive Committee,* Dec. 21, 1917.

[23] All members of the old committee agreed to serve except W. D. Foulke and A. L. Lowell. Professor Thomas H. Reed of the University of California was added to the committee. (*Review,* VII [1918], p. 655.)

[24] *Minutes of Council,* June 4, 1918.

[25] The introductory and concluding chapters were contributed by C. R. Woodruff—"The Municipal Program: Old and New," and "Municipal Development in the United States since 1900" —and he was also the author of the section discussing "The Initiative, Referendum, and Recall." Other chapters were: "Experts in Municipal Government and the New Model Charter," by A. L. Lowell; "Civil Service and Efficiency," by W. D. Foulke; "Constitutional Municipal Home Rule," by A. R. Hatton; "Electoral Provisions of the New Municipal Program," by Mayo Fesler; "The Short Ballot Principle in the Model Charter," by R. S. Childs; "Administrative Organization," by H. G. James; "The Council," by W. B. Munro; "The Franchise Policy of the New Municipal Program," by D. F. Wilcox; "Financial Provisions of the New Municipal Program," by J. A. Fairlie; and "City Planning," by M. N. Baker. The only contributor not a member of the committee was Herbert Harley, secretary of the League's Committee on Municipal Courts, who wrote the chapter entitled, "Business Management For City Courts." In the appendix was printed the report of the League's Committee on Municipal Budgets and Accounting.

[26] *A New Municipal Program,* pp. 302–364.

[27] *A New Municipal Program,* p. 94; W. D. Foulke, "Evolution in City Charter Making," *Review,* IV (1915), pp. 13–25.

[28] *A New Municipal Program,* p. 95.

[29] *Ibid.,* pp. 108, 118.

[30] *Ibid.,* pp. 153–154.

[31] *Ibid.,* p. 33.

[32] *Ibid.,* p. 45.

[33] *Ibid.,* p. 144.

[34] *Ibid.*, p. 177.
[35] *Ibid.*, p. 200.
[36] *Ibid.*, p. 218.
[37] XXXVI (1916), p. 225.
[38] *American Political Science Review,* X (1916), p. 605. See also *American City,* XIV (1916), pp. 513, 515; *Engineering News,* LXXVI (1916), p. 314; *Pacific Municipalities,* XXX (1916), pp. 179–180.
[39] *American City Government* (1925), p. 631.
[40] "John Stuart Mill and the Model City Charter," *Review,* XI (1922), pp. 321–326.
[41] *Handbook of Municipal Government* (1922), pp. 56–57.
[42] *Municipal Government and Administration,* I (1923), pp. 195–196.
[43] *American Journal of Sociology,* XXV (1920), p. 506.
[44] *American Political Science Review,* XV (1921), p. 125.
[45] *Review,* VIII (1919), pp. 442–443.
[46] *Minutes of Council,* Nov. 11, 1924.
[47] M. N. Baker, A. E. Buck, Richard S. Childs, H. W. Dodds, New York; E. A. Cottrell, Stanford University; John A. Fairlie, University of Illinois; Mayo Fesler, Cleveland; A. R. Hatton, Western Reserve University; Charles P. Messick, Trenton, N. J.; W. B. Munro, Harvard University; Thomas H. Reed, University of Michigan; Delos F. Wilcox, Grand Rapids, Mich.; Clinton Rogers Woodruff, Philadelphia.
[48] *Minutes of Council,* Mar. 20, 1925; Nov. 18, 1925.
[49] *A Model City Charter* (rev. ed.; 1927), pp. 3–4.
[50] *Ibid.*, p. 3.
[51] *Minutes of Executive Committee,* Mar. 6, 1930.
[52] *Secretary's Report,* 1929–1930, p. 3.
[53] *Ibid.*
[54] Richard S. Childs, John Bauer, A. E. Buck, New York; M. N. Baker, Montclair, N. J.; Emmett L. Bennett, Alfred

Bettman, Cincinnati; Louis Brownlow, Chicago; Charles A. Carran, East Cleveland; Edwin A. Cottrell, Stanford University; W. F. Day, Staunton, Va.; H. W. Dodds, Princeton University; John N. Edy, Dallas, Texas; John A. Fairlie, University of Illinois; Mayo Fesler, Cleveland; J. P. Harris, University of Washington; A. R. Hatton, Northwestern University; Charles P. Messick, Trenton, N. J.; William B. Munro, California Institute of Technology; Thomas H. Reed, University of Michigan; R. W. Rigsby, Asheville, N. C.; Stephen B. Story, Rochester, N. Y.; Lent D. Upson, Detroit; Clinton Rogers Woodruff, Philadelphia.
[55] *Review,* XX (1931), p. 748; *Minutes of Executive Committee,* Feb. 19, 1932.
[56] *A Model City Charter* (rev. ed.; 1933), pp. 2–3.
[57] *Ibid.*, pp. 4–14.
[58] *Ibid.*, pp. 101–106.
[59] *Ibid.*, p. 2.
[60] Richard S. Childs, New York, chairman; Edwin A. Cottrell, Stanford University, vice-chairman; Arnold Frye, New York, chairman, committee on style and draft; John Bauer, Frederick L. Bird, A. E. Buck, Luther Gulick, Howard P. Jones, Joseph D. McGoldrick, Thomas H. Reed, New York; Charles E. Merriam, Leonard D. White, University of Chicago; Louis Brownlow, Clarence E. Ridley, Chicago; Joseph P. Harris, A. R. Hatton, Northwestern University; Alfred Bettman, Cincinnati; Clarence A. Dykstra, University of Wisconsin; John N. Edy, Harold D. Smith, Washington, D. C.; John A. Fairlie, University of Illinois; Mayo Fesler, Cleveland; Mrs. Siegel W. Judd, Grand Rapids, Mich.; Mrs. Virgil Loeb, St. Louis; William B. Munro, California Institute of Technology; John F. Sly, Princeton University; Charles W. Tooke, New York University; Lent D.

Upson, Detroit; Morton L. Wallerstein, Richmond, Va.

[61] *Review*, XXVI (1937), p. 274; XXVII (1938), p. 126; XXIX (1940), p. 76; XXX (1941), p. 618; *Secretary's Report*, 1936–1937, pp. 9–10; 1937–1938, pp. 18–19; 1938–1939, p. 3; 1939–1940, p. 4; 1940–1941, p. 4.

[62] *Review*, XXXIII (1944), pp. 532–533.

[63] *Ibid.*, XXX (1941), p. 618.

[64] Members of the committee were: Richard S. Childs, chairman, Arnold Frye, Alfred Willoughby, New York; William Anderson, University of Minnesota; E. A. Cottrell, Stanford University; John N. Edy, Houston, Texas; Herbert Emmerich, Chicago; John B. Gage, Kansas City, Mo.; C. A. Harrell, Schenectady; Herman Kehrli, University of Oregon; George R. Sidwell, Michigan Municipal League.

[65] *Secretary's Report*, 1944, p. 5; 1946, p. 5; *Review*, XXXIV (1945), pp. 162, 322. Cf. *A Guide for Charter Commissions* (1947).

[66] Cf. *Model Laws* (1936); *Review*, XXXIII (1944), pp. 531–534, 544.

NOTES TO CHAPTER V

[1] T. H. Reed, *Municipal Government in the United States* (rev. ed.; (1934), p. 118.

[2] See chap. viii.

[3] See chap. iii.

[4] *Proceedings*, 1904, p. 103; 1905, pp. 80–81; 1906, p. 120, 181–193; 1907, pp. 142–165; 1908, pp. 165–242; 1909, pp. 72, 95, 100, 135, 217–228, 463; 1910, pp. 30, 246–280, 308, 555–567.

[5] *City Government by Commission* (1911).

[6] *Ibid.*

[7] *Review*, I (1912), pp. 40–48.

[8] *Ibid.*, III (1914), pp. 44–48, 235–236. Cf. *The Commission Plan and Commission-Manager Plan of Municipal Government* (1914); and *A New Municipal Program* (1919), 12–20.

[9] R. S. Childs, "The City Manager Plan Will Endure," *American City*, LV, No. 5 (May, 1940), pp. 35–36. See also C. C. Maxey, *Urban Democracy* (1929), pp. 108–109; H. A. Stone, D. K. Price, K. H. Stone, *City Manager Government in the United States* (1940), pp. 6–13.

[10] *Review*, V (1916), p. 210. In a letter to Lawrence M. Conant, associate editor of *World's Work*, May 1, 1931, Mr. Childs explained further his connection with the origin of the plan:

"Shortly after I saw your article on Staunton, I conceived the idea that the city manager feature united to the commission plan would provide a new plan analagous to the business corporation and to the German burgomaster set-up, which would be very much superior to the commission plan, which, at that time, was coming rapidly into vogue and bringing with it some advantages as well as some serious defects of organization.

I was then a volunteer secretary of the National Short Ballot Organization, which I had organized in 1909, with Woodrow Wilson as president. I was also secretary of the New York Short Ballot Organization, whose mission was to push for the application of our short ballot ideas in the State of New York. In the latter capacity, I laid out a program for an optional municipal government law, which would make the commission plan available to all the smaller cities of the state, in a form ready for adoption by referendum. I twisted the standard commission form to provide for a city manager and an elaborate bill was drafted by my assistant, H. S. Gilbertson.

I did this without consulting the governing board of the New York Short Ballot Organization and brought the bill to them as a finished piece of work for their endorsement. They declined to endorse it for publication, as part of the association's program, preferring to keep to the simpler strategy of trying to get the minor state officers made appointive—one task at a time, so the bill was left on our hands. Looking around then for some one to father it, we got it sponsored by the Lockport Board of Trade, which introduced it in the legislature. The National Short Ballot Organization, forthwith, gave it generous publicity in its press releases; secured for it the attention of charter commissions all over the country; Woodrow Wilson mentioned it in one of his speeches on a western tour; it was put into a technical book that we published for the aid of charter commissions—Beard's Loose-Leaf Digest of Short Ballot Charters; papers on the "Lockport Plan" were gotten into various civic conventions and magazines; and thus the idea was put on the map in a campaign which went on for ten years under my personal and enthusiastic direction."

[11] I–VII (1912–1918).

[12] See chap. iv.

[13] H. A. Toulmin, *The City Manager* (1915). See also E. A. Fitzpatrick, ed., *Experts in City Government* (1919).

[14] *Minutes of Executive Committee,* Oct. 16, 1914; Dec. 21, 1917; June 25, 1918; *Minutes of Council,* April 19, Nov. 23, 1916; April 12, Nov. 21, 1917; April 24, June 4, 1918; *Review,* VII (1918), pp. 108–109, 235, 653. Cf. J. A. Cohen, "City Managership as a Profession," *Review,* XIII (Supplement, July, 1924), pp. 391–411.

[15] *Secretary's Report,* 1928–1929, p. 7.

[16] In addition to publications previously cited, see Mayo Fesler, "Five Years of City Manager Government in Cleveland," *Review,* XVIII (Supplement, Mar., 1929), pp. 203–220; A. W. Bromage, "Why Some Cities Have Abandoned Manager Charters," *Review,* XIX (1930), pp. 599–603, 761–766; Arch Mandel and W. M. Cotton, "Dayton's Sixteen Years of City Manager Government," *Review,* XIX (Supplement, July, 1930), pp. 497–518; *The City Manager Plan at Work* (1930); *Answers to your Questions About the Manager Plan* (1931); R. S. Childs, "The Best Practice under the City Manager Plan," *Review,* XXII (Supplement, Jan., 1933), pp. 41–44; "Suggested Procedure for Selecting A City Manager," *Review,* XXII (Supplement, Dec., 1933), pp. 629–634; *The*

Cincinnati Plan of Citizen Organization for Political Activity (1934); *Council-Manager Cities During the Depression* (1935); *Progress in City Management, Review,* XXV, No. 2 (Feb., 1936); *Democracy in the Modern World* (1938–1940), Pamphlets Nos. 1–7; *Forms of Municipal Government* (1939); *Who's Boss?* (1940); A. W. Bromage, *Manager Plan Abandonments* (1940); *What Happens to Labor under the Manager Plan* (1940); *What Happens to City Employees under the Manager Plan* (1940); *How Council-Manager Government is Working* (1940); *Town Management in New England* (1940). The League also distributes the following books on manager government: L. D. White, *The City Manager* (1927); C. P. Taft, *City Management: The Cincinnati Experiment* (1933); Murray Seasongood, *Local Government in the United States* (1933).

[17] *Secretary's Report,* 1937–1938, pp. 1–10.

[18] White, *op. cit.,* p. 279; Stone, Price, Stone, *op. cit.,* pp. 23–24.

[19] *Minutes of Executive Committee,* Dec. 18, 1914; Feb. 24, 1917; *Minutes of Council,* April 19, 1916; *Review,* V (1916), p. 175.

[20] *A New Municipal Program* (1919), p. 307.

[21] Section 89.

[22] *Review,* XI (1922), pp. 229–253.

[23] *Minutes of Annual Meeting,* Nov. 10, 1924; *Review,* XIV (1925), p. 17.

[24] *Minutes of Council,* Mar. 20, 1925.

[25] Membership of the Committee also included: C. A. Dykstra, Cincinnati; Dorsey W. Hyde, Jr., Washington, D.C.; Harris S. Keeler, Chicago; Morris Knowles, Pittsburgh; S. Gale Lowrie, University of Cincinnati; Charles McKinley, Reed College; Arthur E. Nelson, St. Paul; Thomas H. Reed, University of Michigan; Clarence G. Shenton, Philadelphia; Flavel Shurtleff, Frank

B. Williams, George H. McCaffrey, New York; Lent D. Upson, Detroit; Hugh K. Wagner, St. Louis.

[26] *Minutes of Executive Committee,* Jan. 5, 1926.

[27] *The Government of Metropolitan Areas* (1930).

[28] *Ibid.,* pp. 3–4, 388–390.

[29] *Review,* XX (1931), p. 38.

[30] *Annals,* CLIV (1931), p. 188.

[31] *American Political Science Review,* XXVI (1932), p. 165.

[32] CVI (April 16, 1931), p. 659.

[33] XXI (1931), p. 177.

[34] Reed, *op. cit.,* chaps. xxii–xxiii.

[35] *City Government in the United States* (1934), p. 443.

[36] Section 82.

[37] Section 83.

[38] Sections 801, 802, 803.

[39] Sections 1102, 1103.

[40] *Secretary's Report,* 1941–1942, pp. 7–9; *Review,* XXXII (1943), pp. 90–91.

[41] *Review,* VI (1917), pp. 182–188.

[42] *Ibid.,* VI (1917), pp. 274.

[43] *Minutes of Executive Committee,* Feb. 24, 1917; June 25, Dec. 12, 1918; *Review,* VII (1918), p. 654; IX (1920), p. 474.

[44] (1) Bill of Rights, Albert Bushnell Hart; (2) Governor and Legislature, single house, state manager, National Short Ballot Organization; (3) Proportional Representation, Proportional Representation League; (4) Budget, Governmental Research Conference; (5) Judiciary, American Judicature Society; (6) Civil Service, National Civil Service Reform League; (7) Municipal Government, Committee on Municipal Program; (8) County Government, Committee on County Government; (9) Initiative and Referendum, National Popular Government League; (10) Taxation, Committee on Taxation; (11) Debt Limitations, A. N. Holcombe; (12) Legislative Procedure, H. W.

Dodds; (13) Limitations on Legislation, Charles A. Beard; (14) Elections and Suffrage, Honest Ballot Association; (15) Labor, Joseph P. Chamberlain; (16) City Planning and Excess Condemnation, Frank B. Williams; (17) Amendments, Herman G. James.

[45] *Review,* VIII (1919), pp. 593, 671, 706–723.

[46] *Ibid.,* VIII (1919), pp. 707–709; *Outlook,* CXXIV (1920), p. 143. Cf. R. S. Childs, "A State Manager Plan," *Review,* VI (1917), pp. 659–663.

[47] *Review,* IX (1920), pp. 691, 711–715; X (1921), pp. 9–10, 226–232.

[48] *Minutes of Council,* Nov. 18, 1921; Cf. *Progress Report on A Model State Constitution* (1921).

[49] Membership of the Committee on State Government included: Charles A. Beard, New Milford, Conn.; A. E. Buck, H. W. Dodds, R. S. Childs, Raymond V. Ingersoll, New York; W. F. Dodd, Chicago; John A. Fairlie, University of Illinois; A. R. Hatton, Western Reserve University; A. N. Holcombe, Harvard University; Isidor Loeb, University of Missouri; Lindsay Rogers, Columbia University; A. E. Sheldon, Lincoln, Neb.; Clinton Rogers Woodruff, Philadelphia. Charles E. Hughes served as chairman until his resignation as League president in the spring of 1921.

[50] *Review,* XVII (1928), p. 723.

[51] *A Model State Constitution* (rev. ed.; 1933), p. 3.

[52] W. B. Graves, *American State Government* (1936), p. 81.

[53] *Review,* XV (1926), pp. 441–444.

[54] *Ibid.,* XIX (1930), pp. 460–462.

[55] *Ibid.,* XVI (1927), pp. 553–554.

[56] W. F. Dodd, *State Government* (2d ed.; 1928), p. 566.

[57] C. G. Haines and B. M. Haines, *Principles and Problems of Government* (3d ed.; 1934), p. 329.

[58] W. B. Munro, *The Government of the United States* (4th ed.; 1936), p. 687.

[59] A. N. Holcombe, *State Government in the United States* (3d ed.; 1931), p. 583.

[60] *Ibid.*, p. 606.

[61] *Review*, XXVIII (1939), p. 682; XXIX (1940), p. 770.

[62] Other members were: Frank Bane, Hubert R. Gallagher, Walter F. Dodd, Chicago; Charles A. Beard, New Milford, Conn.; George C. S. Benson, Northwestern University; A. E. Buck, New York; J. Alton Burdine, University of Texas; Finla G. Crawford, Syracuse University; John A. Fairlie, University of Illinois; Frederick H. Guild, Topeka, Kan.; Arthur N. Holcombe, Harvard University; Rodney L. Mott, Colgate University; Robert S. Rankin, Duke University; Paul T. Stafford, Princeton University; Frank M. Stewart, University of California at Los Angeles.

[63] *Model State Constitution with Explanatory Articles* (4th ed. rev.; 1941); *Review*, XXXI (1942), pp. 92–99.

[64] New members added were: Martin L. Faust, University of Missouri; Samuel C. May, University of California; Lloyd M. Short, University of Minnesota; Roger V. Shumate, University of Nebraska; Edwin E. Witte, University of Wisconsin. Messrs. Charles A. Beard, Finla G. Crawford, and John A. Fairlie were not members of the reconstituted committee.

[65] *Model State Constitution with Explanatory Articles* (4th ed., complete revision, 1941; partial revision, 1946).

[66] *Review*, VIII (Supplement, Nov., 1919), pp. 639–667.

[67] *Ibid.*, IX (Supplement, Nov. 1920), pp. 739–756.

[68] A. E. Buck, *The Reorganization of State Governments in the United States* (1938); *Review*, XXVII (1938), pp. 561–562; *American Political Science Review*, XXXII (1933), pp. 1186–1187.

[69] For other publications in this field, see A. E. Buck, "The Coming of Centralized Purchasing in State Governments," *Review*, IX (Supplement, Feb., 1920), pp. 115–135; and C. E. McCombs, "State Welfare Administration and Consolidated Government," *Review*, XIII (Supplement, Aug., 1924), pp. 461–473.

[70] *Annals*, XLVII (1913), pp. 274–278; *American City*, XI (1914), p. 507; A. W. Bromage, *American County Government* (1933), p. 132.

[71] CXIII (1916), pp. 39–45.

[72] *Minutes of Executive Committee*, Feb. 24, 1917; *Review*, VII (1918), pp. 123–124, 444, 654; IX (1920), pp. 472–473.

[73] *Minutes of Council*, Mar. 20, 1925.

[74] Other members of the committee were: Frank G. Bates, Indiana University; Otho G. Cartwright, New York; James Errant, University of Oklahoma; Luther Gulick, Howard P. Jones, New York; A. R. Hatton, Northwestern University; Wylie Kilpatrick, Clarence E. Ridley, Chicago; J. Noel Macy, White Plains, N.Y.; Samuel C. May, University of California; Benjamin F. Shambaugh, State University of Iowa; Henry M. Waite, Cincinnati.

[75] *Review*, XIX (Supplement, Aug., 1930), pp. 565–579.

[76] *American County Government* (1933), p. 136.

[77] Other members were: William Anderson, University of Minnesota; R. C. Atkinson, Columbus, Ohio; Frank Bane, Clark Foreman, Chicago; Frank G. Bates, Indiana University; Arthur W. Bromage, University of Michigan; John Callahan, Madison, Wis.; Richard S. Childs, Luther Gulick, New York; Edwin A. Cottrell, Stanford University; Harry H. Freeman, Buffalo; Mrs. Walter S. Greenough, Indianapolis; A. R. Hatton, Northwestern University; J. Catron Jones, University of Kentucky;

Mrs. Siegel W. Judd, Grand Rapids, Mich.; Wylie Kilpatrick, Trenton, N.J.; Walter F. Kirk, Port Clinton, Ohio; Harley L. Lutz, Princeton University; Kirk H. Porter, State University of Iowa; Theodore B. Manny, Hugh Reid, Washington, D.C.; C. E. Rightor, Detroit; Walter R. Sharp, University of Wisconsin; Charles P. Taft 2nd, Cincinnati; Robert H. Tucker, Washington and Lee University; Paul W. Wager, University of North Carolina; C. R. White, Ionia, N.Y.

[78] J. A. Fairlie, "The League's Committee on County Government," *Review*, XXI (1932), pp. 519–520.

[79] *Ibid.*

[80] XXI (1932), pp. 525–542. The entire issue was concerned with county government.

[81] See p. 80.

[82] XXII (1933), pp. 467–486.

[83] *Review*, XXIII (Supplement, Feb., 1934), pp. 139–145.

[84] XXIII, No. 10 (1934); XXVIII, No. 2 (1939).

[85] *Review*, XXXVI (1947), p. 62; *Secretary's Report*, 1946, p. 6.

[86] *Secretary's Report*, 1933–1934, p. 9.

[87] *Proceedings*, 1908, pp. 308–327.

[88] His colleagues on the committee were: William H. Allen, Horace E. Deming, New York; Milton J. Foreman, Chicago; George Godard, Hartford, Conn.; Clarence B. Lester, Albany, N.Y.; Oscar Leser, Baltimore; Charles McCarthy, Madison, Wis.; Thomas L. Montgomery, Harrisburg, Pa.; Charles E. Merriam, University of Chicago; Robert T. Paine, Jr., Boston.

[89] *Proceedings*, 1910, pp. 451–459; 1909, p. 477.

[90] *Ibid.*, 1911, pp. 13–15 (*Review*, I, No. 1, Jan., 1912).

[91] *Review*, III (1914), pp. 222–224; *Handbook*, 1914, p. 7; E. W. Crecraft, "The Municipal Reference Library," *Review*, II (1913), pp. 644–653.

[92] *Review*, IV (1915), pp. 176–178; V (1916), pp. 172–174.

[93] *Ibid.*, VI (1917), p. 176.

[94] *Minutes of Council*, April 12, Nov. 21, 1917; April 24, 1918; April 19, 1919; Feb. 18, 1920; *Review*, VII (1918), pp. 236, 653; IX (1920), p. 474.

[95] See p. 52.

[96] *Review*, VII (1918), pp. 109–113. The committee also included: J. C. Dana, Newark, N.J.; Drew B. Hall, Somerville, Mass.; Harrison W. Craver, New York; Arthur E. Bostwick, St. Louis.

[97] Wilfred Bolster, Boston; Roscoe Pound, Harvard University; Hastings H. Hart, Edgar Lauer, William L. Ransom, New York; A. Leo Weil, Pittsburgh; Thomas R. White, Philadelphia.

[98] Cf. Herbert Harley, "The Model Municipal Court," *Review*, III (1914), pp. 57–67. "Business Management for City Courts," *A New Municipal Program* (1919), chap. xiii. *Handbook*, 1914, pp. 6–7; *Review*, IV (1915), pp. 181–184; V (1916), pp. 172, 329, 680; VI (1917), pp. 176–178. See also Herbert Harley, *Criminal Justice—How to Achieve It* (Pocket Civic Series, No. 8, 1922).

[99] Personnel of the committee also included: Newton D. Baker, Cleveland; Francis X. Busch, Walter F. Dodd, Thomas E. Donnelley, Frank J. Loesch, Amos C. Miller, Silas H. Strawn, Charles M. Thomson, Chicago; Richard S. Childs, New York; Raymond Moley, Columbia University; William B. Munro, California Institute of Technology; Frederic A. Ogg, University of Wisconsin; Roscoe Pound, James M. Landis, Harvard University Law School; Carl V. Essery, Detroit; Herbert Harley, Ira E. Robinson, W. F. Willoughby, Washington, D.C.; William G. Hale, University of Southern California Law School; Walter W.

Cook, L. C. Marshall, Institute of Law, Johns Hopkins University; Stuart H. Perry, Adrian, Michigan; Chester Rowell, M. C. Sloss, San Francisco; Murray Seasongood, Cincinnati; Burke Shartel, University of Michigan Law School; Henry U. Sims, Birmingham, Ala.; John H. Wigmore, Northwestern University Law School.

[100] *Secretary's Report,* 1929–1930 to 1935–1936; *Minutes of Executive Committee,* Mar. 26, 1931; *Minutes of Council,* May 14–15, 1932; May 27–28, 1933.

[101] See chaps. iii, iv.

[102] See p. 81.

[103] *Secretary's Report,* 1929–1930, p. 7; 1930–1931, p. 6.

[104] XXI (1932), pp. 12, 94, 176, 229, 312, 357, 434, 564, 601, 671.

[105] William B. Munro, Harvard University, chairman; Harold S. Buttenheim, New York; Frederick L. Hoffman, Newark, N.J.; Herman G. James, University of Texas; Otto Kirchner, Detroit.

[106] *Minutes of Council,* Nov. 21, 1917; June 4, 1918; Feb. 18, 1920; *Minutes of Executive Committee,* Dec. 21, 1917; *Review,* VII (1918), pp. 236, 653; IX (1920), p. 473.

[107] See pp. 89, 90. See also William Anderson, "The Federal Government and the Cities," *Review,* XIII (1924), pp. 288–293.

[108] Other members representative of various group interests were: H. J. Baker, state director of agricultural extension work, Rutgers College; Mrs. La Rue Brown, National League of Women Voters; Paul H. Douglas, University of Chicago; Thomas H. MacDonald, chief, Bureau of Public Roads, U. S. Department of Agriculture; John N. Mackall, chairman, State Road Commission, Maryland; John K. Norton, director of research, National Education Association; S. H. Thompson, president, American Farm Bureau Federation; James T.

Young, University of Pennsylvania.

[109] "Federal Aid to the States," *Review,* XVII (Supplement, Oct., 1928), pp. 619–659.

[110] Because of criticism that two out of six sessions of the program in 1922 dealt with federal problems, a committee was appointed to consider the subject. It recommended that future programs should devote approximately one-half of the sessions to urban problems with the other half divided among county, state, and national questions. The report was accepted by the Council and referred to the program committee. (Cf. *Review,* XII [1923],) pp. 229–231.

[111] B. G. Rosahn, *Housing Management—Its History and Relation to Present Day Housing Problems* (1935); *Social Security,* ed. by J. P. Harris (1936); *Social Security, Progress and Prospects,* ed. by Z. C. Franklin (1937).

NOTES TO CHAPTER VI

[1] "A Democracy That Might Work," *Century,* CXX (1930), pp. 11–17.

[2] See chap. v.

[3] H. P. Jones, "Citizen Groups, Tool of Democracy," *Annals,* CXCIX (1938), pp. 176–182.

[4] See chap. iii.

[5] *Proceedings,* 1900, pp. 212–225; 1901, pp. 184–217.

[6] *Ibid.,* 1902, pp. 35, 348; *Minutes of Executive Committee,* Dec. 13, 1902.

[7] *Proceedings,* 1903, pp. 49–65, 30.

[8] *Ibid.,* 1904, pp. 31, 321–381.

[9] *Draft of a Proposed Municipal Nominating Law* (1904).

[10] *Proceedings,* 1905, pp. 35–40, 293–372, 393. Cf. H. E. Deming, *Municipal Nomination Reform* (Publications of the National Municipal League, Pamphlet No. 14, 1905).

[11] *Proceedings,* 1906, pp. 37–38, 308–348, 446.

[12] *Ibid.*, 1907, pp. 193–222, 407; *Minutes of Executive Committee*, Nov. 19, 1907; *Handbook*, 1914, p. 5.

[13] *Proceedings*, 1908, pp. 75–85, 223–246, 470; 1909, pp. 291–353, 439–440, 464–470, 476; 1910; pp. 328–345, 533–544, 573.

[14] *Minutes of Executive Committee*, Nov. 16, 1908; April 7, 1909; Nov. 14, 1910; April 20, 1911; *Minutes of Council*, under date of November 12, 1913.

[15] See chap. iv.

[16] *Review*, VI (1917), pp. 201–237.

[17] *Ibid.*, VI (1917), pp. 205.

[18] *Minutes of Council*, July 15, 1920.

[19] Membership was as follows: Albert S. Bard, H. W. Dodds, Stephen K. Rapp, Edward R. Finch, New York; Harry Best, University of Kentucky; Mayo Fesler, Brooklyn; Lewis J. Johnson, Harvard University; John C. Lodge, Detroit; F. L. Olson, Minneapolis; Shelby M. Singleton, Chicago; C. G. Hoag, Samuel B. Scott, Clinton Rogers Woodruff, Philadelphia; Ralph S. Boots, University of Nebraska.

[20] R. S. Boots, "The Presidential Primary," *Review*, IX (Supplement, Sept., 1920), pp. 597–617.

[21] *Review*, X (1921), pp. 11–12, 23–31, 87–94, 166–170, 322–324. The addresses by Hughes and Merriam were published as a separate pamphlet, *The Direct Primary* (1921).

[22] "The Outline of an Improved Method of Conducting Elections, with Discussion of the Direct Primary," *Review*, X (1921), pp. 603–616. Cf. several articles on the direct primary, *Review*, XI (1922), pp. 282–290, 332–336, 373–379.

[23] See pp. 81, 84.

[24] Committee personnel was as follows: George H. McCaffrey, Boston; William P. Lovett, Detroit; Raymond V. Ingersoll, H. W. Dodds, Walter T. Arndt, New York; R. F. Griffen, Grand Rapids, Mich.; Raymond Moley, Columbia University.

[25] *Minutes of Council*, Mar. 20, Nov. 18, 1925.

[26] *Ibid.*, April 27, 1926.

[27] Other members were: Albert S. Bard, New York; W. W. Connor, Seattle; Oakley E. Distin, W. P. Lovett, Detroit; Mayo Fesler, Cleveland; Walter Matscheck, Kansas City, Mo.; Harley G. Moorhead, Omaha; H. A. Nichols, Rochester, N.Y.; F. L. Olson, Pittsburgh; Helen M. Rocca, Washington, D.C.; George C. Sikes, Chicago; Thomas R. White, Philadelphia; J. H. Zemansky, San Francisco.

[28] "A Model Registration System," *Review*, XVI (Supplement, Jan. 1927), pp. 45–86. See J. P. Harris, *Registration of Voters in the United States*, Chap. II (1929).

[29] Members of the Committee which supervised the preparation of the report were: Charles E. Merriam, University of Chicago, chairman; Joseph P. Harris, University of Washington, secretary; Albert S. Bard, William M. Chadbourne, New York; Mayo Fesler, Cleveland; Walter Matscheck, Kansas City, Mo.; W. F. Willoughby, Katherine Frederic, Washington, D.C.; Ralph S. Boots, University of Pittsburgh; H. W. Dodds, Princeton University; H. A. Nichols, Rochester, N.Y.; J. H. Zemansky, San Francisco; Harold F. Gosnell, University of Chicago; Edwin E. Witte, Madison, Wis.; Oakley E. Distin, Detroit; William D. McHugh, Omaha; Clarence G. Shenton, Thomas R. White, George H. Hallett, Jr., Philadelphia.

[30] "A Model Election Administration System," *Review*, XIX (Supplement, Sept., 1930), pp. 629–671. See J. P. Harris, *Election Administration in the United States* (1934), chap. ii.

[31] *Review*, XX (1931), pp. 70. *Secretary's Report*, 1929–1930, pp. 1–2; 1930–1931, pp. 1; 1931–1932, p. 1.

[32] See also J. K. Pollock, "Election Administration in Michigan," *Review*, XXIII (Supplement, June, 1934), pp. 343–359.

[33] Membership of the Committee in 1939: Charles E. Merriam, University of Chicago, chairman; Joseph P. Harris, University of California, secretary; Oakley E. Distin, W. P. Lovett, Detroit; Mayo Fesler, Cleveland; George H. Hallett, Jr., New York; Walter Matscheck, Helen M. Rocca, Washington, D.C.; Harley G. Moorhead, Omaha; Thomas R. White, Philadelphia; J. H. Zemansky, San Francisco.

[34] *A Model Registration System* (3d. ed.; 1939), p. 3.

[35] *Secretary's Report*, 1929–1930, p. 7; 1930–1931, p. 6; 1931–1932, p. 7; *Minutes of Executive Committee*, Mar. 26, 1931.

[36] *A Municipal Program*, (1900), pp. 219–220.

[37] *A New Municipal Program* (1919), pp. 95–108, 311–320, 364–366.

[38] *A Model City Charter* (rev. ed.; 1927), pp. 15–24.

[39] *Ibid.* (rev. ed.; 1933), pp. 8–9, 26–40; (5th ed.; 1941), p. 71.

[40] *A Model State Constitution* (rev. ed.; 1933), p. 4; (4th ed.; 1941), p. 6.

[41] R. C. Atkinson, "Principles of a Model County Government," *Review*, XXII (Supplement, Sept., 1933), pp. 472–474.

[42] *Minutes of Annual Meeting*, Nov. 9, 1931; *Minutes of Council*, Nov. 9, 1931.

[43] *Minutes of Executive Committee*, Dec. 4, 1931; Feb. 19, 1932.

[44] *Ibid.*

[45] *Review*, XXV (1936), pp. 43–44.

[46] Membership: C. G. Hoag, Haverford, Pa., chairman; Thomas R. White, Philadelphia; George H. Hallett, Jr., secretary; Albert S. Bard, George H. McCaffrey, H. S. Buttenheim, William Jay Schieffelin, Mrs. F. Louis Slade, New York; Mrs. George Gelhorn, St. Louis; A. R. Hatton, Northwestern University; Lewis J. Johnson, Harvard University; Murray Seasongood, Ralph Holterhoff, Cincinnati; Louis Brownlow, Chicago; Paul H. Douglas, University of Chicago. Mr. Hoag was general secretary-treasurer of the Proportional Representation League from 1912 to 1926, and has been treasurer and honorary secretary since 1926. (*Secretary's Report*, 1931–1932, p. 6).

[47] C. G. Hoag and G. H. Hallett, Jr., *Proportional Representation* (1926); G. H. Hallett, Jr., *Proportional Representation—The Key to Democracy* (1937); William Anderson, "The Constitutionality of Proportional Representation," *Review*, XII (Supplement, Dec., 1923), pp. 745–762; J. P. Harris, "The Practical Workings of Proportional Representation in the United States and Canada," *Review*, XIX (Supplement, May, 1930), pp. 337–383; *Proportional Representation* ("P. R.")— *Effective Voting* (P. R. League Leaflet No. 5, 10th ed., Mar., 1935); *A Primer in Proportional Representation* (mimeo.); *Proportional Representation—Answers to Your Questions* (1939). Cf. *Proportional Representation for the State Legislature* (A reprint of chap. iv of Vol. VII of the Report of the New York State Constitutional Convention Committee appointed by Governor Herbert H. Lehman to collate factual data for the use of the delegates to the Constitutional Convention of 1938).

[48] *A Municipal Program* (1900), pp. 219–220.

[49] *Proceedings*, 1905, pp. 102–107, 384; 1906, pp. 363–387; 1908, pp. 75–85, 223–246; 1909, pp. 309–353; *Review*, I (1912), pp. 204–211, 586–602, 659–661; *ibid.*, II (1913), pp. 467–469; *ibid.*, III (1914), pp. 256–283, 693–701.

[50] *A New Municipal Program* (1919), pp. 159–172, 321–333. See also D. F. Wilcox, *Government by All the People* (1912) ; W. B. Munro, ed., *The Initiative, Referendum and Recall* (National Municipal League Series, 1912) ; and *Review,* V (1916), pp. 380–387; *ibid.,* VI (1917), pp. 387–394, 491–501.

[51] *A Model City Charter* (rev. ed.; 1927), pp. 25–32; (rev. ed.; 1933), pp. 40–50; (4th ed.; 1941), pp. 92–96.

[52] *A Model State Constitution* (1921), pp. 7–9; Atkinson, *op. cit.,* pp. 474, 477–478.

[53] *Review,* VIII (1919), pp. 397–403; *Minutes of Executive Committee,* Sept. 29, 1919; *Minutes of Council,* Dec. 5, 1919; July 15, Dec. 13, 1920; March 28, 1923.

[54] *Review,* VIII (1919), p. 397; XI (1922), p. 226.

[55] *Ibid.,* IX (1920), pp. 146–150; *ibid.,* X (1921), pp. 232–239; *ibid.,* XII (1923), pp. 192–204, 610–622; *ibid.,* XV (1926), pp. 42–65; *ibid.,* XVI (1927), pp. 642–661.

[56] Officers were: Woodrow Wilson, Princeton University, president; Winston Churchill, Cornish, N.H.; Horace E. Deming, New York; Ben B. Lindsey, Denver; William S. U'Ren, Oregon City, Ore.; William Allen White, Emporia, Kan.; John Mitchell, Mt. Vernon, N.Y.; and Clinton Rogers Woodruff, Philadelphia, vice-presidents; Richard S. Childs, New York, secretary-treasurer; and an advisory board consisting of Lawrence F. Abbott, Norman Hapgood, Richard S. Childs, New York; Woodrow Wilson and Henry Jones Ford, Princeton University.

[57] Cf. R. S. Childs, *Short Ballot Principles* (1911) ; *The Short Ballot* (1909) ; *The Story of the Short Ballot Cities* (1910) ; C. A. Beard, ed., *Loose-Leaf Digest of Short Ballot Charters* (1911).

[58] *Review,* IX (1920), p. 270; *Short Ballot Bulletin,* VII, No. 56 (April, 1920) ; H. A. Stone, D. K. Price, K. H. Stone, *City Manager Government in the United States* (1940), pp. 6–7, 21.

[59] *Secretary's Report,* 1929–1930, p. 7.

[60] *The Short Ballot* (1930), p. 30.

[61] Personnel also included: John H. Finley, Princeton University; William F. McDowell, New York; Charles Zueblin, University of Chicago; Robert C. Brooks, Cornell University; E. L. Bogart, Oberlin College; John L. Stewart, Lehigh University; Kendrick C. Babcock, University of California; James T. Young, University of Pennsylvania; Clinton Rogers Woodruff, Philadelphia.

[62] *Proceedings,* 1900, pp. 41–42; 1901, pp. 218–247; 1902, pp. 34, 91–92, 268–291, 348; 1903, pp. 14–16, 222–246, 323; *Handbook,* 1904, pp. 8–9.

[63] Membership of the Committee in 1906 was as follows: L. S. Rowe, University of Pennsylvania, chairman; W. Ward Pierson, University of Pennsylvania, acting chairman; John A. Fairlie, University of Michigan; Clinton Rogers Woodruff, Philadelphia; C. H. Huberich, University of Texas; Frank J. Goodnow, Columbia University; W. B. Munro, Harvard University; James A. Woodburn, University of Indiana; Harry A. Garfield, Princeton University; C. E. Merriam, University of Chicago; William A. Rawles, University of Indiana; S. E. Sparling, University of Wisconsin; Isidor Loeb, University of Missouri; W. A. Schaper, University of Minnesota; James R. Weaver, DePauw University; W. B. Bailey, Yale University.

[64] *Proceedings,* 1904, pp. 59, 242–248, 404; 1905, pp. 180–183, 393; 1906, pp. 416–418, 489; 1907, p. 405.

[65] *Ibid.,* 1908, pp. 73, 355, 348–366, 468.

[66] *Ibid.,* 1908, pp. 355–357; 1909, pp. 476, 479–480.

[67] *Review,* II (1913), pp. 427–438.

[68] *Ibid.,* V (1916), pp. 565–573. In 1916 the Committee consisted of the following: W. B. Munro, Harvard University, chairman; W. B. Bailey, Yale University; C. A. Beard, Columbia University; R. C. Brooks, Swarthmore College; J. A. Fairlie, University of Illinois; H. J. Ford, Princeton University; H. A. Garfield, Williams College; H. G. James, University of Texas; Isidor Loeb, University of Missouri; C. E. Merriam, University of Chicago; T. H. Reed, University of California; L. S. Rowe, University of Pennsylvania; W. A. Schaper, University of Minnesota; B. F. Shambaugh, State University of Iowa; Clinton Rogers Woodruff, Philadelphia.

[69] *Review,* VI (1917), p. 194.

[70] Other members of the Committee were: Charles A. Beard, New Milford, Conn.; H. S. Buttenheim, H. W. Dodds, C. E. Ridley, Luther Gulick, Russell Forbes, New York; John A. Fairlie, University of Illinois; A. C. Hanford, W. B. Munro, Harvard University; O. Garfield Jones, University of Toledo; Arthur E. Morgan, Antioch College; W. E. Mosher, Syracuse University; Thomas H. Reed, University of Michigan; E. A. Cottrell, Stanford University.

[71] *Minutes of Council,* Feb. 3, 1928; *Minutes of Executive Committee,* Aug. 28, 1928; *Secretary's Report,* 1927–1928, p. 2.

[72] *Minutes of Executive Committee,* Dec. 4, 1931; Feb. 19, 1932.

[73] American Political Science Association, *Report of the Committee on Policy* (1930), pp. 127–145.

[74] His associates on the committee were: Isaac S. Wheaton, Princeton, N. J.; Philip Loring Allen, Elliot H. Goodwin, Charles M. Jessup, R. Bayard Cutting, New York; David P. Jones, Minneapolis, Francis R. Cope, Jr., Morris L. Cooke, Robert D. Jenks, Samuel B. Scott, Clinton Rogers Woodruff, Philadelphia; Everett Colby, Orange, N. J.; William Kent, Chicago; F. P. Kippel, Columbia University; A. Julius Freiberg, Cincinnati.

[75] *Proceedings,* 1905, pp. 16, 94, 184–192; 1906, pp. 9–13, 121, 489; 1909, pp. 122.

[76] *Review,* I (1912), p. 509.

[77] Members of the Committee on Intercollegiate Work, 1916–1918, were: William B. Munro, Harvard University, chairman; R. Bayard Cutting, Camillus G. Kidder, New York; Francis B. Sayre, Williams College; Arthur E. Wood, Ann Arbor, Mich.

[78] *Minutes of Executive Committee,* Jan. 27, Nov. 3, 1915; April 19, Dec. 28, 1916; June 25, 1918; *Minutes of Council,* Nov. 23, 1916; April 12, Nov. 21, 1917; June 4, 1918; Feb. 18, 1920. Cf. National Municipal League, Intercollegiate Division, *Social and Civic Activities for College Graduates* (1916); *Review,* IV (1915), pp. 318, 501; *ibid.,* V (1916), pp. 169, 495–496; *ibid.,* VI (1917), pp. 173–174, 193–194, 520–521.

[79] Cf. O. G. Villard, *William Henry Baldwin: A Life of Civic Endeavor* (Pamphlet of the National Municipal League, New Series, No. 1, 1905).

[80] *Review,* XX (1931), p. 435.

[81] *Handbook,* 1914, p. 12.

[82] *Ibid.,* pp. 12–13; *Review,* I (1912), p. 734; *ibid.,* II (1913), p. 715; *ibid.,* IV (1915), pp. 318–319; *ibid.,* V (1916), p. 679.

[83] *Handbook,* 1914, p. 13; *Review,* I (1912), p. 512; *ibid.,* III (1914), p. 618; *ibid.,* V (1916), p. 680.

[84] *Review,* II (1913), p. 715; *ibid.,* III (1914), p. 618.

[85] *Minutes of Executive Committee,* Mar. 24, 1914; *Minutes of Council,* April 22, Dec. 12, 1921; *Review,* XXVI (1937), p. 414.

[86] *Review*, III (1914), p. 618; *ibid.*, XVII (1928), p. 719; *Minutes of Executive Committee*, Dec. 9, 1913; June 12, 1914.

[87] *Review*, XXII (1933), p. 540; *ibid.*, XXIII (1934), p. 2.

[88] Serving also on the committee were: Thomas M. Drown, Lehigh University; John H. Finley, College of the City of New York; Clinton Rogers Woodruff, Franklin S. Edmonds, Oliver P. Cornman, Charles Richardson, Philadelphia; Elmer S. Brown, University of California; John A. Fairlie, University of Michigan; B. F. Buck, Chicago; George H. Martin, Boston; Jesse B. Davis, Detroit; James B. Reynolds, Charles C. Burlingham, Albert Shaw, New York; E. Y. Robinson, Minneapolis; Aaron Gove, Denver; Charles N. Kendall, Indianapolis; James H. Van Sickle, Baltimore; James G. Boone, Cincinnati; Frank J. Goodnow, Columbia University; Charles McMurray, DeKalb, Ill.; Frederick L. Luqueer, Brooklyn; Albert Bushnell Hart, Harvard University.

[89] *Proceedings*, 1903, pp. 14–15, 222–246, 323–324; 1904, pp. 59–68, 249–293, 403; 1905, pp. 11–16, 256–292, 392.

[90] His colleagues were : Frank V. Thompson, South Boston; M. J. O'Shea, John L. Tildsley, New York; Frederic L. Luqueer, Brooklyn; George Groat, Bronx, N.Y.; George H. Martin, Boston.

[91] *Proceedings*, 1907, p. 408; 1908, p. 469; 1909, pp. 24–41, 366–389, 476; *Minutes of Executive Committee*, April 26, 1905.

[92] *Proceedings*, 1911, pp. 5, 17 (*Review*, I, No. 1, Jan., 1912); *Handbook*, 1914, pp. 3–4; *Proceedings*, 1910, p. 572.

[93] *Review*, III (1914), pp. 224–226.

[94] *Review*, III (1914), pp. 346–348. See also National Municipal League, Leaflets, Third Series: No. 1, *What Constitutes Good Citizenship*, by C. E.

Adams, 1911; No. 2, *Training for Citizenship*, 1913; No. 3, *Plan for the Promotion of Civic Education*, 1913; No. 4, *Measuring the Value of Civic Training*, 1913; No. 5, *How Georgia Prepares her Teachers to Teach Citizenship*, 1914; No. 6, *The U. S. Bureau of Education Interest in Better Training for Citizenship*, 1914.

[95] *Review*, IV (1915), pp. 178–179, 186; *ibid.*, V (1916), p. 169; *Minutes of Executive Committee*, Jan. 27, 1915; *The Teaching of Government*, (Report to the American Political Science Association by the Committee on Instruction, 1916), pp. 18–21. In 1914 the committee consisted of Maurice Fels, chairman, J. Lynn Barnard, School of Pedagogy, Philadelphia; Arthur W. Dunn, secretary, James J. Sheppard, New York; Charles A. Beard, Columbia University; John C. Dana, Newark, N. J.; Mabel Hill, Wellesley, Mass.; C. N. Kendall, Trenton, N. J.

[96] *Review*, IX (1920), p. 114; *Minutes of Executive Committee*, Mar. 22, 1919; *Minutes of Council*, April 19, Dec. 5, 1919.

[97] *Review*, XXI (1932), p. 584. An advisory committee of fifteen was created to coöperate with the Council. Representing the League on the advisory committee were: Murray Seasongood, Cincinnati; Charles A. Beard, New Milford, Conn.; Joseph McGoldrick, Columbia University; Charles E. Merriam, University of Chicago; Thomas H. Reed, University of Michigan; Chester H. Rowell, San Francisco.

[98] V, *Constructive Economy in Government* (June–Sept., 1933); VI, *The Crisis in Municipal Finance* (Oct. 1933–Feb. 1934); VII, *Reviving Local Government* (Feb.–June, 1934); VIII, *A New Deal in Local Government* (June–Sept. 1934); IX, *Trends in Government* (Oct. 1934–Jan. 1935); X, *The 44 State Legislatures of 1935* (Feb.–June, 1935);

XI, *Taxation for Prosperity* (June–Sept. 1935) ; XII, *Planning* (Oct. 1935–Jan. 1936).

[99] See pp. 112, 114.

[100] *Minutes of Council,* Nov. 26, 1935.

[101] *Secretary's Report,* 1932–1933, p. 4; 1933–1934, p. 14; 1934–1935, p. 14; 1935–1936, p. 15; *Review,* XXII–XXV (1933–1936), *passim.*

[102] *Proceedings,* 1894–1903, *passim.*

[103] *Ibid.,* 1904, pp. 389–390; 1908, p. 97.

[104] *Ibid.,* 1906, pp. 424–453; 1908, pp. 85–121; 1909, pp. 450–464.

[105] *Ibid.,* 1909, pp. 450–464.

[106] In 1914 the committee had forty-eight members, with Addison L. Winship, Boston, chairman; Winston Paul, Jersey City, N. J., secretary; and H. Marie Dermitt, Allegheny County, Treasurer.

[107] *Proceedings,* 1910, pp. 516–532, 575–576; *Handbook,* 1914, pp. 2–3; *Review,* I (1912), pp. 18, 147; *ibid.,* III (1914), pp. 162–163; *ibid.,* IV (1915), pp. 192–195; *ibid.,* V (1916), pp. 190–193; *ibid.,* VI (1917), pp. 192–193; *ibid.,* VII (1918), pp. 129–130; *ibid.,* VIII (1919), pp. 106–107.

[108] *Handbook,* 1914, p. 8; *Minutes of Council,* Nov. 12, 1913; *Minutes of Executive Committee,* Dec. 9, 1913.

[109] *Preliminary Report of Committee on Plan of Political Organization* (1914) ; *Review,* IV (1915), p. 190. In addition to Mr. Weil, members of the committee, in 1914, were: Robert S. Binkerd, Richard S. Childs, Frederic C. Howe, New York; Stoughton Cooley, Chicago; J. Lionberger Davis, St. Louis; Cyrus D. Foss, Jr., Clinton Rogers Woodruff, Philadelphia; Charles E. Merriam, University of Chicago; George R. Nutter, A. L. Winship, Boston; Elliott H. Pendleton, Cincinnati.

[110] *Minutes of Council,* April 27, 1926.

[111] Committee membership also included: Harold S. Buttenheim, Sidney Harris, H. W. Marsh, George H. McCaffrey, R. E. McGahen, New York; Mayo Fesler, Cleveland; Belle Sherwin, Washington, D.C.; Lent D. Upson, Detroit.

[112] *Secretary's Report,* 1928–1929, p. 4; 1929–1930, p. 3; 1930–1931, p. 4; 1931–1932, p. 4; 1932–1933, p. 5.

[113] Ralph Holterhoff, Edna Strohm, Cincinnati; Grace R. Howe, S. Norwalk, Conn.; Walter J. Millard, New York; W. Earl Weller, Rochester, N. Y., were the rest of the Committee.

[114] *The Cincinnati Plan of Citizen Organization for Political Activity* (1934). A revised edition was issued as a pamphlet in 1941.

[115] *Secretary's Report,* 1928–1929 to 1935–1936, *passim.*

[116] Members of the subcommittee were: J. W. Esterline, Indianapolis, chairman; Forest Frank, Cincinnati, secretary; Edward Fenias, Newark, N. J.; Julian G. Hearne, Jr., Wheeling, West Va.; George H. Hallett, Jr., Walter J. Millard, Alfred Willoughby, New York. (*Review,* XXVIII [1939], p. 818.)

[117] Committee membership included: Thomas H. Reed, University of Michigan, chairman; A. R. Hatton, Northwestern University; Henry Bentley, Cincinnati; H. S. Buttenheim, New York; J. W. Esterline, Indianapolis; C. E. Merriam, University of Chicago.

[118] *Minutes of Executive Committee,* Feb. 19, June 17, 1932; *Minutes of Council,* May 14–15, 1932; *Secretary's Report,* 1931–1932, pp. 6–7.

[119] *Retrenching in State and Local Expenditures* (Government Series Lecture No. 10, Nov. 15, 1932) ; *Review,* XXI (1932), pp. 664–665.

[120] *Review,* XXII (1933), pp. 157–158, 219–220, 255, 258; *Minutes of Executive Committee,* Jan. 27, Feb. 9, 1933; *Minutes of Council,* May 27–28, 1933.

[121] Vice-chairmen were: Harold S. Buttenheim, Mrs. F. Louis Slade, New York; C. R. Mann, Washington, D.C.; Carl H. Milam, Chicago; and members included: Mrs. Hugh Bradford, Belle Sherwin, Washington, D.C.; Louis Brownlow, Chicago; Lee F. Hanmer, New York; Mrs. Charles C. Rumsey, Georgetown, S. C.

[122] *Citizens' Councils for Constructive Economy* (1933); *A Citizens' Council— Why and How?* (1933); *Citizens' Councils in Action* (1933); *Committee on Citizens' Councils for Constructive Economy* (1933).

[123] See C. W. Edwards, *Citizens' Councils in Alabama* (1934).

[124] V to VIII. See p. 109.

[125] *Secretary's Report*, 1932–1933, pp. 6–7; 1933–1934, pp. 11, 14–16; *Report of the Committee on Citizens' Councils for Constructive Economy* (mimeo., May 15, 1934); *Review*, XXII (1933), pp. 306, 354, 462, 531–532; *ibid.*, XXIII (1934), pp. 131, 192, 240, 640.

[126] Other members were: Lee F. Hanmer, New York; R. A. Kent, University of Louisville; Carl H. Milam, Chicago; Alonzo G. Grace, Univ. of Rochester.

[127] *Secretary's Report*, 1934–1935, pp. 11, 14–15; *Minutes of Council*, Nov. 26, 1935; *Review*, XXV (1936), pp. 51–53, 59, 92–95.

[128] *Secretary's Report*, 1935–1936, pp. 13, 15; 1936–1937, p. 11; *Minutes of Council*, Nov. 16, 1936; *Review*, XXV (1936), p. 442.

[129] *Review*, XXVIII (1939), pp. 492, 754; *Secretary's Report*, 1938–1939, pp. 1, 5.

[130] *Citizens' Councils, A Device to Mobilize the Forces of Each Community in the Interest of More Effective Citizenship* (1939), and *A Program to Improve the Quality of Government by Improving the Quality of Citizenship* (1939).

[131] *Review*, XXIX (1940), p. 5.

[132] *Review*, XXII (1933), pp. 354, 406.

[133] *Improved Assessment Technique* (Dec., 1934); *Reporting Governmental Costs* (Feb., 1935).

[134] *Review*, XXIII (1934), pp. 185, 446; *ibid.*, XXIV (1935), pp. 49–50.

[135] *Ibid.*, XXIV (Supplement, May, 1935), pp. 290–305.

[136] See pp. 112–113.

[137] *Report of the Secretary, National Pay Your Taxes Campaign Committee* (Mimeo., Jan., 1934; June, 1934; Aug., 1935). See also *Secretary's Report*, 1932–1933, p. 7; 1933–1934, p. 16; 1934–1935, p. 15.

[138] *Review*, XXV (1936), pp. 390, 442; *ibid.*, XXIV (1940), pp. 151, 288; *Secretary's Report* 1935–1936, p. 12; 1936–1937, p. 10; 1937–1938, p. 19.

[139] Cf. *What's in the Proposed Constitution?* (1938).

[140] *Review*, XXVI (1937), p. 414; *Secretary's Report*, 1936–1937, pp. 10–11; 1937–1938, pp. 19–20.

[141] *Minutes of Council*, Nov. 15, 1939; *Minutes of Executive Committee*, Feb. 15, 1940; *Secretary's Report*, 1938–1939, p. 2.

[142] *Review*, XXIX (1940), pp. 150–151, 288, 356–358, 711; *Proceedings of the Conference on American Self-Government held at Indiana University, May 13 and 14, 1940* (mimeo.); *Secretary's Report*, 1939–1940, pp. 3–4.

[143] *Review*, XXVIII (1939), p. 608. *Secretary's Report*, 1938–1939, p. 1; 1939–1940, p. 9.

[144] *Secretary's Report*, 1940–1941, pp. 8–10.

[145] *Review*, XXXIII (1944), p. 116.

[146] *Ibid.*, XXXV (1946), p. 567. Cf. P. P. Womer, *Citizenship and the New Day* (1945).

[147] *Secretary's Report*, 1946, p. 3.

NOTES TO CHAPTER VII

[1] *Proceedings*, 1910, pp. 209–213.
[2] Circular Letter, July 28, 1936.
[3] *Proceedings of the Philadelphia Conference* (1894), pp. 123–133. For other articles on civil service, see *Proceedings*, 1896, pp. 162–191; 1897, pp. 133–144; 1900, pp. 136–146; 1908, pp. 215–222; 1910, pp. 304–316, 577–580.
[4] "Permanent Officials in Municipal Government," *Proceedings*, 1908, pp. 215–222.
[5] *Review*, I (1912), pp. 33–39, 124.
[6] *Ibid.*, I (1912), pp. 549–561, 639–649.
[7] *Minutes of Executive Committee*, Dec. 9, 1913; Jan. 7, 1914; *Handbook*, 1914, p. 8; *A New Municipal Program* (1919), pp. 269–281.
[8] *Review*, III (1914), pp. 304–326; *ibid.*, IV (1915), pp. 26–31, 171, 191–192; *ibid.*, V (1916), pp. 266–272, 574–585; *ibid.*, VI (1917), pp. 197–198, 692–707; *ibid.*, VII (1918), pp. 14–19, 266–272, 365–371, 583–591. See also W. C. Beyer, "Employment Standardization in the Public Service," *Review*, IX (Supplement, June, 1920), pp. 391–403; E. A. Fitzpatrick, ed., *Experts in City Government* (National Municipal League Series, 1919).
[9] *Review*, VII (1918), pp. 14–19, 235, 653; *ibid.*, IX (1920), p. 472; *Minutes of Council*, Nov. 21, 1917; April 24, 1918; *Minutes of Executive Committee*, June 25, 1918.
[10] *Review*, IX (1920), p. 200; *Minutes of Council*, Feb. 18, 1920. Members of the committee: Arthur N. Pierson, New Jersey State Senate, chairman; George B. Buck, H. W. Dodds, Darwin R. James, Lawson Purdy, Albert de Roode, New York; E. O. Griffenhagen, Chicago; William G. Rice, Albany, N. Y.; Clinton Rogers Woodruff, Philadelphia; Don C. Sowers, Akron, Ohio; Paul Studenski, Newark, N. J.

[11] *Review*, XI (1922), pp. 97–124, 145–146, 355–357.
[12] *Secretary's Report*, 1921–1922, p. 6.
[13] *Minutes of Council*, Dec. 5, 1919.
[14] *Review*, X (1921), pp. 10–11, 386–391.
[15] *Minutes of Annual Meeting*, Nov. 23, 1922.
[16] *Review*, XII (1923), pp. 109–111.
[17] *Minutes of Council*, Mar. 28, 1923; *Review*, XII (1923), p. 441.
[18] *Review*, XII (1923), pp. 441–513.
[19] *Minutes of Annual Meeting*, Nov. 16, 1923.
[20] *Minutes of Council*, Mar. 28, 1923; *Minutes of Executive Committee*, April 5, 1923.
[21] *The Merit System in Government* (1926); *Review*, XV (1926), pp. 189–190.
[22] W. C. Beyer, "Municipal Salaries under the Changing Price Level," *Review*, XV (Supplement, Mar., 1926), pp. 187–200.
[23] W. E. Mosher and Sophie Polah, "Extent, Costs and Significance of Public Employment in the United States," *Review*, XXI (Supplement, Jan., 1932), pp. 51–75; R. M. Gallagher, "Public Personnel Problems and the Depression," *Review*, XXII (Supplement, April, 1933), pp. 199–215; S. H. Ordway, Jr., and J. C. Laffan, "Approaches to the Measurement and Reward of Effective Work of Individual Government Employees," *Review*, XXIV (Supplement, Oct., 1935), pp. 557–601.
[24] *Minutes of Executive Committee*, Feb. 19, 1932; *Minutes of Council*, May 14–15, 1932.
[25] *Minutes of Executive Committee*, Mar. 26, 1935. Members of the committee were: Charles P. Taft, Cincinnati, chairman; Luther Gulick, vice-chairman, Richard Kyle, secretary, John B. Andrews, H. Eliot Kaplan, New York; Edgar Dawson, Hunter College; Arthur

W. Macmahon, Columbia University; Wallace Sayre, New York University; G. Lyle Belsley, Clarence E. Ridley, Chicago; Mrs. Walter S. Greenough, Indianapolis; Morris B. Lambie, Harvard University; Mrs. Virgil M. Loeb, St. Louis; Charles P. Messick, Ellen C. Potter, Trenton, N. J.; Samuel H. Ordway, Jr., Washington, D. C.; James K. Pollock, University of Michigan.

[26] *Review,* XXIV (1935), p. 420; *ibid.,* XXVI (1937), p. 54; *ibid.,* XXVII (1938), pp. 126, 242; *ibid.,* XXVIII (1939), p. 268; *Secretary's Report,* 1934–1935, p. 11; 1935–1936, p. 12; 1936–1937, p. 8; 1937–1938, p. 18.

[27] *Proceedings,* 1904, pp. 15–31, 47, 294–304, 404.

[28] *Ibid.,* 1905, pp. 20–24, 393; 1906, pp. 487–488.

[29] Committee personnel: Lawson Purdy, chairman, John G. Agar, Horace E. Deming, Clarence H. Kelsey, George F. Seward, New York; Richard H. Dana, Cambridge, Mass.; Frederick N. Judson, St. Louis; Clinton Rogers Woodruff, Philadelphia; Edwin R. A. Seligman, Columbia University.

[30] *Proceedings,* 1907, pp. 223–316, 403–404.

[31] *Ibid.,* 1910, pp. 346–352, 573; *Handbook,* 1914, p. 6.

[32] *Proceedings,* 1911, pp. 6, 10–11 (*Review,* I, No. 1, Jan., 1912).

[33] Cf. R. E. Cushman, *Excess Condemnation* (National Municipal League Series, 1917).

[34] *Proceedings,* 1912, pp. 23–25 (*Review,* II, No. 1, Jan., 1913).

[35] *Minutes of Council,* July 8, 1912; Nov. 17, 1915.

[36] *Review,* V (1916), pp. 175–179.

[37] *Ibid.,* VI (1917), pp. 178–181. Members: Robert M. Haig, Columbia University, chairman, Walter T. Arndt, C. C. Williamson, Herbert S. Swan, New York; Mayo Fesler, Cleveland; William A. Rawles, Indiana University.

[38] *Review,* VIII (Supplement, Sept., 1919), pp. 511–527. Reprinted as No. 1 of the League's Technical Pamphlets, several editions were issued, the third in 1923 and the fourth in 1929.

[39] *Review,* XI (1922), pp. 7–10. Members of the committee were: Luther Gulick, chairman, A. C. Pleydell, New York; Harris S. Keeler, Chicago; Mabel Newcomer, Vassar College; William A. Rawles, Indiana University; Robert M. Haig, Columbia University.

[40] *Review,* XI (1922), pp. 43–58.

[41] *Ibid.,* XII (Supplement, May, 1923), pp. 273–282.

[42] *Ibid.,* IX (1920), p. 473.

[43] *Minutes of Council,* Dec. 5, 1919; Feb. 18, 1920; April 22, 1921; Nov. 11, 1924; Mar. 20, 1925; *Minutes of Executive Committee,* Oct. 9, 1924.

[44] Other members, several of whom represented the Investment Bankers' Association, were: F. Seymour Barr, J. J. English, Luther Gulick, D. V. Raymond, New York; Robert H. Bradley, Newark, N.J.; Walter R. Darby, Trenton, N. J.; John A. Fairlie, University of Illinois; Alden H. Little, St. Louis, Mo.; Benjamin I. Taylor, Harrison, N. Y.; Arthur N. Pierson, New Jersey State Senate.

[45] *Review,* XVI (Supplement, Feb., 1927), pp. 135–150.

[46] *Secretary's Report,* 1926–1927, p. 10; 1927–1928, p. 4.

[47] *Minutes of Executive Committee,* Mar. 26, Dec. 4, 1931.

[48] Other members were: F. Seymour Barr, Philip H. Cornick, Lawson Purdy, Herbert S. Swan, Chester B. Marslich, New York; Paul V. Betters, Herbert U. Nelson, Clarence E. Ridley, Herbert D. Simpson, Chicago; Carl H. Chatters, Detroit; Welles A. Gray, Washington, D. C.; John S. Harris, Toledo; Walter Matscheck, Kansas City, Mo.; Edward Nugent, Elizabeth, N. J.; Walter S. Schmidt, Cincinnati; Harold A. Stone,

Los Angeles; Benjamin I. Taylor, Harrison, N. Y.; C. W. Tooke, New York University.

[49] *Secretary's Report*, 1931–1932, p. 6; 1932–1933, p. 6; 1933–1934, p. 11; 1934–1935, p. 11; 1935–1936, p. 13.

[50] Personnel also included: Philip A. Benson, Henry R. Chittick, Philip H. Cornick, E. Fleetwood Dunstan, Raymond Greer, John S. Linen, Frank H. Morse, Lawson Purdy, Sanders Shanks, Jr., New York; Carl H. Chatters, Chicago; John H. Fertig, Harrisburg, Pa.; Mark Graves, Albany, N. Y.; Henry F. Long, Boston; Harley L. Lutz, Princeton University; J. H. Thayer Martin, Trenton, N. J.; Seabury C. Mastick, Pleasantville, N. Y.; Lent D. Upson, Detroit; John A. Zangerle, Cleveland; Harry A. Freiberg, Cincinnati.

[51] *Review*, XXIV (Supplement, May, 1935), pp. 290–305.

[52] *Secretary's Report*, 1934–5, p. 11.

[53] XXII, No. 6 (1933); XXV, No. 6 (1936); XXVII, No. 6 (1938); XXIV, No. 11 (1935).

[54] See pp. 35–36, 58–59, 69–70, 81, 114.

[55] See also E. S. Corwin, "Constitutional Tax Exemption," *Review*, XIII (Supplement, Jan., 1924), pp. 51–67; J. W. Martin, "The Administration of Gasoline Taxes in the United States," *Review*, XIII (Supplement, Oct., 1924), pp. 587–600; Paul Studenski, *Public Borrowing* (National Municipal League Monograph Series, 1930); H. H. Freeman, "How American Cities are Retrenching in Time of Depression," *Review*, XXI (Supplement, April, 1932), pp. 267–281; J. M. Leonard, *The Direct Tax Burden on Low Income Groups* (1939); F. G. Crawford, *The Administration of the Gasoline Tax in the United States* (Municipal Administration Service, Nos. 7, 15, 30; 1928, 1930, 1932); C. H. Chatters, *The Enforcement of Real Estate Tax Liens* (Municipal Adminis-

tration Service, No. 10, 1928); C. E. Reeves, *The Appraisal of Urban Land and Buildings* (Municipal Administration Service, No. 11, 1931).

[56] *Proceedings*, 1896, pp. 226–235.

[57] *Ibid.*, 1898, pp. 8, 12, 254–256.

[58] *Ibid.*, 1899, pp. 96–168.

[59] *Ibid.*, 1900, pp. 52–59, 239–256.

[60] *Ibid.*, 1901, p. 248.

[61] *Ibid.*, 1901, pp. 51, 248–314; 1902, pp. 17–30, 292–329, 348; 1903, pp. 17–21, 247–297, 323; 1904, pp. 49–55, 191–241, 404–405; 1905, pp. 206–255, 393; 1906, pp. 207–243, 488–489; 1907, pp. 404–405; 1908, pp. 328–347, 470.

[62] Committee personnel: Edward M. Hartwell, Chairman, Harvey S. Chase, Boston; Frederick A. Cleveland, M. N. Baker, Horace E. Deming, E. M. Sells, H. W. Wilmot, Edgar J. Leavy, New York; Harry B. Henderson, Cheyenne, Wyo.; J. W. Jenks, Cornell University; Samuel E. Sparling, University of Wisconsin; Howard C. Beck, Detroit; L. G. Powers, Washington, D. C.; Clinton Rogers Woodruff, William M. Lybrand, Philadelphia; Jacob H. Hollander, Johns Hopkins University; Frank J. Goodnow, E. R. A. Seligman, Columbia University.

[63] *Minutes of Executive Committee*, Nov. 16, 1908.

[64] *Proceedings*, 1905, pp. 221–222, 231–234.

[65] *Handbook*, 1914, pp. 5–6.

[66] *Proceedings*, 1907, pp. 407.

[67] *Minutes of Executive Committee*, April 7, 1909.

[68] *Minutes of Council*, Nov. 23, 1916; Nov. 21, 1917.

[69] *Ibid.*, Dec. 5, 1919.

[70] *Minutes of Business Meetings*, Nov. 18, 1921.

[71] *Minutes of Council*, Nov. 11, 1924.

[72] *Minutes of Executive Committee*, Dec. 17, 1936; *Review*, XXVI (1937), p. 2.

[73] *Review,* XXIX (1940), p. 86. The League's advisory group consisted of Carter W. Atkins, Hartford, Conn.; R. E. Miles, Columbus, Ohio; C. E. Rightor, Washington, D. C.; L. D. Upson, Detroit.

[74] *Proceedings,* 1909, pp. 68–69, 205–216, 258–283, 475.

[75] *Ibid.,* 1910, pp. 203–245, 473–489, 515, 573.

[76] *Ibid.,* 1910, pp. 203–213, 573. Other members were: William H. Allen, M. N. Baker, New York; Jesse D. Burks, Clinton Rogers Woodruff, Philadelphia; Allen T. Burns, Pittsburgh; Harvey S. Chase, Charles F. Gettemy, Boston; Frederick A. Cleveland, L. G. Powers, Washington, D. C.; Charles E. Merriam, University of Chicago; B. M. Rastall, University of Wisconsin.

[77] *Proceedings,* 1911, pp. 5, 6, 12–13 (*Review,* I, No. 1, Jan., 1912).

[78] *Minutes of Executive Committee,* Nov. 13, 1911.

[79] *Proceedings,* 1912, pp. 13–20 (*Review,* II, No. 1, Jan., 1913). Cf. J. D. Burks, "Efficiency Standards in Municipal Management," *Review,* I (1912), pp. 364–371.

[80] *Minutes of Council,* July 8, 1912.

[81] *Review,* III (1914), pp. 218–222.

[82] *Ibid.,* IV (1915), pp. 185–186; *ibid.,* V (1916), p. 180. In 1914 the committee members were: George Burnham, Jr., chairman, William B. Hadley, Philadelphia; Harvey S. Chase, L. G. Powers, Washington, D. C.; Frederick A. Cleveland, New York; John A. Fairlie, University of Illinois; Charles F. Gettemy, Boston; J. L. Jacobs, Chicago; W. F. Willoughby, Princeton University. (*Handbook,* 1914, pp. 5–6).

[83] *A New Muncipal Program* (1919), pp. 367–378.

[84] *Review,* V (1916), pp. 403–410, 631–637; *ibid.,* VI (1917), pp. 395–398, 485–491, 707–719; *ibid.,* VII (1918), pp. 167–173; *ibid.,* VIII (1919),

pp. 360–365, 406–411, 422–435, 572–573; *ibid.,* IX (1920), pp. 219–233, 538–545; *ibid.,* X (1921), pp. 382–385, 568–573; *ibid.,* XI (1922), pp. 428–437; *ibid.,* XII (1923), pp. 58–66, 119–122; *ibid.,* XIII (1924), pp. 19–25.

[85] *Minutes of Council,* Jan. 21, 1927. With some changes the membership of the Committee on Municipal Borrowings was retained; the other members included: A. E. Buck, Arthur J. Edwards, Luther Gulick, D. V. Raymond, New York; Walter R. Darby, Trenton, N. J.; Mark Graves, Albany, N. Y.; Clyde L. King, University of Pennsylvania; George M. Link, Minneapolis; H. P. Seidemann, Washington, D. C.; L. D. Upson, Detroit; Arthur N. Pierson, New Jersey State Senate.

[86] Governmental Research Conference, *Proceedings,* 1927 (mimeo.), pp. 152–165.

[87] *Review,* XVII (Supplement, July, 1928), pp. 437–445.

[88] *Secretary's Report,* 1927–1928, pp. 2, 4; 1928–1929, p. 2. Other publications of the League and the Municipal Administration Service in this field should be noted: L. D. Upson and C. E. Rightor, "Standards of Financial Administration," *Review,* XVII (Supplement, Feb., 1928), pp. 119–132; Joseph McGoldrick, "The Board of Estimate and Apportionment of New York City," *Review,* XVIII (Supplement, Feb., 1929), pp. 125–152, reprinted, revised, May, 1932; Wylie Kilpatrick, *State Administrative Review of Local Budget Making* (Municipal Administrative Service, No. 3, 1927); *State Supervision of Local Budgeting* (1939); C. E. Rightor, *The Preparation of a Long-Term Financial Program* (Municipal Administration Service, No. 5, 1927); A. E. Buck, *Budgeting for Small Cities* (Municipal Administration Service, No. 23, 1931); *Public Budgeting* (1929).

[89] II (1913), pp. 239–254.

⁹⁰ *Review,* IX (Supplement, Feb., 1920), pp. 115–135.

⁹¹ *Ibid.,* XIII (1924), pp. 631–641.

⁹² *Secretary's Report,* 1930–1931, p. 2; *Review,* XIX (1930), p. 490.

⁹³ Russell Forbes, *Centralized Purchasing* (1931); *The Organization and Administration of a Governmental Purchasing Office* (1932); *Governmental Purchasing* (1929); *Purchasing for Small Cities* (Municipal Administration Service, No. 25, 1932).

⁹⁴ Personnel of the committee is given in *Review,* XXVII (1938), pp. 253, 260.

⁹⁵ *Review,* XXVI (1937), p. 274; *ibid.,* XXVII (1938), p. 242; *ibid.,* XXXVI (1947), p. 62; *Secretary's Report,* 1936–1937, p. 9; 1937–1938, p. 18; 1938–1939, p. 3; 1939–1940, p. 9; 1946, p. 5; *Minutes of Council,* Nov. 16, 1936; Nov. 17, 1937; Nov. 30, 1938; Nov. 15, 1939.

⁹⁶ *Review,* II (1913), pp. 160–166; *ibid.,* III (1914), pp. 474–483, 538–547; *ibid.,* IV (1915), pp. 383–397; *ibid.,* V (1916), pp. 89–92, 388–394, 638–642; *ibid.,* VI (1917), pp. 57–63, 325–365, 463–465, 598–604; *ibid.,* VII (1918), pp. 605–613; *ibid.,* IX (1920), pp. 21–31; *ibid.,* X (1921), pp. 39–50; *ibid.,* XI (1922), pp. 27–33; *ibid.,* XII (1923), pp. 77–82; *ibid.,* XIII (1924), pp. 103–110; *ibid.,* XIV (1925), pp. 307–314; *ibid.,* XV (1926), pp. 342–349; *ibid.,* XVI (1927), pp. 369–373.

⁹⁷ See chaps. iii, iv.

⁹⁸ E. M. Bassett, "Zoning," *Review,* IX (Supplement, May, 1920), pp. 315–341, revised 1922; H. S. Swan, "The Law of Zoning," *Review,* X (Supplement, Oct., 1921), pp. 519–536; F. B. Williams, "The Law of the City Plan," (Technical Pamphlets, No. 8, revised 1922); Thomas Adams, "Modern City Planning," *Review,* XI (1922), pp. 157–177; H. S. Swan and G. W. Tuttle, "Land Subdivisions and the City Plan," *Review,* XIV (Supplement, July, 1925),

pp. 437–462; E. P. Goodrich, "Airports as a Factor in City Planning," *Review,* XVII (Supplement, Mar., 1928), pp. 181–194; H. S. Swan, "Theory and Practice in Building Lines under Eminent Domain," *Review,* XX (Supplement, Sept., 1931), pp. 557–566.

⁹⁹ *Minutes of Council,* Dec. 5, 1919.

¹⁰⁰ *Minutes of Annual Meeting,* Nov. 17–19, 1920. This arrangement continued until 1925.

¹⁰¹ *Review,* XI (1922), pp. 255–256, 307.

¹⁰² *Minutes of Executive Committee,* Nov. 16, 1908.

¹⁰³ *Review,* X (1921), pp. 67–70; *Minutes of Annual Meeting,* Nov. 17–19, 1920; *Minutes of Council,* Dec. 13, 1920.

¹⁰⁴ *Minutes of Council,* Dec. 12, 1921; Jan. 21, 1927; *Review,* X (1921), pp. 440–441, 448–449; *ibid.,* XII (1923), pp. 102–104, 215–217, 340–341, 562–563, 682–685, 735–736; *ibid.,* XIII (1924), pp. 128–130, 182–184, 246–248, 371–373.

¹⁰⁵ *Review,* XXVI (1937), pp. 214, 462. Members of the League's City Planning Committee were: Ernest P. Goodrich, chairman, William Exton, Jr., secretary, Harry B. Brainerd, Harold S. Buttenheim, Harold M. Lewis, Richard Schermerhorn, Jr., Flavel Shurtleff, Herbert S. Swan, Frank B. Williams, New York; Wayne D. Heydecker, Albany, N. Y.

¹⁰⁶ *Review,* XXVII (1938), p. 245.

¹⁰⁷ *Proceedings,* 1894–5, pp. 125–8.

¹⁰⁸ *Ibid.,* 1894–1910, *passim.*

¹⁰⁹ See chap. iii.

¹¹⁰ *Proceedings,* 1905, p. 19.

¹¹¹ *Minutes of Executive Committee,* April 28, 1905; April 7, 1909.

¹¹² *Proceedings,* 1910, pp. 449–451, 574.

¹¹³ *Minutes of Executive Committee,* Nov. 14, 1910; *Minutes of Business Committee,* Dec. 4, 1910.

[114] *Proceedings*, 1911, pp. 5, 17 (*Review*, I, No. 1, Jan., 1912). For the report see C. L. King, ed., *The Regulation of Municipal Utilities*, (National Municipal League Series, 1912), chap. ix.

[115] *Review*, I (1912), pp. 630–638; *ibid.*, II (1913), pp. 11–38; *Proceedings*, 1912, pp. 31–32 (*Review*, II, No. 1, Jan., 1913).

[116] *Review*, III (1914), pp. 13–27, 239–243. From 1910 to 1920 the Committee on Municipal Franchises underwent several reorganizations. In 1914 personnel consisted of: Delos F. Wilcox, New York, chairman; Edward W. Bemis, Chicago; Robert Treat Paine, Abraham E. Pinanski, Boston; J. W. S. Peters, Kansas City, Mo.; Charles Richardson, Philadelphia. (*Handbook*, 1914, p. 5).

[117] *Review*, IV (1915), pp. 180–181.

[118] *Municipal Home Rule and a Model City Charter* (3d ed.; Nov. 15, 1915), pp. 41–55.

[119] *Review*, V (1916), pp. 172, 190.

[120] See chap. iv.

[121] *A New Municipal Program* (1919), chap. x.

[122] *Review*, VI (1917), pp. 31–40, 181.

[123] *Ibid.*, VII (1918), pp. 122, 151–158.

[124] *Ibid.*, VII (1918), pp. 444, 531–533, 545–552.

[125] *Minutes of Executive Committee*, Dec. 12, 1918; *Minutes of Council*, April 19, 1919.

[126] *Review*, VII (1918), pp. 545–552; *ibid.*, VIII (1919), pp. 235–243, 282–290, 481–493, 546–550, 606–614, 676–679; *ibid.*, IX (1920), pp. 13–16, 78–83, 357–364, 545–553; *ibid.*, X (1921), pp. 176–183. See also several articles by D. F. Wilcox, and others, *Review*, VIII (1919), pp. 33–48, 542–546, 562–566; *ibid.*, IX (1920), pp. 622–623, 633–636, 705–711, 765–772; *ibid.*, X (1921), pp. 324–327, 417–422, 506–510. The series on the five-cent fare was resumed in 1926–1927, with articles dealing with Pittsburgh, Toronto, Chicago, Minneapolis, St. Paul, Cincinnati, and Toledo. (*Review*, XV [1926], pp. 459–465, 530–536, 595–601, 644–650, 699–706; *ibid.*, XVI [1927], pp. 250–255.)

[127] Members of the committee: Delos F. Wilcox, Elmhurst, N. Y., chairman; Alfred Bettman, Cincinnati; John P. Fox, New York; John A. Harzfeld, Kansas City, Mo.; Stiles P. Jones, Minneapolis; William M. Leiserson, Toledo; George C. Sikes, Chicago; Clinton Rogers Woodruff, Philadelphia.

[128] *Review*, IX (Supplement, April, 1920), pp. 251–267.

[129] *Ibid.*, X (Supplement, Feb., 1921), pp. 111–139.

[130] *Ibid.*, X (1921), pp. 470–474, 498–502, 563–567; *ibid.*, XI (1922), pp. 21–27, 76–79, 140–144; *ibid.*, XIV (1925), pp. 215–220, 284–287, 506–511, 749–753.

[131] *Ibid.*, XV (1926), pp. 188, 232. For other publications of the League, see: C. L. King, ed., *The Regulation of Municipal Utilities* (National Municipal League Series, 1912); D. F. Wilcox, "Electric Light and Power as a Public Utility," *Review*, XIV (Supplement, Mar., 1925), pp. 191–204; O. C. Hormell, "Electricity in Great Britain—A Study in Administration," *Review*, XVII (Supplement, June, 1928), pp. 363–385; A. B. Knapp, "Water Power in New York State," *Review*, XIX (Supplement, Feb., 1930), pp. 125–150; John Bauer, ed., *Public Utility Problems* (a symposium of articles reprinted from the *Review*, XXIII, No. 11, Nov., 1934); and three publications of the Municipal Administration Service: John Bauer, *Standards for Modern Public Utility Franchises* (No. 17, 1930); D. F. Wilcox, *The Administration of Municipally Owned Utilities* (No. 22, 1931); F. L.

Bird, *The Management of Small Municipal Lighting Plants* (No. 28, 1932).

[132] *Minutes of Executive Committee,* Dec. 10, 1932; Mar. 26, 1935; *Minutes of Council,* Sept. 19–20, 1932.

[133] *Review,* XVII (1928), pp. 251, 304.

[134] *Minutes of Council,* Jan. 21, 1927; *Minutes of Executive Committee,* Jan. 26, 1927.

[135] *Minutes of Executive Committee,* June 17, 1932.

[136] *Proceedings,* 1906, pp. 391–398.

[137] *Minutes of Executive Committee,* April 27, 1906.

[138] *Proceedings,* 1909, pp. 53–63, 157–178; 1910, pp. 281–303, 545–554.

[139] *Minutes of Executive Committee,* Nov. 14, 1910.

[140] *Proceedings,* 1911, pp. 5–6 (*Review,* I, No. 1, Jan., 1912).

[141] *Review,* I (1912), p. 332.

[142] *Proceedings,* 1894–1895, pp. 492–499.

[143] *Ibid.,* 1905, pp. 197–205.

[144] *Ibid.,* 1907, pp. 82, 317–381.

[145] *Ibid.,* 1908, pp. 8–21, 378–387; 1909, pp. 433–438; 1910, pp. 446–449.

[146] *Ibid.,* 1911, pp. 5, 13 (*Review,* I, No. 1, Jan., 1912); *Review,* I (1912), pp. 49–53, 71–73, 240–245, 331; *ibid.,* II (1913), pp. 200–209; *ibid.,* III (1914), pp. 107–109.

[147] Personnel in 1914 included: M. N. Baker, chairman, Graham R. Taylor, John Ihlder, New York; Selskar M. Gunn, Massachusetts Institute of Technology; E. O. Jordan, University of Chicago; E. C. Levy, Richmond, Va.; Charles E. A. Winslow, University of the City of New York. (*Handbook,* 1914, p. 7).

[148] *Review,* II (1913), pp. 509–511, 716–717; *ibid.,* XIII (1924), pp. 249–250, 369–370, 529–530; *ibid.,* XIV (1925), pp. 319–321.

[149] *Proceedings,* 1908, pp. 49–72, 421–443; 1910, pp. 395–438.

[150] *Minutes of Executive Committee,* Nov. 14, 1910.

[151] *Proceedings,* 1911, pp. 5, 17–19 (*Review,* I, No. 1, Jan., 1912); *Review,* I (1912), pp. 332, 680–685; *ibid.,* II (1913), pp. 275–279, 629–638; *ibid.,* III (1914), pp. 232–235, 505–516; *ibid.,* IV (1915), pp. 80–83, 179–180.

[152] Membership in 1914 was: Camillus G. Kidder, Orange, N. J., chairman; F. Spencer Baldwin, Boston University; John Koren, Boston; Maynard N. Clement, Albany, N. Y.; Albert H. Hall, Minneapolis; A. R. Hatton, Western Reserve University; S. C. Mitchell, Columbia, S. C.; Walter T. Sumner, Chicago. (*Handbook,* 1914, p. 7).

[153] Other members were: Frank Bane, Louis Brownlow, Simeon E. Leland, Henry W. Toll, Chicago; A. E. Buck, Fred G. Clark, Leonard V. Harrison, Howard P. Jones, Elizabeth Laine, New York; Thomas C. Desmond, Newburgh, N. Y.; John W. Eggleston, Norfolk, Va.; Lavinia Engle, Baltimore; Mark Graves, Albany, N. Y.; Arnold B. Hall, Washington, D. C.; Seabury C. Mastick, Pleasantville, N. Y.; C. H. Morrissett, Richmond, Va.; Lent D. Upson, Detroit; John G. Winant, Concord, N. H.; Marshall E. Dimock, University of Chicago.

[154] "Liquor Control: Principles, Model Law," *Review,* XXIII (Supplement, Jan., 1934), pp. 47–78.

[155] *Review,* XXIV (Supplement, Jan., 1935), pp. 63–79.

[156] *Secretary's Report,* 1935–1936, p. 12.

[157] Other members were: Jane Addams, Chicago; Allen T. Burns, Pittsburgh; Henry C. Campbell, Milwaukee; John Collier, Woods Hutchinson, Henry M. Leipziger, Clarence A. Perry, E. W. Stitt, New York; Samuel M. Crothers, Cambridge, Mass.; George M. Forbes, Paul Moore Strayer, Rochester, N. Y.; Mrs. Mary V. Grice, Philadelphia;

Charles W. Holman, Dallas, Texas; Charles E. Knowles, Buffalo; E. D. Martin, Columbus, Ohio; Livy S. Richard, Boston; Miss L. S. Stearns, Madison, Wis.; Brand Whitlock, Toledo; Charles Zueblin, Winchester, Mass.

[158] E. J. Ward, ed., *The Social Center* (1913). See also *Proceedings*, 1909, pp. 35–41, 123; 1910, pp. 353–374, 464–473, 574; *Handbook*, 1914, p. 4.

[159] *Proceedings*, 1909, pp. 51–53, 142–156; 1910, pp. 375–384.

[160] *Review*, V (1916), pp. 183–187. The Committee consisted of: Frances A. Keller, chairman, Mary Antin, Julius Henry Cohen, Frederic C. Howe, New York; D. E. Cole, Cleveland; Julius Rosenwald, Chicago.

[161] Membership: Clyde L. King, University of Pennsylvania, chairman; Arthur J. Anderson, editor, *Pennsylvania Farmer*; C. M. Arthur, Pennsylvania State College; H. B. Fullerton, Medford, N. Y.; Cyrus C. Miller, New York; Paul Work, Cornell University.

[162] *Review*, IV (1915), p. 186; *ibid.*, V (1916), p. 175; *ibid.*, VI (1917), p. 175; *Handbook*, 1914, p. 8; *The Relation of the City to Its Food Supply* (1915); *Public Markets in the United States* (1917); C. L. King, *Lower Living Costs in Cities* (National Municipal League Series, 1915). See also F. W. Ryan and Miller McClintock, "Municipal Control of Retail Trade in the United States," *Review*, XXIV (Supplement, Dec., 1935), pp. 723–769.

[163] *Review*, X (Supplement, Nov., 1921), pp. 583–600.

[164] *Ibid.*, XX (Supplement, July, 1931), pp. 485–506.

[165] Committee personnel included: Jay B. Nash, New York University, chairman; LeRoy E. Bowman, Harold S. Buttenheim, Lee F. Hanmer, New York; Louis Brownlow, Chicago; W. P. Capes, Albany, N. Y.; Randolph O. Huus, Friends' University.

[166] XXV, Nos. 3, 4 (1936).

[167] Cf. *Social Security, Progress and Prospects*, ed. by Z. C. Franklin (1937); and the *Review*, for January, 1938, which was entirely on "The Relief Problem."

[168] *Proceedings*, 1909, pp. 196–204.

[169] *Minutes of Executive Committee*, April 17, 1931.

[170] C. S. Ascher, "Elements of a Low-Cost Housing Law and Its Administration," *Review*, XXII (Supplement, Feb., 1933), pp. 85–113; B. G. Rosahn, *Housing Management—Its History and Relation to Present Day Housing Problems* (1935); E. B. Drellich and Andrée Emery, *Rent Control in War and Peace* (1939). See also G. N. Thompson, *The Preparation and Revision of Local Building Codes* (Municipal Administration Service, No. 2, 1927); and "Fitz-Elwyne's Assize of Buildings," *Review*, XVII (Supplement, Sept., 1928), pp. 555–563.

[171] See C. E. Ridley, *The Public Works Department in American Cities* (Municipal Administration Service, No. 13, 1929).

[172] *Review*, XXIII (1934), p. 80. Committee consisted of the following: Harold S. Buttenheim, chairman, Frank B. Williams, secretary, Flavel Shurtleff, New York; Harland Bartholomew, St. Louis; Russell Van Nest Black, Princeton, N. J.; Louis Brownlow, Jacob L. Crane, Chicago; Otto T. Mallery, Philadelphia; John Nolen, Cambridge, Massachusetts.

[173] *Minutes of Executive Committee*, Aug. 28, 1928.

[174] Members were: W. Earl Weller, chairman, Stephen B. Story, Rochester, N. Y.; Emmett L. Bennett, secretary, John B. Blandford, Cincinnati; Robert T. Crane, University of Michigan; John N. Edy, Berkeley, Calif.; Welles A. Gray, New York; Walter Matscheck, Kansas City, Mo.

[175] *Secretary's Report,* 1933–1934, p. 10; 1934–1935, p. 11; 1935–1936, p. 12.

[176] *Minutes of Executive Committee,* Dec. 21, 1917; *Minutes of Council,* Dec. 5, 1919; *Review,* VII (1918), p. 655. Other members were: H. Marie Dermitt, Pittsburgh; R. P. Farley, Baltimore; C. M. Fassett, Spokane, Wash.; A. R. Hatton, Raymond Moley, Western Reserve University; E. I. Lewis, Indianapolis; J. Horace McFarland, Harrisburg, Pa.; W. B. Munro, Harvard University; J. G. Schmidlapp, Cincinnati; Mrs. V. G. Simkhovitch, New York; Don C. Sowers, Akron, Ohio; Harrison G. Otis, Auburn, Me.

[177] Publication No. 19.

[178] See also Wylie Kilpatrick, *Reporting Municipal Government* (Municipal Administration Service, No. 9, 1928).

[179] *Review,* XXX (1941), p. 618; *ibid.,* XXXI (1942), p. 70; *Secretary's Report,* 1941–1942, p. 6.

[180] *Review,* I (1912), pp. 364–371.

[181] *Review,* I (1912), pp. 21–32; *ibid.,* XI (1922), pp. 274–281, 317–320; *ibid.,* XII (1923), pp. 119–122, 163–164, 223–225, 336–338; *ibid.,* XIII (1924), pp. 152–157, 534–535; *ibid.,* XIV (1925), pp. 400–403; *ibid.,* XVI (1927), pp. 223–226.

[182] *Secretary's Report,* 1926–1927, p. 12; *Review,* XVI (1927), p. 430.

[183] *Review,* XVII (1928), pp. 195, 436.

[184] See also C. E. Ridley, *Measuring Municipal Government; Suggested Standards for Measuring the Results of Fire, Health, Police and Public Works Departments* (Municipal Administration Service, No. 4, 1927) ; and Governmental Research Association, *Proceedings,* 1929, pp. 91–93 (mimeo.).

[185] *Review,* XIX (1930), pp. 493–494.

[186] Cf. Committee on Uniform Street Sanitation Records, International Association of Street Sanitation Officials, *The Measurement and Control of Municipal Sanitation* (1930).

[187] See C. E. Ridley and H. A. Simon, *Measuring Municipal Activities* (1938).

[188] *Proceedings,* 1908, pp. 122–129; 1909, pp. 284–290.

[189] *Review,* I (1912), pp. 364–371, 420–425; *ibid.,* II (1913), pp. 39–47, 48–56.

[190] See p. 118.

[191] *Proceedings,* 1910, pp. 203–213, 474–480, 573.

[192] See p. 128.

[193] *Review,* V (1916), p. 193; *ibid.,* VI (1917), pp. 174, 194–197; *ibid.,* VII (1918), pp. 127–129, 332–334, 446–448; Norman H. Gill, *Municipal Research Bureaus* (1944), p. 86.

[194] Regarding the aid of the League to the governmental research movement, Professor H. G. Hodges, University of Cincinnati, said: *"The National Municipal League,* founded a decade before the advent of the research bureau, shifted an enlarged portion of its activity to local administration, coincident with the rise of the research bureau. Operating on a national scale, and armed with ten years' experience in the general field of local government, it lent more than superficial aid and comfort to the purposes of the scattered local bureaus. As an established medium for disseminating information on government, it increased their factual facilities and gave wide publicity to their labors." (*City Management,* [1939], p. 738.)

[195] "The Next Step in the Organization of Municipal Research," *Review,* XI (1922), pp. 274–281.

[196] *Ibid.,* XIII (1924), p. 5; *Minutes of Executive Committee,* July 25, 1923.

[197] *Minutes of Council,* Nov. 11, 1924; *Review,* XIV (1925), p. 13.

[198] *Review,* XVII (1928), p. 387.

[199] See pp. 266–267.

[200] This description of the organization and activities of the Municipal Administration Service is based largely on the annual reports of the director, avail-

able only in typed or mimeographed form.

[201] *Review,* XXII (1933), p. 156. Cf. Governmental Research Association, "The Search for Facts in Government," *Review,* XXII (Supplement, June, 1933), pp. 301–305; C. A. Beard, *Government Research, Past, Present and Future* (Municipal Administration Service, No. 1, 1926).

[202] *Review,* XXII (1933), p. 576; *Minutes of Council,* Nov. 9, 1933; *Minutes of Executive Committee,* Nov. 28, 1933; *Secretary's Report,* 1933–1934, p. 2.

[203] *Minutes of Executive Committee,* Nov. 28, 1933.

[204] *Ibid.,* April 20, Oct. 25, 1934.

[205] Among the communities employing the Service were: Mount Vernon, Mount Pleasant, Cortlandt, Greenburgh, Harrison, Yonkers, Nassau County, New York; Toledo, Ohio; Lehigh County, Pennsylvania; Norwalk, Connecticut; Asbury Park, Dumont, Jersey City, Kearny, Lyndhurst, North Bergen, Teaneck, Essex County, New Jersey; Coral Gables, Jacksonville, St. Petersburg, Winter Park, Florida; Atlanta and Fulton County, Savannah, Georgia; Brookline, New Bedford, Massachusetts.

[206] *Review,* XXIII (1934), pp. 40, 128–292; *ibid.,* XXIV (1935), p. 82; *ibid.,* XXV (1936), pp. 103, 223, 373, 425–426, 741; *ibid.,* XXVI (1937), pp. 214, 251, 447; *ibid.,* XXVII (1938), p. 66.

[207] See pp. 258–260.

[208] *Minutes of Executive Committee,* June 30, 1928; June 27, 1939; *Minutes of Council,* Nov. 30, 1938.

[209] *Secretary's Report,* 1937–1938, pp. 30–31.

[210] *Review,* XXVIII (1939), pp. 188–189; *ibid.,* XXIX (1940), pp. 151, 163, 791; *ibid.,* XXX (1941), p. 134; *ibid.,* XXXII (1943), pp. 150–151; *ibid.,* XXXIII (1944), pp. 2, 6; *ibid.,* XXXIV (1945), pp. 301–302, 317, 434; *ibid.,* XXXV (1946), p. 390.

NOTES TO CHAPTER VIII

[1] *Secretary's Report,* 1928–1929, p. 5; 1939–1940, p. 2.

[2] Article II, sec. 2.

[3] *Proceedings,* 1901, p. 319.

[4] Article II, sec. 1.

[5] *Review,* XXIII (1934), p. 649.

[6] *Minutes of Council,* Nov. 21, 1917.

[7] *Review,* VII (1918), pp. 106, 115–122.

[8] *Report of the Survey Committee to the National Municipal League,* June 5, 1918, pp. 24–27. (Hereafter cited as *Report of Survey Committee.)*

[9] See "Drastic Proposals for a New National Municipal League," *Review,* X (1921), pp. 554–557.

[10] *Proceedings,* 1911, p. 6 (*Review,* I, No. 1, Jan., 1912).

[11] Harold W. Dodds resigned as secretary of the League in 1928 but continued as editor of the *Review* until 1933. (*Minutes of Executive Committee,* May 21, 1928). The Survey Committee in 1918 had recommended the separation of executive and editorial work.

[12] Present editorial staff consists of: Alfred Willoughby, editor; Elsie S. Parker, assistant editor; contributing editors: John Bauer, Public Utilities; George H. Hallett, Jr., William Redin Woodward, Proportional Representation; H. M. Olmsted, City, State and Nation; John E. Bebout, Research; Wade S. Smith, Taxation and Finance; Elwyn A. Mauck, County and Township; Richard S. Childs; and fifty-six state correspondents.

[13] The following are typical subjects: city councils, mayors, state legislatures, public utility problems, city manager government, registration of voters, initiative and referendum, municipal treatment of vice, city planning, tax rates, bonded debt, cost of government, home rule, city-county consolidation, civic education, municipal labor policies, and town management.

14 Topics and dates of special issues have been: Reconstruction (Jan., 1919); Improved Methods of Election (Dec., 1921); Special Assessments (Feb., 1922); Pensions (April, 1922); City Planning (June, 1922); Metropolitan Communities (Aug., 1922); Report of Civil Service Committee (Aug., 1923); County Government (Aug., 1932; Oct., 1934; Oct. 1936; Feb., 1939); Municipal Debt (June, 1933; June, 1936; June, 1938); Public Utilities (Nov., 1934); Real Estate Tax Limitation (Nov., 1935); City Management (Feb., 1936); Social Security (Mar., April, 1936); The Relief Problem (Jan., 1938); European Local Government (Sept., 1936); Chicago Convention Number (Nov., 1929); Cleveland Convention Number (Oct., 1930); Convention Issue (Jan., Dec., 1939; Jan., 1941; Jan., 1942); Fiftieth Anniversary Issue (Nov., 1944).

15 *Report of Survey Committee* (1918), pp. 13–17.

16 The annual meeting in 1919 authorized the Council to select a more suitable name for the magazine. (*Review*, IX [1920], p. 99.)

17 *Report of Survey Committee* (1918), p. 16.

18 *Minutes of Executive Committee*, Mar. 22, 1919; Dec. 23, 1920; *Minutes of Council*, Dec. 13, 1920; April 22, 1921; *Review*, VIII (1919), p. 211.

19 *Minutes of Council*, Nov. 12, 1929; Feb. 21–22, 1931; Nov. 9, 1933; Nov. 30, 1938; *Review*, VIII (1919), p. 211; *ibid.*, X (1921), pp. 554–557.

20 *Proceedings*, 1911, p. 6 (*Review*, I, No. 1, Jan., 1912).

21 *Report of Survey Committee* (1918), p. 25.

22 *Review*, VIII (1919), p. 211.

23 *Report of Survey Committee* (1918), p. 16.

24 A special subscription rate is offered to students and a number of teachers require students to subscribe during the college year.

25 *Minutes of Council*, Nov. 17, 1915.

26 *Review*, XI (1922), p. 127.

27 See pp. 253–258.

28 *Report of Survey Committee* (1918), pp. 24–29.

29 See pp. 251–252.

30 *Minutes of Executive Committee*, July 19, 1938; *Secretary's Report*, 1937–1938, pp. 1–4.

31 *Minutes of Executive Committee*, Jan. 20, 1906.

32 *Report of Survey Committee* (1918), pp. 18–20.

33 See pp. 260–261.

34 *Minutes of Executive Committee*, Mar. 6, 1930.

35 See p. 261.

36 *Proceedings*, 1905, p. iv.

37 For complete list of League publications, see pp. 249–266.

38 *Secretary's Report*, 1927–1928 to 1939–1940, *passim; ibid.*, 1948, p. 13.

39 *Proceedings*, 1908, p. 45.

40 *Secretary's Report*, 1926–1927, p. 10.

41 *Ibid.*, 1928–1929, pp. 5–6; 1929–1930, p. 4.

42 *Ibid.*, 1937–1938, p. 21.

43 *Ibid.*, p. 21.

44 *Ibid.*, 1926–1927 to 1936–1937, *passim.* From 1931 to 1937 members of the staff at the secretariat made approximately 1,700 addresses.

45 See pp. 105–106.

46 *Review*, XI (1922), pp. 379–385.

47 *Minutes of Council*, Feb. 21–22, 1931.

48 See pp. 108–109.

49 *Minutes of Executive Committee*, Mar. 20, 1938; *Minutes of Council*, Nov. 30, Dec. 30, 1938.

50 *Proceedings*, 1901, p. 318.

51 *Ibid.*, 1900, p. 90.

52 *Ibid.*, 1903, pp. 86, 307; 1906, p. 123.

53 *Ibid.*, 1908, pp. 449, 464.

[54] *Ibid.*, 1894–1895, p. 70; 1896, p. iv; 1897, p. 61–62; 1900, p. 88.

[55] See pp. 113–114.

[56] See ch. iii.

[57] C. R. Woodruff, "The Nationalization of Municipal Movements," *Annals*, XXI (1903), p. 254.

[58] *Review*, X (1921), p. 557.

[59] *Secretary's Report*, 1929–1930, p. 7.

[60] *A Municipal Program* (1900), pp. 152, 156.

[61] *Review*, VIII (1919), p. 460. Cf. R. S. Childs, "A Democracy That Might Work," *Century*, CXX (1930), pp. 11–17.

[62] *Minutes of Council*, Nov. 18, 1914; Nov. 21, 1917; Feb. 21–22, 1931; Dec. 30, 1938; *Minutes of Executive Committee*, April 17, Dec. 4, 1931; *Review*, IX (1920), p. 99.

[63] See pp. 111–113, 144–145, 152, 155.

[64] *Report of Survey Committee* (1918), p. 29.

[65] *Review*, VI (1917), p. 630 *ibid.*, IX (1920), p. 407.

[66] *Minutes of Council*, April 22, 1921.

[67] *Cleveland Plain Dealer*, Feb. 15, 1920; H. A. Stone, D. K. Price, K. H. Stone, *City Manager Government in the United States* (1940), pp. 23–24.

[68] See pp. 183–184.

[69] *Minutes of Council*, Dec. 13, 1920; April 25, Nov. 11, 1930; May 14–15, 1932; *Minutes of Executive Committee*, Mar. 6, 1930.

[70] Membership of the committee: Howard Strong, Wilkes-Barre, Pa., chairman; Harold S. Buttenheim, H. S. Braucher, New York; L. D. Upson, Detroit; H. M. Waite, Cincinnati.

[71] *Report of Committee on Local Branches* (mimeo., 1930).

[72] *Secretary's Report*, 1937–1938, pp. 6–8.

[73] *Ibid.*, 1935–1936, p. 4.

[74] *Review*, X (1921), p. 329.

[75] *Ibid.*, XXIX (1940), pp. 2, 75.

[76] Cf. Public Administration Clearing House, *Public Administration Organizations* (5th ed.; 1941).

[77] *The Government of American Cities* (4th ed.; 1926), pp. 428, 433. See also William Anderson, *American City Government* (1925), pp. 217–219, chap. xxiv; A. F. Macdonald, *American City Government and Administration*, (rev. ed.; 1936), chap. xxi; T. H. Reed, *Municipal Government in the United States* (rev. ed.; 1934), chap. ix; Harold Zink, *Government of Cities in the United States* (1939), chap. xiv; R. H. Wells, *American Local Government* (1939), pp. 40–46; W. B. Graves, *American State Government* (1936), pp. 150–160; W. B. Munro, "Civic Organizations," *Encyclopedia of the Social Sciences* (1930), III, pp. 498–502; L. W. Lancaster, *Government in Rural America* (1937), pp. 401–409.

[78] See p. 148.

[79] See pp. 110, 141.

[80] *Annals*, CXCIX (1938), pp. 183–189.

[81] See pp. 75–76.

[82] *Minutes of Executive Committee*, April 29, 1908.

[83] *Review*, I (1912), pp. 603–610.

[84] *Ibid.*, III (1914), p. 616. The original committee was composed of Richard S. Childs, Robert S. Binkerd, New York; Edward M. Sait, Columbia University.

[85] *Review*, VII (1918), pp. 107–108, 444.

[86] *Ibid.*, XIV (1925), p. 121; *ibid.*, XV (1926), p. 567.

[87] *Ibid.*, XVIII (1929), pp. 1, 116–119, 344–346.

[88] See pp. 139, 140, 142. See H. D. Smith and G. C. S. Benson, "Associations of Cities and of Municipal Officials," *Urban Government* (1939), Pt. IV (Vol. I of the Supplementary Report of the Urbanism Committee to the National Resources Committee).

[80] See pp. 102–106, 150.

[90] Harvard University, 1902, 1924; University of Michigan, 1903; Brown University, 1907; University of Cincinnati, 1909.

[91] *Minutes of Council,* Nov. 21, 1917.

[92] See pp. 108–109.

[93] *Review,* I (1912), pp. 78–79; *ibid.,* II (1913), p. 135; *ibid.,* III (1914), pp. 216–217; *Proceedings,* 1909, p. 17.

[94] *Minutes of Executive Committee,* Dec. 17, 1936; *Review,* XXIII (1934), pp. 362, 450.

[95] *Secretary's Report,* 1924–1925, p. 5; 1926–1927, p. 10.

[96] *Proceedings,* 1901, p. 46. See Woodruff, *op. cit.,* pp. 252–260.

[97] *Proceedings,* 1902, pp. 260–267; 1903, pp. 7–11, 85–86, 202–221, 305–309; 1904, pp. 110, 405; 1905, pp. 92, 394; 1906, p. 490. League representatives were: Charles Richardson, Clinton Rogers Woodruff, Philadelphia; William P. Bancroft, Wilmington.

[98] *Minutes of Executive Committee,* Jan. 24, 1907.

[99] *Proceedings,* 1907, pp. 65–75, 385–387; *Review,* IV (1915), pp. 8–9, 626–632.

[100] *Review,* VI (1917), pp. 191, 246–254.

[101] *Minutes of Council,* Nov. 21, 1917.

[102] *Report of Survey Committee* (1918), pp. 34–35.

[103] *Minutes of Council,* May 14–15, 1932.

[104] *Proceedings,* 1897, pp. 118–128, 133–144; 1908, pp. 413–420.

[105] Members of the committee were: George Burnham, Jr., Philadelphia, chairman; Frank N. Hartwell, Louisville; Oliver McClintock, Pittsburgh; E. M. Thresher, Dayton; Samuel B. Capen, Boston; William P. Bancroft, Wilmington.

[106] *Proceedings,* 1901, pp. 43–46.

[107] *Ibid.,* 1900, pp. 81–82; 1901, pp. 64–65; 1902, pp. 97–98; 1903, pp. 306–307; 1905, pp. 93–94; 1908, p. 145; 1910, pp. 76–77.

[108] See pp. 113–114.

[109] See p. 130.

[110] J. A. Vieg, "Advice for Municipal Reformers," *Public Opinion Quarterly,* I (Oct., 1937), pp. 91–92.

[111] A. F. Howe, "Organized Labor Favorable to City Manager Plan," *Review,* XII (1923), pp. 165–167.

[112] Stone, Price, Stone, *op. cit.,* pp. 26–27.

[113] *Secretary's Report,* 1937–1938, pp. 4–5. See League pamphlets, *What Happens to Labor under the Manager Plan* (1940), and *What Happens to City Employees under the Manager Plan* (1940).

[114] *Proceedings,* 1907, pp. 22–23, 407–408.

[115] *Ibid.,* 1912, p. 2 (*Review,* II, No. 1, Jan., 1913).

[116] *Minutes of Council,* July 11, 1912; *Review,* IV (1915), pp. 171, 174–176. The committee was composed of Mrs. Florence Kelley, New York, chairman; Mrs. Samuel B. Sneath, Tiffin, Ohio; Jane Campbell, Mrs. John M. Oakley, Clinton Rogers Woodruff, Philadelphia.

[117] *Review,* X (1921), pp. 327–330.

[118] *Ibid.,* XXV (1936), p. 310.

[119] *Proceedings,* 1894–1895, p. 262; 1899, p. 251.

[120] *Ibid.,* 1903, p. 303.

[121] *Ibid.,* 1906, p. iv.

[122] *Review,* XXII (1933), p. 595.

[123] *City Government,* III (July, 1897), pp. 9–13.

[124] Woodruff, *op. cit.,* p. 256.

[125] *Sanford* (Me.) *Herald,* June 12, 1929; *Ryan's Weekly* (Tacoma, Wash.), April 13, 1929.

[126] *Burlington* (Ia.) *Gazette,* Mar. 18, 1924.

[127] *Montclair* (N. J.) *Times,* Oct. 12, 1934.

[128] *Review,* XVIII (1929), p. 284.

[129] *Ibid.,* XXI (1932), p. 140.

[130] Quoted in leaflet, *The Influence of the National Municipal League* (1910), pp. 8–9.

[131] Jan. 27, 1912.

[132] *State Government* (1922), p. 409.

[133] *County and Township Government in the United States* (1922), p. xiii.

[134] T. H. Reed and Paul Webbink, *Documents Illustrative of American Municipal Government* (1926), p. 301.

[135] *Municipal Government in the United States* (rev. ed.; 1934), p. 214.

[136] Macdonald, *op. cit.*, p. 368.

[137] *A Study of Research in Public Administration* (mimeo., 1930), p. 133.

[138] *The Government of American Cities* (4th ed.; 1926), p. 423.

[139] Anderson, *op. cit.*, pp. 631–632.

NOTES TO CHAPTER IX

[1] See p. 204.

[2] See p. 206.

[3] New York *Times*, Feb. 15, 1905; *American Bar Association Journal*, XIV (1928), pp. 127–132.

[4] See pp. 16–17, 19–20.

[5] F. M. Stewart, *The National Civil Service Reform League* (1929), pp. 17–18.

[6] *Review*, X (1921), p. 447; *Proceedings*, 1910, p. 490.

[7] Stewart, *op. cit.*, pp. 64–65.

[8] See p. 51.

[9] *Review*, XXIV (1935), pp. 310, 368.

[10] *Ibid.*, VII (1918), p. 232; *Who's Who in America*, XXI (1940–1941), p. 2114.

[11] *Review*, IX (1920), p. 61; *Who's Who in America*, XXI (1940–1941), pp. 1327–1328.

[12] *Review*, X (1921), p. 203; *ibid.*, XXXVII (1948), p. 520.

[13] L. D. White, *The City Manager* (1927), pp. 78–82; *Who's Who in America*, XXI (1940–1941), p. 2654; *Review*, XXXIII (1944), p. 438.

[14] *Who's Who in America*, XXI (1940–1941), p. 2079; *Review*, XXXII (1943), p. 122.

[15] See pp. 75, 219–220.

[16] *Review*, XX (1931), p. 683; *Who's Who in America*, XXI (1940–1941), p. 567.

[17] *Review*, XVIII (1929), pp. 68–75; *ibid.*, XX (1931), p. 683; *ibid.*, XXIII (1934), p. 642; *Who's Who in America*, XXI (1940–1941), p. 2311.

[18] *Review*, XXII (1933), pp. 116, 259; *ibid.*, XXIII (1934), p. 642; *Who's Who in America*, XXI (1940–1941), p. 782.

[19] *Who's Who in America*, XXI (1940–1941), p. 826; *Survey Graphic*, XXVI (1937), pp. 204–206; *Review*, XXXIV (1945), p. 162.

[20] *Review*, XXX (1941), p. 70; *ibid.*, XXXV (1946), p. 158; *ibid.*, XXXVI (1947), p. 606; *Who's Who in America*, XXI (1940–1941), p. 2798; *Reader's Digest*, XXXVIII (June, 1941), pp. 115–118.

[21] *Who's Who in America*, XXIII (1944–1945), p. 604; *Review*, XXXV (1946), p. 566.

[22] *Report of Survey Committee*, (1918), p. 5.

[23] *Who's Who in America*, XXI (1940–1941), p. 2822. *Review*, XXXVII (1948), p. 126.

[24] *Review*, IX (1920), pp. 62–65, 98; *ibid.*, VIII (1919), pp. 271, 329.

[25] *Who's Who in America*, XXI (1940–1941), p. 782.

[26] *Review*, XXII (1933), p. 218; *ibid.*, XXVI (1937), p. 214; *Who's Who in America*, XXI (1940–1941), p. 950.

[27] *Who's Who in America*, XXI (1940–1941), p. 1414; *Minutes of Executive Committee*, June 27, 1939; *Review*, XXVIII (1939), p. 408; *ibid.*, XXXII (1943), pp. 122, 414; *ibid.*, XXXIV (1945), p. 434; *ibid.*, XXXV (1946),

p. 334; *ibid.*, XXXVI (1947), p. 2; *ibid.*, XXXVII (1948), p. 520.

[28] *Who's Who in America,* XXV (1948–1949), p. 2702; *Review,* XXXVI (1947), p. 602.

[29] *Report of Survey Committee,* (1918), pp. 11–13.

[30] See p. 148. The following facetious statement of the plight of the Secretary was contributed by Mr. Woodruff and printed in the *Review* for May, 1930, under the caption, "The Secretary's Lament."

If the secretary writes a letter, it is too long.
If he sends a postal, it is too short.
If he issues a pamphlet, he's a spendthrift.
If he attends a committee meeting, he is butting in.
If he stays away, he is a shirker.
If the attendance at a meeting is slim, he should have called the members up.
If he does call them, he is a pest
If he duns a member for his dues, he is insulting.
If he does not collect, he is lazy.
If a meeting is a howling success, the program committee is praised.
If it's a failure, the Secretary is to blame.
If he asks for advice, he is incompetent, and if he does not, he is bull-headed.
Ashes to ashes,
    Dust to dust,
If the others won't do it,
    The Secretary must.

[31] *Review,* XXIII (1934), p. 501.

[32] *Ibid.,* VIII (1919), p. 213.

[33] *Minutes of Executive Committee,* Mar. 22, 1919; *Minutes of Council,* April 19, 1919.

[34] *Who's Who in America,* XX (1938–1939), p. 1313.

[35] *Review,* IX (1920), pp. 61, 98.

[36] *Ibid.,* XI (1922), p. 1; *Wall Street Journal,* Jan. 28, 1927.

[37] See p. 206.

[38] *Handbook,* 1904, pp. 35–38; 1914, p. 2; *Minutes of Executive Committee,* April 28, 1904.

[39] See p. 204.

[40] *Report of Survey Committee* (1918), pp. 5–7.

[41] See pp. 139, 140.

[42] *Report of Survey Committee* (1918), pp. 7–9.

[43] Because of war conditions no annual meetings were held in 1942, 1943, 1944, and 1945. In November, 1946, the first postwar National Conference on Government, in celebration of the fiftieth anniversary of the National Municipal League, was held in Philadelphia.

[44] *Report of Survey Committee* (1918), p. 21.

[45] *Municipal Government in the United States* (rev. ed.; 1934), p. 130; *Review,* IX (1920), pp. 61–62.

[46] *Report of Survey Committee* (1918), pp. 23–24.

[47] *Minutes of Council,* June 6, 1918; April 19, 1919; Dec. 13, 1920; Nov. 11, 1924; Nov. 30, 1938; *Minutes of Executive Committee,* April 30, 1936.

[48] *What the League is Doing* (1940), pp. 1–2; *Review,* XXIX (1940), pp. 2, 86, 150, 224; *Secretary's Report,* 1939–1940, pp. 6–7.

[49] *Handbook,* 1904, p. 35. Forty-five local reform associations were listed in the appendix to the *Proceedings of the Philadelphia Conference* (1894). League records indicated the existence of 176 associations in 1895; 267 in 1896; 463 in 1900; 600 in 1902; 892 in 1905; 1149 in 1906; and 1320 in 1907.

[50] Fifteen affiliated associations organized the League in 1894. In 1895 there were 52 affiliated societies; 86 in 1897; 119 in 1900; 115 in 1901; 87 in 1903; 135 in 1907; 154 in 1908; 191 in 1910; and 227, with an enrolled membership of 198,000, in 1913.

[51] *Constitution and By-Laws of the National Municipal League, as Amended by the Seventeenth Annual Meeting, held in Richmond, Va., November 14th, 1911* (1912), Art. III.

[52] *Review,* IX (1920), p. 168.

[53] *Secretary's Report,* 1946, p. 22; 1948, pp. 1, 14.

[54] *Review,* IX (1920), pp. 169–170.
[55] *Secretary's Report,* 1935–1936, p. 12; 1936–1937, p. 10; 1937–1938, p. 19; *Review,* XXV (1936), pp. 390, 442; *ibid.,* XXVI (1937), p. 414; *ibid.,* XXVII (1938), pp. 2, 126, 186, 242, 350, 478; *ibid.,* XXIX (1940), pp. 151, 288.
[56] *What's in the Proposed Constitution?* (1938).
[57] *Review,* XXVI (1937), p. 2.
[58] *Minutes of Council,* Dec. 13, 1920; April 25, Nov. 11, 1930; May 14–15, 1932; *Minutes of Executive Committee,* Mar. 6, 1930.
[59] Members of the committee were: Howard Strong, Wilkes-Barre, Pa., chairman; H. S. Buttenheim, H. S. Braucher, New York; Lent D. Upson, Detroit; H. M. Waite, Cincinnati.
[60] *Report of Committee on Local Branches* (mimeo., 1930).
[61] See p. 159.
[62] *Minutes of Business Committee,* Jan. 13, June 5, 1911; *Minutes of Executive Committee,* April 26, 1905; April 20, 1911; Feb. 20, 1919; *Minutes of Council,* April 19, 1919; Mar. 28, 1923.
[63] *Report of Survey Committee* (1918), pp. 9–10.
[64] *Review,* IX (1920), p. 405.
[65] See p. 143.
[66] *Minutes of Executive Committee,* Feb. 24, 1934.
[67] *Minutes of Council,* Dec. 30, 1938; *Minutes of Executive Committee,* Dec. 27, 1938; May 22, June 27, 1939; *Review,* XXVIII (1939), p. 2.
[68] *Review,* XXVIII (1939), p. 569.
[69] *Proceedings,* 1894–1895, p. 183.
[70] *Ibid.,* 1900, pp. 7–8.
[71] *Report of Survey Committee* (1918), pp. 29–30, 32.
[72] *Comparative Report of Income of the National Municipal League* (mimeo., Mar. 1, 1935).
[73] *Reports of Audit.*
[74] *Financing Program of the National Municipal League,* 1 (mimeo., May 14, 1947).
[75] A special Committee on Endowment reported in 1911 that a permanent endowment was desirable, but the committee had grave doubts whether a public appeal for funds for endowment would be successful at that time. (*Minutes of Executive Committee,* April 20, 1911).
[76] *Handbook,* 1904, p. 36. In 1894 the secretary was authorized by the Executive Committee to ask all affiliated associations for contributions. In 1904–1905, the Executive Committee adopted a plan of asking each city represented in the Executive Committee to subscribe a definite quota for the support of the League. (*Minutes of Executive Committee,* Oct. 6, 1894; April 27, 1904; April 26, 1905).
[77] See pp. 77, 112, 142.
[78] *Review,* XXVII (1938), p. 186.
[79] President Childs, in 1931, commented on the difficulty of getting individual contributions: "We have learned from a long, unsatisfactory experience that the number of wealthy individuals who are interested in government reform on a national scale is very, very limited. It is not particularly difficult to persuade an individual to contribute to a reform campaign in his local community. It is extremely difficult to persuade that individual to contribute to an organization which may use his money to bring about a governmental reform in some far off community." (Letter to Morris Knowles, July 24, 1931).
[80] *Minutes of Executive Committee,* Dec. 16, 1898; April 7, 1909; *Minutes of Council,* Nov. 12, 1913; April 24, 1918.
[81] *Minutes of Council,* Feb. 21–22, 1931; *Minutes of Executive Committee,* Mar. 26, April 17, 1931.

[82] *Secretary's Report,* 1926–1927, p. 3; 1928–1929, p. 9; 1929–1930, pp. 6–7; 1930–1931, p. 8; 1936–1937, p. v.

[83] *Ibid.,* 1926–1927, p. 4.

[84] See pp. 157–159.

[85] *Secretary's Report,* 1930–1931, p. 7.

[86] *Minutes of Council,* Nov. 11, 1946.

[87] *Minutes of Executive Committee,* Nov. 26, 1946; *Review,* XXXVI (1947), p. 2.

[88] *Financing Program of the National Municipal League,* (mimeo., May 14, 1947).

[89] *Review,* XXXVI (1947), pp. 602, 606; *ibid.,* XXXVIII (1949), p. 64; *Secretary's Report,* 1947, pp. 1–2; *ibid.,* 1948, pp. 1–3.

[90] *Constitution,* Arts. IV, V, IX.

[91] See pp. 113–114.

[92] *Secretary's Report,* 1936–1937, p. v.

[93] *Report of Survey Committee* (1918), pp. 31–33.

[94] *Review,* X (1921), pp. 554–557.

[95] See pp. 164–166.

[96] *Minutes of Council,* Nov. 21, 1917.

[97] *Review,* VII (1918), pp. 116–117.

[98] *Ibid.,* VII (1918), pp. 443.

[99] *Report of Survey Committee* (1918), pp. 1–2.

[100] *Review,* X (1921), pp. 554–557.

[101] *Minutes of Council,* Nov. 11, 1930.

[102] *Minutes of Meeting of the Vice Presidents and Council,* Feb. 21–22, 1931.

[103] See p. 79.

[104] *Report of Survey Committee* (1918), pp. 34–35.

[105] *Review,* XII (1923), pp. 229–231. The committee was composed of L. D. Upson, Detroit, chairman; John A. Fairlie, University of Illinois; Mayo Fesler, Morton D. Hull, Chicago; Charles E. Merriam, University of Chicago.

[106] See pp. 99–100, 147, 150.

NOTES TO CHAPTER X

[1] W. B. Munro, *The Government of American Cities* (4th ed.; 1926), p. 431.

[2] *Ibid.*

[3] T. H. Reed, *Municipal Government in the United States* (rev. ed.; 1934), p. 115.

[4] L. D. White, *Trends in Public Administration* (1933), pp. 17, 211–212.

[5] *Urban Government,* pp. 3–4 (Volume I of the Supplementary Report of the Urbanism Committee to the National Resources Committee, 1939). See also White, *op. cit.,* chap. xv.

[6] Harold Zink, *Government of Cities in the United States* (1939), chap. xiv.

[7] *Modern Democracies* (1921), II, 138–140.

[8] Munro, *op. cit.,* pp. 431–432.

[9] Reed, *op. cit.,* p. 330.

[10] William Anderson, *American City Government* (1925), p. 648.

[11] *Ibid.,* chap. xxiv; Munro, *op. cit.,* chap. xxii; Reed, *op. cit.,* chaps. ix, xx; A. F. Macdonald, *American City Government and Administration,* (rev. ed.; 1936), chap. xxi; Zink, *op. cit.,* chap. xxxii; R. H. Wells, *American Local Government* (1939), chap. ii; *Annals,* CXCIX (1938), pp. 171–189; Public Administration Clearing House, *Public Administration Organizations,* (5th ed.; 1941); W. B. Graves, *American State Government* (1936), pp. 150–160.

[12] See articles by John G. Winant, Charles A. Beard, Clinton Rogers Woodruff, Richard S. Childs, Harold W. Dodds, Murray Seasongood, in the Fiftieth Anniversary issue of the *Review,* XXXIII, No. 10 (Nov., 1944).

[13] *The Influence of the National Municipal League* (1910).

[14] *Secretary's Report,* 1936–1937, pp. iii–iv.

[15] *Ibid.,* 1937–1938, p. 1.

[16] See pp. 170–171.

[17] *Proceedings,* 1903, p. 307.

Bibliography

PUBLICATIONS OF THE NATIONAL MUNICIPAL LEAGUE

Periodicals and Serials

Minutes of the Board of Delegates
Minutes of the Executive Committee
Minutes of the Business Committee
Minutes of the Council

The League Constitution of 1894 created a Board of Delegates and an Executive Committee. A small Business Committee to exercise the powers of the Executive Committee ad interim was created in 1904 by resolution of the Executive Committee. Under the constitution, as amended at the 1911 meeting, the Board of Delegates was abolished, and the Executive Committee was renamed the Council and the Business Committee became the Executive Committee.

Minutes of the first meeting of the Board of Delegates of the League held in New York City, May 28–29, 1894, were typed. Minutes of subsequent meetings were incorporated in the printed annual volumes of the Proceedings of the National Conference for Good City Government and the Annual Meeting of the National Municipal League.

Minutes of the Executive Committee, Business Committee, and Council have been recorded in typed or mimeographed form.

National Municipal Review, vol. 1 from Jan., 1912. Qtly. Jan., 1912 to Oct., 1916; Bi-monthly, Jan., 1917 to Mch., 1919; Mo., May, 1919–1941; Mo., except Aug., 1942–. Publication office: 150 Fremont St., Worcester, Mass.; Editorial and Business office: 299 Broadway, New York 7, N. Y.

Proceedings

The Proceedings of the National Conference for Good City Government held at Philadelphia January 25–26, 1894, together with a bibliography of municipal government and reform and a brief statement concerning the objects and methods of municipal reform organizations in the United States, was published by the Municipal League of Philadelphia in 1894.

Minutes of the first meeting of the Board of Delegates of the League held in New York City, May 28–29, 1894, were typed.

From 1895 to 1910 sixteen volumes of Proceedings of the National Conference for Good City Government and the Annual Meeting of the National Municipal League were published by the League.

A summary of the proceedings of the annual meetings of the League from 1911 to 1918 was printed in the *National Municipal Review* for Jan., 1912; Jan., 1913; Jan., 1914; Jan., 1915; Jan., 1916; Jan., 1917; Jan., 1918; and July, 1918.

Formal accounts of the League meetings since 1918 have not been published. The *Review* has frequently printed brief comments on the meetings, including the business session, and in it have appeared many papers delivered before the annual conferences. Typed minutes of the proceedings of the annual business meeting have been made since 1918.

The Proceedings of the Annual Meeting of the Governmental Research Association (mimeographed) for 1927, 1928, 1929, contain the papers and discussions of several sessions held jointly with the League.

Secretary's Report

The annual report of the Secretary of the League, including a review of the progress of governmental reform, was published in the annual volume of Proceedings from 1895 to 1910, and was continued in the *National Municipal Review* from 1911 to 1920. Since 1920 the report has been presented in typed or mimeographed form, except those for 1927–1928, 1929–1930, and 1930–1931, which were published in the *Review*. No report was issued in 1943 and 1945.

Leaflets

1. Woodruff, Clinton R. *The National Municipal League.* 1898.
2. *The National Municipal League— What It is Doing; What Others Have to Say About it.* 1899.
3. Gladden, Washington, *Civic Religion.* 1899. Five editions.
4. *What Others are Saying of the National Municipal League.* ca. 1900.
5. Bonaparte, Charles J. *The Essential Element in Good City Government.* 1901. Three editions.
6. Deming, Horace E. *Public Service by Citizens in Private Station.* 1902. Three editions.

Leaflets, New Series

1. Villard, Oswald G. *William Henry Baldwin, a Life of Civic Endeavor.* 1905. 2d ed., 1909.

2. Deming, Horace E. *Public Service by Private Citizens.* 3d ed., 1906; 4th ed., 1910.
3. McFarland, John H. *The Ignorance of Good Citizens.* 1906. Reprinted from the *Outlook,* v. 82 (1906), pp. 271–273.
4. Butler, John A. *The National Municipal League.* 1907. 2d ed., 1909.
5. Fesler, Mayo. *Civic Philistinism.* 1908.
6. Bonaparte, Charles J. *The Field of Labor of the National Municipal League.* 1908.
7. English, H.D.W. *The Functions of Business Bodies in Improving Civic Conditions.* 1909.
8. Woodruff, Clinton R. *The National Municipal League's Work for Charter Reform.* 1909.
9. Hodges, George. *The Value of a Vote.* 1910.
10. Schurz, Carl. *The Relation of Civil Service Reform to Municipal Reform.* 1910. Reprinted from *Proceedings of the Philadelphia Conference for Good City Government,* 1894, pp. 123–133.
11. Palmer, John M. *The Man in the Pigeonhole.* 1910.
12. Foulke, William D. *The Mission of the National Municipal League.* 1914.

Leaflets, Third Series

1. Adams, Charles E. *What Constitutes Good Citizenship.* 1911
2. Dunn, Arthur W. *Training for Citizenship.* 1913.
3. Committee on Civic Education. *Plan for the Promotion of Civic Education.* 1913.
4. ———. *Measuring the Value of Civic Training.* 1913.
5. ———. *How Georgia Prepares her Teachers to Teach Citizenship.* 1914.

6. ———. *The United States Bureau of Education Interested in Better Training for Citizenship.* 1914.

Democracy in the Modern World Leaflets Nos. 1–7 of a Series on Making Democracy Work. 1938–1940.

Pamphlets

1. Dole, Charles F. *City Government and the Churches.*

   Richardson, Charles. *What a Private Citizen Can Do For Good City Government.* 1894. Five editions.
2. Bonaparte, Charles J. *Address to the Public. Constitution and By-Laws of the National Municipal League.* 1894. Five editions.
3. Schurz, Carl. *The Relation of Civil Service Reform to Municipal Reform.* 1894. Three editions. Reprinted from *Proceedings of the Philadelphia Conference for Good City Government,* 1894, pp. 123–133.
4. *Constitutions and By-Laws of Leading Municipal Reform Organizations Including Those of the Municipal League of Philadelphia, City Club of New York, Baltimore Reform League, Civic Federation of Chicago, Good Government Club of San Francisco, Law Enforcement Society of Brooklyn, and Civic Club of Philadelphia.* 1895. Two editions.
5. Ritchie, Ryerson. *Commercial Organizations and Municipal Reform.* 1897.
6. Capen, Samuel B. *The Closing Work of the Nineteenth Century.* 1899. Two editions.
7. Deming, Horace E. *A Municipal Program.* 1901. Reprinted from *Annals,* v. 17 (1901), pp. 431–443.
8. Ames, Herbert B. *The City Problem—What is It?*

   Root, E. T. *Christian Citizenship.* 1901.*

   These titles (as one) and the one following are both listed as No. 8.)

8. McFarland, John H. *Harrisburg's Advance: a Lesson to Smaller Municipalities Presented at the Boston Conference in Connection with 70 Lantern Slides.* 1902.
9. Deming, Horace E. *The Meaning and Importance of Nomination Reform.* 1903.
10. Hartwell, Edward M. *Uniform Municipal Accounting and Statistics.* 1903.
11. Woodruff, Clinton R. *A Year's Disclosure and Development.* 1904.
12. Rowe, Leo S. *University and Collegiate Instruction and Research in Municipal Government.* 1904.
13. Purdy, Lawson. *Municipal Taxation.* 1904.
14. Deming, Horace E. *Municipal Nomination Reform.* 1905. Reprinted from *Annals,* v. 25 (1905), pp. 203–217.

Campaign Pamphlets
(formerly Pocket Civic Series).

Answers to Your Questions about the Manager Plan. 1931. Numerous editions and reprints.

Bromage, Arthur W. *Why Some Cities Have Abandoned Manager Charters.* Reprinted from *National Municipal Review,* v. 19, no. 9 (Sept., 1930), pp. 599–603; and v. 19, no. 11 (Nov., 1930), pp. 761–766.

———. *Manager Plan Abandonments: Why 25 Communities Shelved Council-Manager Government.* 1940.

Childs, Richard S. *Ramshackle County Government—the Plague Spot of American Politics.* 1921. Numerous editions and reprints. Pocket Civic Series no. 4.

———. *Best Practice under the Manager Plan: Role of Voters, Press, Council and Manager.* rev. ed., 1939.

———. *The County Manager Plan, with a Review of the Efforts to Adopt It.* 1925. Numerous editions and reprints.

————. *The Short Ballot, a Movement to Simplify Politics*. 1921. Numerous editions and reprints.

The City Manager Plan at Work: What Those Who Live in Manager Cities Think of their Government. c. 1930.

Council-Manager Cities During the Depression. c. 1935.

Forms of Municipal Government: How Have They Worked? c. 1939. Reprinted, 1944.

Harley, Herbert. *Criminal Justice— How to Achieve It*. Supplement to the *National Municipal Review*, v. 11, no. 3. March, 1922. Pocket Civic Series no. 8.

How Council-Manager Government is Working: As Described by Newspapermen in 30 Cities. 1940.

Proportional Representation: Answers to Your Questions. 1939.

Quick, Herbert. *A New Kind of County Government*. 1925.

The Story of the City-Manager Plan, the Most Democratic Form of Municipal Government. 1921. Numerous editions and reprints. Pocket Civic Series no. 3.

What Happens to Labor under the Manager Plan. 1940. Reprinted, 1944.

What Happens tu City Employees under the Manager Plan. 1940.

Who's Boss: A Story in Pictures about the Citizen and his City Government. 1940.

Citizens' Councils Pamphlets

National Federation of Citizens' Councils; in Affiliation with the National Municipal League. *Making Democracy Work—The Citizens' Council Plan; a Device to Mobilize the Forces of Each Community in the Interest of More Effective Citizenship*. 1936.

National Municipal League. *Citizens' Councils; a Device to Mobilize the Forces of Each Community in the In-*

terest of More Effective Citizenship. 1939.

National Municipal League. Committee on Citizens' Councils for Constructive Economy. *Citizens' Councils for Constructive Economy*. 1933.

————. *Citizens' Councils in Action; Achievements and Possibilities When Civic Groups Unite for Constructive Economy in Government and for the Support of Essential Community Services*. 1933.

————. *Citizens' Councils News Bulletin*. v. 1, nos. 1–6. Oct. 1933–June, 1934. mimeo.

————. *A Citizen's Council Why and How?; a Device to Unite Civic Groups in Their Common Aim to Achieve Economy in Local Government Without Sacrifice of Essential Services*. 1933.

————. *Committee on Citizens' Councils for Constructive Economy of the National Municipal League*. 1933.

————. *Report*. May 15, 1934. mimeo.

National Municipal League and Federation of Citizens' Organizations. *A Program to Improve the Quality of Government by Improving the Quality of Citizenship*. 1939.

Seasongood, Murray and Hatton, A. R. *Retrenching in State and Local Expenditures: A Summary of the Report of the Committee on Constructive Economy of the National Municipal League*. Government Series Lecture No. 10, delivered November 15, 1932. Chicago, University of Chicago Press, 1932.

National Pay-Your-Taxes Campaign Pamphlets

Campaign Manual: Suggestions and Methods for Reducing Tax Delinquency by Organizing a Local Pay Your Taxes Campaign. 1934. rev. ed., 1935. mimeo.

Facts About the Pay Your Taxes Campaign. ca. 1935.

Information Bulletin. v. 1–2, Dec., 1933–March, 1935. mimeo.

Improved Assessment Technique, Including a Description of the Brunswick, Georgia, Reassessment Project in Work Relief. 1934. No. 1 in a Series on Current Tax Problems.

Pay Your Taxes Campaign. ca. 1933.

Publicity Handbook: Detailed Suggestions for the Publicity Chairman of a Local Pay Your Taxes Campaign Committee. 1935. mimeo.

Report of the Secretary, National Pay Your Taxes Campaign Committee. Jan., 1934; June, 1934; Aug., 1935. mimeo.

Reporting Governmental Costs: Informing Taxpayers with the Tax Dollar Leaflet. 1935. No. 2 in a Series on Current Tax Problems.

Radio Addresses

"You and Your Government" Series

Broadcasts over a nation-wide network of the National Broadcasting Company presented by the Committee on Civic Education by Radio of the National Advisory Council on Radio in Education and the American Political Science Association, in coöperation with the National Municipal League. Published by the National Municipal League, New York.

V. *Constructive Economy in Government.*
Fifteen broadcasts delivered June 20–September 26, 1933. c. 1934.

VI. *The Crisis in Municipal Finance.*
Nineteen broadcasts delivered October 3, 1933–February 6, 1934. c. 1934.

VII. *Reviving Local Government.*
Nineteen broadcasts delivered February 13–June 19, 1934. c. 1934.

VIII. *A New Deal in Local Government.*
Fourteen broadcasts delivered June 26–September 25, 1934. c. 1936.

IX. *Trends in Government.*
Eighteen broadcasts delivered October 2, 1934–January 29, 1935. c. 1936.

X. *The 44 State Legislatures of 1935.*
Nineteen broadcasts delivered February 5–June 11, 1935. c. 1936.

XI. *Taxation for Prosperity.*
Fifteen broadcasts delivered June 18–September 24, 1935. c. 1936.

XII. *Planning.*
Eighteen broadcasts delivered October 1, 1935–January 28, 1936. c. 1936.

Reference and Research Pamphlets

(Many publications which are so classified by the League are elsewhere listed as Supplements to the *National Municipal Review* and as Technical Pamphlets.)

Bauer, John. *Postwar Planning for Metropolitan Utilities: a Series of Articles from the National Municipal Review.* 1945.

Bauer, John, ed. *Public Utility Problems: a Symposium of Articles Reprinted from the National Municipal Review November 1934.* c. 1934.

Citizen Organization for Political Activity: The Cincinnati Plan. rev., 1941.

City Growing Pains: a Series of Discussions of Metropolitan Area Problems Originally Published in the National Municipal Review. 1941.

Committee on a Program of Model Fiscal Legislation for Local Governments. *Model Accrual Budget Law.* 1946.

Committee on Election Administration. *A Model Registration System: Report.* Prepared by Joseph P. Harris. 3d rev. ed., 1939.

Committee on Municipal Borrowings. *A Model Bond Law.* 2d. ed., 1929.

Committee on Municipal Program. *A Model City Charter and Municipal Home Rule.* Final ed. March 15, 1916.

———. *A Model City Charter with Home Provisions Recommended for State Constitutions.* Final ed., March, 1922.

———. *A Model City Charter with Home Rule Provisions Recommended for State Constitutions.* rev. ed., 1927.

———. *A Model City Charter with Home Rule Provisions Recommended for State Constitutions.* rev. ed., 1933.

Committee on Revision of the Model City Charter. *Model City Charter.* 5th ed. rev., 1941.

Committee on State Government. *A Model State Constitution; Reprinted with Explanatory Articles.* 1924.

———. *A Model State Constitution; with Explanatory Articles.* rev. ed., 1928.

———. *A Model State Constitution; with Explanatory Articles.* rev. ed., 1933.

———. *Model State Constitution; with Explanatory Articles.* 4th ed. rev., 1941.

———. *Model State Constitution; with Explanatory Articles.* 4th ed. partial revision, 1946.

———. *Progress Report on a Model State Constitution. Presented . . . at Chicago, November 18, 1921, Subject to Further Amendment and Improvement in Draftsmanship.* 1921.

DAWSON, EDGAR, ed. *Outlines of Responsible Government: Some Constructive Proposals.* 1923. 3d ed. 1924.

The Direct Primary, an Appraisal of What the Primary has Accomplished, and a Proposal for a Modified System of Nominations.

1. "Recent Tendencies in Primary Election Systems," Charles E. Merriam.

2. "The Fate of the Direct Primary," Charles E. Hughes. *ca.* 1921.

Draft of a State Civil Service Law. Prepared by National Civil Service Reform League and National Municipal League. 1939.

DRELLICH, EDITH B. and EMERY, ANDRÉE. *Rent Control in War and Peace: a Study Prepared for the Laws and Administration Committee of the Citizens' Housing Council of New York.* 1939.

FRANKLIN, ZILPHA C., ed. *Social Security: Progress and Prospects.* c. 1937.

HARRIS, JOSEPH P., ed. *Social Security: a Symposium of Articles Reprinted from the National Municipal Review for March and April 1936.* c. 1936.

KILPATRICK, WYLIE. *State Supervision of Local Budgeting.* 1939.

LEONARD, JAMES M. *The Direct Tax Burden on Low Income Groups.* 1939.

Model Laws. c. 1936. Nine Model Laws Prepared by Committees of the National Municipal League.

A Model State Civil Service Law. Prepared by National Civil Service League, Civil Service Assembly of United States and Canada, and National Municipal League. 1946.

NUNN, WILLIAM L. *Local Progress in Labor Peace: a Series of Articles Originally Published in the National Municipal Review, with an Introduction by C. A. Dykstra.* 1941.

PURDY, LAWSON. *Why We Need Excess Condemnation: a Boon to the Property Owner—a Blessing to the Public.* Reprinted from the National Municipal Review, v. 12, no. 7 (July, 1923), pp. 363–368.

ROSAHN, BEATRICE G. *Housing Management—Its History and Relation to Present Day Housing Problems.* c. 1935.

Town Management in New England: a Series of Articles Originally Pub-

lished in the National Municipal Review. 1940.

WEIDNER, EDWARD W. *The American County—Patchwork of Boards.* 1946.

Technical Pamphlets

(Issued as supplements, whole numbers, or reprints from the *National Municipal Review.*)

1. PURDY, LAWSON. *The Assessment of Real Estate.* Supplement, v. 8, no. 7 (Sept., 1919), pp. 511–527; 3d. ed., 1923; 4th. ed., 1929.
2. BUCK, ARTHUR E. *Administrative Consolidation in State Governments.* Supplement, v. 8, no. 9 (Nov., 1919), pp. 639–667; 2d. ed., 1922; 3d. ed., 1924; 4th. ed., 1928; 5th. ed., 1930.
3. ———. *The Coming of Centralized Purchasing in State Governments.* Supplement, v. 9, no. 2 (Feb., 1920), pp. 115–135.
4. Committee on Public Utilities. *A Correct Public Policy Toward the Street Railway Problem: Report.* Supplement, v. 9, no. 4 (April, 1920), pp. 251–267.
5. BASSETT, EDWARD M. *Zoning.* Supplement, v. 9, no. 5 (May, 1920), pp. 315–341; rev. ed., 1922.
6. BEYER, WILLIAM C. *Employment Standardization in the Public Service.* Supplement, v. 9, no. 6 (June, 1920), pp. 391–403.
7. BOOTS, RALPH S. *The Presidential Primary.* Supplement, v. 9, no. 9 (Sept., 1920), pp. 597–617.
8. WILLIAMS, FRANK B. *The Law of the City Plan.* Supplement, v. 9, no. 10 (Oct., 1920), pp. 663–690; rev. ed., 1922.
9. MATHEWS, JOHN M. *Administrative Reorganization in Illinois.* Supplement, v. 9, no. 11 (Nov., 1920), pp. 739–756.
10. *Service at Cost for Street Railways: A Symposium.* Supplement, v. 10, no. 2 (Feb., 1921), pp. 111–139.

11. SWAN, HERBERT S. *The Law of Zoning.* Supplement, v. 10, no. 10 (Oct., 1921), pp. 519–536; rev. ed., 1922.
12. CAPARN, HAROLD A. *State Parks.* Supplement, v. 10, no. 11 (Nov., 1921), pp. 583–600.
13. Committee on Electoral Reform. *A Model Election System and the Direct Primary: Pro and Con.* v. 10, no. 12 (Dec., 1921), pp. 603–616.
14. HUGHES, CHARLES E. *The Fate of the Direct Primary.* Reprint, v. 10, no. 1 (Jan., 1921), pp. 23–31.
15. ADAMS, THOMAS. *Modern City Planning: its Meaning and Methods.* v. 11, no. 6 (June, 1922), pp. 157–177.
16. Committee on Sources of Revenue. *Special Assessments.* v. 11, no. 2 (Feb., 1922), pp. 43–58; 2d. ed., 1923; 3d. ed., 1929.
17. Committee on Pensions. *Pensions in Public Employment: Report.* Prepared by Paul Studensky. v. 11, no. 4 (April, 1922), pp. 97–124.
18. MAXEY, CHESTER C. *The Political Integration of Metropolitan Communities.* v. 11, no. 8 (Aug., 1922), pp. 229–253.
19. Committee on Sources of Revenue. *Minor Highway Privileges as a Source of Revenue: Report.* Supplement, v. 12, no. 5 (May, 1923), pp. 273–282.
20. McCOMBS, CARL E. *State Welfare Administration and Consolidated Government.* Supplement, v. 13, no. 8 (Aug., 1924), pp. 461–473.
21. *New Charter Proposals for Norwood, Massachusetts.* Introduction by Frederick A. Cleveland. Supplement, v. 12, no. 7 (July, 1923), pp. 405–440.
22. Special Committee on Civil Service. *Employment Management in Municipal Civil Service: Report.* v. 12, no. 8 (Aug., 1923), pp. 441–513.
23. ANDERSON, WILLIAM. *The Constitutionality of Proportional Repre-*

sentation. Supplement, v. 12, no. 12 (Dec., 1923), pp. 745–762.

24. CORWIN, EDWARD S. *Constitutional Tax Exemption.* Supplement, v. 13, no. 1 (Jan., 1924), pp. 51–67.

25. MARTIN, JAMES W. *The Administration of Gasoline Taxes in the United States.* Supplement, v. 13, no. 10 (Oct., 1924), pp. 587–600.

26. WILCOX, DELOS F. *Electric Light and Power as a Public Utility.* Supplement, v. 14, no. 3 (March, 1925), pp. 191–204.

27. SWAN, HERBERT S. and TUTTLE, GEORGE W. *Land Subdivisions and the City Plan.* Supplement, v. 14, no. 7 (July, 1925), pp. 437–462.

28. BEYER, WILLIAM C. *Municipal Salaries under the Changing Price Level.* Supplement, v. 15, no. 3 (March, 1926), pp. 187–200.

Supplements to the National Municipal Review

ANDERSON, WILLIAM. *The Constitutionality of Proportional Representation.* v. 12, no. 12 (1923), pp. 745–762.

ASCHER, CHARLES S. *Elements of a Low-Cost Housing Law and its Administration.* v. 22, no. 2 (Feb., 1933), pp. 85–113.

ATKINSON, RAYMOND C. *Principles of a Model County Government: Report no. 2 of the Committee on County Government of the National Municipal League.* v. 22, no. 9 (Sept., 1933), pp. 465–486.

BASSETT, EDWARD M. *Zoning.* v. 9, no. 5 (May, 1920), pp. 315–341.

BEYER, WILLIAM C. *Employment Standardization in the Public Service.* v. 9, no. 6 (June, 1920), pp. 391–403.

———. *Municipal Salaries Under the Changing Price Level.* v. 15, no. 3 (March, 1926), pp. 187–200.

BOOTS, RALPH S. *The Presidential Primary: A Comprehensive Examination of the Presidential Primary at*

Work with Proposals of Reform. v. 9, no. 9 (Sept., 1920), pp. 597–617.

BROMAGE, ARTHUR W. *Recommendations on Township Government: Report no. 3 of the Committee on County Government of the National Municipal League.* v. 23, no. 2 (Feb., 1934), pp. 139–145.

BUCK, ARTHUR E. *Administrative Consolidation in State Governments.* v. 8, no. 9 (Nov., 1919), pp. 639–667.

———. *The Coming of Centralized Purchasing in State Governments.* v. 9, no. 2 (Feb., 1920), pp. 115–135.

CAPARN, HAROLD A. *State Parks: an Account of the Widening Movement to Preserve for All the People Choice Bits of Nature with Scenic, Historical, Recreational and Educational Values.* v. 10, no. 11 (Nov., 1921), pp. 583–600.

CHILDS, RICHARD S. *The Best Practice under the City Manager Plan.* v. 22, no. 1 (Jan., 1933), pp. 41–44.

CHILDS, RICHARD S., DODDS, HAROLD W., and REED, THOMAS H. *Suggested Procedure for Selecting a City Manager: to Aid City Councils in the Process of Selecting a Qualified Manager.* v. 22, no. 12 (Dec., 1933), pp. 629–634.

Cleveland Citizens League. Executive Board. *Five Years of City Manager Government in Cleveland.* v. 18, no. 3 (March, 1929), pp. 203–220.

COHEN, JOSEPH A. *City Managership as a Profession.* v. 13, no. 7 (July, 1924), pp. 391–411.

Committee on County Government. *A Model County Manager Law.* v. 19, no. 8 (Aug., 1930), pp. 565–579.

Committee on Election Administration. *A Model Election Administration System: Report.* Prepared by Joseph P. Harris. v. 19, no. 9 (Sept., 1930), pp. 629–671.

Committee on Election Administration. *A Model Registration System: Re-*

port. Prepared by Joseph P. Harris. v. 16, no. 1 (Jan., 1927), pp. 45–86; revised and reprinted, Feb., 1931.

Committee on Federal Aid to the States. *Federal Aid to the States: Report.* Prepared by Austin F. Macdonald. v. 17, no. 10 (Oct., 1928), pp. 619–659; reprinted, March, 1931.

Committee on Liquor Control Legislation. *Liquor Control, Principles, Model Law: Report.* v. 23, no. 1 (Jan., 1934), pp. 47–78.

———. *Liquor Taxes and the Bootlegger: Report.* Prepared by Paul Studenski. v. 24, no. 1 (Jan., 1935), pp. 63–79.

Committee on a Model Municipal Budget Law. *A Model Municipal Budget Law.* v. 17, no. 7 (July, 1928), pp. 437–445.

Committee on a Model Tax Collection Law. *A Model Real Property Tax Collection Law: Report.* v. 24, no. 5 (May, 1935), pp. 290–305.

Committee on Municipal Borrowings. *A Model Bond Law.* v. 16, no. 2 (Feb., 1927), pp. 135–150.

Committee on Play and Recreation Administration. *Standards of Play and Recreation Administration: Report.* Prepared by Jay B. Nash. v. 20, no. 7 (July, 1931), pp. 485–506.

Committee on Public Utilities. *A Correct Public Policy Toward the Street Railway Problem:* Report. v. 9, no. 4 (April, 1920), pp. 251–267.

Committee on Sources of Revenue. *Minor Highway Privileges as a Source of City Revenue: Report.* v. 12, no. 5 (May, 1923), pp. 273–282.

CORWIN, EDWARD S. *Constitutional Tax Exemption: The Power of Congress to Tax Income from State and Municipal Bonds.* v. 13, no. 1 (Jan., 1924), pp. 51–67.

Fitz-Elwyne's Assize of Buildings, I Richard I (1189) (The Pioneer Building Ordinance). Introduction by

Charles W. Tooke. v. 17, no. 9 (Sept., 1928), pp. 555–563.

FREEMAN, HARRY H. *How American Cities are Retrenching in Time of Depression.* v. 21, no. 4 (April, 1932), pp. 267–281.

GALLAGHER, RAYMOND M. *Public Personnel Problems and the Depression: How Civil Service Commissions are Meeting New Problems.* v. 22, no. 4 (April, 1933), pp. 199–215.

GOODRICH, E. P. *Airports as a Factor in City Planning.* v. 17, no. 3 (March, 1928), pp. 181–194.

Governmental Research Association. *The Search for Facts in Government: How Citizens Can Participate Constructively and Effectively in the Improvement of Government.* v. 22, no. 6 (June, 1933), pp. 301–305.

HARLEY, HERBERT. *Criminal Justice, How to Achieve It.* v. 11, no. 3 (March, 1922).

HARRIS, JOSEPH P. *The Practical Workings of Proportional Representation in the United States and Canada.* v. 19, no. 5 (May, 1930), pp. 337–383; reprinted, Feb., 1931.

Harvard University. Bureau for Research in Municipal Government. *Municipal Control of Retail Trade in the United States.* v. 24, no. 12 (Dec. 1935), pp. 723–769.

HORMELL, ORREN C. *Electricity in Great Britain—A Study in Administration.* v. 17, no. 6 (June, 1928), pp. 363–385.

JONES, HOWARD P. *Constitutional Barriers to Improvement in County Government: Report No. 1 of the Committee on County Government of the National Municipal League.* v. 21, no. 8 (Aug., 1932), pp. 525–542.

KNAPP, A. BLAIR. *Water Power in New York State.* v. 19, no. 2 (Feb., 1930), pp. 125–150.

MCCOMBS, CARL E. *State Welfare Administration and Consolidated Gov-*

ernment. v. 13, no. 8 (Aug., 1924), pp. 461–473.

McGOLDRICK, JOSEPH, *The Board of Estimate and Apportionment of New York City.* v. 18, no. 2 (Feb., 1929), pp. 125–152; reprinted and revised, May, 1932.

MANDEL, ARCH, and COTTON, WILBUR M. *Dayton's Sixteen Years of City Manager Government: an Appraisal of a Pioneer Venture.* v. 19, no. 7 (July, 1930), pp. 497–518.

MARTIN, JAMES W. *The Administration of Gasoline Taxes in the United States.* v. 13, no. 10 (Oct., 1924), pp. 587–600.

MATHEWS, JOHN M. *Administrative Reorganization in Illinois.* v. 9, no. 11 (Nov., 1920), pp. 739–756.

MITZLAFF, *German Cities Since the Revolution of 1918.* v. 15, no. 11 (Nov., 1926), pp. 679–691.

MOSHER, WILLIAM E., and POLAH, SOPHIE. *Extent, Costs and Significance of Public Employment in the United States.* v. 21, no. 1 (Jan., 1932), pp. 51–75.

National Municipal Review. *Index.* Beginning with vol. 19, 1930, the annual index has been issued as a Supplement to the January issue, except for 1932, when it was issued as a Supplement to the February, 1933, issue.

New Charter Proposals for Norwood, Massachusetts Submitted to the Special Committee on Charter Revision of the Citizens Committee of One Hundred of Norwood. Introduction by Frederick A. Cleveland. v. 12, no. 7 (July, 1923), pp. 405–440.

ORDWAY, SAMUEL H. JR., and LAFFAN, JOHN C. *Approaches to the Measurement and Reward of Effective Work of Individual Government Employees.* v. 24, no. 10 (Oct., 1935), pp. 557–601.

POLLOCK, JAMES K. *Election Administration in Michigan: an Exploratory Study.* v. 23, no. 6 (June, 1934), pp. 343–359.

Preliminary Program of the Bicentennial Conference on Planning, Parks, and Government, Washington, D. C., September 18th. to 25th., 1932. v. 21, no. 9 (Sept., 1932).

PURDY, LAWSON. *The Assessment of Real Estate.* v. 8, no. 7 (Sept., 1919), pp. 511–527.

Report on Activities and Accomplishments of National Municipal League from November 1, 1930, to October 31, 1931. By Russell Forbes, Secretary. v. 20, no. 12 (Dec., 1931), pp. 745–753.

Report on Work of National Municipal League from November 1, 1929, to October 31, 1930. By Russell Forbes, Secretary. v. 20, no. 1 (Jan., 1931).

Service at Cost for Street Railways: A Symposium. v. 10, no. 2 (Feb., 1921), pp. 111–139.

SWAN, HERBERT S. *The Law of Zoning.* v. 10, no. 10 (Oct., 1921), pp. 519–536.

———. *Theory and Practice in Building Lines Under Eminent Domain.* v. 20, no. 9 (Sept., 1931), pp. 557–566.

SWAN, HERBERT S., and TUTTLE, GEORGE W. *Land Subdivisions and the City Plan.* v. 14, no. 7 (July, 1925), pp. 437–462.

UPSON, LENT D., and RIGHTOR, CHARLES E. *Standards of Financial Administration.* v. 17, no. 2 (Feb., 1928), pp. 119–132.

WILCOX, DELOS F. *Electric Light and Power as a Public Utility.* v. 14, no. 3 (March, 1925), pp. 191–204.

WILLIAMS, FRANK B. *The Law of the City Plan.* v. 9, no. 10 (Oct., 1920), pp. 663–690.

Consultant Service Reports

Asbury Park, New Jersey. *Financial and Administrative Survey of Asbury Park, New Jersey: A Report to the*

Protective Committee for Security Holders of the City of Asbury Park, New Jersey. 1935. mimeo.

Atlanta and Fulton County, Georgia. *The Governments of Atlanta and Fulton County, Georgia. A Report of a Complete Administrative and Financial Survey of the Several Departments and Activities of the City of Atlanta and Fulton County to the Board of Commissioners of Roads and Revenues of Fulton County, the Mayor and General Council of the City of Atlanta, the Atlanta Chamber of Commerce. February 5, 1938.* Atlanta, Atlanta Chamber of Commerce, 1938. litho.

Augusta, Georgia. Reed, Thomas H. and Reed, Doris D. *Report to the Citizens: A Survey of the Government of the City of Augusta, Georgia.* Augusta, Georgia, Augusta Citizens Union, 1945.

Bar Harbor, Maine. *Survey of the Government of Bar Harbor, Maine.* 1939. mimeo.

Brookline, Massachusetts. *A Report of a Brief Survey of the Park and Recreation Activities of the Town of Brookline, Massachusetts.* Brookline, Massachusetts, Brookline Taxpayers' Association. 1937.

Cincinnati, Ohio. Reed, Thomas H. and Reed, Doris D. *The Government of Cincinnati, 1924–1944; An Appraisal. A Report to the Stephen H. Wilder Foundation, Public Affairs Division.* Cincinnati, The Stephen H. Wilder Foundation, 1944.

Cleveland, Ohio. Reed, Thomas H. and Reed, Doris D. *Financing a Postwar Public Improvement Program for Greater Cleveland: A Report to the Cleveland Bureau of Governmental Research and the Metropolitan Cleveland Development Council.* 1946. mimeo.

Coral Gables, Florida. *Financial and Administrative Survey of the City of Coral Gables, Florida.* Coral Gables, Florida, The City Clerk, 1934.

Cortlandt, New York. *Financial and Administrative Survey of the Town of Cortlandt, New York.* 1934. mimeo.

Dumont, New Jersey. *A Brief Financial Survey of the Borough of Dumont, New Jersey.* 1935. mimeo.

Essex County, New Jersey. Reed, Thomas H. *Twenty Years of Government in Essex County, New Jersey.* New York, Appleton-Century, 1938.

Greenburgh, New York. *A Brief Financial and Administrative Survey of the Town of Greenburgh, N. Y.* 1934. mimeo.

Harrison, New York. *A Brief Financial and Administrative Survey of The Town of Harrison, N.Y.* 1934. mimeo.

Inverness, Florida. *Refunding Proposal for the City of Inverness, Florida.* 1936. mimeo.

Kearny, New Jersey. *A Brief Financial and Administrative Survey of the Town of Kearny, N. J.,* 1934, mimeo.

Lehigh County, New York. *The Fiscal Affairs of Lehigh County: A Report to the Committee of Fifty on Taxation of the Allentown Chamber of Commerce.* 1934. mimeo.

Lyndhurst, New Jersey. *A Brief Financial and Administrative Survey of the Township of Lyndhurst, New Jersey, with a Plan of Refunding.* 1935.

Mount Pleasant, New York. *A Brief Financial and Administrative Survey of the Town of Mount Pleasant, N. Y.* 1934. mimeo.

Mount Vernon, New York. *A Survey of the Financial Condition of the City of Mount Vernon, N. Y., Including the Board of Education.* 1934. mimeo.

Nassau County, New York. *Nassau County Survey.* 1934. mimeo. Volume I, General Report and Recommendations.

New Bedford, Massachusetts. *Survey of the City Government of New Bedford, Massachusetts: A Report to the Non-Partisan Citizens Charter Committee.* New Bedford, Massachusetts, The Standard-Times, 1938.

North Bergen, New Jersey. *A Brief Financial and Administrative Survey of the Township of North Bergen, New Jersey.* 1934. mimeo.

Passaic, New Jersey. *A Report on Administration and Finance in All Departments and in the Schools of the City of Passaic, New Jersey.* 2 vol. Passaic, New Jersey, Passaic Renters and Taxpayers Association, 1941. mimeo.

Polk County, Florida. *A Survey and Refunding Plan for Nine Road and Bridge Districts of Polk County, Florida.* 1936. mimeo.

Rome, New York. Reed, Thomas H. and Reed, Doris D. *Report to the Chamber of Commerce of a Brief Administrative and Financial Survey of Rome, New York.* 1942. typed.

Savannah, Georgia. *A Brief Financial Survey of the City of Savannah, Georgia.* Savannah, Savannah Evening Press, July 30, 1937, pp. 16–17.

St. Petersburg, Florida. *Financial and Administrative Survey of the City of St. Petersburg, Florida.* 1936. mimeo.

Teaneck, New Jersey. *A Brief Financial Survey of the Township of Teaneck, New Jersey.* 1935. mimeo.

Wallingford, Connecticut. Reed, Thomas H. and Reed, Doris D. *Report of a Survey of the Town and Borough of Wallingford, Conn.* 1943. mimeo.

White Plains, New York. *Report on Survey of Principal Administrative Departments of the City of White Plains, New York.* 1940. mimeo.

Wicomico County, Maryland. Mauck, Elwyn A. *Report of a Brief Administrative Survey of Wicomico County, Maryland.* 1947. mimeo.

Winter Park, Florida. *A Brief Financial and Administrative Survey of the City of Winter Park, Florida.* 1934. mimeo.

Woodbridge, New Jersey. *A Financial Survey and Refunding Plan, Township of Woodbridge, New Jersey.* 1936. mimeo.

Yonkers, New York. Reed, Thomas H. and Associates. *A Brief Financial and Administrative Survey of the City of Yonkers.* 1933. mimeo.

Yonkers, New York. *Report on the Financial Condition of the City of Yonkers, New York.* 1934. mimeo.

National Municipal League Series of Books

BEARD, MARY R. *Woman's Work in Municipalities.* New York, Appleton, 1915.

BIRD, CHARLES S., JR. ed. *Town Planning for Small Communities.* New York, Appleton, 1917.

CUSHMAN, ROBERT E. *Excess Condemnation.* New York, Appleton, 1917.

FITZPATRICK, EDWARD A. ed. *Experts in City Government.* New York, Appleton, 1919.

JAMES, HERMAN G. *Municipal Functions.* New York, Appleton, 1917.

KING, CLYDE L. *Lower Living Costs in Cities; a Constructive Programme for Urban Efficiency.* New York, Appleton, 1915.

KING, CLYDE L. ed. *The Regulation of Municipal Utilities.* New York, Appleton, 1912.

MUNRO, WILLIAM B. ed. *The Initiative, Referendum, and Recall.* New York, Appleton, 1912.

NOLEN, JOHN. ed. *City Planning; a Series of Papers Presenting the Essential Elements of a City Plan.* New York, Appleton, 1916.

———. *City Planning; a Series of Papers Presenting the Essential Elements of a City Plan.* 2d ed. New York, Appleton, 1929.

TAYLOR, GRAHAM R. *Satellite Cities; a Study of Industrial Suburbs.* New York, Appleton, 1915.

TOULMIN, HARRY A., JR. *The City Manager, a New Profession.* New York, Appleton, 1915.

WARD, EDWARD J. ed. *The Social Center.* New York, Appleton, 1913.

WOODRUFF, CLINTON R. ed. *A New Municipal Program.* New York, Appleton, 1919.

——— *City Government by Commission.* New York, Appleton, 1911.

National Municipal League Monograph Series

(Published by National Municipal League, New York).

BUCK, ARTHUR E. *Municipal Budgets and Budget Making.* 1925.

CORWIN, EDWARD S. *The President's Removal Power under the Constitution.* 1927.

Conference Committee on the Merit System. *The Merit System in Government: Report.* 1926.

STUDENSKI, PAUL. *Public Borrowing.* 1930.

WILCOX, DELOS F. *Depreciation in Public Utilities; Relation of Accrued Depreciation to Annual Depreciation and Maintenance.* 1925.

Other Books Published or Distributed by The National Municipal League

A Municipal Program: Report of a Committee of the National Municipal League, Adopted by the League, November 17, 1899, Together with Explanatory and Other Papers. New York, Macmillan, 1900.

BARTHOLOMEW, HARLAND. *Urban Land Uses: Amounts of Land Used and Needed for Various Purposes by Typical American Cities; an Aid to Scientific Zoning Practice.* Cambridge, Harvard University Press, 1932.

BEARD, CHARLES A., ed. *Loose Leaf Digest of Short Ballot Charters; a Documentary History of the Commission Form of Municipal Government.* New York, The Short Ballot Organization, c. 1911.

BUCK, ARTHUR E. *Public Budgeting; a Discussion of Budgetary Practice in the National, State and Local Governments of the United States.* New York, Harper, 1929.

———. *Reorganization of State Governments in the United States.* New York, Columbia University Press, 1938.

CHILDS, RICHARD S. *Short Ballot Principles.* Boston, Houghton Mifflin, c. 1911.

Committee on Metropolitan Government. *The Government of Metropolitan Areas in the United States.* Prepared by Paul Studenski. New York, National Municipal League, c. 1930.

CRANE, ROBERT T. *Loose-Leaf Digest of City Manager Charters.* New York, National Municipal League, 1923.

Democracy Must Think: an Informal Round-table Discussion on Public Opinion in a Democracy at the National Municipal League's Forty-fourth Annual Conference on Government. New York, Columbia University Press, 1939.

FORBES, RUSSELL. *Governmental Purchasing.* New York, Harper, 1929.

FORD, GEORGE B. *Building Height, Bulk and Form; How Zoning Can Be Used as a Protection against Uneconomic Types of Buildings on High-Cost Land.* Cambridge, Harvard University Press, 1931.

GILBERTSON, HENRY S. *The County, the "Dark Continent" of American Politics.* New York, The National Short Ballot Organization, 1917.

HARRIS, JOSEPH P. *Registration of Voters in the United States.* Washington, The Brookings Institution, 1929.

HUBBARD, HENRY V., McCLINTOCK, MILLER, and WILLIAMS, FRANK B. *Airports: Their Location, Administration and Legal Basis.* Cambridge, Harvard University Press, 1930.

HALLETT, GEORGE H. *Proportional Representation—The Key to Democracy.* With the cooperation of Clarence G. Hoag. Washington, National Home Library Foundation, 1937.

——. *Proportional Representation— The Key to Democracy.* 2d rev. ed. New York, National Municipal League, 1940.

HOAG, CLARENCE G., and HALLETT, GEORGE H. *Proportional Representation.* New York, Macmillan, 1926.

LOVETT, WILLIAM P. *Detroit Rules Itself.* Boston, R. Q. Badger, c. 1930.

REED, THOMAS H. *Municipal Government in the United States.* rev. ed. N. Y., Appleton-Century, c. 1934.

——. *Municipal Management.* New York, McGraw-Hill, 1941.

SEASONGOOD, MURRAY. *Local Government in the United States; a Challenge and an Opportunity.* Cambridge, Harvard University Press, 1933.

TAFT, CHARLES P. *City Management: the Cincinnati Experiment.* New York, Farrar & Rinehart, c. 1933.

WALKER, HARVEY. *Federal Limitations upon Municipal Ordinance Making Power.* Columbus, Ohio State University Press, 1929.

WHITE, LEONARD D. *The City Manager.* Chicago, University of Chicago Press, c. 1927.

WHITTEN, ROBERT H., and ADAMS, THOMAS. *Neighborhoods of Small Homes; Economic Density of Low-Cost Housing in America and England.* Cambridge, Harvard University Press, 1931.

WOMER, PARLEY P. *Citizenship and the New Day.* New York, Abingdon-Cokesbury Press, 1945.

Other Publications of the National Municipal League

(Included are League promotion circulars and leaflets, reprints of Conference addresses and reports, and miscellaneous publications.)

BURNHAM, GEORGE. *Business Bodies and Municipal Reform.* ca. 1906.

CHASE, HARVEY S. *Budgets and Balance Sheets, the Practical Application of Sound Accounting Principles and Methods to Municipal Book-keeping.* ca. 1910.

——. *Uniform Municipal Accounting, Uniform Municipal Reporting, Uniform Municipal Budgets; Address ... before the Conference Upon Uniform Legislation, Washington, January 19, 1910.* 1910.

Cincinnati Meeting of the National Municipal League as Viewed in Cincinnati. ca. 1909.

City Co-operation. 1910.

City Manager Plan; Information and Campaign Service. 1921.

The Commission Plan and Commission-Manager Plan of Municipal Government; an Analytical Study by a Committee of the National Municipal League. 1914.

Committee on Franchises. *Report.* n.d.

——. Sub-Committee. *Suggestions for a Model Street Railway Franchise.* ca. 1911.

Committee on Instruction in Municipal Government in American Educational Institutions. *Report.* 1901.

——. *Second Report.* 1902.

Committee on Local Branches. *Report.* 1930. mimeo.

Committee on Municipal Budgets and Accounting. *Report.* Nov. 23, 1916.

Committee on Municipal Program. *The Commission Manager Plan, City Government,* March 15, 1916; Constructed by Ralph D. Kern. Cleveland, Distributed by Committee of Fifteen, Investigating the City Manager Plan for Cleveland, c. 1917.

————. *Constitutional Amendment and Municipal Corporations Act.* 1899.

————. *A Model City Charter and Municipal Home Rule, Tentative Drafts of the Sections Dealing with the Constitutional Provisions, the Council, Nominations and Elections, Preferential Ballot, Recall, Initiative, Referendum, Proportional Representation, City Manager, Administrative Departments, Civil Service Board, Financial Provisions and Franchises... Presented at the Twentieh Annual Meeting of the National Municipal League Held at Baltimore, November 20, 1914 and Revised at the Meeting of the Committee Held in New York, April 8, and 9, 1915, and on September 14, 1915, and again Presented to the League at its Annual Meeting in Dayton, November, 1915, and Further Revised by the Committee at its Meeting in Philadelphia, December 27 and 28, 1915.* Jan. 15, 1916.

————. *Model City Charter & Municipal Home Rule, Tentative Drafts of the Sections Dealing with the Council, City Manager, Civil Service and Efficiency, Initiative, Referendum, Recall, Electoral Provisions and Constitutional Amendments...Presented at the Twentieth Annual Meeting of the National Municipal League held at Baltimore, November 20, 1914, and Revised at the Meeting of the Committee held in New York, April 8 and 9, 1915.* June 15, 1915.

————. *Municipal Home Rule and a Model City Charter, Tentative Drafts of the Sections Dealing with the Constitutional Provisions, the Council, Nominations and Elections, Preferential Ballot, Recall, Initiative, Referendum, Proportional Representation, City Manager, Administrative Departments, Civil Service Board, Financial Provisions and Franchises... Presented at the Twentieth Annual*

Meeting of the National Municipal League Held at Baltimore, November 20, 1914, and Revised at the Meeting of the Committee held in New York, April 8 and 9, 1915, and on September 14, 1915. 3d ed. Nov. 15, 1915.

————. *Tentative Drafts of the Sections Dealing with the Council, City Manager, Civil Service and Efficiency Board and Constitutional Amendments ... Presented at the Twentieth Annual Meeting of the National Municipal League held at Baltimore, November 20, 1914.* Dec. 1, 1914.

————. *Tentative Outline The Commission Manager Plan City Government. Constructed by LeRoy Hodges.* Dec. 1, 1914.

Committee on Plan of Political Organization. *Preliminary Report. Annual Meeting ... Baltimore November 18, 19, 20, 21, 1914.* 1914.

Committee on Taxation. *State Revenue and Municipal Home Rule.* 1905.

Committee on Uniform Municipal Accounting and Statistics. *Report.* 1901.

Comparative Report of Income of the National Municipal League. March 1, 1935. mimeo.

Conference on American Self-Government. *Proceedings ... held at Indiana University, May 13 and 14, 1940.* 1940. mimeo.

Constitution and By-Laws of the National Municipal League, As Amended by the Seventeenth Annual Meeting, held in Richmond, Va., November 14th 1911. 1912.

Constitutional Amendment and Municipal Corporations Act Submitted by the Special Committee of the National Municipal League ... to the Meeting of the League Held at Columbus, O., November, 1898. 1898.

"... *the divine right of government* ..." ca. 1930.

Draft of a Proposed Municipal Nominating Law. Submitted to the Na-

tional Municipal League at its Annual Meeting held April 27th, 28th, and 29th, 1904. 1904.

Executive Committee. *Address to the Friends of Good Government throughout the United States, October 20, 1897.* 1897.

———. *Report of Horace E. Deming, Chairman, Presented at Pittsburgh, November 16, 1908.* Reprinted from the *Proceedings of the Pittsburgh Conference for Good City Government,* 1908, pp. 44–49.

Executive Committee and Treasurer. *Report for the Fiscal Year Ending April 1, 1907.*

———. *Report for the Fiscal Year Ending April 1, 1908.*

Financing Program of the National Municipal League. May 14, 1947. mimeo.

FLACK, HORACE E. *Municipal Reference Libraries.* Reprinted from the *Proceedings of the Pittsburgh Conference for Good City Government,* 1908, pp. 308–316.

The Goal and The Way. Oct., 1918.

Governors by Birthright. 1943.

GUTHRIE, WILLIAM B. *The City and County of Denver, a Paper Read at the Detroit Meeting of the National Municipal League in November, 1917.* ca. 1917.

Hand Book of the National Municipal League, 1894–1904. 1904.

Hand Book of the National Municipal League. 1914.

HARLEY, HERBERT. *The Model Municipal Court, a Paper Read at the Annual Meeting of the National Municipal League held at Toronto, Nov. 11–15, 1913.* ca. 1913.

HATTON, AUGUSTUS R. *The Liquor Traffic and City Government.* Reprinted from the *Proceedings of the Pittsburgh Conference for Good City Government,* 1908, pp. 421–443.

The Influence of the National Municipal League, 1909.

Intercollegiate Division. *Social and Civic Activities for College Graduates.* 1916.

KING, CLYDE L. *Lower Living Costs in Cities.* n.d.

The League's Work. ca. 1906.

LIGHTHALL, W. D. *A Tribute to the National Municipal League.* 1914.

McFARLAND, JOHN H. *The Awakening of Harrisburg. Some Account of the Improvement Movement Begun in 1902; with the Progress of the Work to the End of 1906.* Originally presented at the Boston Conference of the National Municipal League in 1902, and printed as its Pamphlet No. 8. Now revised and brought up to date by the author, with additional illustrations, and published in cooperation with the Municipal League of Harrisburg and the Harrisburg Board of Trade, by the National Municipal League. 1906.

The Membership of the National Municipal League. 1908.

Memorandum on Financial Needs of the National Municipal League. Sept., 1930. mimeo.

MESSICK, CHARLES P. *Building Careers in Government, Address for the 41st Annual Conference on Government of the National Municipal League, Providence, R. I., Nov. 26, 1935.* 1935. mimeo.

National Municipal League. 1905.

The National Municipal League, 1894–1907. 1907.

National Municipal League, National Civil Service Reform League and Civil Service Assembly of the United States and Canada. *Suggested Draft of a State Civil Service Law.* Preliminary and tentative. 1938. mimeo.

The National Municipal League, North American Building, Philadelphia. n.d.

National Municipal League; Outstanding National Sponsor of Improvements in Local Government. ca. 1936.

National Municipal League; Report on Audit of Accounts. 1921–. Typed. Report made annually by a firm of accountants and auditors.

National Municipal League: A Thirty Years' Retrospect and a Look Ahead. 1925.

National Municipal Review; A New Magazine of Civics with Uncommon Editorial Resources. 1918.

The National Municipal League's Work; Analyzed by Functions, Subjects and Methods. Feb. 19, 1931. mimeo.

New York State Committee. Special Committee on the New York State Constitution. *What's in the Proposed Constitution? A Summary of the Amendments Submitted by the New York State Constitutional Convention of 1938.* c. 1938.

PAINE, ROBERT T. JR. *The Elimination of National Party Designations from Municipal Ballots.* Reprinted from the *Proceedings of the Cincinnati Conference for Good City Government,* 1909, pp. 291–308.

———. *The Initiative, the Referendum and the Recall in American Cities.* Reprinted from the *Proceedings of the Pittsburgh Conference for Good City Government,* 1908, pp. 223–246.

A Primer in Proportional Representation. ca. 1938. mimeo.

Proportional Representation Demonstration Ballot Cards. n.d. mimeo.

Public Markets in the United States: Second Report of a Committee of the National Municipal League. Figures Revised to March 15, 1917. 1917.

Reasons for Supporting the National Municipal League. ca. 1911.

The Relation of the City to Its Food Supply: Report of a Committee of the National Municipal League. November 19, 1914. 1915.

Revamping Local Government. ca. 1933.

Rules for Counting Ballots in Private Elections under the Hare System of Proportional Representation. Jan., 1946. mimeo.

SEASONGOOD, MURRAY. *How Political Gangs Work, and Some Recent Trends in Municipal Government.* 1932. Reprinted from *Harvard Graduates' Magazine,* v. 38 (1929–1930), pp. 261–272; and v. 39 (1930–1931), pp. 141–155.

Step by Step to Better Government. 1934.

The Study of City Government in American Colleges and Universities. ca. 1906.

Survey Committee. *Report: a Survey of the League's Activities and Opportunities; Recommendations for extending Its Usefulness. Report made at the Annual Meeting in New York June 5, 1918.* 1918.

To Those Interested in Honest and Efficient Government. ca. 1916.

Tomorrow's Problems Are Today's Challenge; The "Why" of Membership in the National Municipal League. 1935.

WAITE, HENRY M. *The Commission-Manager Plan in Actual Operation: a Discussion.* 1915.

WEIL, A. LEO. *Awakened Social Conscience, the Interests' Best Preparation for Post-War Conditions. Paper read at ... Annual Meeting in New York, June 5, 1918.* 1918.

WELSH, HERBERT. *The Call to Arms of Municipal Leagues and Good Government Clubs, an address Delivered before the National Municipal League Convention held at Minneapolis Dec. 8, 1894.* ca. 1894.

What is Being Done to Secure Improved Conditions for Our Cities. 1903.

What The League is Doing: Report to Members of the National Municipal League for the months of January, February, March, April, 1940. 1940.

What the National Municipal League Aims to Accomplish. ca. 1902.

WOODRUFF, CLINTON R. *The National Municipal League and the Committee of Ten.* 1897.

——. *A Statement to the National Municipal League.* Nov. 1, 1911. *The Work of the League, 1894–1895.* 1905.

PUBLICATIONS OF THE MUNICIPAL ADMINISTRATION SERVICE

Monograph Series

1. BEARD, CHARLES A. *Government Research, Past, Present, and Future.* 1926.
2. THOMPSON, GEORGE N. *The Preparation and Revision of Local Building Codes.* 1927.
3. KILPATRICK, WYLIE. *State Administrative Review of Local Budget Making: an Examination of State Supervision of Local Taxes and Bonds in Indiana and Iowa.* 1927.
4. RIDLEY, CLARENCE E. *Measuring Municipal Government: Suggested Standards for Measuring the Results of Fire, Health, Police and Public Works Departments.* 1927.
5. RIGHTOR, CHARLES E. *The Preparation of a Long-Term Financial Program.* 1927.
6. GREENMAN, E. D. *Codification of Ordinances.* 1928.
7. CRAWFORD, FINLA G. *The Administration of the Gasoline Tax in the United States.* 1928.
8. POST, ADOLPH J., and MCCAFFREY, GEORGE H. *Street Name Signs.* 1928.
9. KILPATRICK, WYLIE. *Reporting Municipal Government.* 1928.
10. CHATTERS, CARL H. *The Enforcement of Real Estate Tax Liens.* 1928.
11. REEVES, CUTHBERT E. *The Appraisal of Urban Land and Buildings: a Working Manual for City Assessors.* 1931.
12. HAVENNER, GEORGE C. *Photostat Recording.* 1928.
13. RIDLEY, CLARENCE E. *The Public Works Department in American Cities.* 1929.
14. CROSSER, CALLENDER A., and GRAY, WELLES A. *Municipal Motor Equipment.* 1929.
15. CRAWFORD, FINLA G. *The Administration of the Gasoline Tax in the United States.* rev. ed., 1930.
16. MCCLINTOCK, MILLER, and WILLIAMS, SIDNEY J. *Municipal Organization for Street Traffic Control.* 1930.
17. BAUER, JOHN. *Standards for Modern Public Utility Franchises.* 1930.
18. HUUS, RANDOLPH O., and CLINE, DOROTHY I. *Municipal, School and University Stadia.* 1931.
19. National Committee on Municipal Reporting. *Public Reporting With Special Reference to Annual, Departmental, and Current Reports of Municipalities.* 1931.
20. NICHOLSON, JOSEPH W. *House Number Signs.* 1931.
21. TRULL, EDNA. *Municipal Auditoriums.* 1931.
22. WILCOX, DELOS F. *The Administration of Municipally Owned Utilities.* 1931.
23. BUCK, ARTHUR E. *Budgeting for Small Cities.* 1931.
24. BETTERS, PAUL V. *Federal Services to Municipal Governments.* 1931.
25. FORBES, RUSSELL. *Purchasing for Small Cities.* 1932.
26. MCCRACKEN, DWIGHT. *Traffic Regulation in Small Cities.* 1932.
27. TRULL, EDNA. *The Administration of Regulatory Inspectional Services in American Cities.* 1932.
28. BIRD, FREDERICK L. *The Management of Small Municipal Lighting Plants.* 1932.
29. SLY, JOHN F., FORDHAM, JEFFERSON B., and SHIPMAN, GEORGE A. *The*

Codification and Drafting of Ordinances for Small Towns. 1932.

30. CRAWFORD, FINLA G. *The Administration of the Gasoline Tax in the United States.* 3d ed., 1932.

Statistical Series

1. CRANDALL, ESTHER. *Salaries of Policemen and Firemen in 35 Cities, 1928.* Reprinted from the *National Municipal Review* v. 17, no. 5 (May, 1928), pp. 268–279.

2. *Salaries and Conditions of Employment for Firemen and Policemen in 49 Cities, 30,000 to 100,000 Population, 1929.* Reprinted from the *American City,* v. 42 no. 3 (March, 1930), pp. 169, 171, 173; and v. 42, no. 4 (April, 1930), pp. 108–109.

3. MARTIN, JAMES W., and STEPHENSON, C. M. *Taxation of Private and Common-Carrier Motor Vehicles by Municipalities.* 1931.

4. *Selected List of Recent Municipal Research Reports.* 1931.

5. BIRD, FREDERICK L. *The Present Financial Status of 135 Cities in the United States and Canada.* 1931.

6. RICHTOR, CHARLES E. *Comparative Tax Rates of 290 Cities, 1931.* Reprinted from the *National Municipal Review,* v. 20, no. 12 (Dec., 1931), pp. 703–718.

7. WOLFF, DAVID. *Salaries and Conditions of Employment of Police Forces in 245 Cities in the United States and Canada.* 1932.

Mimeographed Series

(Abstracts of the Research Reports listed below.)

1. STONE, DONALD C. *A New Efficiency Rating System.* Cincinnati Bureau of Municipal Research. 1927. Abstracted, 1927.

2. CARTER, LEYTON E. *Government Responsibility in the Fields of Social Work.* Abstracted, 1927.

3. CROSSER, CALLENDER A. *Financing the Des Moines City Plan.* Des Moines Bureau of Municipal Research. 1927. Abstracted, 1927.

4. MATSCHECK, WALTER. *Special Assessment Procedure.* Kansas City Public Service Institute. 1927. Abstracted, 1928.

5. Syracuse Municipal Research Commission. *The Selection of Patrolmen in Syracuse, New York.* 1929. Abstracted, 1929.

6. Buffalo Municipal Research Bureau, Inc. *Report on the Survey of the Buffalo City Hospital.* 1929. Abstracted, 1929.

7. New York State Bureau of Municipal Information. *Model Noise Ordinance.* Reprinted, 1930.

8. Detroit Bureau of Governmental Research. *The Condemnation Procedure of Twenty-Three Cities.* 1928. Abstracted, 1930.

9. Los Angeles County Bureau of Efficiency. *Survey of the Purchasing and Stores Department, County of Los Angeles.* 1928. Abstracted, 1930.

10. Cincinnati Bureau of Governmental Research. *The Regulation of Minor Highway Privileges.* 1929. Abstracted, 1930.

11. MADDOX, W. ROLLAND. *Municipal Licenses for Hawkers and Peddlers and Transient Merchants.* Michigan Municipal League. 1930. Abstracted, 1930.

12. *Regulation of Miniature Golf Courses.* Compiled from Reports by State Leagues of Municipalities. 1930.

13. OSTROW, E. K. *Selected Bibliography on Garbage and Refuse Disposal.* 1930.

14. League of Wisconsin Municipalities. *Model Ordinance for the Regulation of Junk Dealers. The Regulation of Municipal Sales of Obsolete and Scrap Materials.* Reported by Joseph W. Nicholson. 1931.

BOOKS

ADAMS, HENRY. *The Education of Henry Adams, An Autobiography.* Boston, Houghton Mifflin, c. 1918.

American Political Science Association. COMMITTEE ON INSTRUCTION. *The Teaching of Government: Report.* New York, Macmillan, 1916.

——. Committee on Policy. *Report.* Menasha, Wis., Banta, 1930.

ANDERSON, WILLIAM. *American City Government.* New York, Holt, c. 1925.

BAKER, MOSES N. *Municipal Engineering and Sanitation.* New York, Macmillan, c. 1901.

BEARD, CHARLES A. *American City Government: A Survey of Newer Tendencies.* New York, Century, 1912.

——. *Contemporary American History, 1877–1913.* New York, Macmillan, c. 1914.

BIRD, FREDERICK L. and RYAN, FRANCES M. *The Recall of Public Officers: A Study of the Operation of the Recall in California.* New York, Macmillan, 1930.

BROMAGE, ARTHUR W. *American County Government.* New York, Holston House, c. 1933.

BRYCE, JAMES. *Modern Democracies.* New York, Macmillan, 1921. 2 vols.

——. *The American Commonwealth.* New York, Macmillan, 1888. 2 vols.

CONKLING, ALFRED R. *City Government in the United States.* New York, Appleton, 1894.

CRAWFORD, FINLA G. *Readings in American Government.* New York, Knopf, 1927.

DEMING, HORACE E. *The Government of American Cities; A Program of Democracy; A Study of Municipal Organization and of the Relation of the City to the State. Also a Reprint of the Municipal Program of the National Municipal League.* New York, Putnam, 1909.

DEVLIN, THOMAS C. *Municipal Reform in the United States.* New York, Putnam, 1896.

DILLON, JOHN F. *Treatise on the Law of Municipal Corporations.* Chicago, Cockcroft and Co., 1872.

——. *Commentaries on the Law of Municipal Corporations.* 5th ed. rev. Boston, Little, 1911. 5 vols.

DODD, WALTER F. *State Government.* New York, Century, c. 1922.

EATON, DORMAN B. *The Government of Municipalities.* New York, Macmillan, 1899.

FAIRLIE, JOHN A. *Essays in Municipal Administration.* New York, Macmillan, 1908.

——. *Municipal Administration.* New York, Macmillan, 1901.

FASSETT, CHARLES M. *Handbook of Municipal Government.* New York, Crowell, c. 1922.

GILL, NORMAN N. *Municipal Research Bureaus; A Study of the Nation's Leading Citizen-Supported Agencies.* Foreword by Lent D. Upson. Washington, American Council on Public Affairs, c. 1944.

GOODNOW, FRANK J. *Comparative Administrative Law: An Analysis of the Administrative Systems, National and Local, of the United States, England, France and Germany.* New York, Putnam, 1893. 2 vols.

——. *Municipal Home Rule; a Study in Administration.* New York, Macmillan, 1895.

——. *Municipal Problems.* New York, Macmillan, 1897.

GRAVES, WILLIAM B. *American State Government.* Boston, Heath, c. 1936.

GREER, SARAH. *A Bibliography of Public Administration.* Pt. I. New York, Institute of Public Administration, Columbia University, 1933.

GRIFFITH, ERNEST S. *The Modern Development of City Government in the United Kingdom and the United*

States. London, Oxford University Press, 1927. 2 vols.

HADDOW, ANNA. *Political Science in American Colleges and Universities, 1636–1900*. Edited with an Introduction and Concluding Chapter by William Anderson. New York, Appleton-Century, c. 1939.

HAINES, CHARLES G. and HAINES, BERTHA M. *Principles and Problems of Government*. 3d ed. New York, Harper, 1934.

HARRIS, JOSEPH P. *Election Administration in the United States*. Washington, The Brookings Institution, 1934.

HODGES, HENRY G. *City Management; Theory and Practice of Municipal Administration*. New York, Crofts, 1939.

HOLCOMBE, ARTHUR N. *State Government in the United States*. 3d. ed. New York, Macmillan, 1931.

KNEIER, CHARLES M. *City Government in the United States*. New York, Harper, 1934.

LANCASTER, LANE W. *Government in Rural America*. New York, Van Nostrand, 1937.

MACDONALD, AUSTIN F. *American City Government and Administration*. rev. ed. New York, Crowell, c. 1936.

———. *American State Government and Administration*. New York, Crowell, c. 1934.

MATHEWS, JOHN M. *American State Government*. New York, Appleton, 1924.

MAXEY, CHESTER C. *Urban Democracy*. Boston, Heath, c. 1929.

MERRIAM, CHARLES E. *American Political Ideas: Studies in the Development of American Political Thought, 1865–1917*. New York, Macmillan, 1920.

MERRIAM, CHARLES E. and GOSNELL, HAROLD F. *The American Party System; An Introduction to the Study of Political Parties in the United States*. rev. ed. New York, Macmillan, 1929.

MUNRO, WILLIAM B. *A Bibliography of Municipal Government in the United States*. Cambridge, Harvard University Press, 1915.

———. *Municipal Government and Administration*. New York, Macmillan, 1923. 2 v.

———. *The Government of American Cities*. 4th ed. New York, Macmillan, 1926.

———. *The Government of the United States; National, State, and Local*. 4th ed. New York, Macmillan, 1936.

NEVINS, ALLAN. *The Emergence of Modern America; 1865–1878*. New York, Macmillan, 1927.

PARSONS, FRANK. *The City for the People; or, the Municipalization of the City Government and Local Franchises*. Philadelphia, Taylor, 1899.

PATTON, CLIFFORD W. *The Battle for Municipal Reform; Mobilization and Attack, 1875–1900*. Introduction by Arthur M. Schlesinger. Washington, American Council on Public Affairs, c. 1940.

PEEL, ROY V. ed. *Better City Government*. Philadelphia, American Academy of Political and Social Science, 1938. *Annals*, v. 199 (Sept., 1938).

PFIFFNER, JOHN M. *Public Administration*. New York, Ronald, c. 1935.

PINANSKI, ABRAHAM E. *The Street Railway System of Metropolitan Boston*. New York, McGraw, 1908.

PORTER, KIRK H. *County and Township Government in the United States*. New York, Macmillan, 1922.

Public Administration Organizations: A Directory of Unofficial Organizations in the Field of Public Administration in the United States and Canada. Chicago, Public Administration Clearing House, 1941.

REED, THOMAS H. *Municipal Management*. New York, McGraw-Hill, 1941.

REED, THOMAS H. and WEBBINK, PAUL. *Documents Illustrative of American*

Municipal Government. New York, Century, c. 1926.

REGIER, CORNELIUS C. *The Era of the Muckrakers.* Chapel Hill, University of North Carolina Press, 1932.

RIDLEY, CLARENCE E. and SIMON, HERBERT A. *Measuring Municipal Activities; A Survey of Suggested Criteria for Appraising Administration.* Chicago, The International City Managers' Association, 1938.

SCHLESINGER, ARTHUR M. *The Rise of the City, 1878–1898.* New York, Macmillan, 1933.

STEWART, FRANK M. *The National Civil Service Reform League, History, Activities, and Problems.* Austin, University of Texas Press, 1929.

STONE, HAROLD A., PRICE, DON K., STONE, KATHRYN H. *City Manager Government in the United States; A Review After Twenty-Five Years.* Chicago, Public Administration Service, 1940.

TOLMAN, WILLIAM H. *Municipal Reform Movements in the United States.* New York, Revell, 1895.

U. S. National Resources Committee. Urbanism Committee. *Urban Government. Volume I of the Supplementary Report of the Urbanism Committee to the National Resources Committee.* Washington, U.S. Govt. Printing Office, 1939.

WEBER, ADNA F. *The Growth of Cities in the Nineteenth Century; A Study in Statistics.* New York, Macmillan, 1899.

WELLS, ROGER H. *American Local Government.* New York, McGraw-Hill, 1939.

WERNER, MORRIS R. *Tammany Hall.* Garden City, N.Y., Doubleday-Doran, 1928.

WHITE, LEONARD D. *Trends in Public Administration.* New York, McGraw-Hill, 1933.

WILCOX, DELOS F. *Government by All the people; or The Initiative, The Referendum and The Recall as Instruments of Democracy.* New York, Macmillan, 1912.

———. *The American City: A Problem in Democracy.* New York, Macmillan, 1904.

———. *The Study of City Government; An Outline of the Problems of Municipal Functions, Control and Organization.* New York, Macmillan, 1897.

ZINK, HAROLD. *City Bosses In The United States; A Study of Twenty Municipal Bosses.* Durham, Duke University Press, 1930.

———. *Government of Cities in the United States.* New York, Macmillan, 1939.

ARTICLES

BALDWIN, HENRY DE FOREST. "Municipal Problems: A Discussion of the Model Charter of the National Municipal League." *Municipal Affairs,* v. 3 (1899), pp. 3–17.

BROOKS, ROBERT C. "A Bibliography of Municipal Administration and City Conditions." *Municipal Affairs,* v. 1 (1897), pp. 1–224.

CAPEN, SAMUEL B. "The Boston Municipal League." *American Journal of Politics,* v. 5 (1894), pp. 1–13.

CHILDS, RICHARD S. "A Democracy that Might Work; How Out of a Multitude of Preoccupied Voters to Secure an Obedient Government." *Century,* v. 120 (1930), pp. 11–17.

———. "The City Manager Plan Will Endure." *American City,* v. 55 (May, 1940), pp. 35–36.

CHOATE, JOSEPH H. "James C. Carter: Seventeenth President of Association." *American Bar Association Journal.* v. 14 (1928), pp. 127–132.

"The City Manager—and the Next Step." *American City,* v. 12 (1915), pp. 1–2.

"A City Set on A Hill; An Account of the First American Conference on Reconstruction Problems, Rochester, November 20–22." *Survey*, v. 41 (1918), pp. 241–242.

"Civic Week in Pittsburgh." *Charities and the Commons*, v. 21 (1908–1909), pp. 329–337.

"Constructive Municipal Economy vs. Indiscriminate Reduction of Expenditures." *American City*, v. 47 (Dec., 1932), pp. 47–48.

"Convention of the National Municipal League." *American City*, v. 5 (1911), pp. 374–378.

DEMING, HORACE E. "A Municipal Program." *Annals*, v. 17 (1901), pp. 441–443.

DODDS, HAROLD W. "City Government Grows Up." *Survey*, v. 67 (1931–1932), pp. 9–11, 50, 52, 57.

———. "Metropolitan Regions— Chaos? Annexation? or Federation?" *American City*, v. 44 (Jan., 1931), pp. 144–145.

———. "New Model City Charter Now Available." *American City*, v. 37 (1927), pp. 599–600.

———. "Outline of History and Activities of National Municipal League." *Cambridge Tribune*, November 15, 1924.

DURAND, EDWARD D. "Council Government Versus Mayor Government." *Political Science Quarterly*, v. 15 (1900), pp. 426–451, 675–709.

FAIRLIE, JOHN A. "The Problems of City Government from the Administrative Point of View." *Annals*, v. 27 (1906), pp. 132–154.

FORBES, RUSSELL. "The Work of the National Municipal League." *Proceedings Fifth Meeting The American Municipal Association* (1929), pp. 72–83, Lawrence, Kansas, American Municipal Association, 1929.

GREENLAW, EDWIN A. "Office of Mayor in the United States." *Municipal Affairs*, v. 3 (1899), pp. 33–60.

"High Lights of the National Municipal League Meeting." *Public Management*, v. 14 (1932), pp. 328–329.

IHLDER, JOHN. "Municipal Week at Springfield." *Survey*, v. 37 (1916–1917), pp. 264–266.

JOHNSON, W. TEMPLETON. "The National Municipal League." *Survey*, v. 28 (1912), pp. 601–602.

JONES, HOWARD P. "Challenge to the Governed." *Independent Woman*, v. 13 (1934), pp. 377, 402–405.

———. "Citizens' Councils for Constructive Economy." *Recreation*, v. 28 (1934–1935), pp. 487–489, 506.

———. "Citizen Groups, Tool of Democracy." *Annals*. v. 199 (1938), pp. 176–182.

———. "City League Scans States." *State Government*, v. 9 (1936), p. 14.

———. "Constructive vs. Destructive Economy in Government." *American City*, v. 47 (Oct., 1932), pp. 83–84.

———. "The Crisis in Local Government." *Survey*, v. 68 (1932), pp. 510–511.

———. "Model Law for County Manager Government Now Available." *American City*, v. 43 (Aug., 1930), p. 118.

———. "Modernizing the Political 'Dark Continent' of County Government." *American City*, v. 49 (Nov., 1934), pp. 57–58.

———. "A New Aid for City Charter Modernization."—*American City*, v. 48 (April, 1933), p. 40.

———. "Rural Municipalities of Tomorrow." *Survey*, v. 67 (1931–1932), pp. 37, 57–59, 61, 63.

"Last Issue of the Short Ballot Bulletin—We Consolidate with the 'National Municipal Review.'" *Short Ballot Bulletin*, v. 7, no. 56 (April, 1920).

LEA, HENRY C. "For Good City Government." *Harper's Weekly*, v. 38, pt. 1 (1894), p. 79.

"Making Government More Effective for Social Control." *Public Management*, v. 16 (1934), pp. 419–420.

"A Model Charter." *Pacific Municipalities*, v. 30 (1916), pp. 179–180.

"A Model City Charter." *Outlook*, v. 60 (1898), pp. 894–895.

"A Model for State Constitutions." *Outlook*, v. 124 (1920), p. 143.

"A Model Form of County Government." *American City*, v. 32 (1925), p. 541.

"Model Judiciary Article and Comment Thereon." *Journal of the American Judicature Society*, v. 26 (1942), pp. 51–60.

"Modern Charter Provisions for Curing Slums and Blighted Areas." *American City*, v. 48 (April, 1933), p. 48.

"Modern City Charters." *Municipal Record* (San Francisco), v. 9 (April 20, 1916), p. 121.

"Municipal Reform." *Encyclopedia of Social Reform*, ed. by William D. P. Bliss, New York, Funk and Wagnalls, 1897, pp. 907–910.

"The Municipal Reformers." *City Government*, v. 9 (1900), pp. 104–105.

MUNRO, WILLIAM B. "Civic Organizations." *Encyclopedia of the Social Sciences*, v. 3 (1930), pp. 498–502.

———. "Municipal Government." *Encyclopedia of the Social Sciences*, v. 11 (1933), pp. 105–117.

"The National Conference for Good City Government." *Annals*, v. 4 (1893–1894), pp. 850–856.

"National Municipal League." *American City*, v. 13 (1915), pp. 547–549.

"National Municipal League." *American City*, v. 22 (1920), p. 134.

"National Municipal League." *Annals*, v. 13 (1899), pp. 267–269.

"National Municipal League." *Annals*, v. 15 (1900), pp. 122–126.

"National Municipal League Fifty Years Old." *American City*, v. 59 (Feb., 1944), p. 61.

"National Municipal League Holds Fortieth Annual Convention this Month." *American City*, v. 49 (Nov., 1934), p. 73.

"National Municipal League Visits Canada." *Survey*, v. 31 (1913), pp. 304–305.

"The National Municipal Reform League." *Annals*, v. 5 (1894–1895), pp. 636–639.

"Needed—the Power of Excess Condemnation." *American City*, v. 29 (1923), p. 346.

"A New 'Model' for City Charters." *Survey*, v. 36 (1916), p. 225.

PRICHARD, FRANK P. "The Study of the Science of Municipal Government." *Annals*, v. 2 (1891–1892), pp. 450–457.

"Public Utility and Franchise Policy in a Model City Charter." *American City*, v. 14 (1916), p. 166.

"Public Utility Extensions and the Resettlement of Outstanding Franchises." *American City*, v. 9 (1913), pp. 533–536.

"Reconstruction at Rochester." *Nation*, v. 107 (1918), pp. 648–649.

RICHARDSON, CHARLES. "The National Conference for Good City Government." *Independent*, v. 46, pt. 1 (Feb. 8, 1894), p. 166.

ROEDER, ADOLPH. "Good Government Conference; National Municipal League." *American Magazine of Civics*, v. 8 (1896), pp. 656–657.

ROHER, MIRIAM. "National Municipal League Holds 45th National Conference." *Public Management*, v. 21 (1939), pp. 370–371.

ROWE, LEO S. "Meeting of the National Municipal League." *Annals*, v. 8 (1896), pp. 188–190.

SEYBOLD, G. B. "National Conference on Government Held in Toledo." *Public Management*, v. 18 (1936), p. 372.

SEYBOLD, GENEVA. "Dykstra of Cincinnati: Portrait of a Scholar in Action." *Survey Graphic,* v. 26 (1937), pp. 204–206.

SHAW, ALBERT. "Our 'Civic Renaissance.'" *Review of Reviews,* v. 11 (1895), pp. 415–427.

"Summary of Model Municipal Budget Law Drafted by National Municipal League." *State and Local Budgetary Methods; A Report of the Committee on State and Local Taxation Expenditures.* Washington, Chamber of Commerce of the United States. 1935, pp. 31–32.

TAYLOR, GRAHAM R. "The Cincinnati Civic Convention." *Survey,* v. 23 (1909), pp. 321–328.

THOMPSON, E. N. "Making Democracy Work is Theme of Conference on Government." *Public Management,* v. 22 (1940), pp. 368–369.

"The Toronto Meeting of the National Municipal League." *American City,* v. 9 (1913), pp. 573–575.

"The Twentieth Century City." *Survey,* v. 33 (1914), p. 280.

VIEG, JOHN A. "Advice for Municipal Reformers." *Public Opinion Quarterly,* v. 1, no. 4 (Oct., 1937), pp. 87–92.

WALKER, CHARLES R. "Winant of New Hampshire." *Atlantic Monthly,* v. 167 (1941), pp. 548–554.

WELSH, HERBERT. "A Definite Step Toward Municipal Reform." *Forum,* v. 17 (1894), pp. 179–185.

———. "The Movement for Good City Government." *American Journal of Politics,* v. 5 (1894), pp. 67–75.

WHITE, ANDREW D. "The Government of American Cities." *Forum,* v. 10 (1890), pp. 357–372.

WILCOX, DELOS F. "A Proposed Municipal Program." *City Government,* v. 7 (1899), pp. 140–142.

WILLOUGHBY, ALFRED. "Citizenship Conferences Sponsored by National Municipal League." *Public Management,* v. 22 (1940), pp. 85–86.

———. "National Municipal League Holds Forty-third Annual Conference." *Public Management,* v. 19 (1937), p. 377.

———. "Selling Democracy, Taking Polls, and Relief Discussed at League Meeting." *Public Management,* v. 21 (1939), pp. 21–22.

WOODFORD, ARTHUR B. "The Municipal League of Philadelphia." *Social Economist,* v. 2 (1891–1892), pp. 366–369.

WOODRUFF, CLINTON R. "After-War Problems—Respective Obligations of National, State and Local Governments." *American City,* v. 19 (1918), pp. 352–354.

———. "The Activities of Civic Organizations for Municipal Improvement in the United States." *Annals,* v. 25 (1905), pp. 359–401.

———. "An American Municipal Program." *Political Science Quarterly,* v. 18 (1903), pp. 47–58.

———. "Charter-Making in America." *Atlantic Monthly,* v. 103 (1909), pp. 628–639.

———. "Cleveland Conference for Good City Government." *American Magazine of Civics,* v. 7 (1895), pp. 167–171.

———. "Good City Government." *Public Opinion,* v. 18 (1895), p. 536.

———. "The Good Government Conference." *Harper's Weekly,* v. 43, pt. 2 (1899), p. 1219.

———. "How to Promote the Civic Efficiency of Commercial Organizations." *American City,* v. 11 (1914), pp. 133–135.

———. "The Movement for Municipal Reform." *North American Review,* v. 167 (1898), pp. 410–417.

———. "Municipal Government Now and a Hundred Years Ago." *Popular*

Science Monthly, v. 58 (1900–1901), pp. 60–68.

———. "The Municipal League of Philadelphia." *American Journal of Sociology,* v. 11 (1905–1906), pp. 336–358.

———. "Municipal Progress: 1904–1905." *Annals,* v. 27 (1906), pp. 191–199.

———. "Municipal Review 1907–1908." *American Journal of Sociology,* v. 14 (1908–1909), pp. 465–496.

———. "Municipal Review, 1908–1909." *American Journal of Sociology,* v. 15 (1909–1910), pp. 502–535.

———. "Municipal Review 1909–1910." *American Journal of Sociology,* v. 16 (1910–1911), pp. 485–518.

———. "The National Municipal League." *Proceedings of the American Political Science Association,* v. 5 (1909), pp. 131–148.

———. "The National Municipal League." *American City,* v. 1 (1909), pp. 109–112.

———. "The National Municipal League." *Yale Review,* v. 7 (1898–1899), pp. 213–216.

———. "The National Municipal League." *Harper's Weekly,* v. 41, pt. 1 (1897), p. 510.

———. "The National Municipal League." *Municipal Journal and Engineer,* v. 10 (1901), pp. 77–78.

———. "National Municipal Organization." *World Today,* v. 8 (1905), pp. 614–618.

———. "The Nationalization of Municipal Movements." *Annals,* v. 21 (1903), pp. 252–260.

———. "The Philadelphia Municipal League." *American Journal of Politics,* v. 5 (1894), pp. 287–294.

———. "Practical Municipal Progress." *American Journal of Sociology,* v. 12 (1906–1907), pp. 190–215.

———. "The Progress of Municipal Reform." *Municipal Affairs,* v. 1 (1897), pp. 301–316.

———. "Progress of Municipal Reform." *Review of Reviews,* v. 12 (1895), pp. 202–203.

———. "The Progress of Municipal Reform, 1894–5." *American Magazine of Civics,* v. 7 (1895), pp. 66–73.

———. "The Progress of Municipal Reform in Philadelphia." *Harper's Weekly,* v. 38 (1894), p. 1019.

———. "Provisions of a Model City Charter." *American City,* v. 14 (1916), pp. 513–515.

———. "Recent Municipal Progress in the United States," in Bliss, William D. P., ed. *The New Encyclopedia of Social Reform,* New York, Funk and Wagnalls, 1908, pp. 795–800. Also contains: "Municipal Reform," pp. 800–801; "National Municipal League," p. 809.

———. "The Reformer-in-Chief of Our Municipalities." *World Today,* v. 20 (1911), p. 311.

———. "A Review of Municipal Events, 1906–7." *American Journal of Sociology,* v. 13 (1907–1908), pp. 455–488.

———. "Secretaries of State Leagues to Confer at Baltimore." *American City,* v. 10 (1914), pp. 547–548.

———. "A Year's Municipal Activities." *Municipal Journal and Engineer,* v. 10 (1901), pp. 208–210.

———. "A Year's Municipal Development." *Engineering News,* v. 44 (1900), pp. 194–195.

———. "A Year's Municipal Development." *American Journal of Sociology,* v. 6 (1900–1901), pp. 532–549.

YOUNG, JAMES T. "University Instruction in Municipal Government." *Municipal Journal and Engineer,* v. 11 (1901), pp. 5–6.

Administration Service for the Year Ending August 31, 1930." *Proceedings Seventh Meeting The American Municipal Association*, 1931, pp. 54–59. Lawrence, Kansas, American Municipal Association, 1931.

THOMAS, WILLIAM H. *The Recent Prohibition Movement in the South; Address before the National Municipal League, Richmond, Va. November 13–19, 1911.* Reprinted from Montgomery *Journal*, November 16, 1911. Montgomery, Alabama, The Paragon Press, 1911.

WOODRUFF, CLINTON R. *Constitutional Development and Municipal Life; a Paper Read Before the Eighteenth Annual Meeting of the State Bar Association of Indiana, Held at Indianapolis, Indiana, July 8 and 9, 1914.* ca. 1914.

Index

Abbott, Grace, 138
Academy of Political Science of New York, 164
Accounting, uniform, League's work on, 126–129
Adams, Henry, on general conditions of national life in post-Civil War period, 2
Administrative code, model municipal, League's work on, 139
Administrative service: Municipal Program, 35; New Municipal Program, 56; Model City Charter, 5th ed. (1941), 68–69
Advance Club of Providence, 20, 212n, 213n
Allen, William H., 102, 140, 223n, 235n; urges bureau of research on municipal administration, 141
Allied Stores Corporation, 187
American Academy of Political and Social Science, 4, 164
American City Planning Institute, 131, 132
American Civic and Planning Association, 132
American Civic Association, 131, 132, 136–137, 148, 162, 166, 182, 190
American Economic Association, 4, 120
American Institute of Civics, 12, 14, 212n
American Institute of Park Executives, 131
American Judicature Society, 90–91, 162, 221n
American League for Civic Improvement, 165
American Legislators' Association, 143, 162, 182
American Library Association, 90, 162
American Municipal Association, 139, 140, 142, 143, 148, 163, 182
American Park and Outdoor Art Association, 165
American Political Science Association, 4, 79, 83, 103, 104, 108, 109, 120, 144, 156, 164, 182
American Proportional Representation League. See Proportional Representation League
American Public Utilities Bureau, 135
American Public Welfare Association, 143
American Society for Municipal Improvements, 162, 164, 165
American Society of Planning Officials, 132
Anderson, William, 104, 206, 219n, 222n; appraisal of League, 63, 171; on improvement in city government in past fifty years, 199
Appeal of League, nature, 156–159
Appleton, D. & Co., publisher of *National Municipal League Series*, 151

Architectural League, 165
Arents, George, 187
Ascher, Charles S., 80, 143
Association of Governmental Research Agencies. *See* Governmental Research Association
Associations, local, in League, 183–184
Associations touching municipal problems, founding, 4
Atkinson, R. C., 88, 222n

Baker, Frederick E., 206
Baker, M. N., 126, 127, 137, 164, 216n, 218n, 234n, 235n, 238n; on Municipal Program, 47–48; on city planning under New Municipal Program, 62
Baldwin, Henry de Forest, 136; on Municipal Program, 46–47
Baldwin, William H. Jr., 105
Baltimore Reform League, 12, 20, 212n, 213n
Baltimore Tax-Payers' Association, 212n
Bancroft, William P., 207, 244n
Barnard, J. Lynn, 108, 229n
Bassett, Edward M., 124
Bassett, William A., 125, 139
Bauer, John, 135, 218n, 241n
Baxter, Sylvester, 202, 212n
Beard, Charles A., 74, 75, 140, 142, 221n, 222n, 228n, 229n; on New Municipal Program, 63; on nonpartisanship, 96
Beard, Mary Ritter, 167
Bebout, John E., 179, 241n
Beebe, James L., 206
Belsley, G. Lyle, 122, 233n
Bemis, Edward W., 23, 132, 214n, 237n
Bennett, Emmett L., 66, 139, 218n, 239n
Bentley, Henry, 111, 188, 230n
Bettman, Alfred, 121, 132, 218n, 237n
Beyer, William C., 66, 121
Beyle, Herman C., 139
Billings, John S., 136
Binkerd, Robert S., 124, 230n, 243n
Bird, Charles S., Jr., 131
Bird, Frederick L., 142, 145, 160, 206, 218n
Blucher, Walter, 132
Board of Delegates, League: first meeting, 19–20; discontinued, 22, 179
Board of Trade: of Minneapolis, 20, 212n; of Reading, 212n